Shojo Beat

DAYTIME SHOOTING STAR

Story & Art by
Mika Yamamori

6

CONTENTS

STORY THUS FAR

Suzume Yosano is a first-year in high school. Born in the country, she grew up living a free and easy life. Due to family circumstances, she was forced to transfer to a school in Tokyo. Lost on her first day in the city, she is found by a man who later turns out to be her homeroom teacher, Mr. Shishio.

Suzume gradually develops feelings for him.

The appearance of Shishio's ex-girlfriend Tsubomi, and Shishio's everyday words and actions, soon have Suzume declaring her love to him, though he turns her down. To avoid getting her hopes up, Suzume tries to keep her distance from Shishio, who continues to send mixed messages. When he notices this, Shishio corners Suzume to explain that he wasn't spending time with her out of pity but because he *wanted* to be with her—which causes Suzume to cry tears of joy.

With both of them on the same page, Suzume makes plans for the two of them to celebrate Shishio's birthday together. Unfortunately, she lacks the funds for a gift, so she gets a part-time job. But Shishio isn't too keen on the idea...

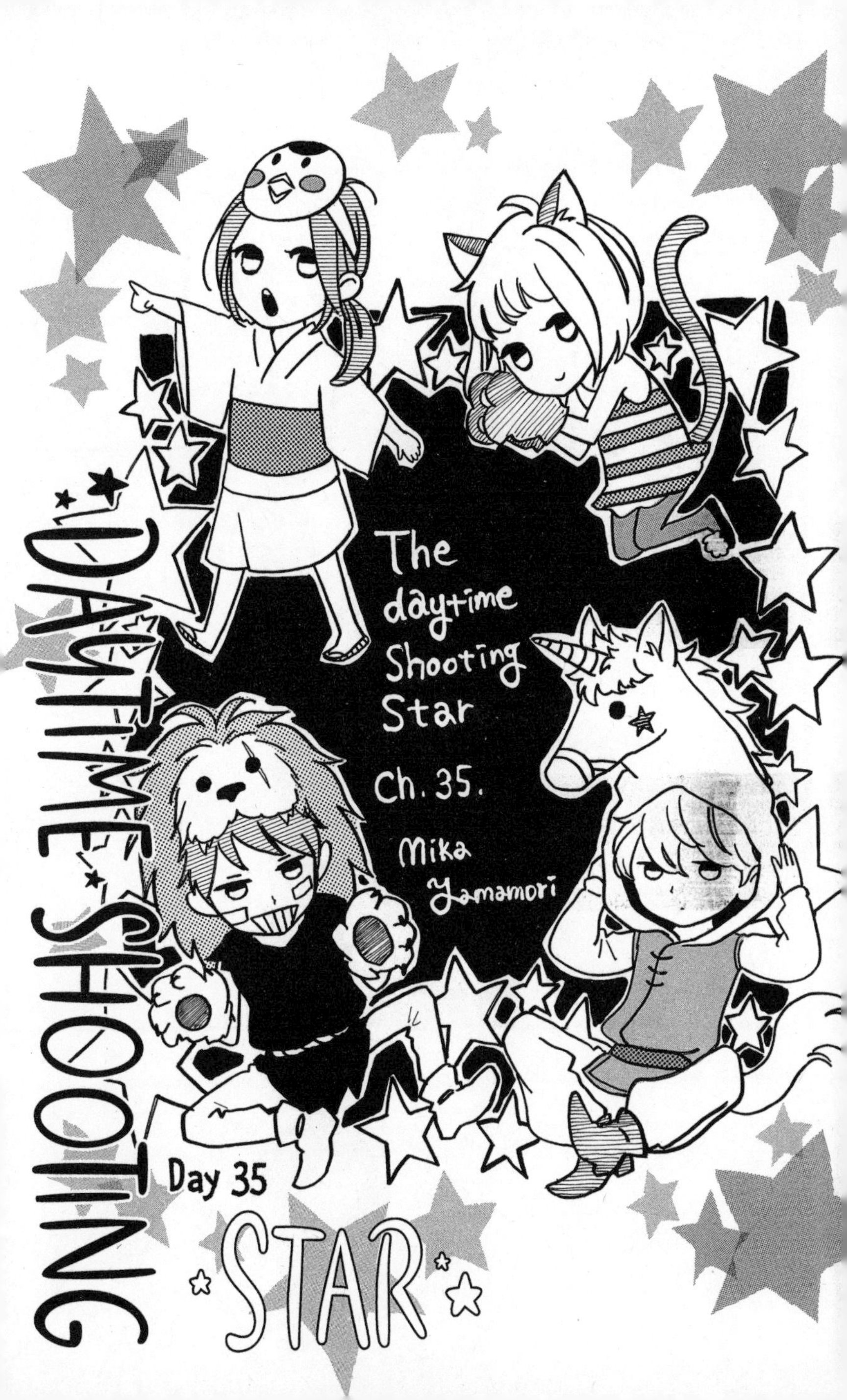
DAYTIME SHOOTING
STAR
Day 35
The daytime Shooting Star
Ch. 35.
Mika Yamamori

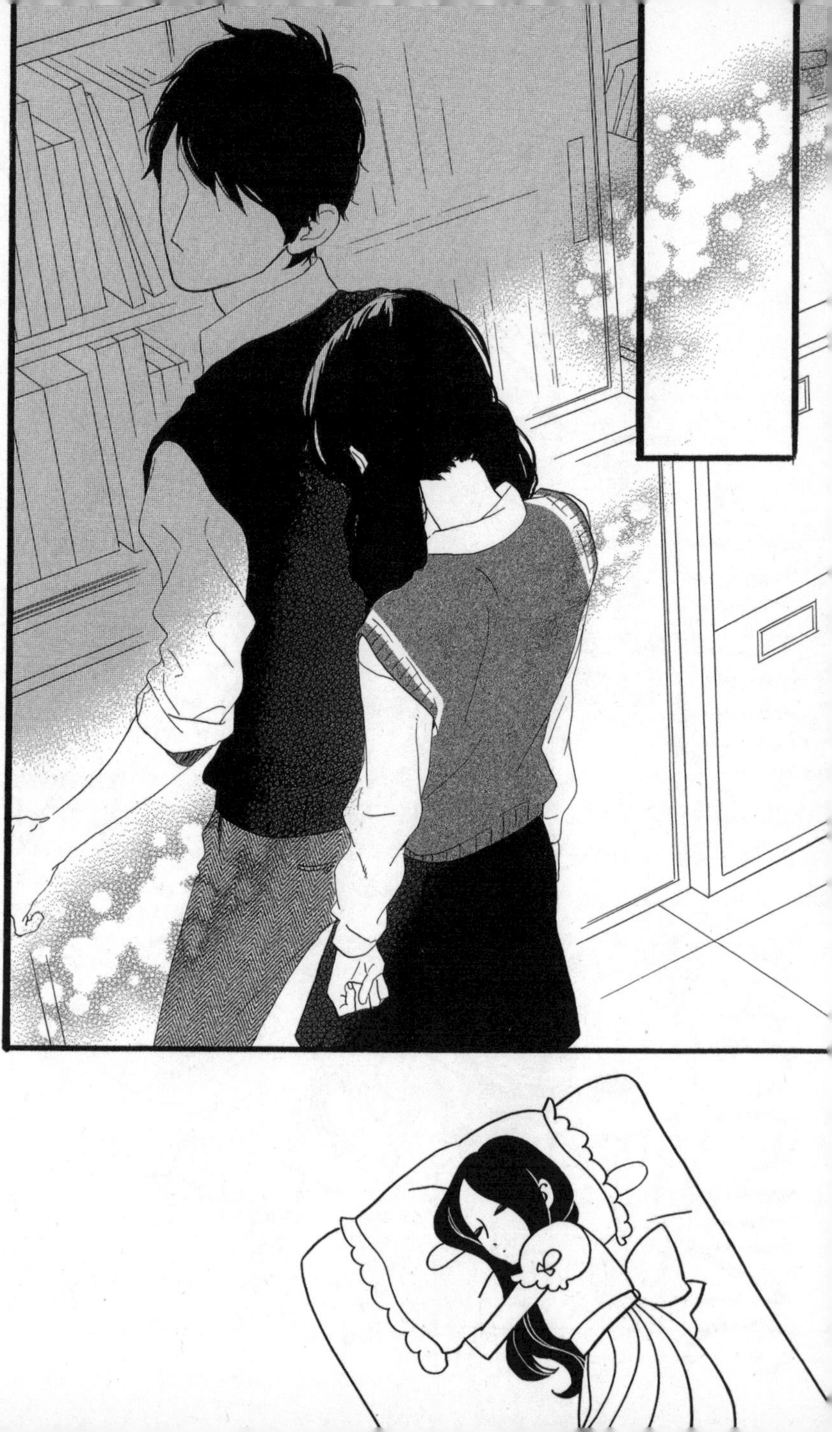

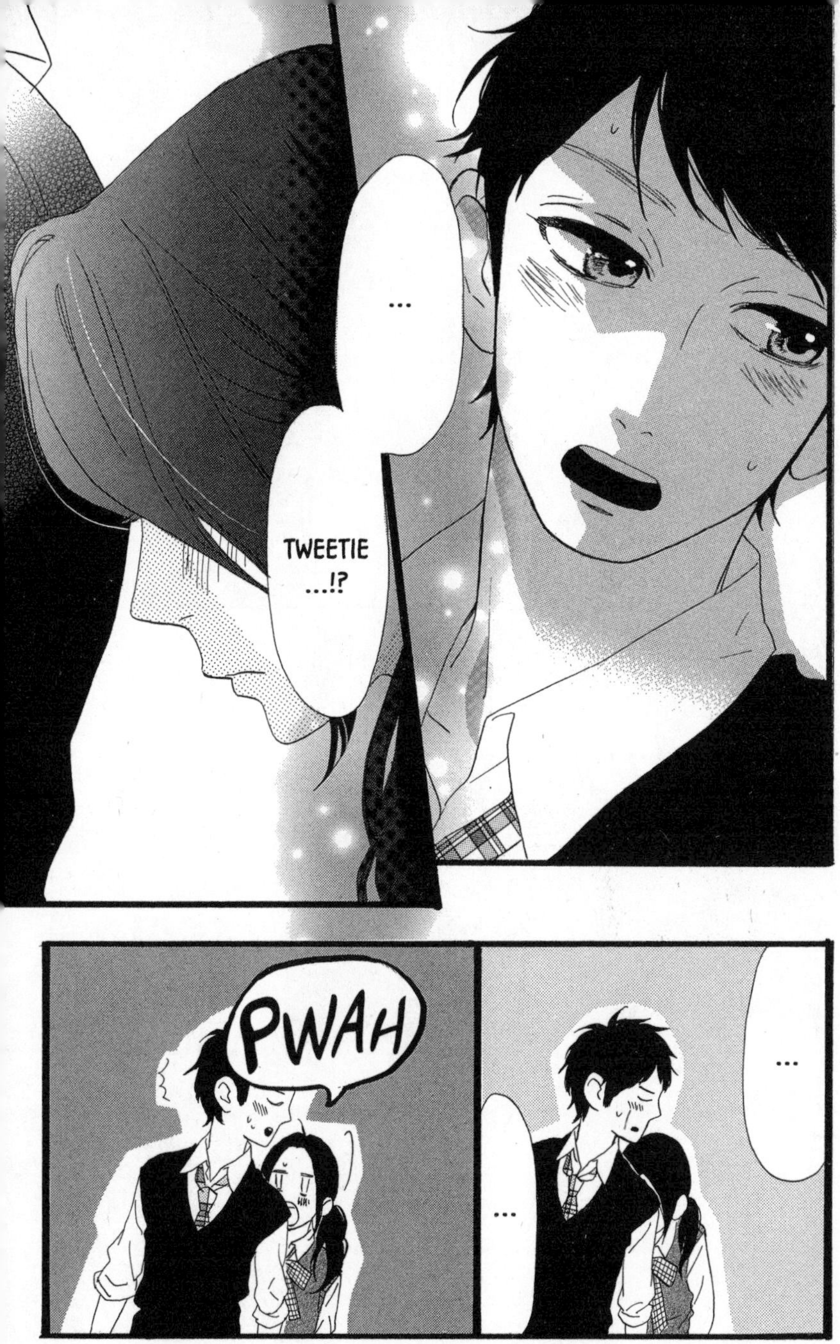
...
TWEETIE ...!?
...
...
PWAH

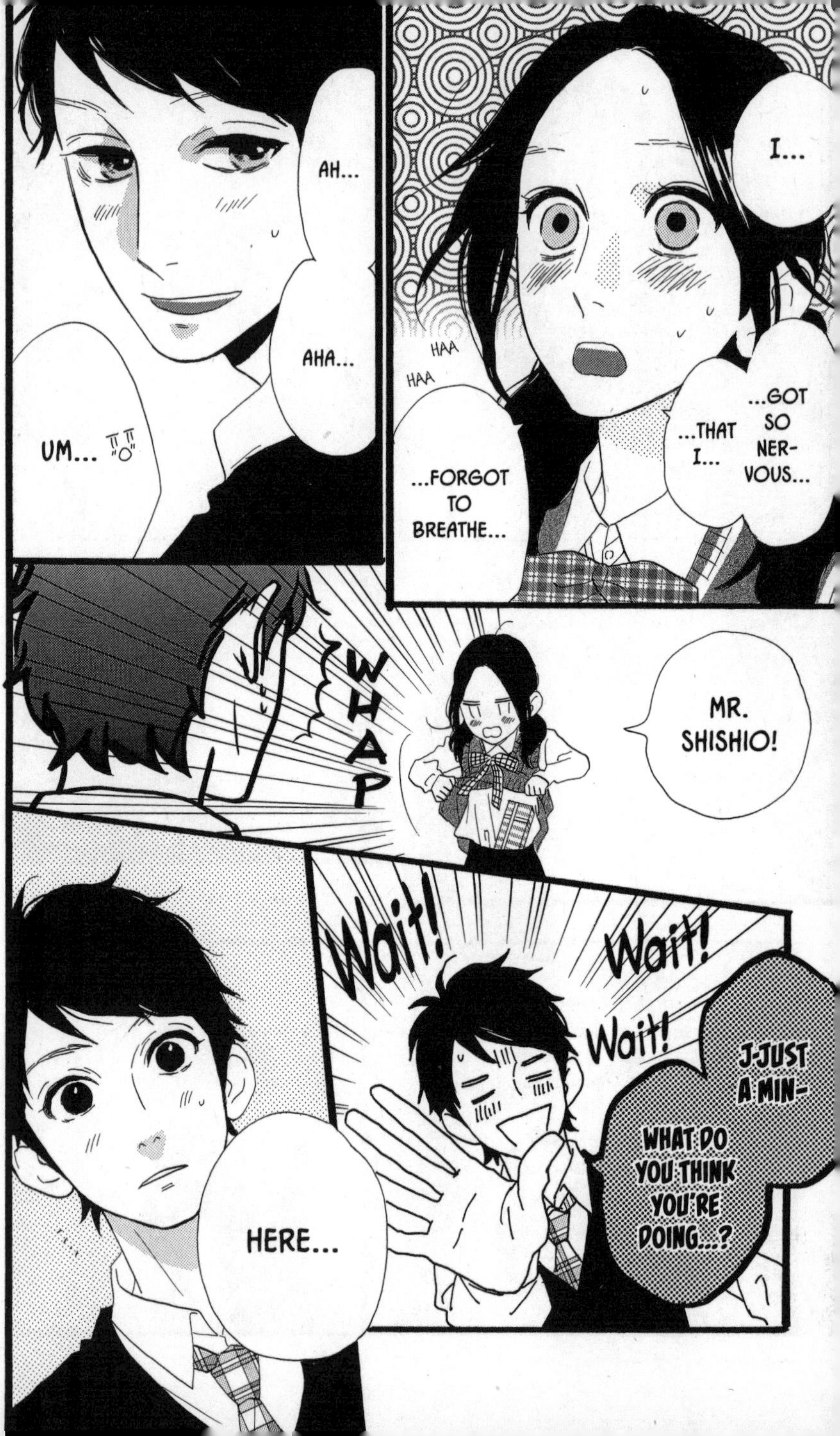

I...
...GOT SO NER-VOUS...
...THAT I...
HAA
HAA
...FORGOT TO BREATHE...
AH...
AHA...
UM...
MR. SHISHIO!
WHAP
Wait!
Wait!
Wait!
J-JUST A MIN-
WHAT DO YOU THINK YOU'RE DOING...?
HERE...

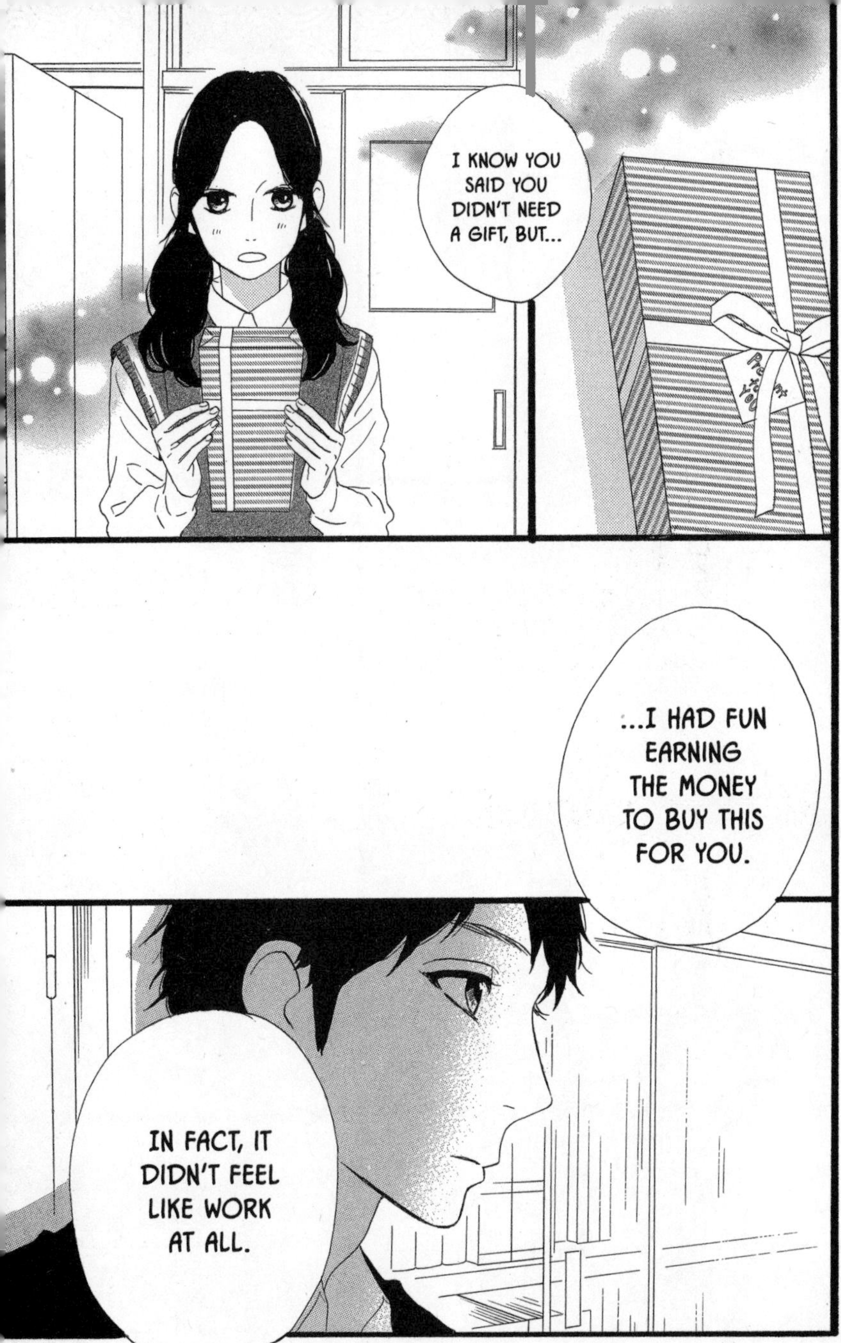
I KNOW YOU SAID YOU DIDN'T NEED A GIFT, BUT...
...I HAD FUN EARNING THE MONEY TO BUY THIS FOR YOU.
IN FACT, IT DIDN'T FEEL LIKE WORK AT ALL.

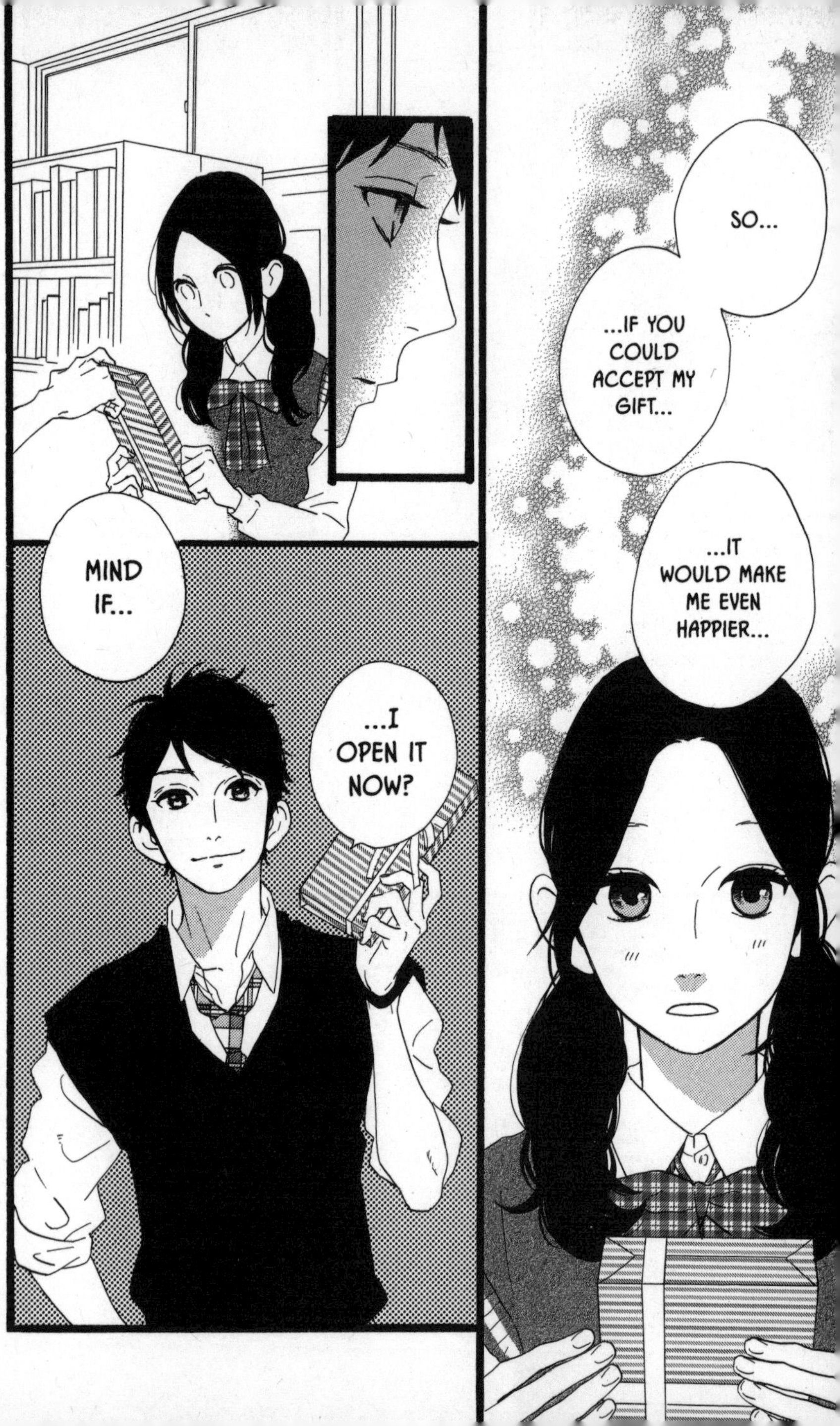
SO...
...IF YOU COULD ACCEPT MY GIFT...
...IT WOULD MAKE ME EVEN HAPPIER...
MIND IF...
...I OPEN IT NOW?

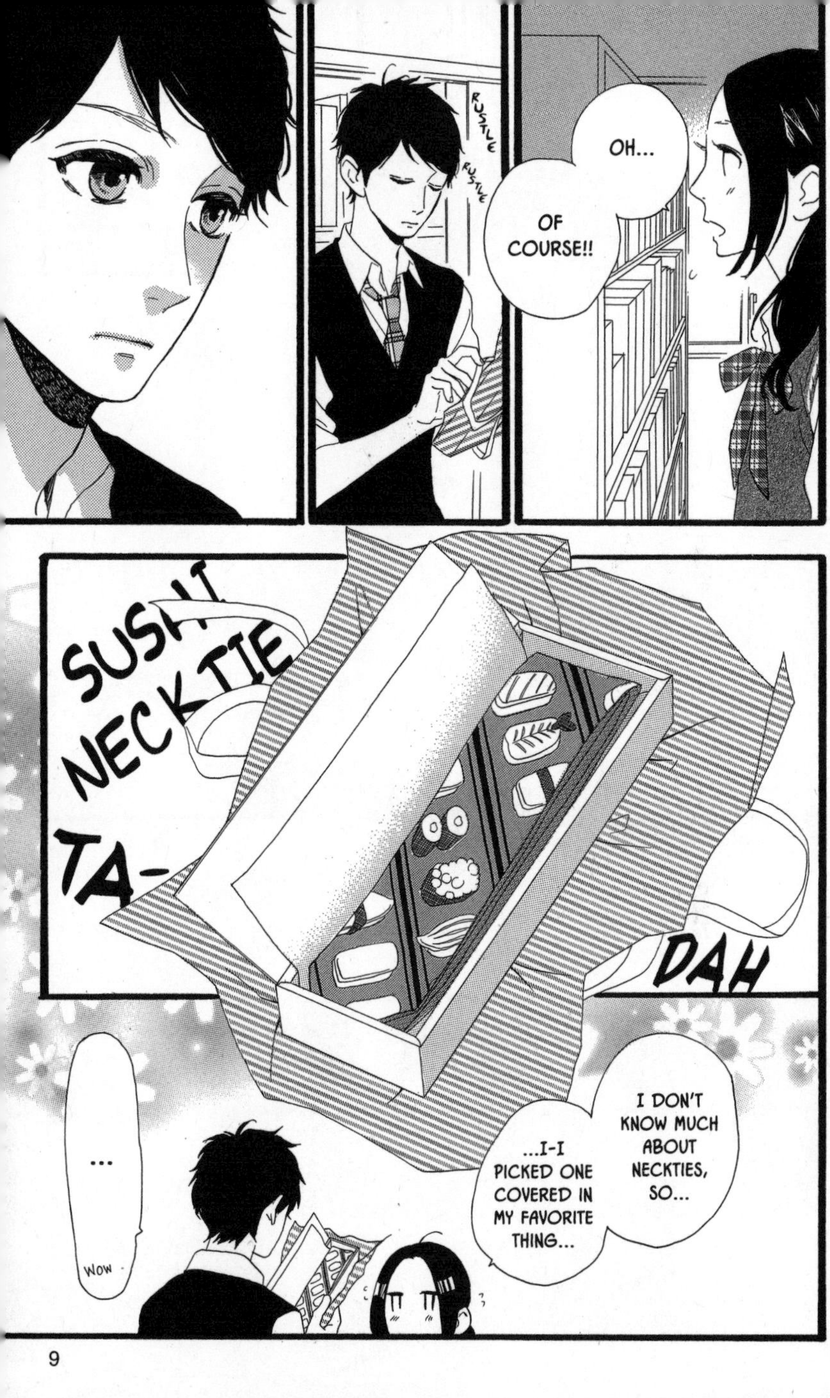
OH...
OF COURSE!!
RUSTLE
RUSTLE
SUSHI NECKTIE
TA-
DAH
I DON'T KNOW MUCH ABOUT NECKTIES, SO...
...I-I PICKED ONE COVERED IN MY FAVORITE THING...
...
WOW

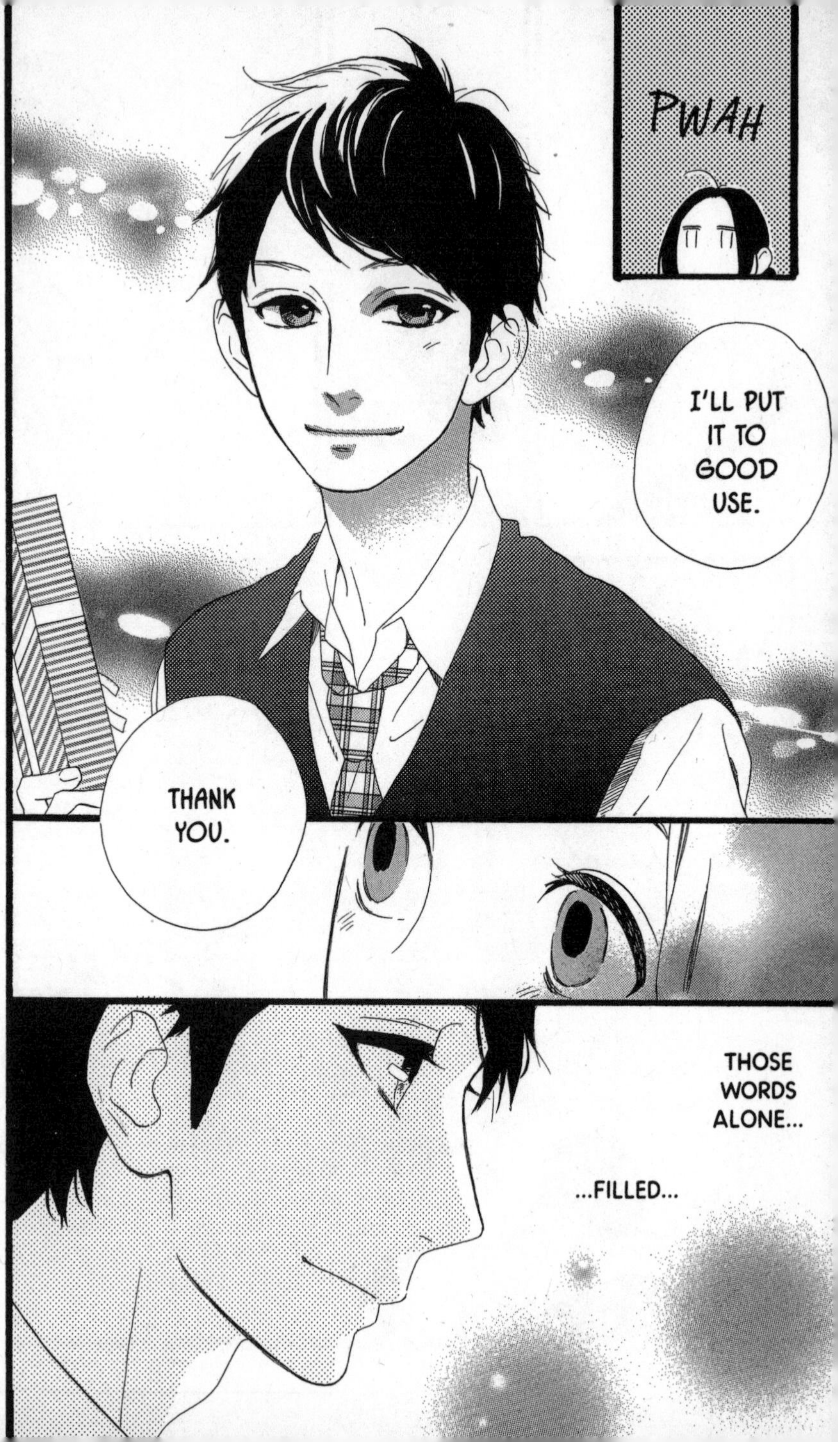
PWAH
I'LL PUT IT TO GOOD USE.
THANK YOU.
THOSE WORDS ALONE...
...FILLED...

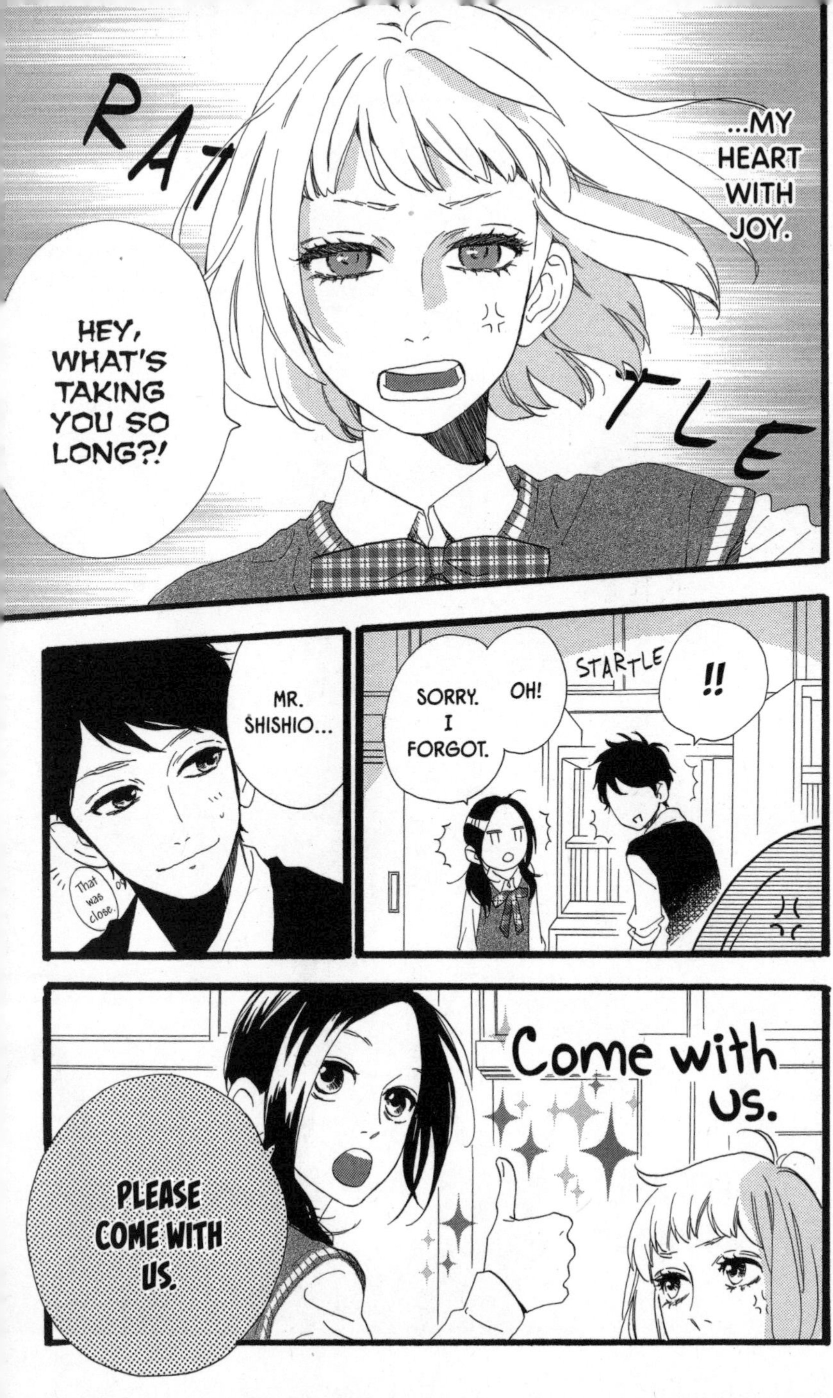
...MY HEART WITH JOY.
RATTLE
HEY, WHAT'S TAKING YOU SO LONG?!
!!
STARTLE
OH!
SORRY. I FORGOT.
MR. SHISHIO...
That was close.
Come with us.
PLEASE COME WITH US.

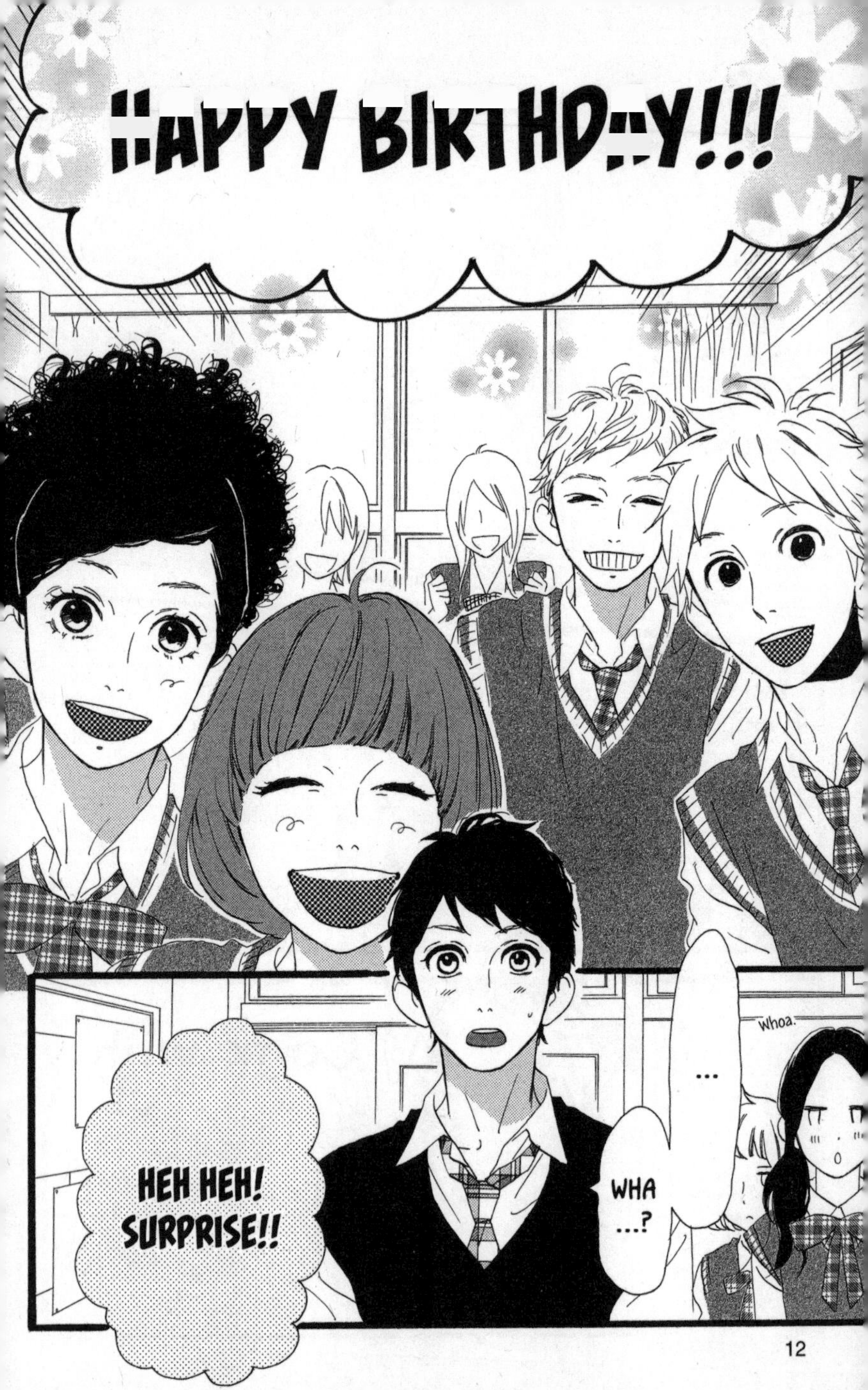
HAPPY BIRTHDAY!!!
Whoa.
...
WHA ...?
HEH HEH! SURPRISE!!

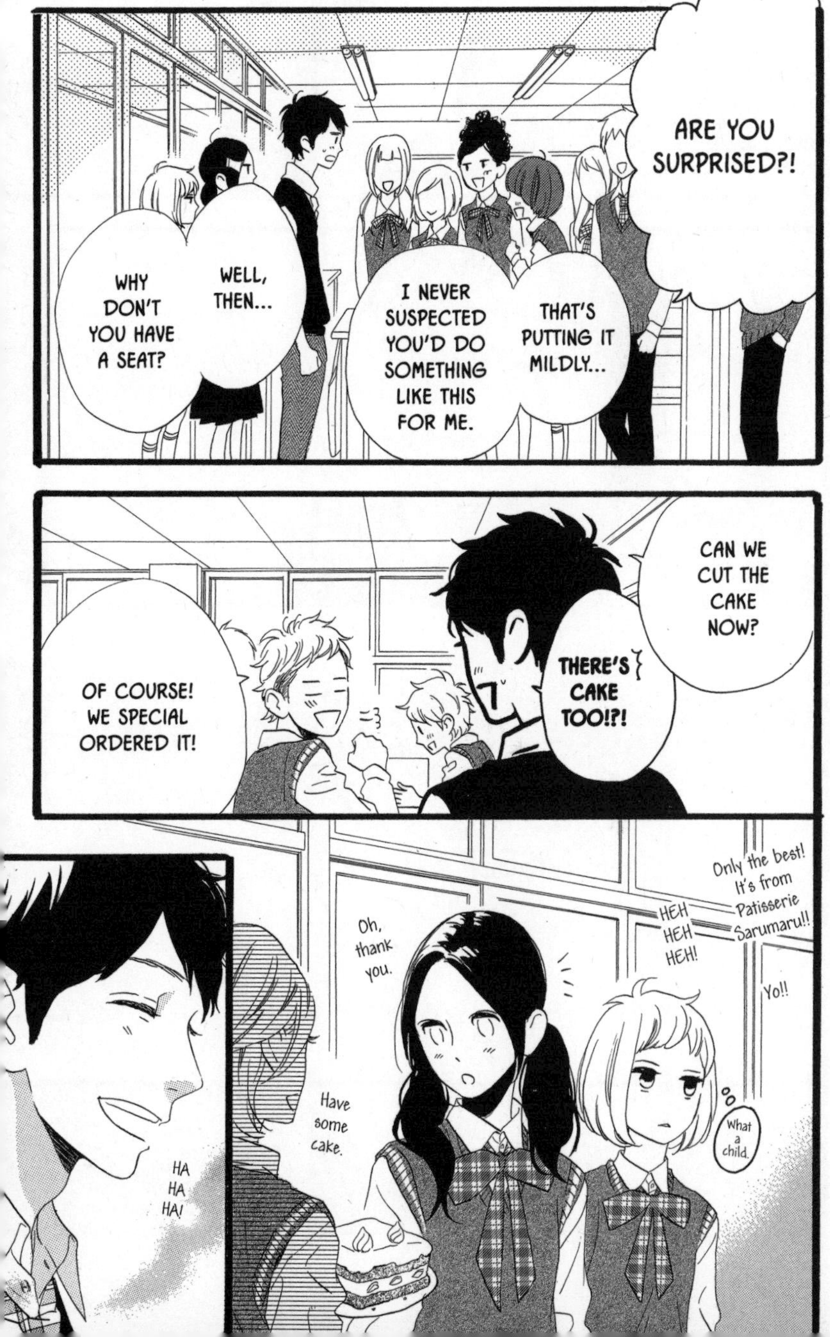
ARE YOU SURPRISED?!
THAT'S PUTTING IT MILDLY...
I NEVER SUSPECTED YOU'D DO SOMETHING LIKE THIS FOR ME.
WELL, THEN...
WHY DON'T YOU HAVE A SEAT?
CAN WE CUT THE CAKE NOW?
THERE'S CAKE TOO!?!
OF COURSE! WE SPECIAL ORDERED IT!
Only the best! It's from Patisserie Sarumaru!!
HEH HEH HEH!
Yo!!
Oh, thank you.
What a child.
Have some cake.
HA HA HA!

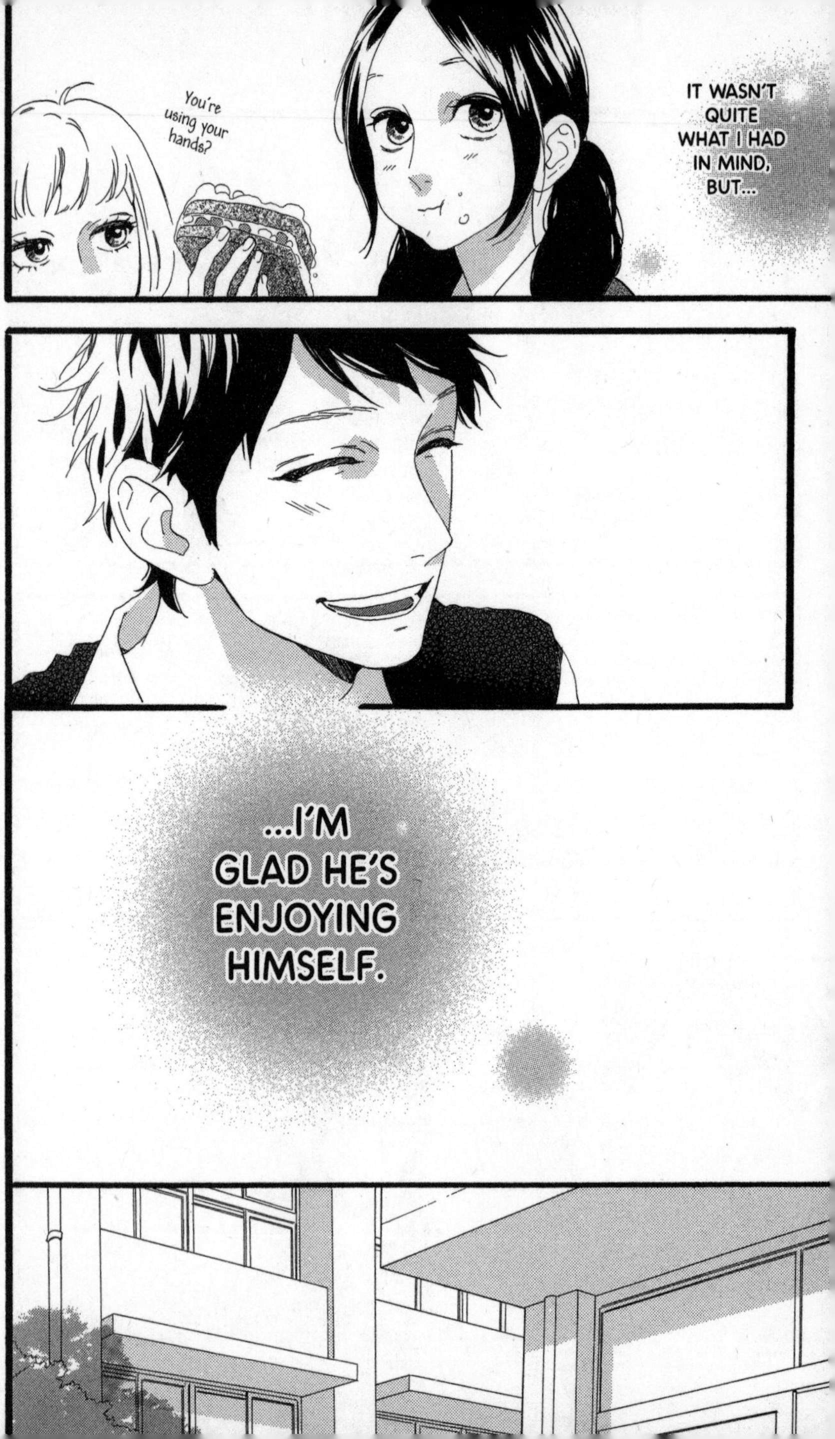
IT WASN'T QUITE WHAT I HAD IN MIND, BUT...
You're using your hands?
...I'M GLAD HE'S ENJOYING HIMSELF.

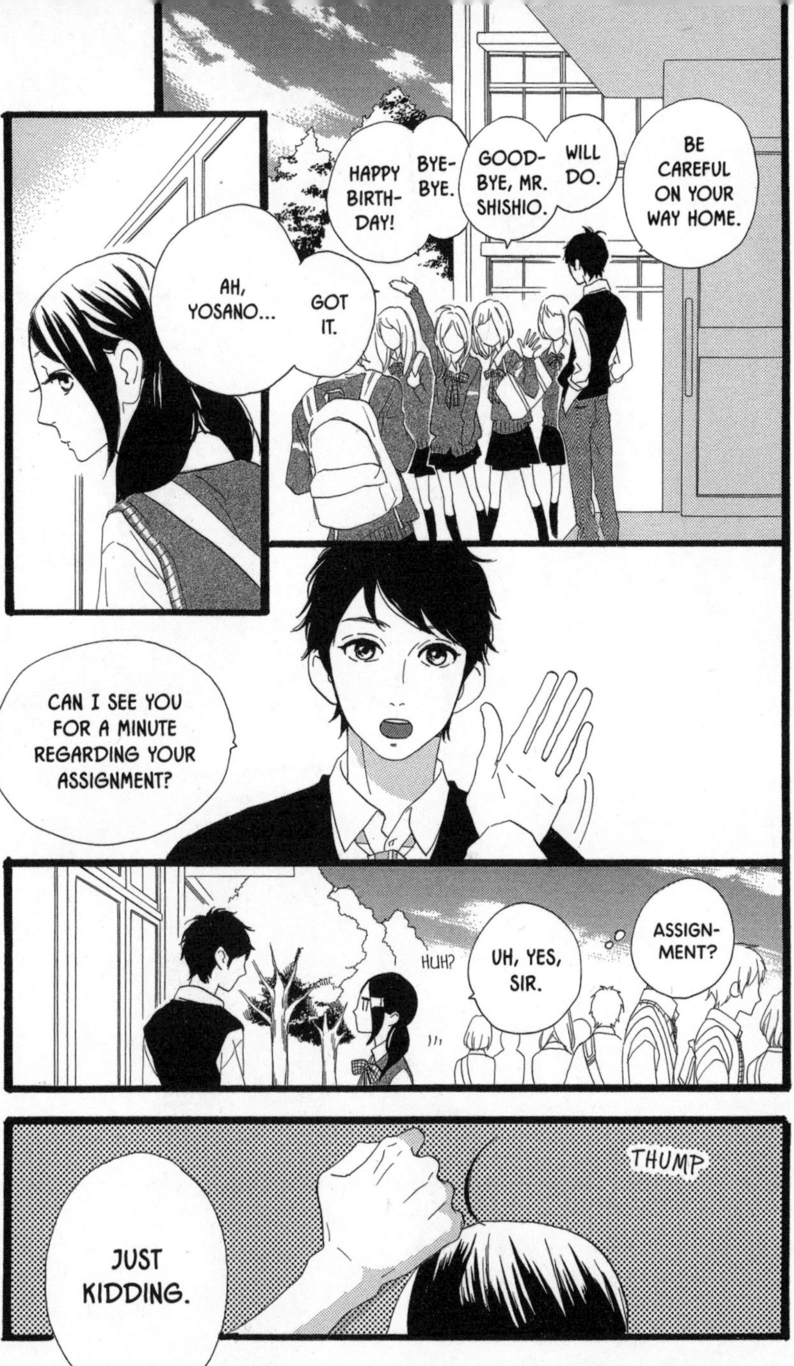
BE CAREFUL ON YOUR WAY HOME.
WILL DO.
GOOD-BYE, MR. SHISHIO.
BYE-BYE.
HAPPY BIRTH-DAY!
GOT IT.
AH, YOSANO...
CAN I SEE YOU FOR A MINUTE REGARDING YOUR ASSIGNMENT?
ASSIGN-MENT?
UH, YES, SIR.
HUH?
THUMP
JUST KIDDING.

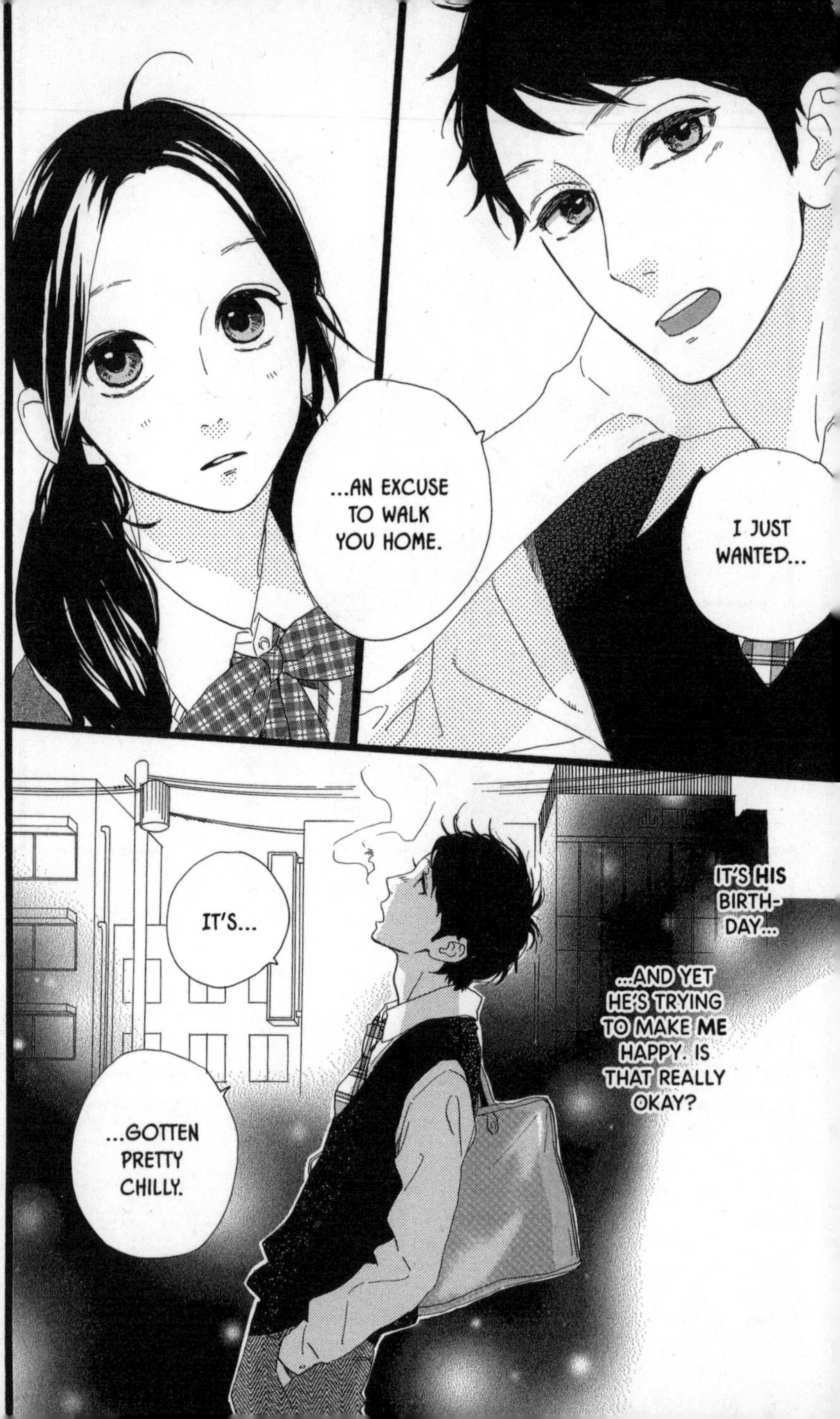
I JUST WANTED...
...AN EXCUSE TO WALK YOU HOME.
IT'S HIS BIRTH-DAY...
...AND YET HE'S TRYING TO MAKE ME HAPPY. IS THAT REALLY OKAY?
IT'S...
...GOTTEN PRETTY CHILLY.

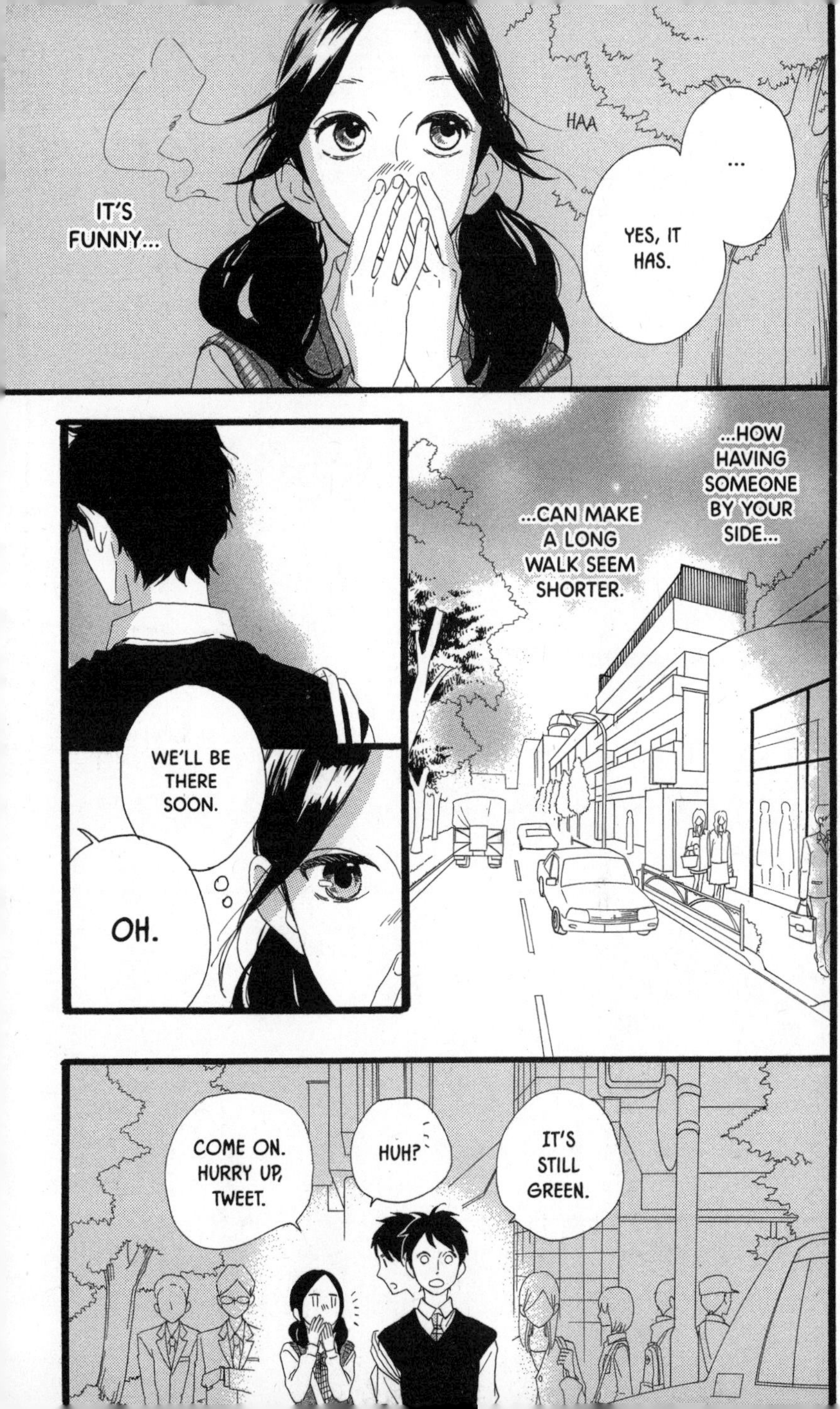
HAA
...
YES, IT HAS.
IT'S FUNNY...
...HOW HAVING SOMEONE BY YOUR SIDE...
...CAN MAKE A LONG WALK SEEM SHORTER.
WE'LL BE THERE SOON.
OH.
IT'S STILL GREEN.
HUH?
COME ON. HURRY UP, TWEET.

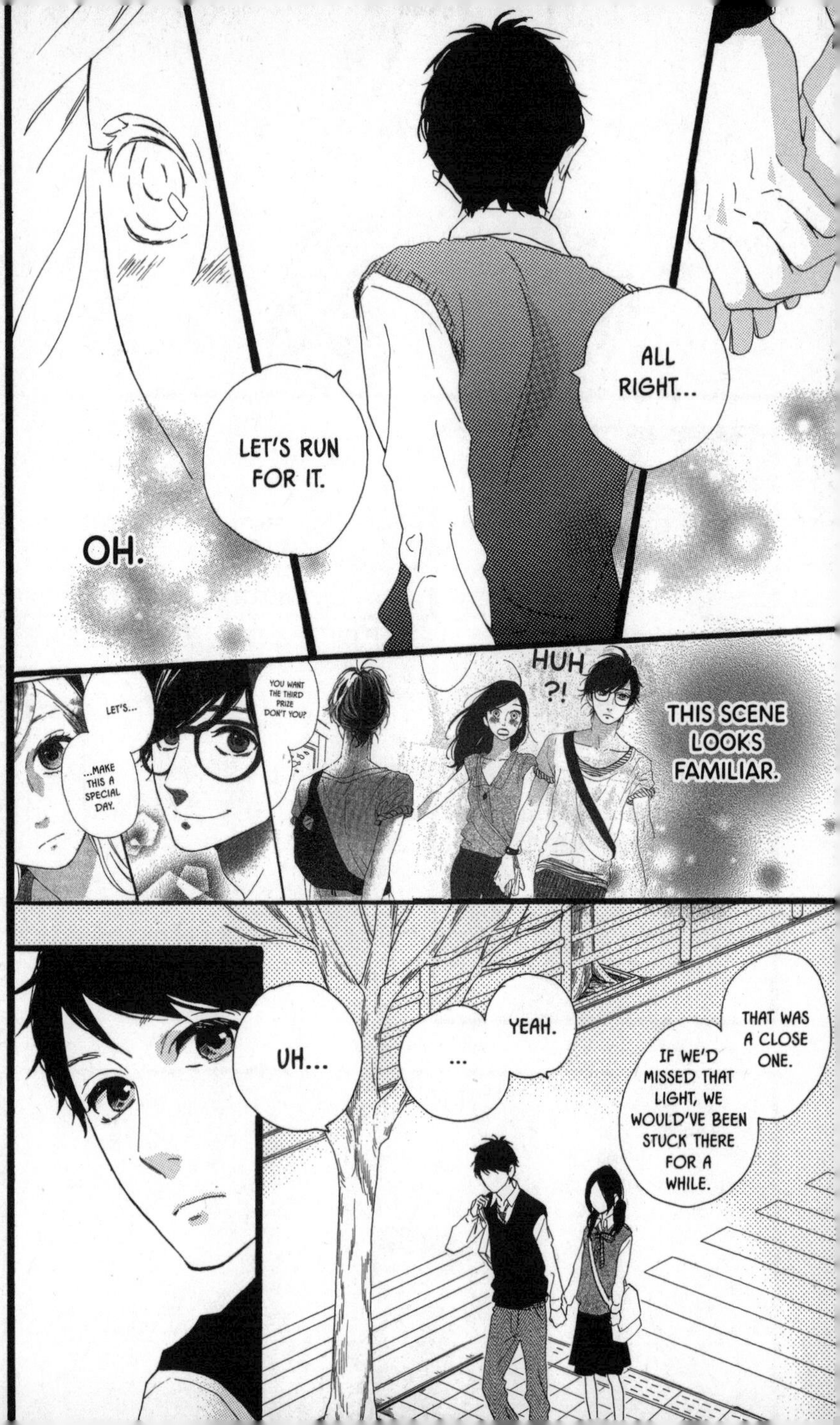
ALL RIGHT...
LET'S RUN FOR IT.
OH.
THIS SCENE LOOKS FAMILIAR.
HUH ?!
YOU WANT THE THIRD PRIZE DON'T YOU?
LET'S...
...MAKE THIS A SPECIAL DAY.
THAT WAS A CLOSE ONE.
IF WE'D MISSED THAT LIGHT, WE WOULD'VE BEEN STUCK THERE FOR A WHILE.
YEAH.
...
UH...

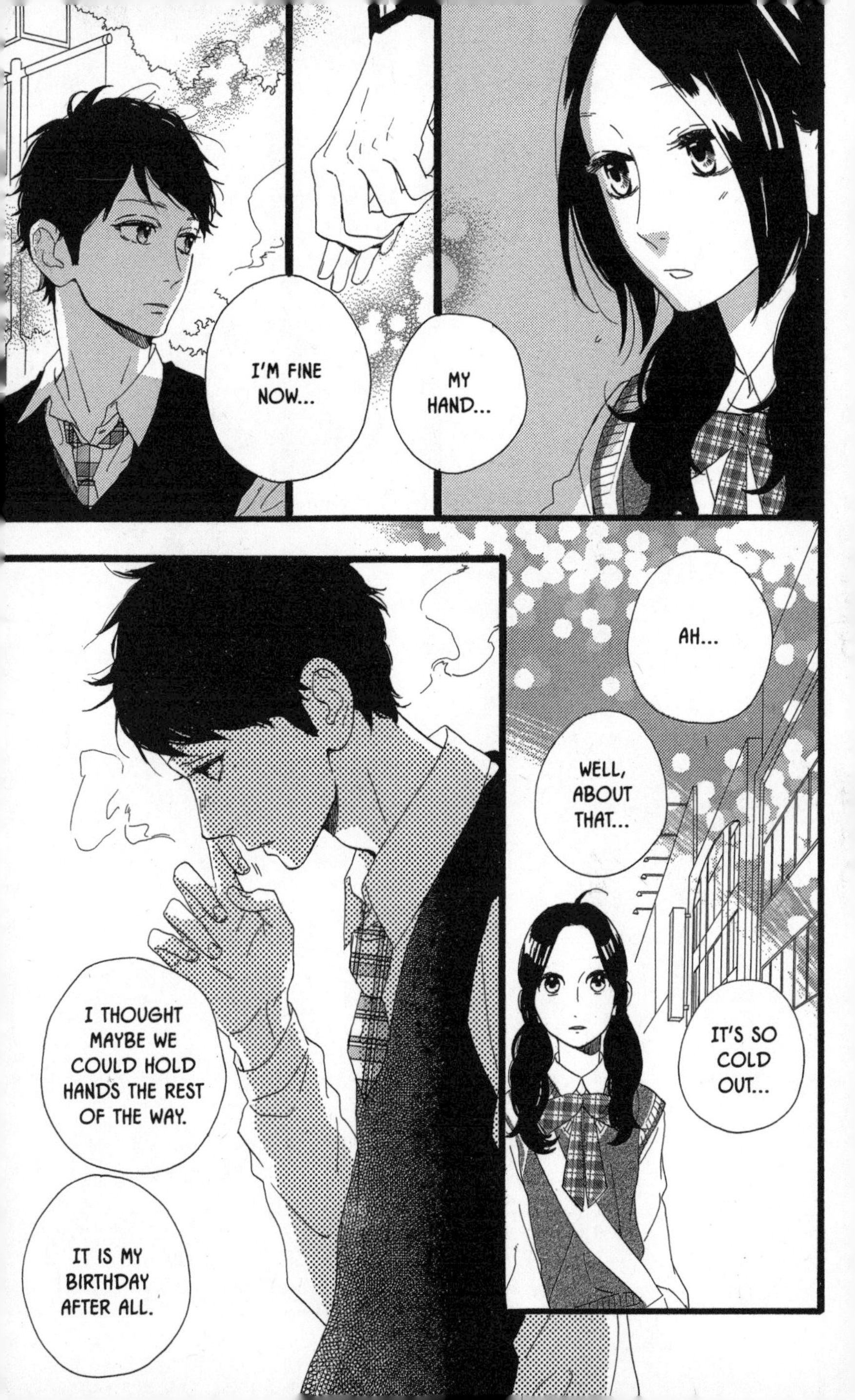
MY HAND...
I'M FINE NOW...
AH...
WELL, ABOUT THAT...
IT'S SO COLD OUT...
I THOUGHT MAYBE WE COULD HOLD HANDS THE REST OF THE WAY.
IT IS MY BIRTHDAY AFTER ALL.

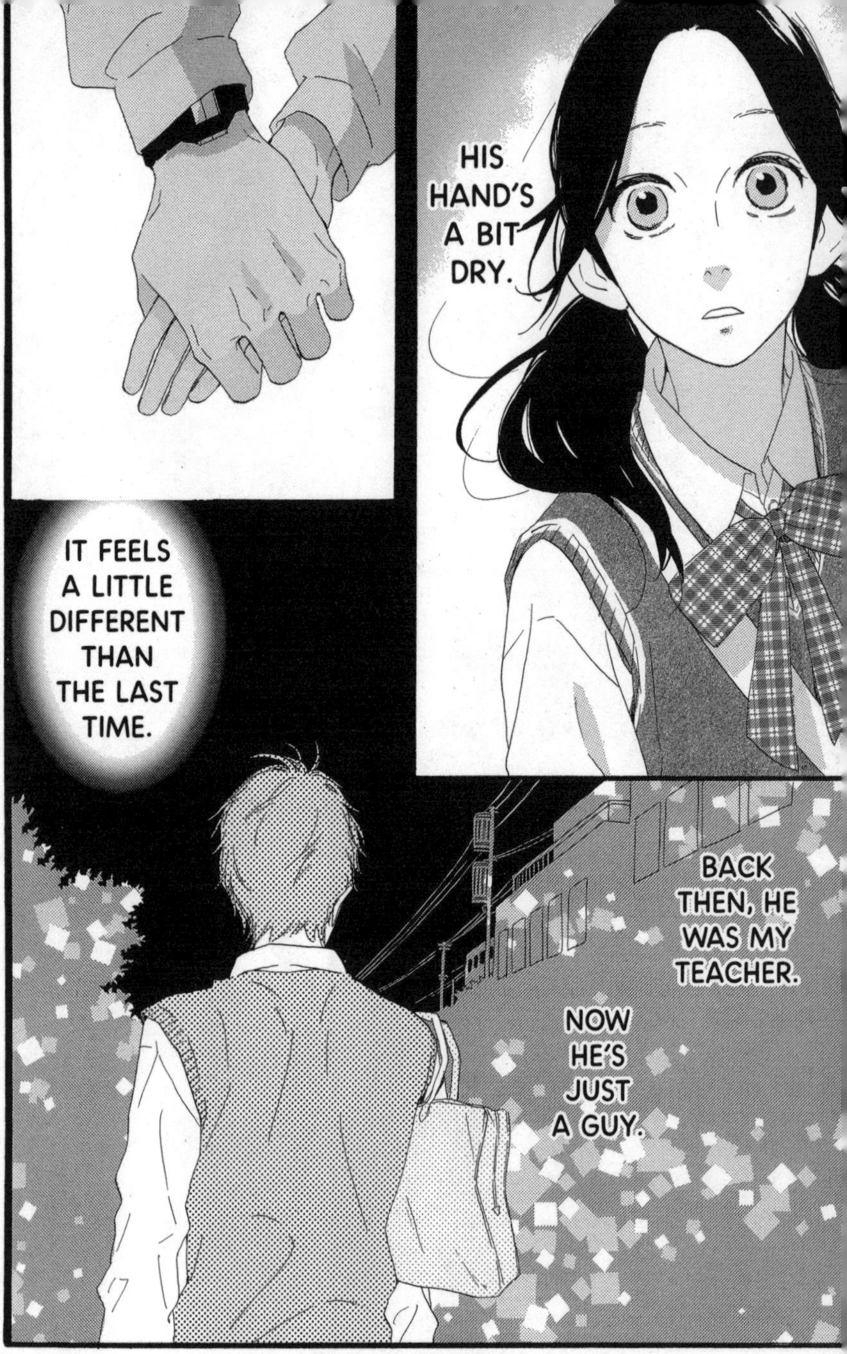
HIS HAND'S A BIT DRY.
IT FEELS A LITTLE DIFFERENT THAN THE LAST TIME.
BACK THEN, HE WAS MY TEACHER.
NOW HE'S JUST A GUY.

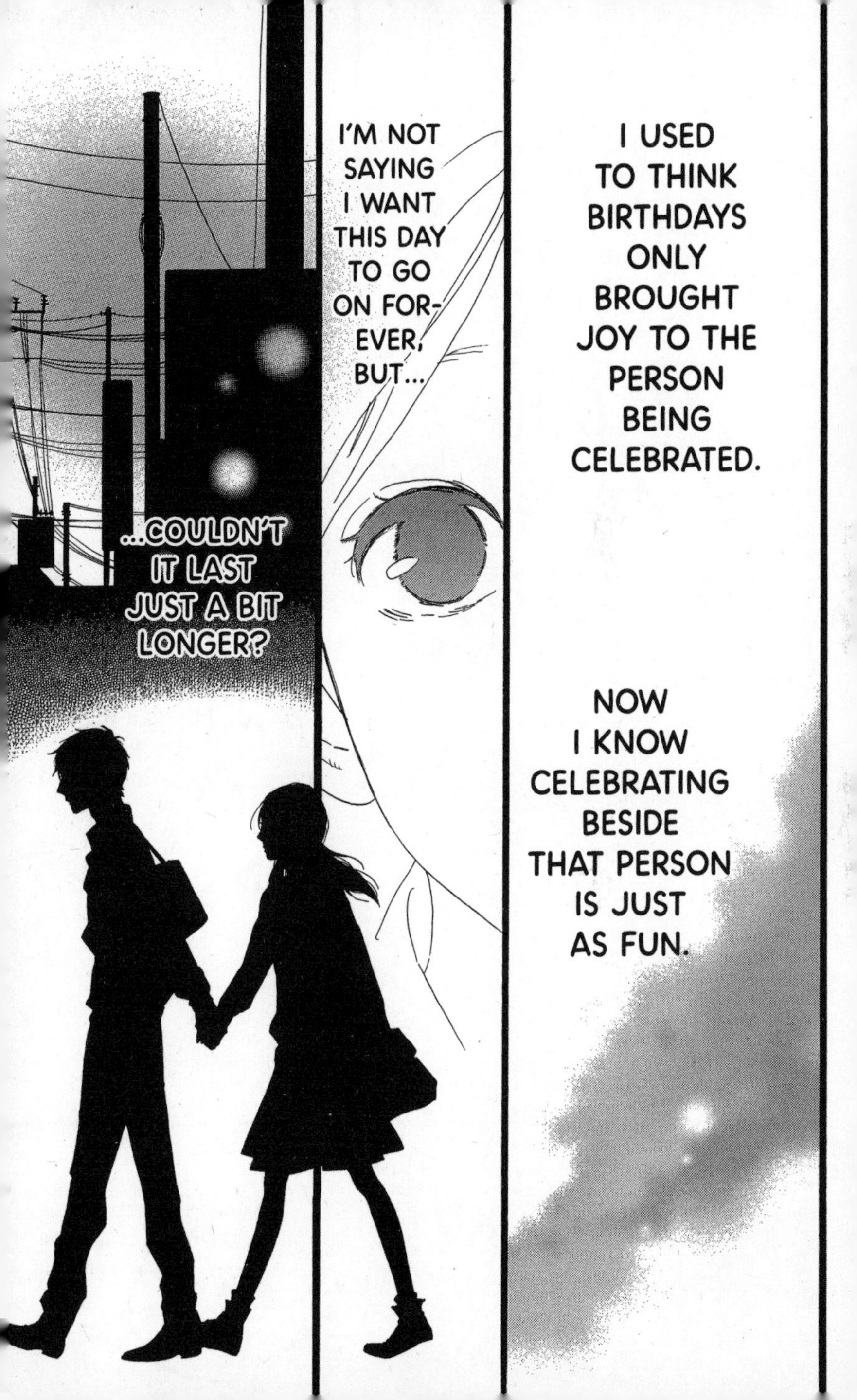
I USED TO THINK BIRTHDAYS ONLY BROUGHT JOY TO THE PERSON BEING CELEBRATED.
NOW I KNOW CELEBRATING BESIDE THAT PERSON IS JUST AS FUN.
I'M NOT SAYING I WANT THIS DAY TO GO ON FOR-EVER, BUT...
...COULDN'T IT LAST JUST A BIT LONGER?

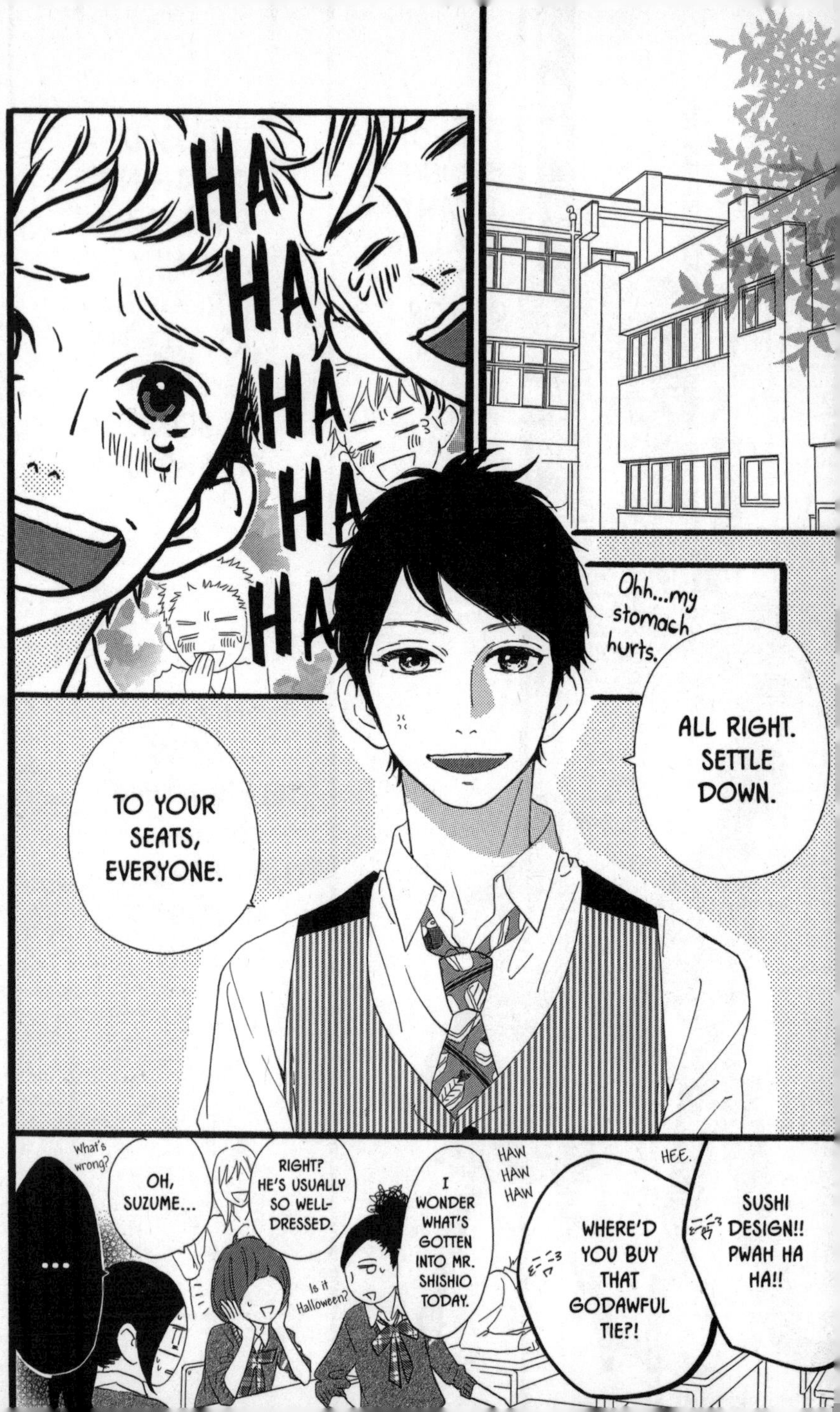
HA HA HA HA HA
Ohh...my stomach hurts.
ALL RIGHT. SETTLE DOWN.
TO YOUR SEATS, EVERYONE.
SUSHI DESIGN!! PWAH HA HA!!
HEE.
WHERE'D YOU BUY THAT GODAWFUL TIE?!
HAW HAW HAW
I WONDER WHAT'S GOTTEN INTO MR. SHISHIO TODAY.
Is it Halloween?
RIGHT? HE'S USUALLY SO WELL-DRESSED.
OH, SUZUME...
What's wrong?
...

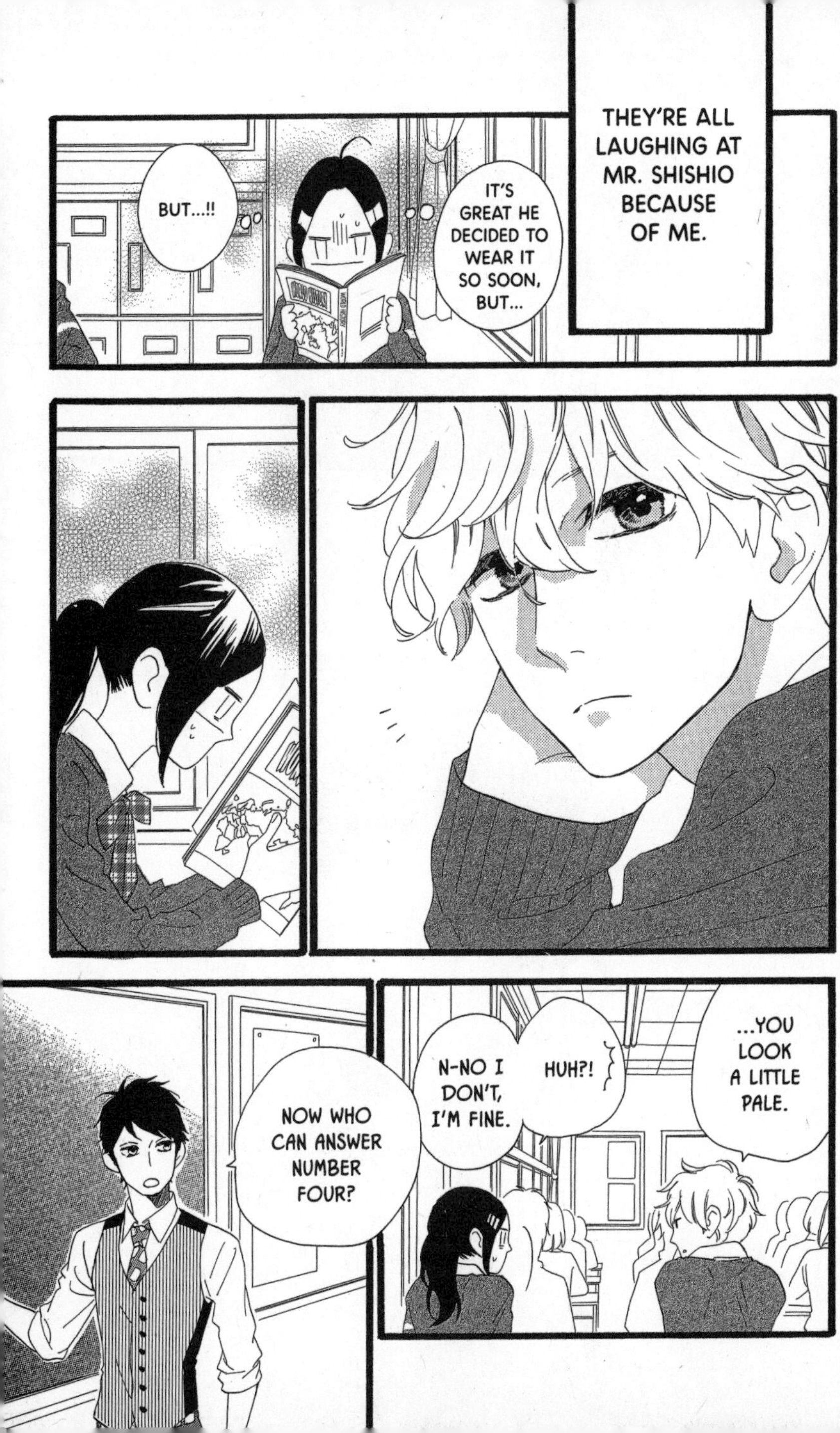
THEY'RE ALL LAUGHING AT MR. SHISHIO BECAUSE OF ME.
IT'S GREAT HE DECIDED TO WEAR IT SO SOON, BUT...
BUT...!!
...YOU LOOK A LITTLE PALE.
HUH?!
N-NO I DON'T, I'M FINE.
NOW WHO CAN ANSWER NUMBER FOUR?

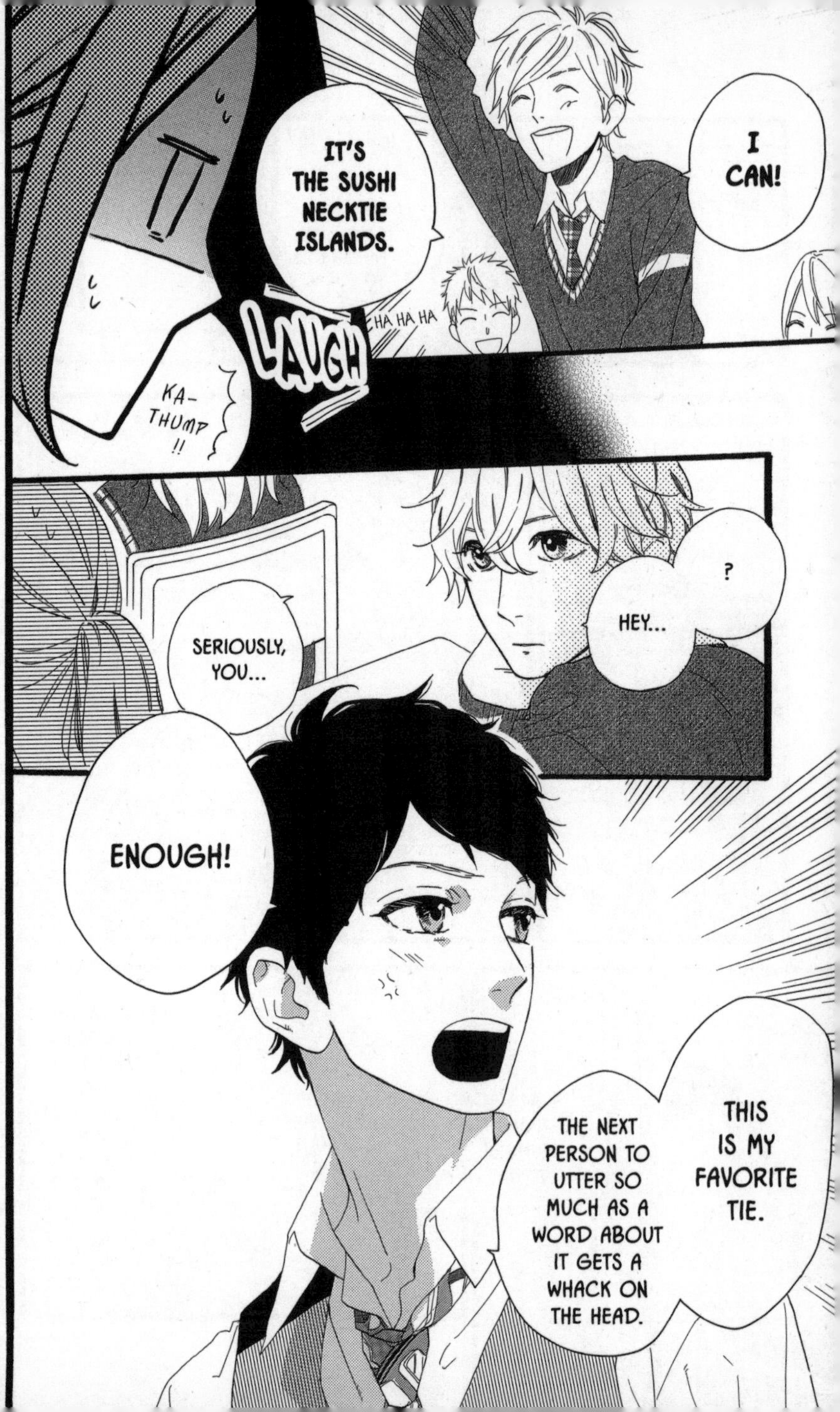
I CAN!
IT'S THE SUSHI NECKTIE ISLANDS.
HA HA HA
LAUGH
KA-THUMP !!
?
HEY...
SERIOUSLY, YOU...
THIS IS MY FAVORITE TIE.
THE NEXT PERSON TO UTTER SO MUCH AS A WORD ABOUT IT GETS A WHACK ON THE HEAD.
ENOUGH!

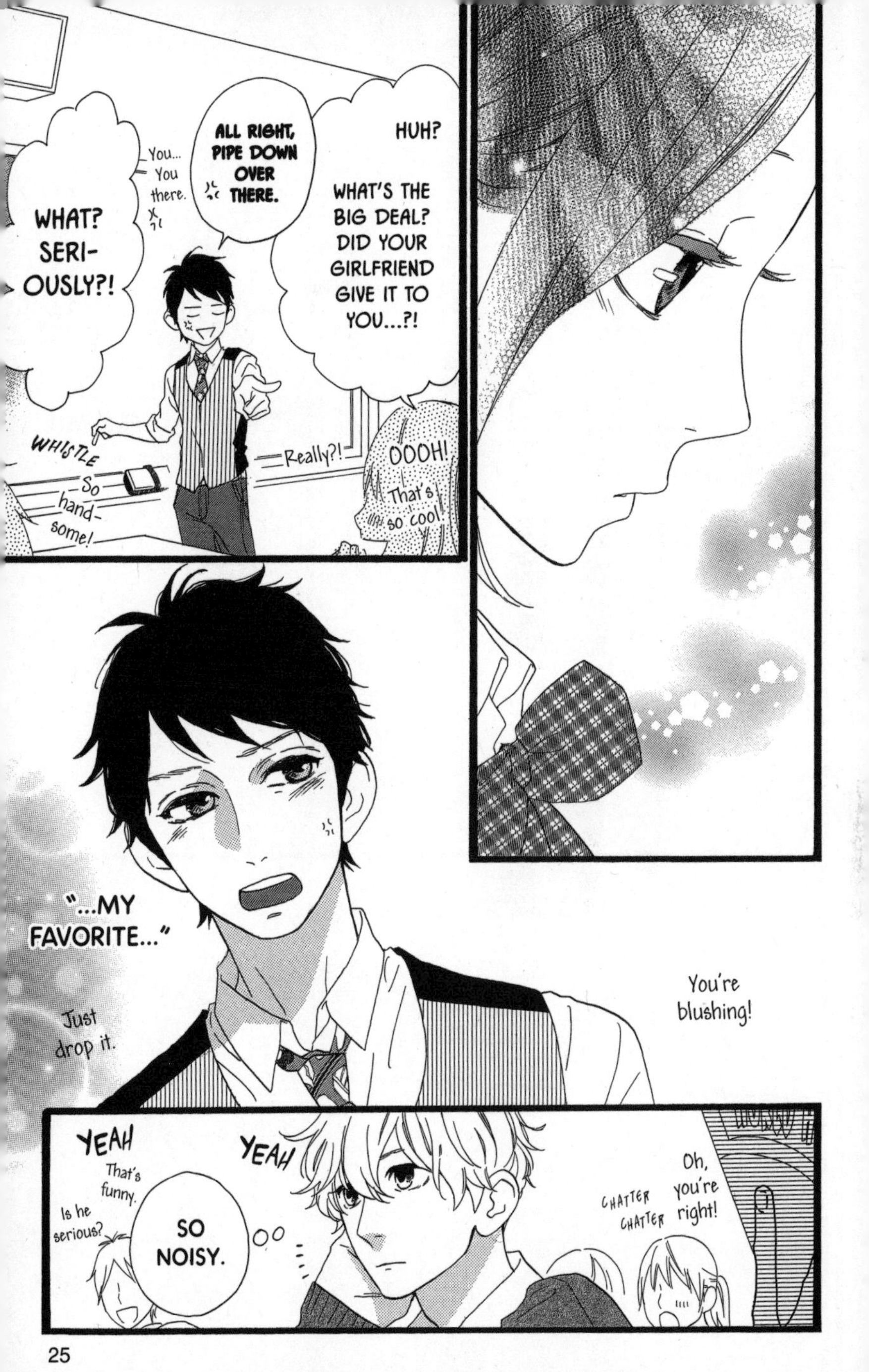
HUH?
WHAT'S THE BIG DEAL? DID YOUR GIRLFRIEND GIVE IT TO YOU...?!
ALL RIGHT, PIPE DOWN OVER THERE.
You... You there.
WHAT? SERI-OUSLY?!
OOOH!
That's so cool!
Really?!
WHISTLE
So hand-some!
You're blushing!
"...MY FAVORITE..."
Just drop it.
Oh, you're right!
CHATTER CHATTER
YEAH
SO NOISY.
YEAH
That's funny.
Is he serious?

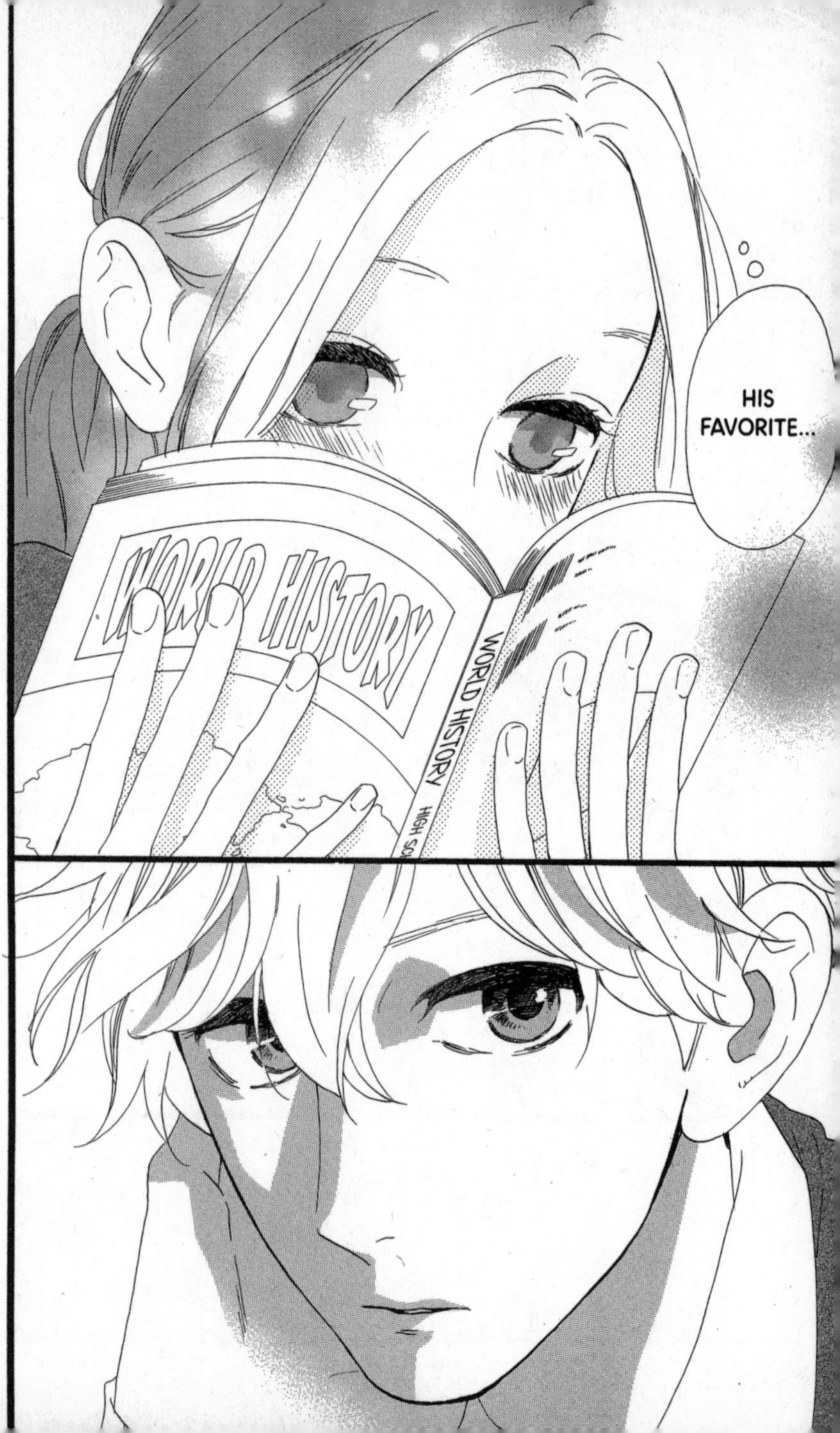
HIS FAVORITE...
WORLD HISTORY
WORLD HISTORY
HIGH SCH

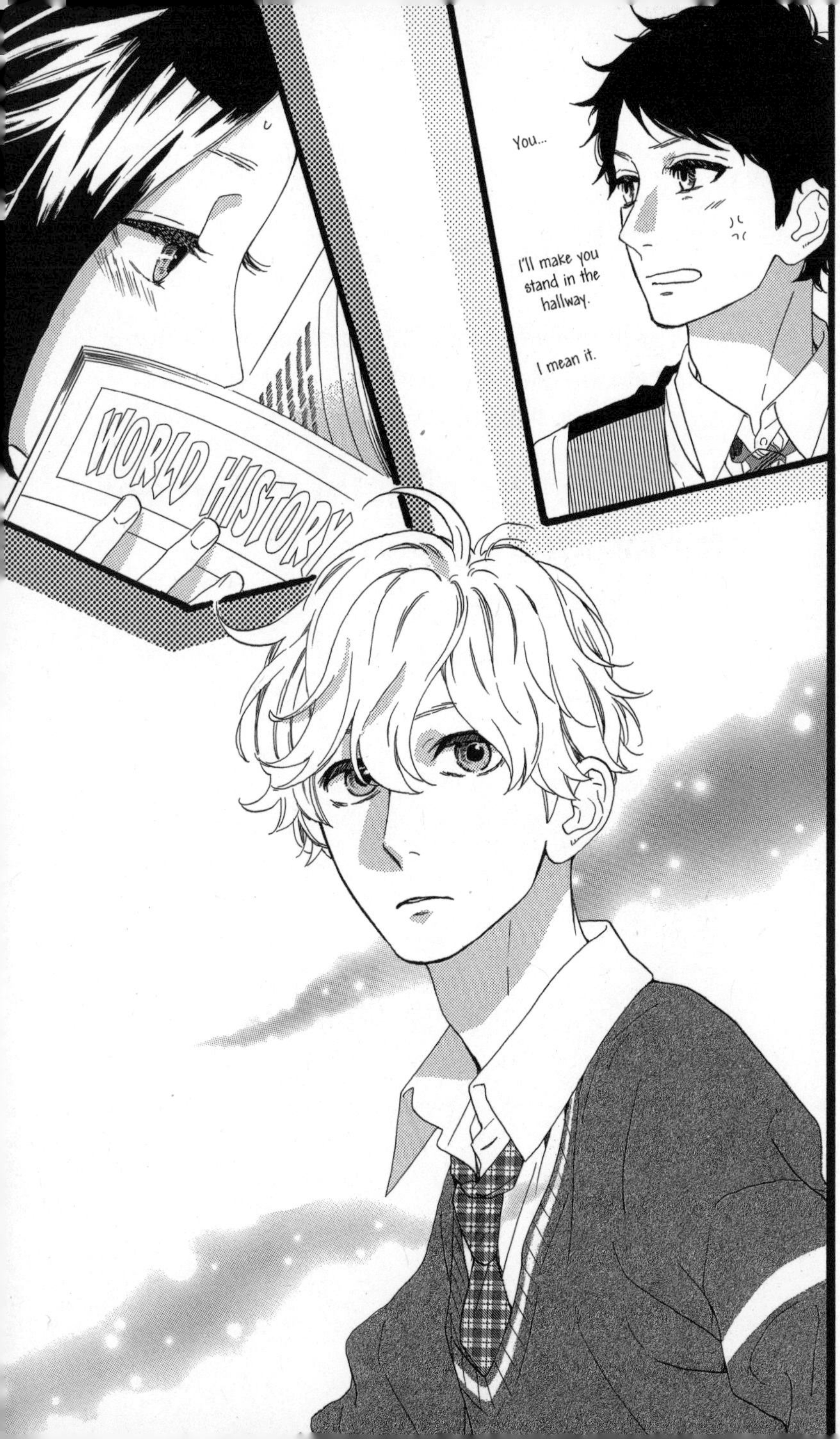
You...
I'll make you stand in the hallway.
I mean it.
WORLD HISTORY

And so...

We've reached volume 6 already! Thank you all. It's thanks to you that I've gotten this far. Thank you very much. ₊₄
There's one more thing I'd like to say:

This is not an official statement on Mamura's growth...!!

> But he does seem to be the one who's matured the most...

Well, there are still more volumes to come. I hope you'll stick with me until the end.

Yahoo!

I'm jumping for joy.

HOP   HOP

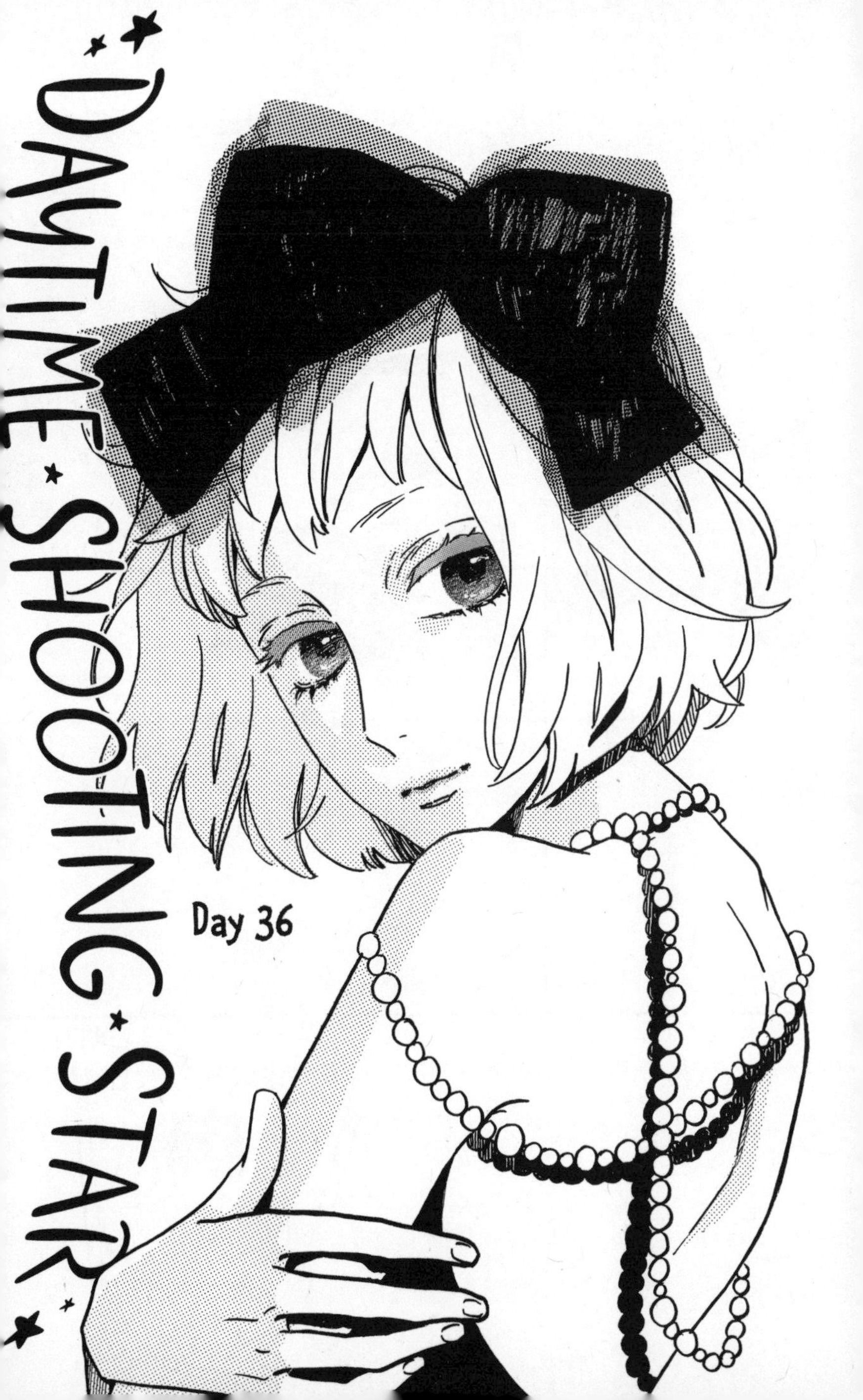
DAYTIME SHOOTING STAR
Day 36

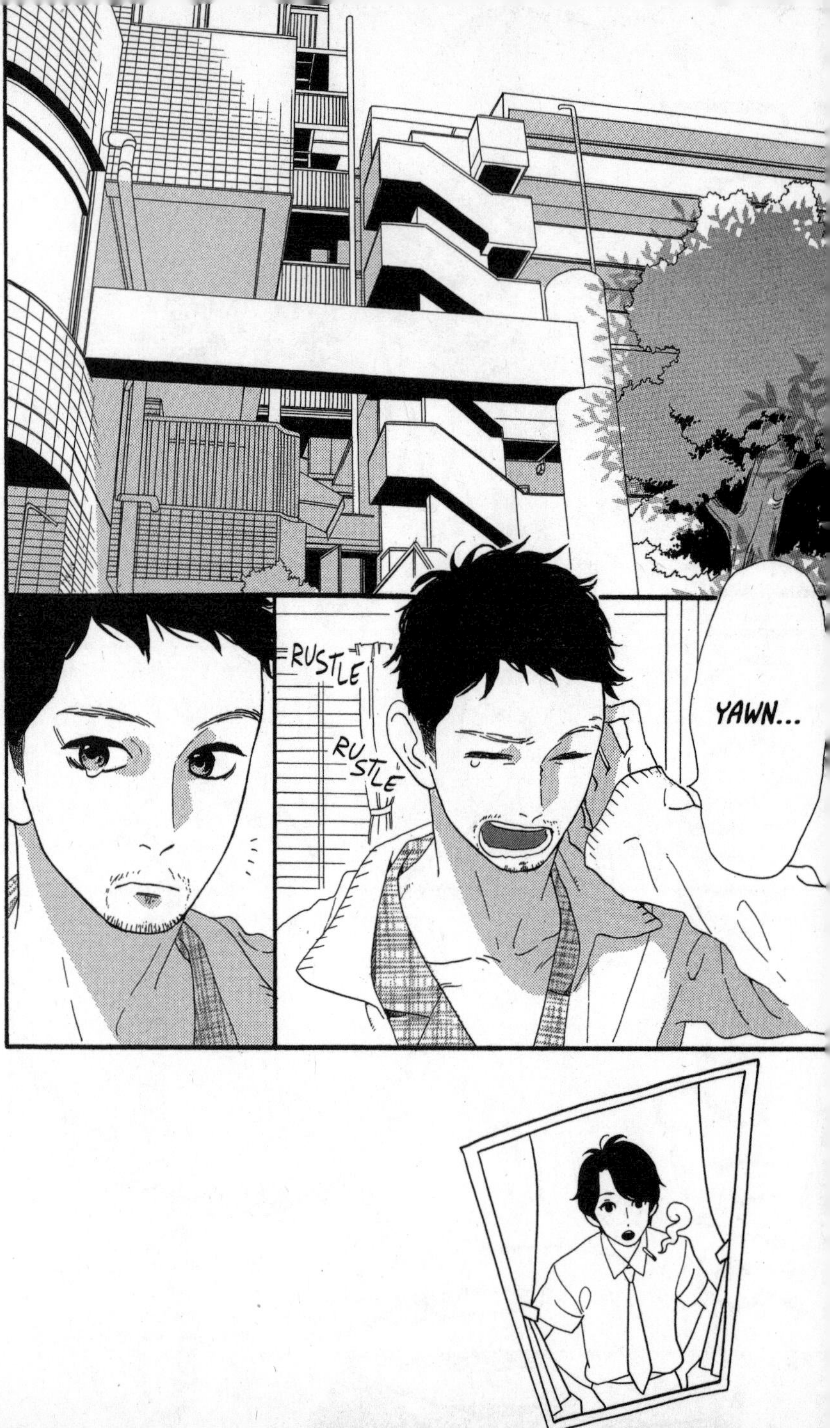
YAWN...
RUSTLE
RUSTLE

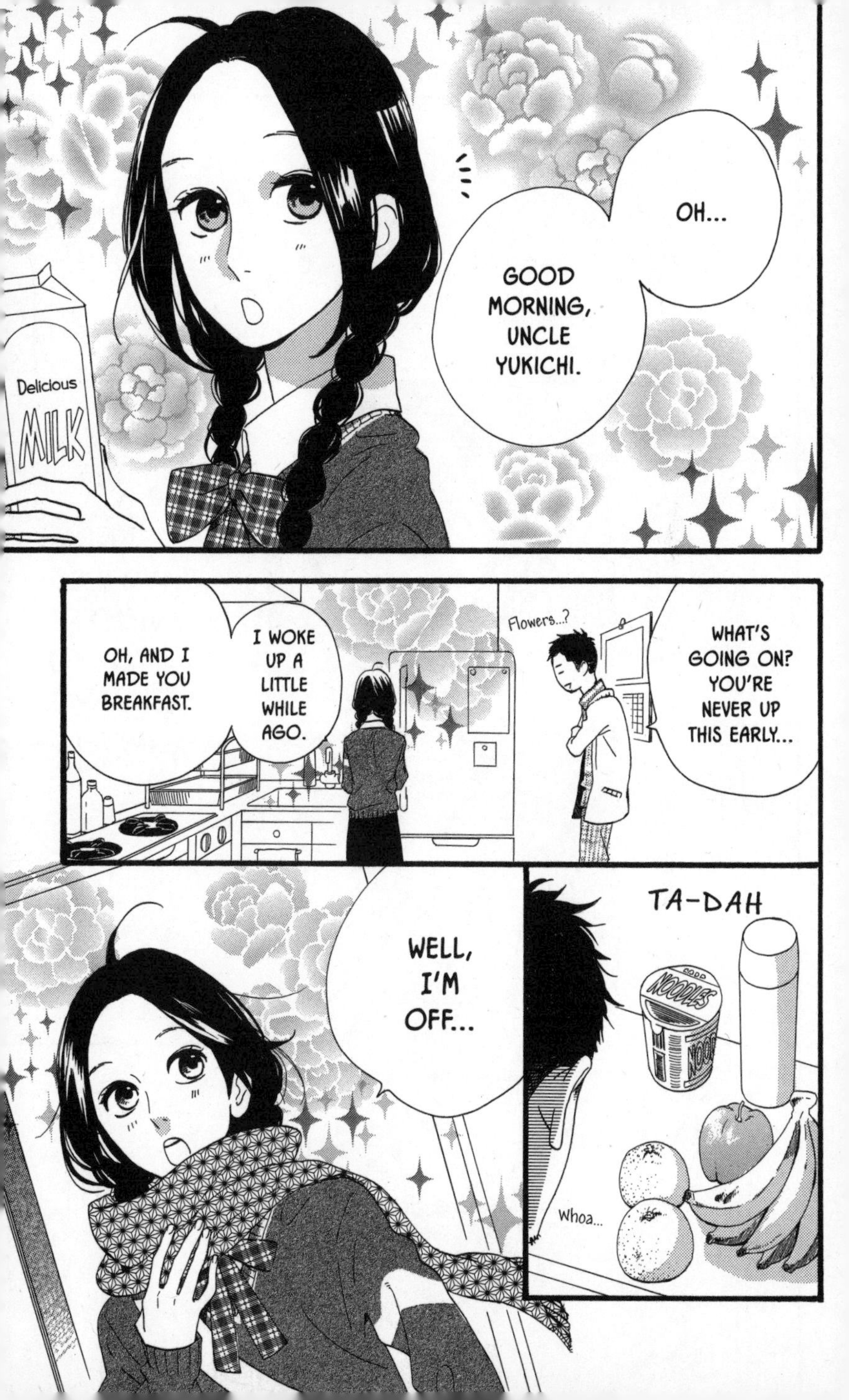
OH...
GOOD MORNING, UNCLE YUKICHI.
Delicious MILK
WHAT'S GOING ON? YOU'RE NEVER UP THIS EARLY...
Flowers...?
I WOKE UP A LITTLE WHILE AGO.
OH, AND I MADE YOU BREAKFAST.
TA-DAH
NOODLES
Whoa...
WELL, I'M OFF...

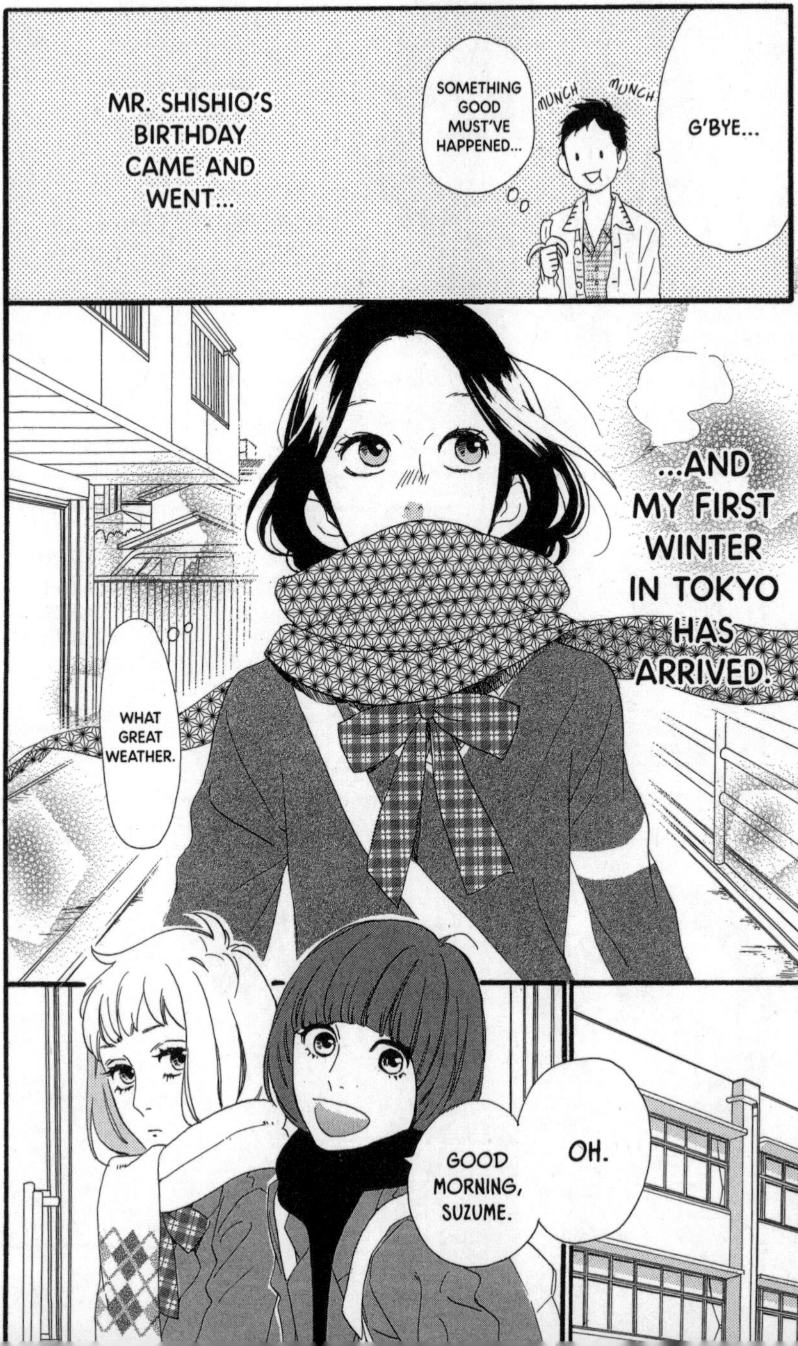
G'BYE...
MUNCH
MUNCH
SOMETHING GOOD MUST'VE HAPPENED...
MR. SHISHIO'S BIRTHDAY CAME AND WENT...
...AND MY FIRST WINTER IN TOKYO HAS ARRIVED.
WHAT GREAT WEATHER.
OH.
GOOD MORNING, SUZUME.

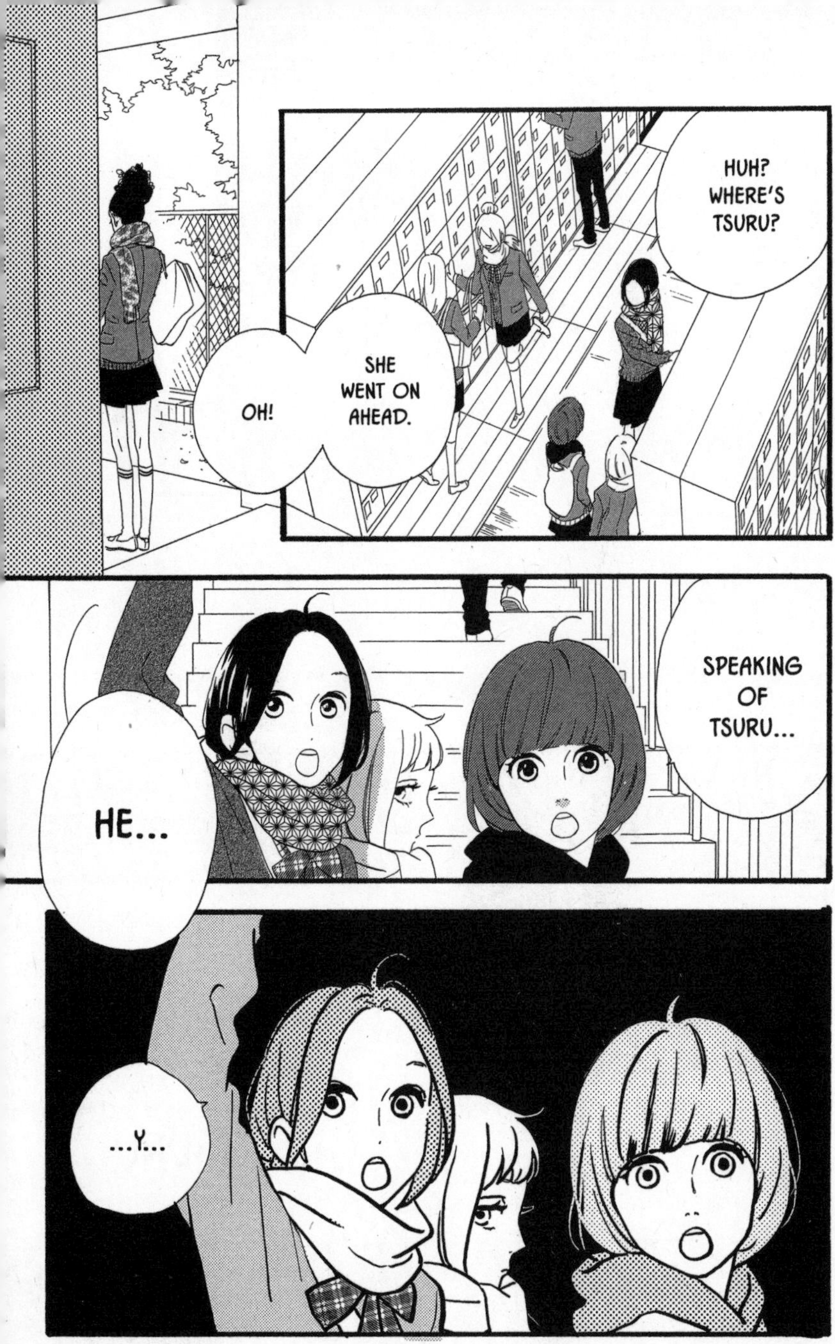
HUH? WHERE'S TSURU?
SHE WENT ON AHEAD.
OH!
SPEAKING OF TSURU...
HE...
...Y...

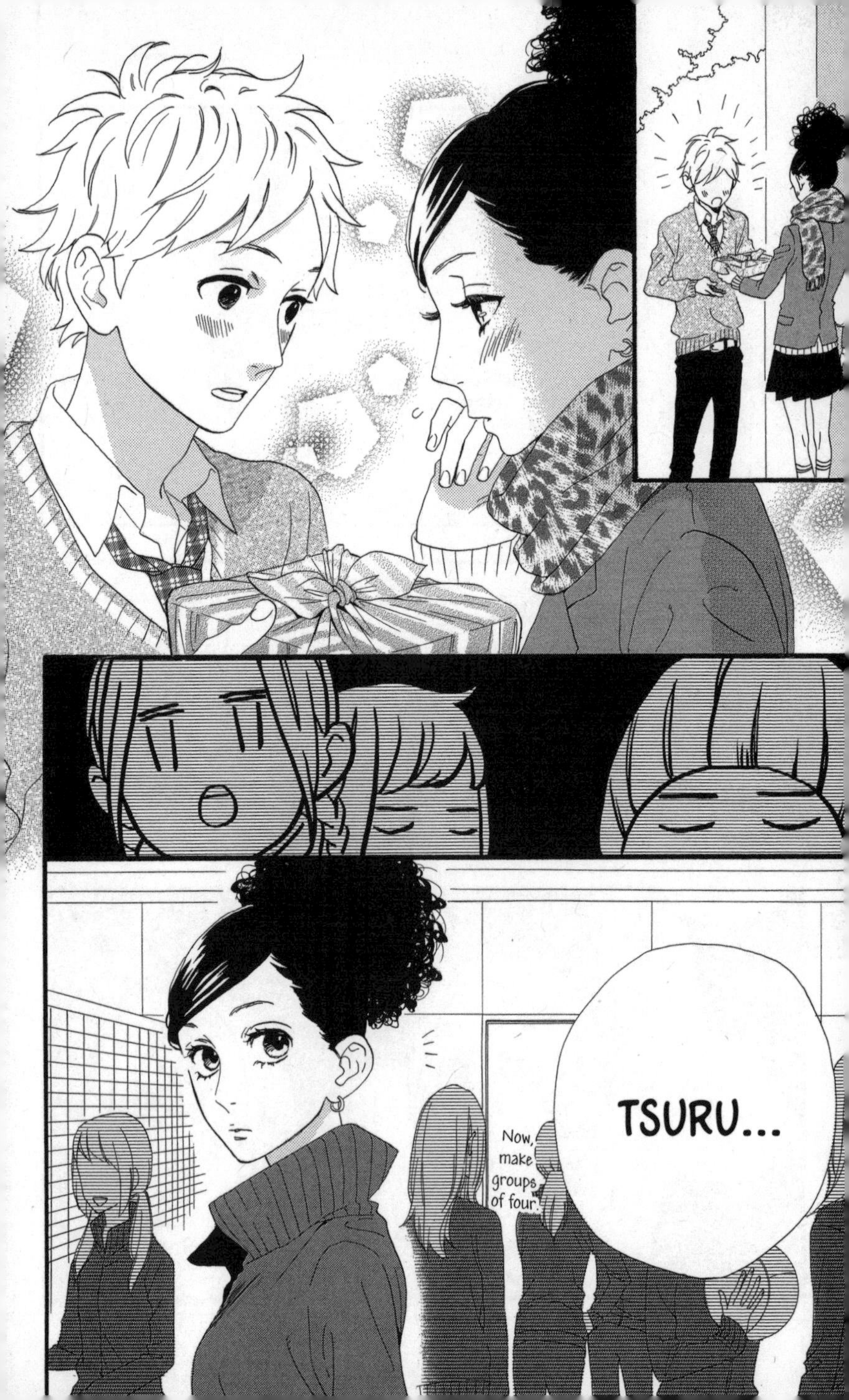

TSURU...
Now, make groups of four.

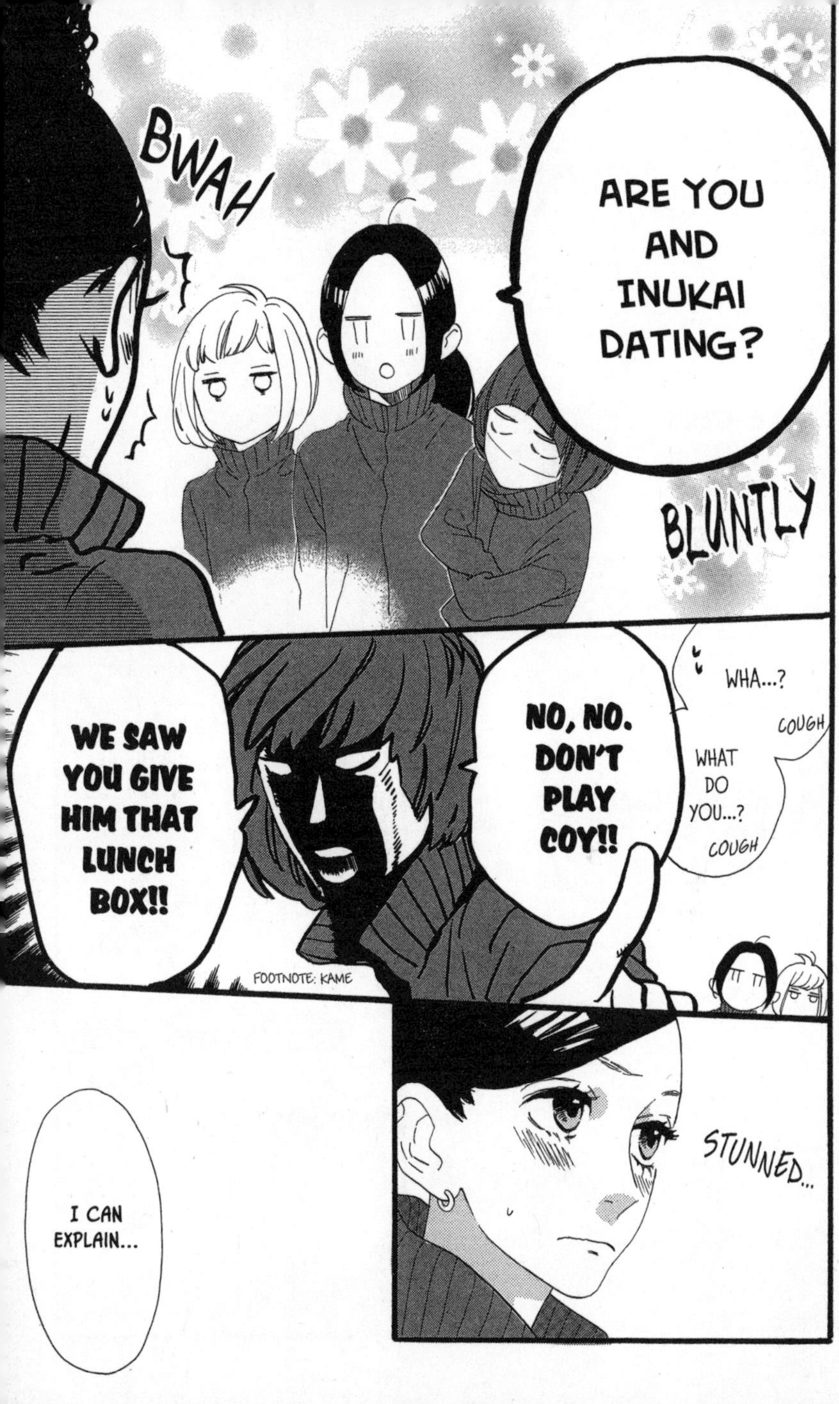
ARE YOU AND INUKAI DATING?
BLUNTLY
BWAH
WHA...?
COUGH
WHAT DO YOU...?
COUGH
NO, NO. DON'T PLAY COY!!
WE SAW YOU GIVE HIM THAT LUNCH BOX!!
FOOTNOTE: KAME
STUNNED...
I CAN EXPLAIN...

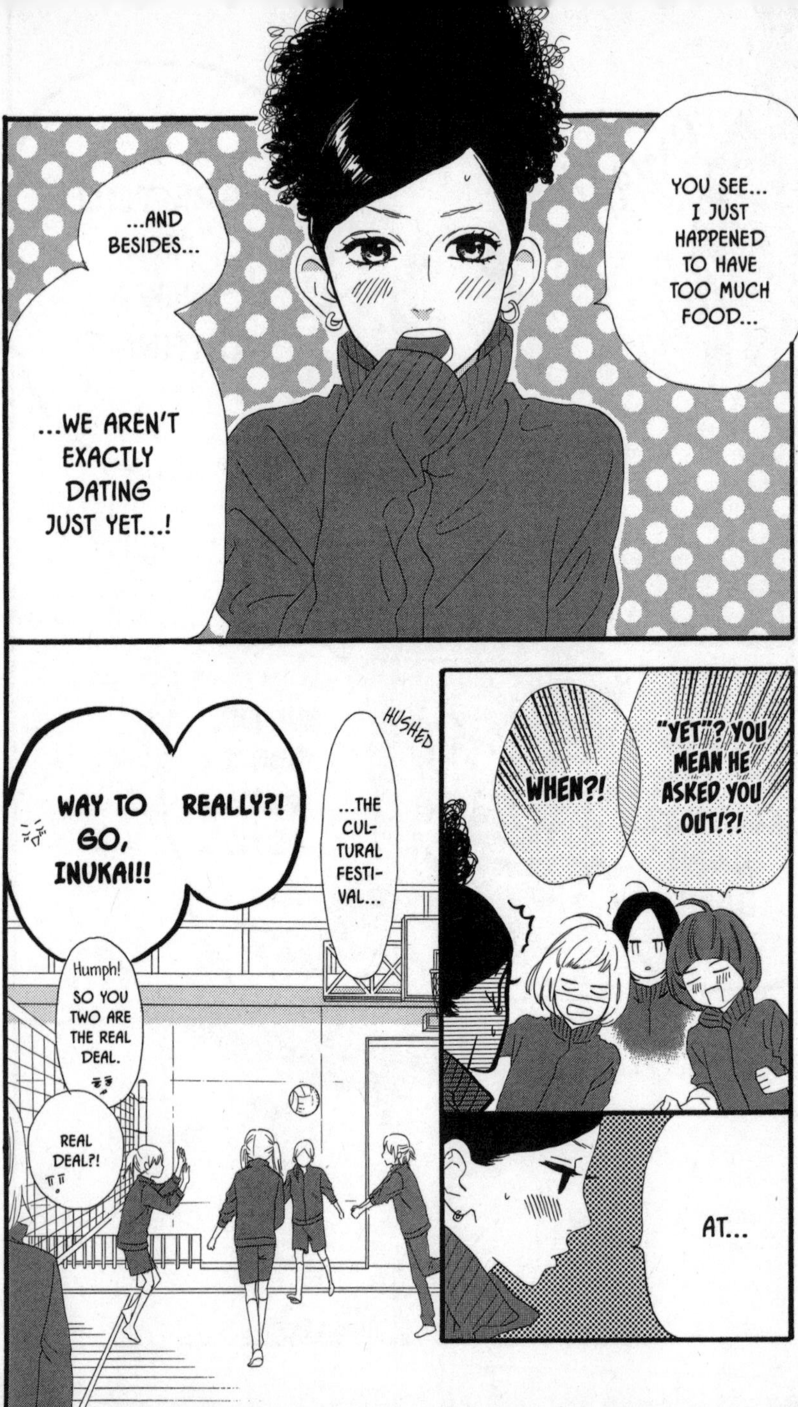
YOU SEE... I JUST HAPPENED TO HAVE TOO MUCH FOOD...
...AND BESIDES...
...WE AREN'T EXACTLY DATING JUST YET...!
"YET"? YOU MEAN HE ASKED YOU OUT!?!
WHEN?!
AT...
HUSHED
...THE CUL-TURAL FESTI-VAL...
REALLY?!
WAY TO GO, INUKAI!!
Humph! SO YOU TWO ARE THE REAL DEAL.
REAL DEAL?!

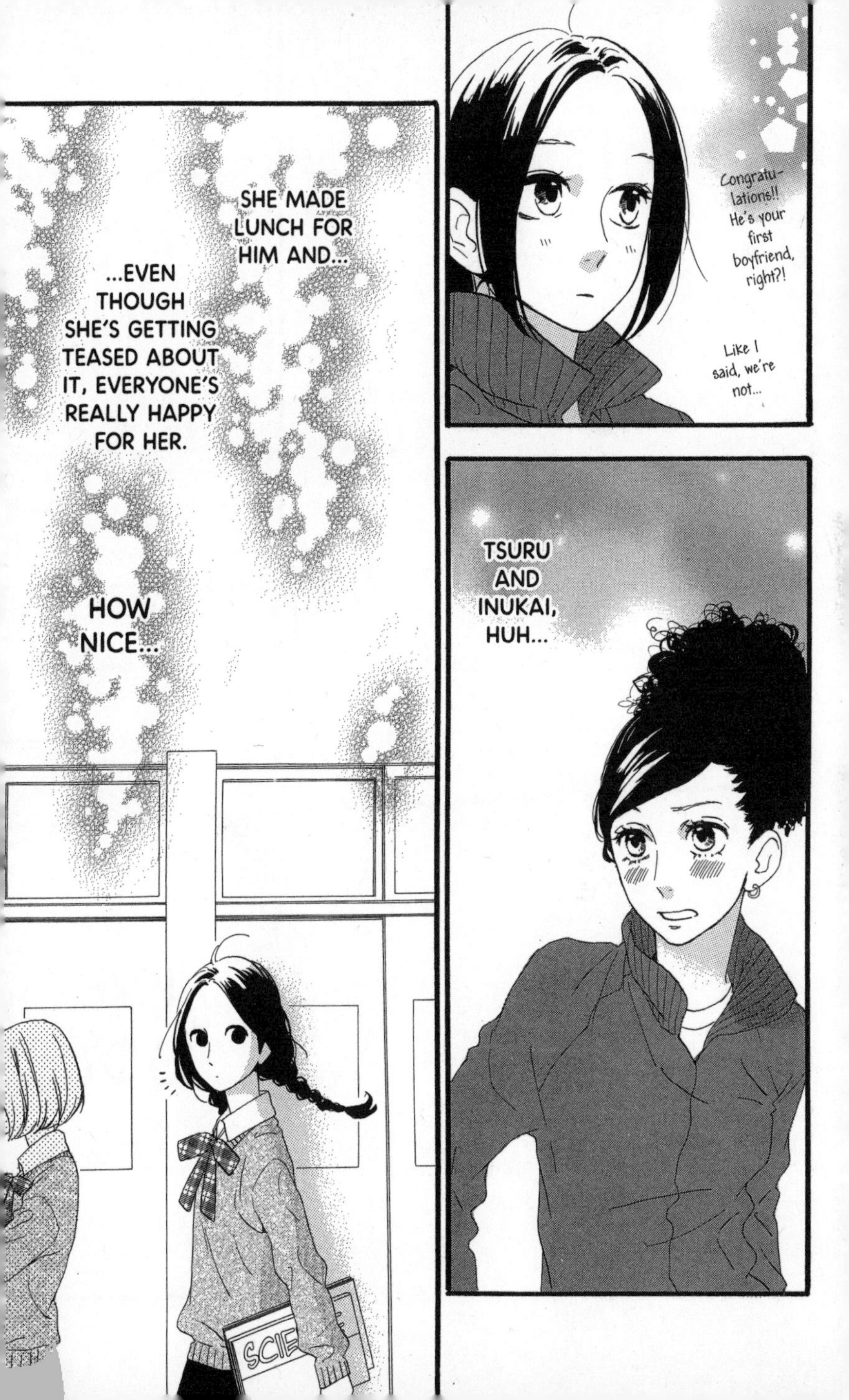
Congratu-lations!! He's your first boyfriend, right?!
Like I said, we're not...
TSURU AND INUKAI, HUH...
SHE MADE LUNCH FOR HIM AND...
...EVEN THOUGH SHE'S GETTING TEASED ABOUT IT, EVERYONE'S REALLY HAPPY FOR HER.
HOW NICE...
SCIE

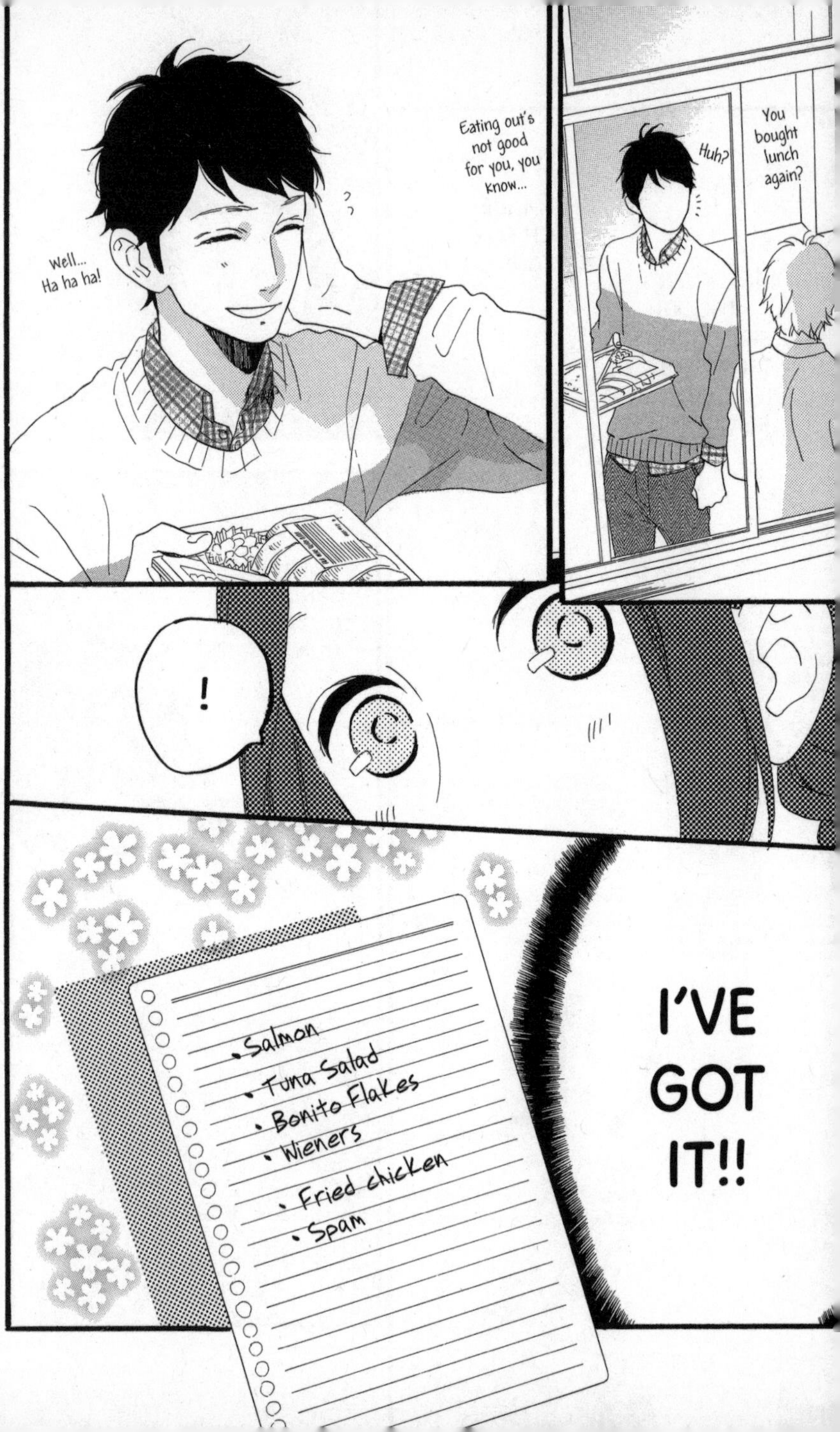
You bought lunch again?
Huh?
Eating out's not good for you, you know...
Well... Ha ha ha!
!
I'VE GOT IT!!
• Salmon
• Tuna Salad
• Bonito Flakes
• Wieners
• Fried chicken
• Spam

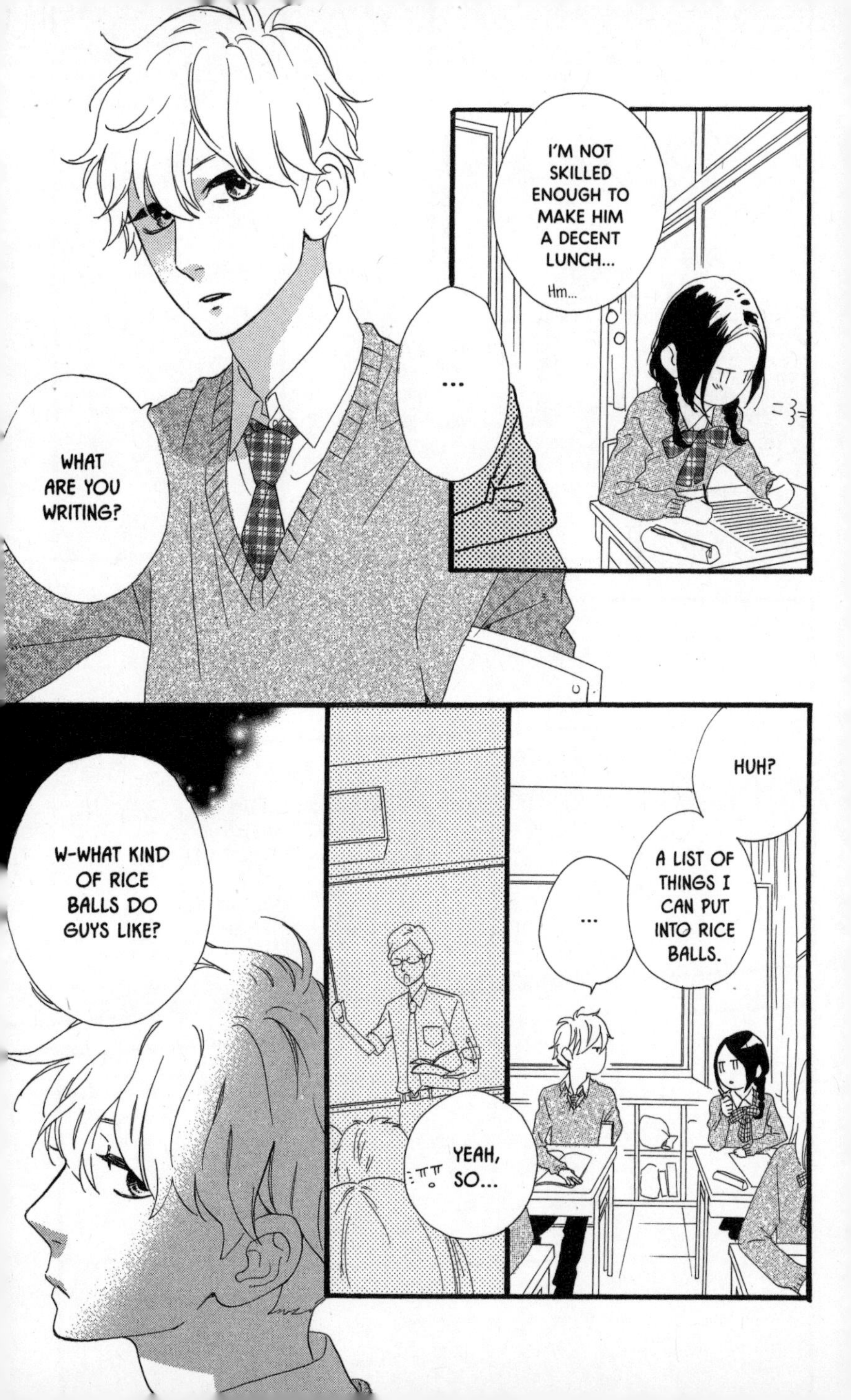
I'M NOT SKILLED ENOUGH TO MAKE HIM A DECENT LUNCH...
Hm...
...
WHAT ARE YOU WRITING?
HUH?
A LIST OF THINGS I CAN PUT INTO RICE BALLS.
...
YEAH, SO...
W-WHAT KIND OF RICE BALLS DO GUYS LIKE?

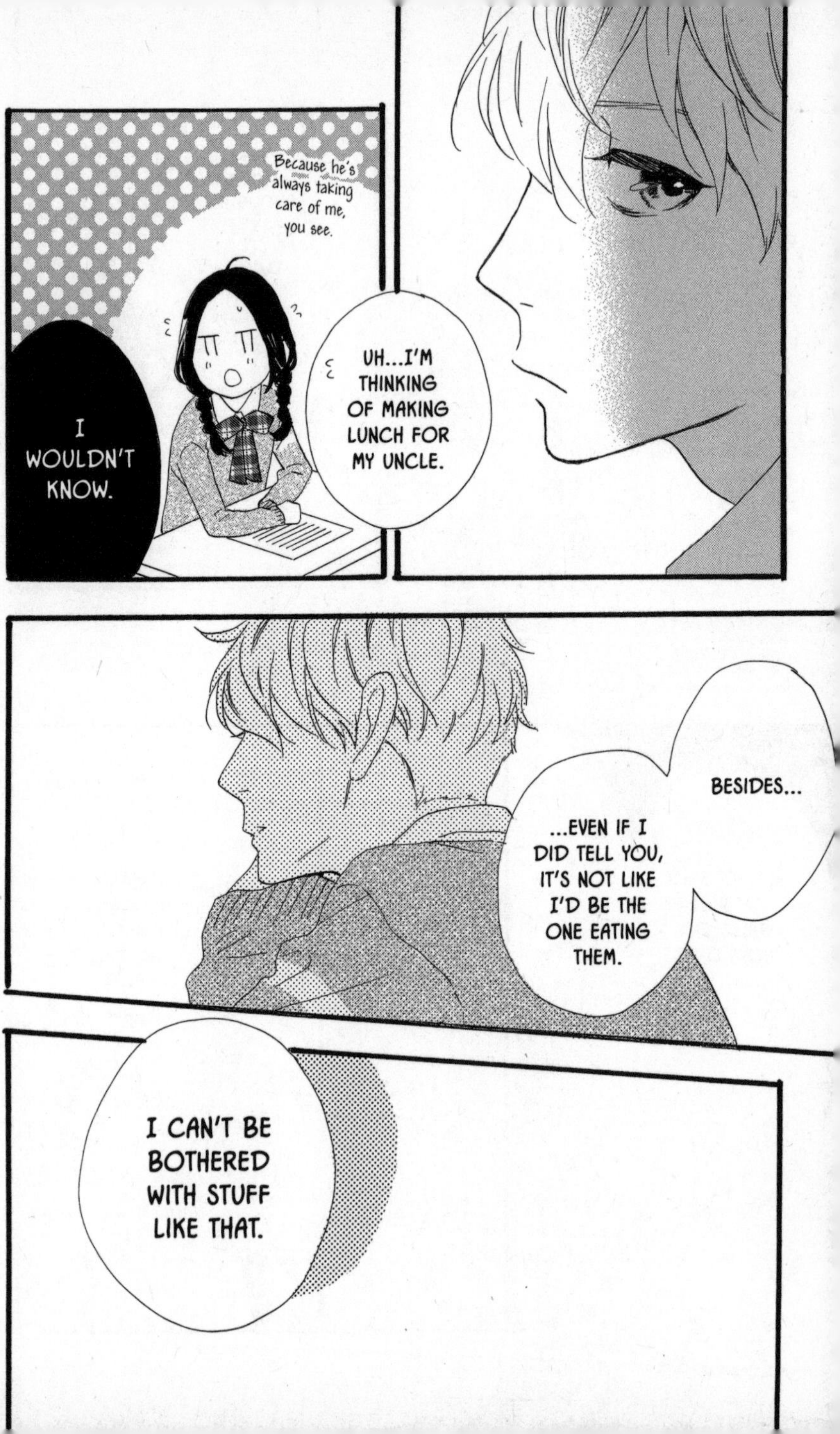
UH...I'M THINKING OF MAKING LUNCH FOR MY UNCLE.
Because he's always taking care of me, you see.
I WOULDN'T KNOW.
BESIDES...
...EVEN IF I DID TELL YOU, IT'S NOT LIKE I'D BE THE ONE EATING THEM.
I CAN'T BE BOTHERED WITH STUFF LIKE THAT.

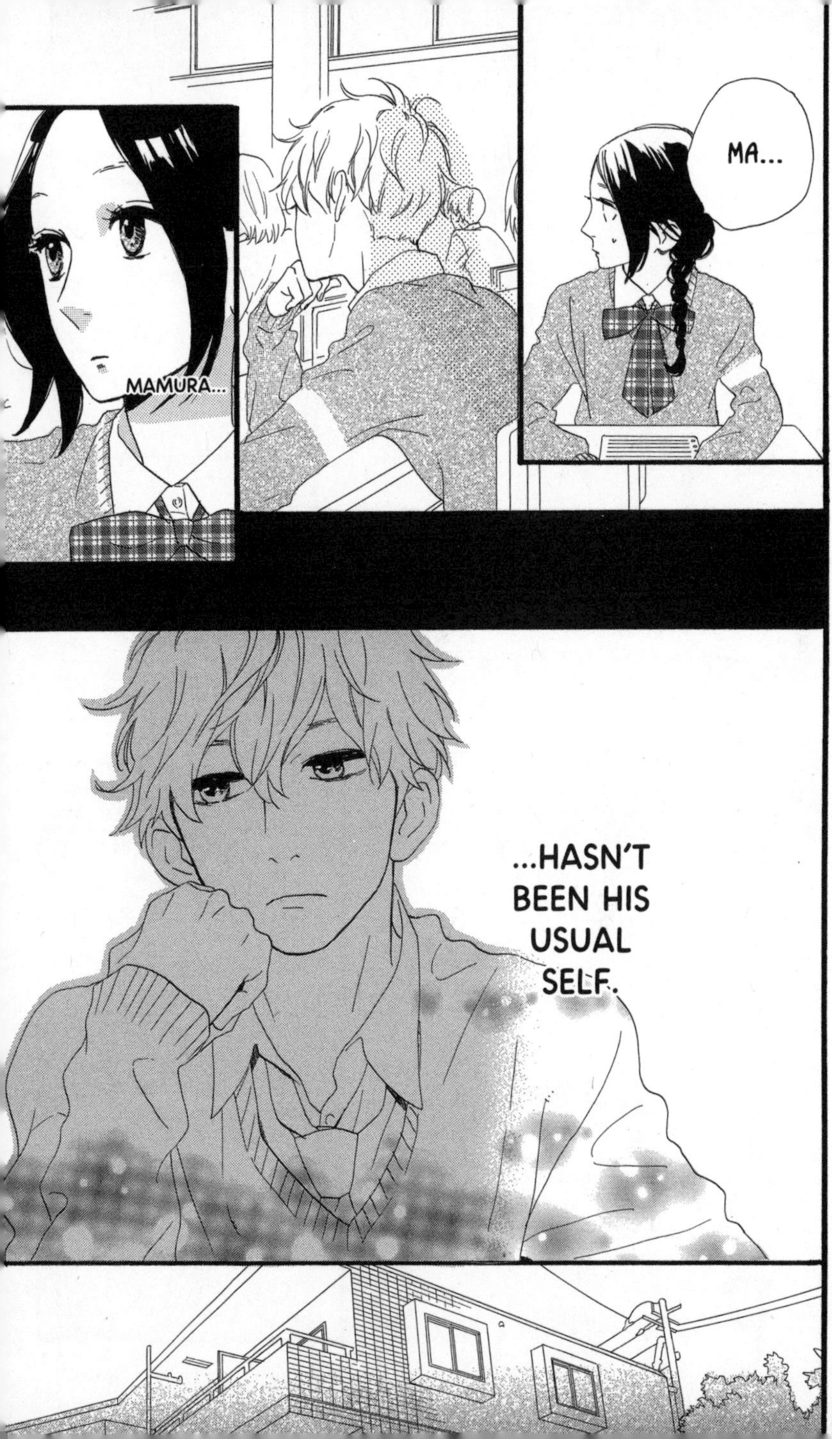
MA...
MAMURA...
...HASN'T BEEN HIS USUAL SELF.

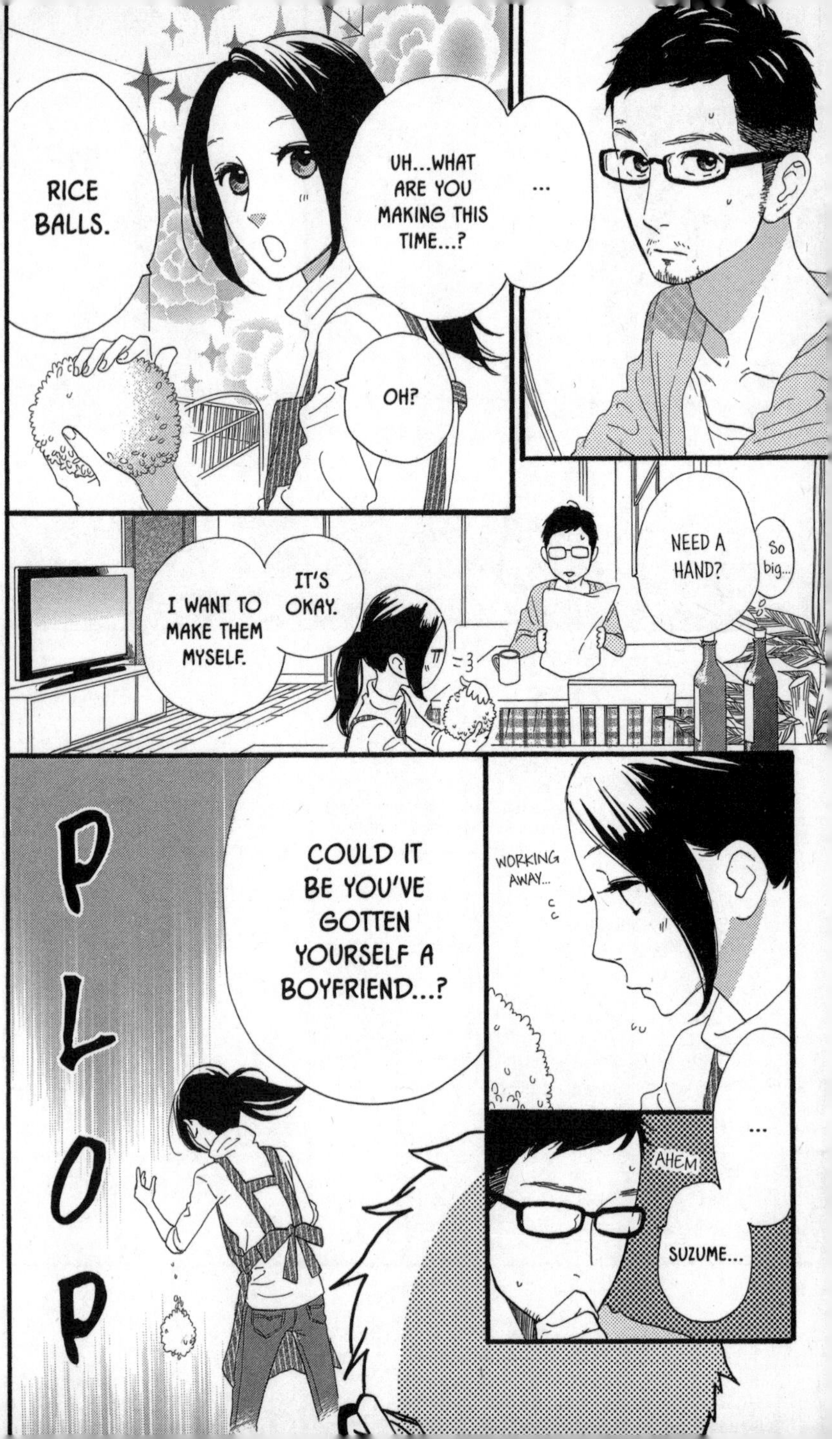
...
UH...WHAT ARE YOU MAKING THIS TIME...?
OH?
RICE BALLS.
So big...
NEED A HAND?
IT'S OKAY.
I WANT TO MAKE THEM MYSELF.
WORKING AWAY...
...
AHEM
SUZUME...
COULD IT BE YOU'VE GOTTEN YOURSELF A BOYFRIEND...?
PLOP

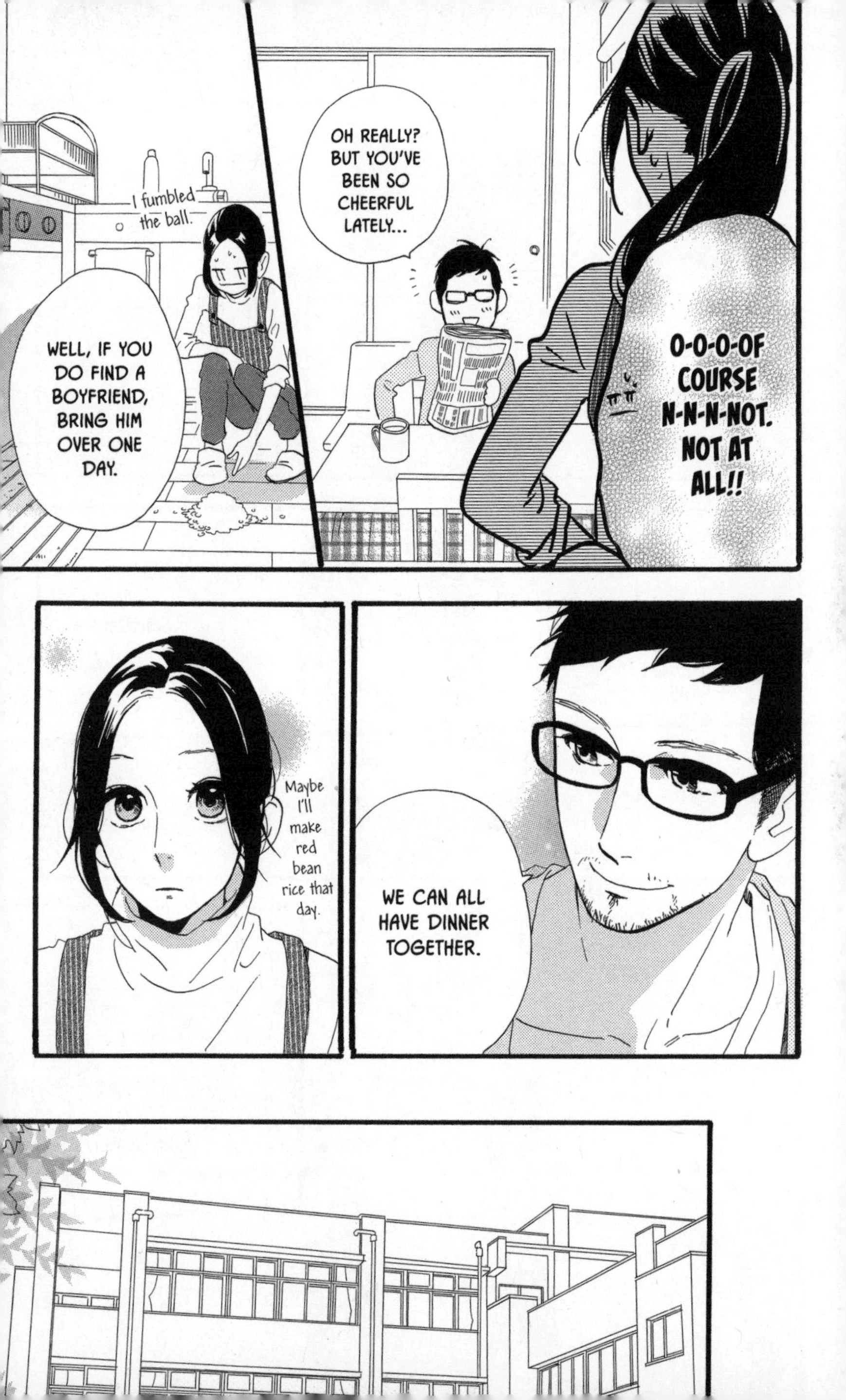
O-O-O-OF COURSE N-N-N-NOT. NOT AT ALL!!
OH REALLY? BUT YOU'VE BEEN SO CHEERFUL LATELY...
I fumbled the ball.
WELL, IF YOU DO FIND A BOYFRIEND, BRING HIM OVER ONE DAY.
WE CAN ALL HAVE DINNER TOGETHER.
Maybe I'll make red bean rice that day.

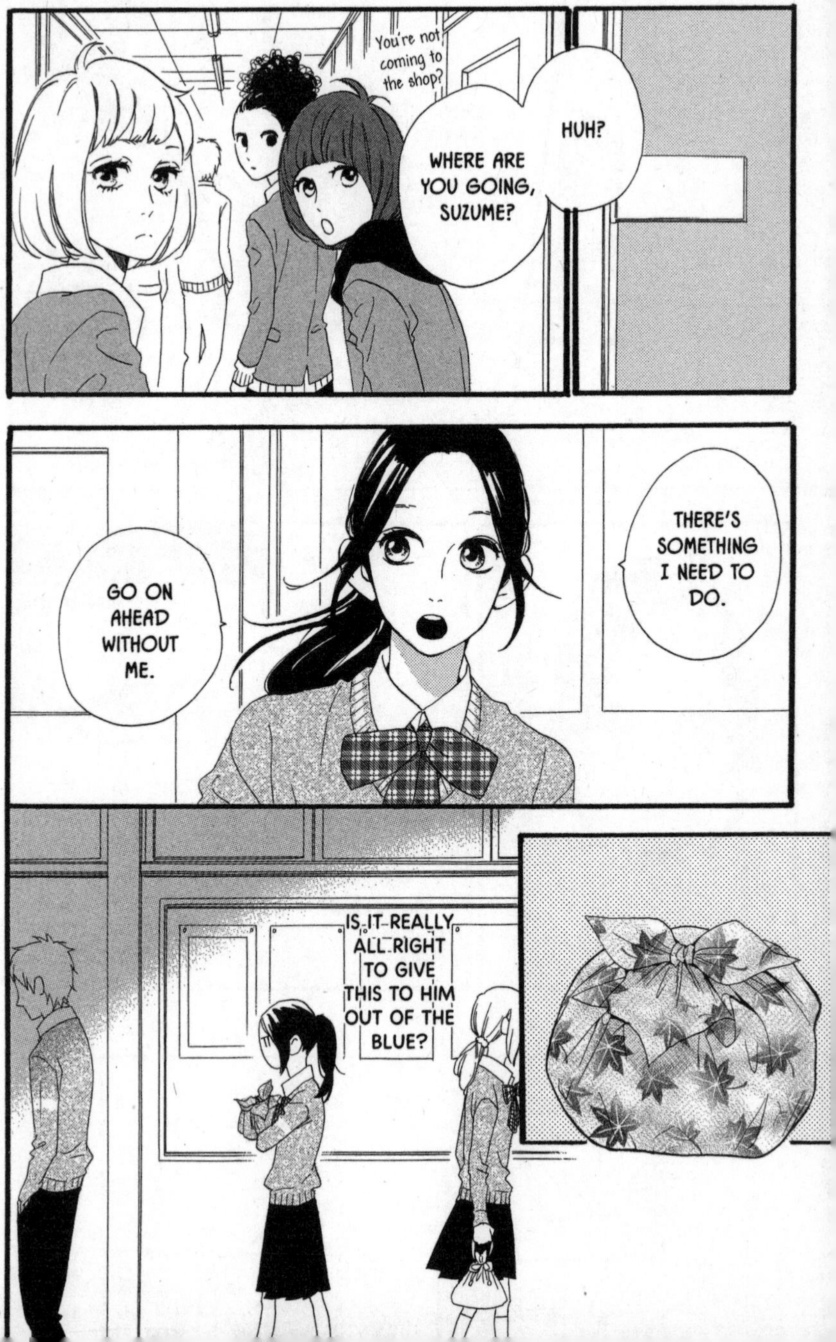
HUH?
You're not coming to the shop?
WHERE ARE YOU GOING, SUZUME?
THERE'S SOMETHING I NEED TO DO.
GO ON AHEAD WITHOUT ME.
IS IT REALLY ALL RIGHT TO GIVE THIS TO HIM OUT OF THE BLUE?

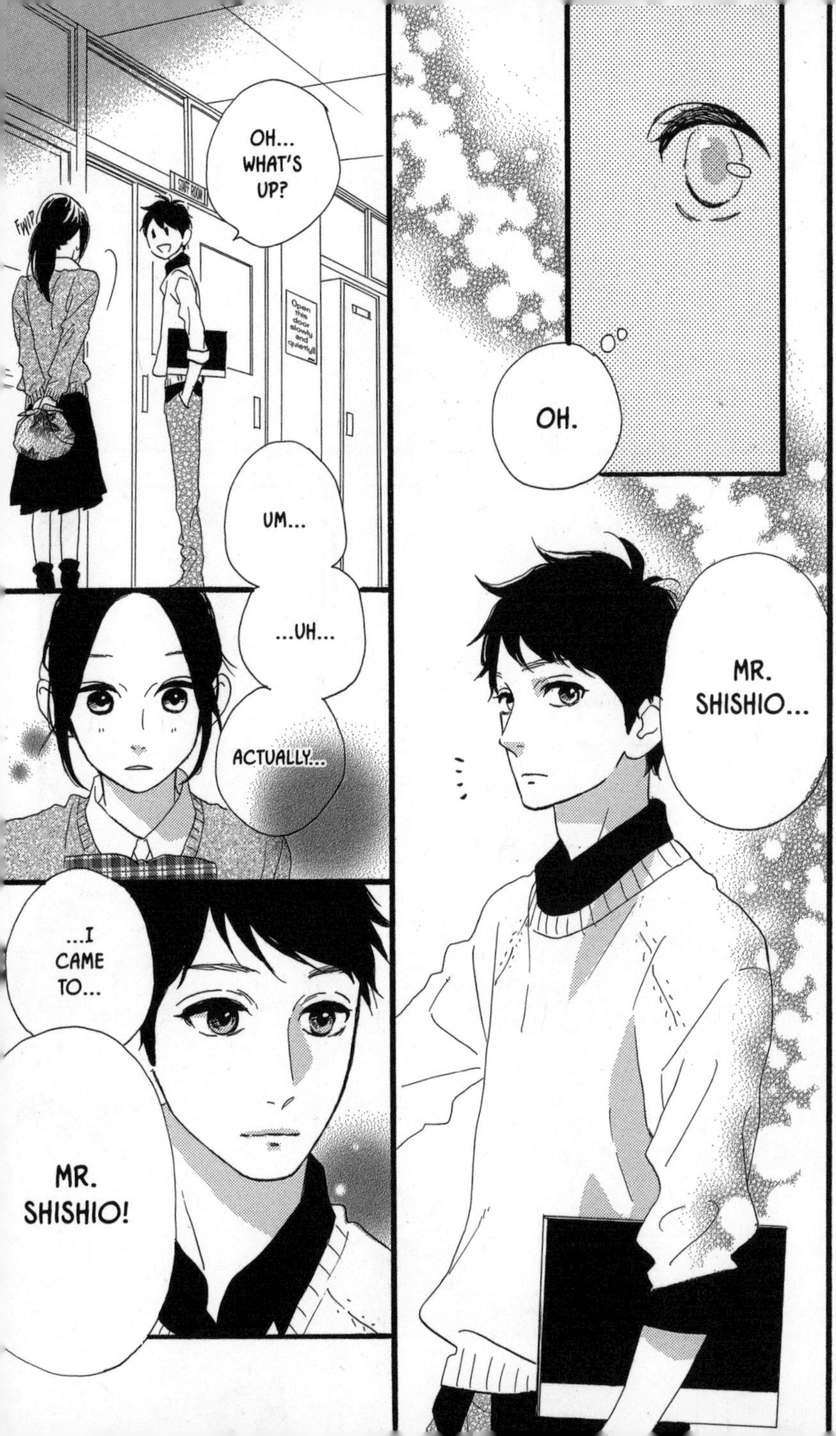
OH.
MR. SHISHIO...
FWIP
STAFF ROOM
OH... WHAT'S UP?
Open this door slowly and quietly!!
UM...
...UH...
ACTUALLY...
...I CAME TO...
MR. SHISHIO!

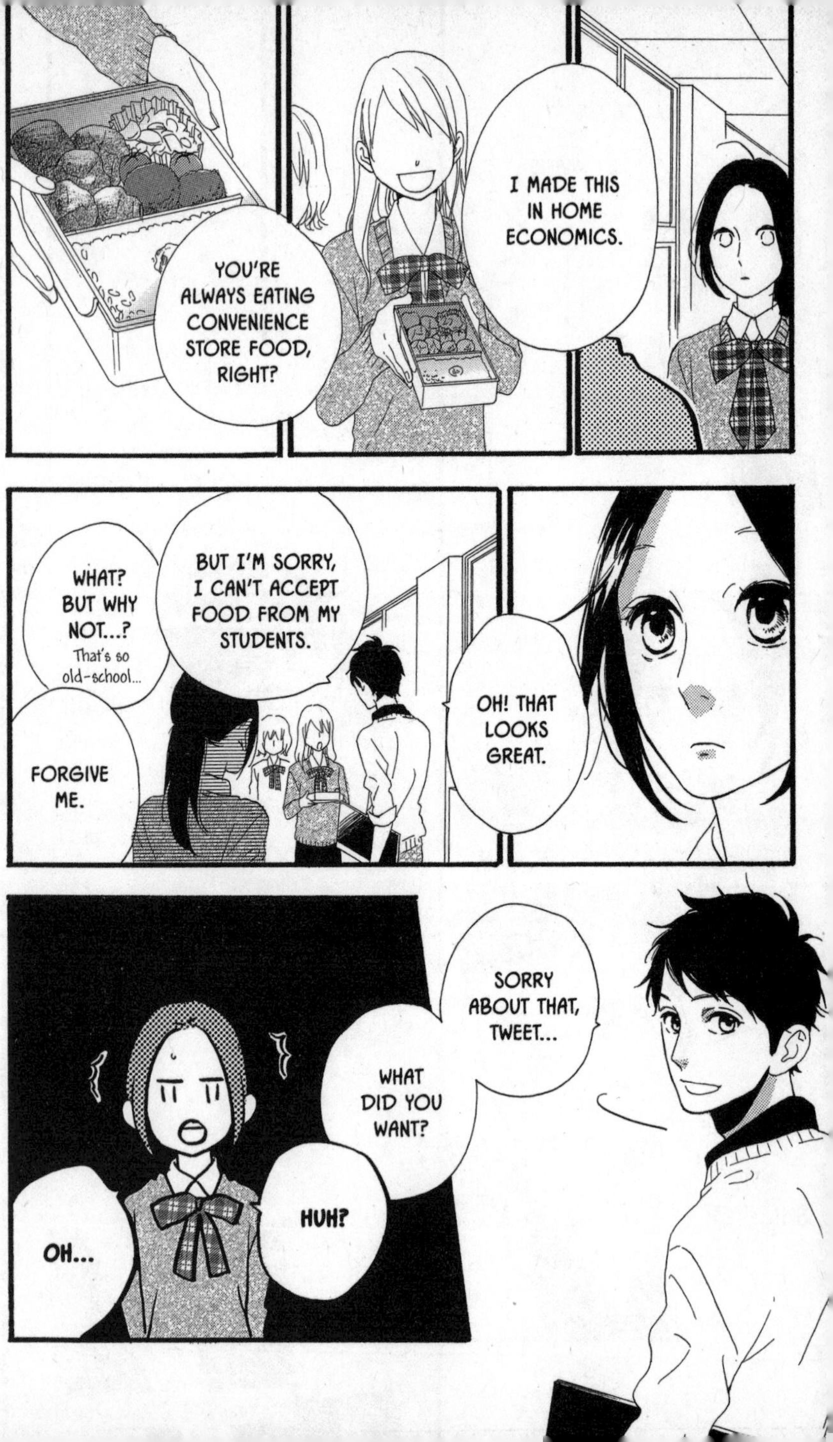
I MADE THIS IN HOME ECONOMICS.
YOU'RE ALWAYS EATING CONVENIENCE STORE FOOD, RIGHT?
OH! THAT LOOKS GREAT.
BUT I'M SORRY, I CAN'T ACCEPT FOOD FROM MY STUDENTS.
WHAT? BUT WHY NOT...?
That's so old-school...
FORGIVE ME.
SORRY ABOUT THAT, TWEET...
WHAT DID YOU WANT?
HUH?
OH...

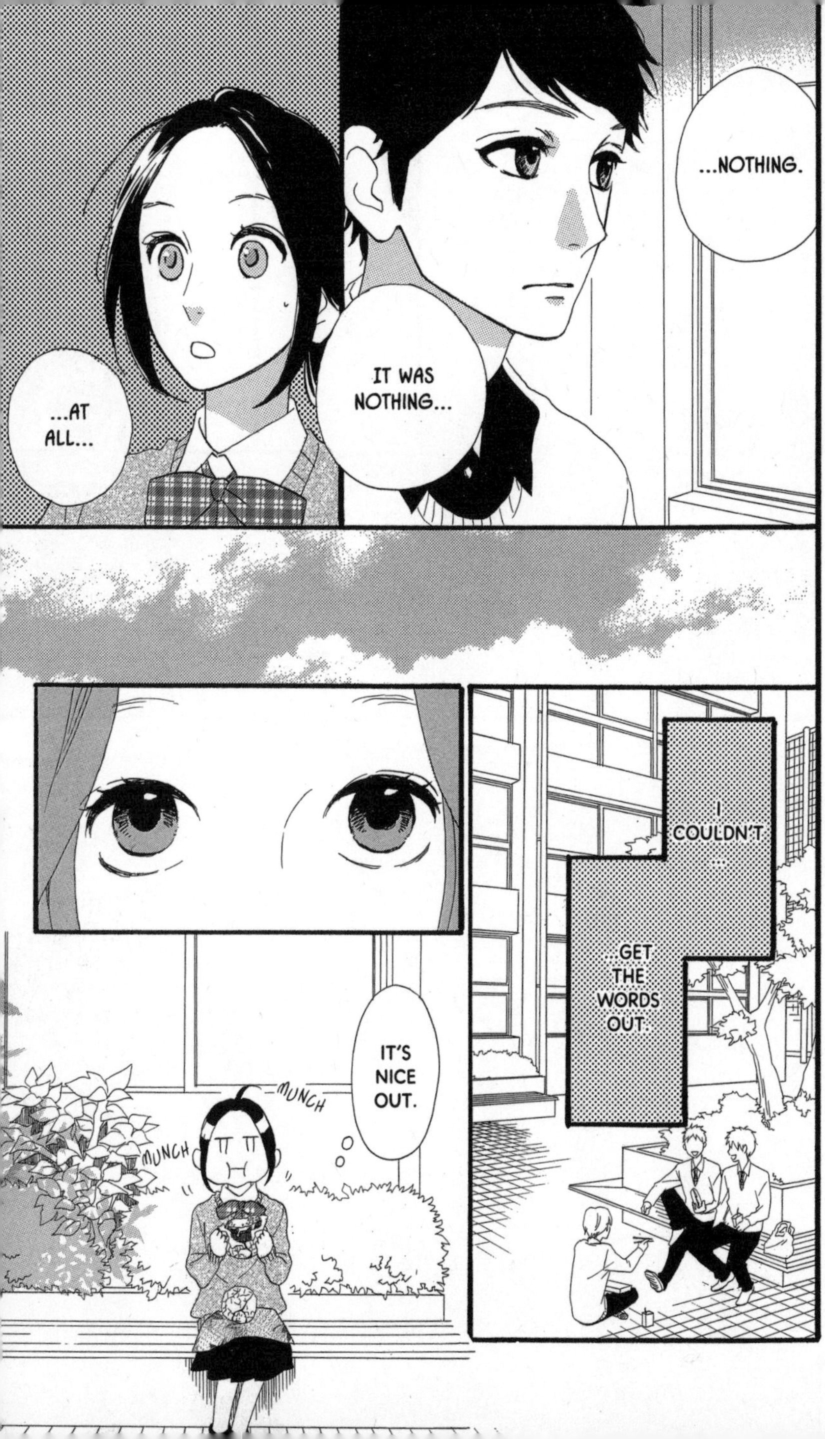
...NOTHING.
IT WAS NOTHING...
...AT ALL...
I COULDN'T
GET THE WORDS OUT
MUNCH
MUNCH
IT'S NICE OUT.

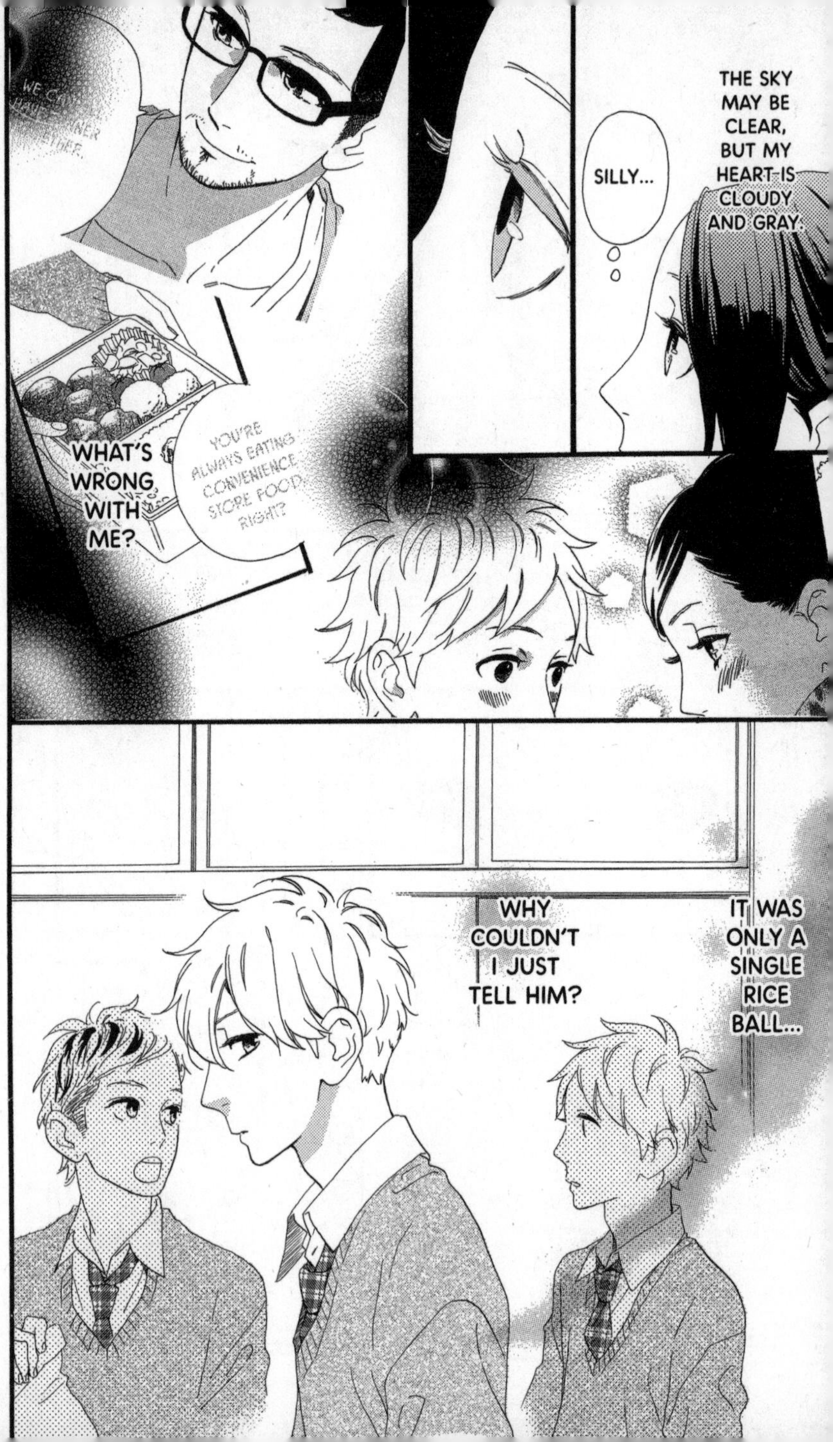
THE SKY MAY BE CLEAR, BUT MY HEART IS CLOUDY AND GRAY.
SILLY...
YOU'RE ALWAYS EATING CONVENIENCE STORE FOOD, RIGHT?
WHAT'S WRONG WITH ME?
IT WAS ONLY A SINGLE RICE BALL...
WHY COULDN'T I JUST TELL HIM?

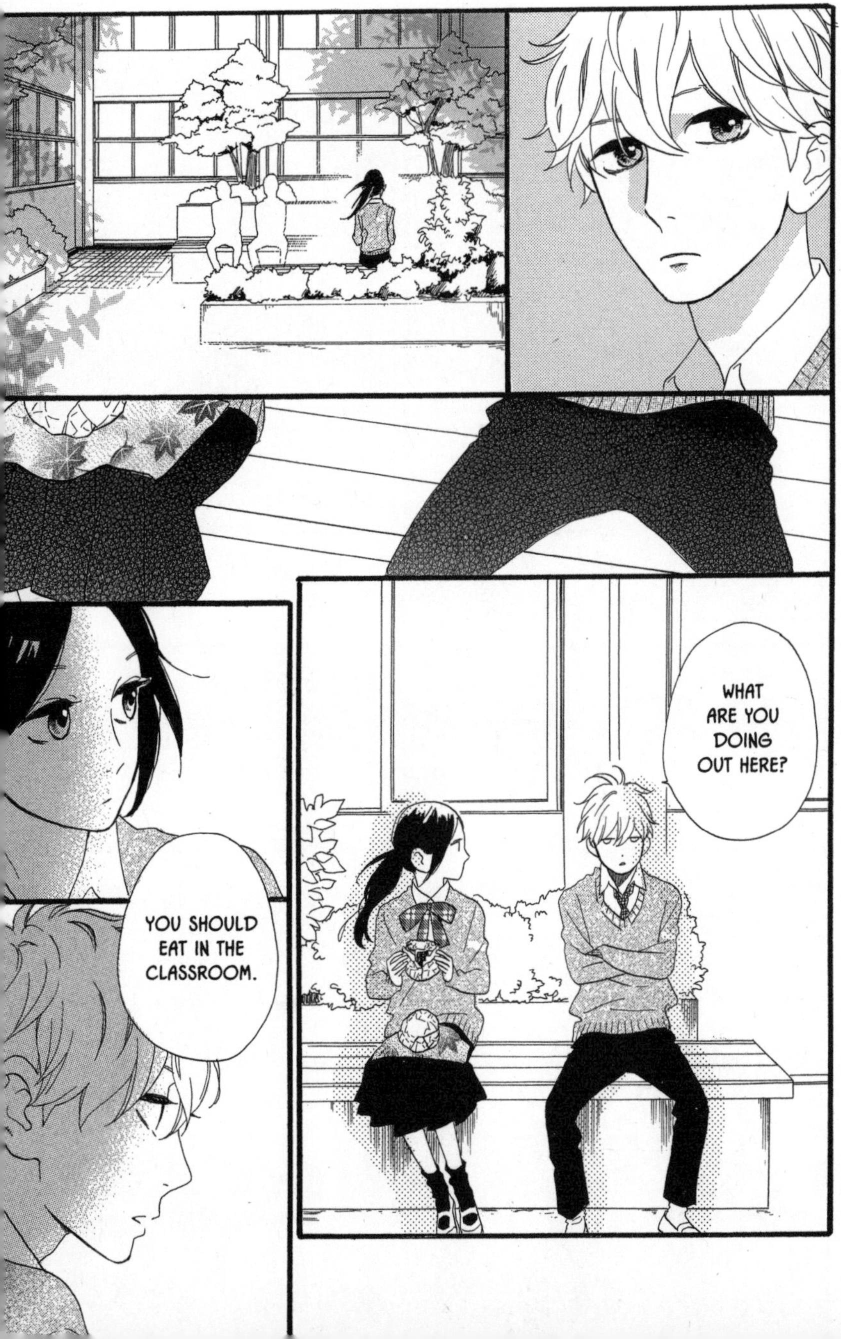
WHAT ARE YOU DOING OUT HERE?
YOU SHOULD EAT IN THE CLASSROOM.

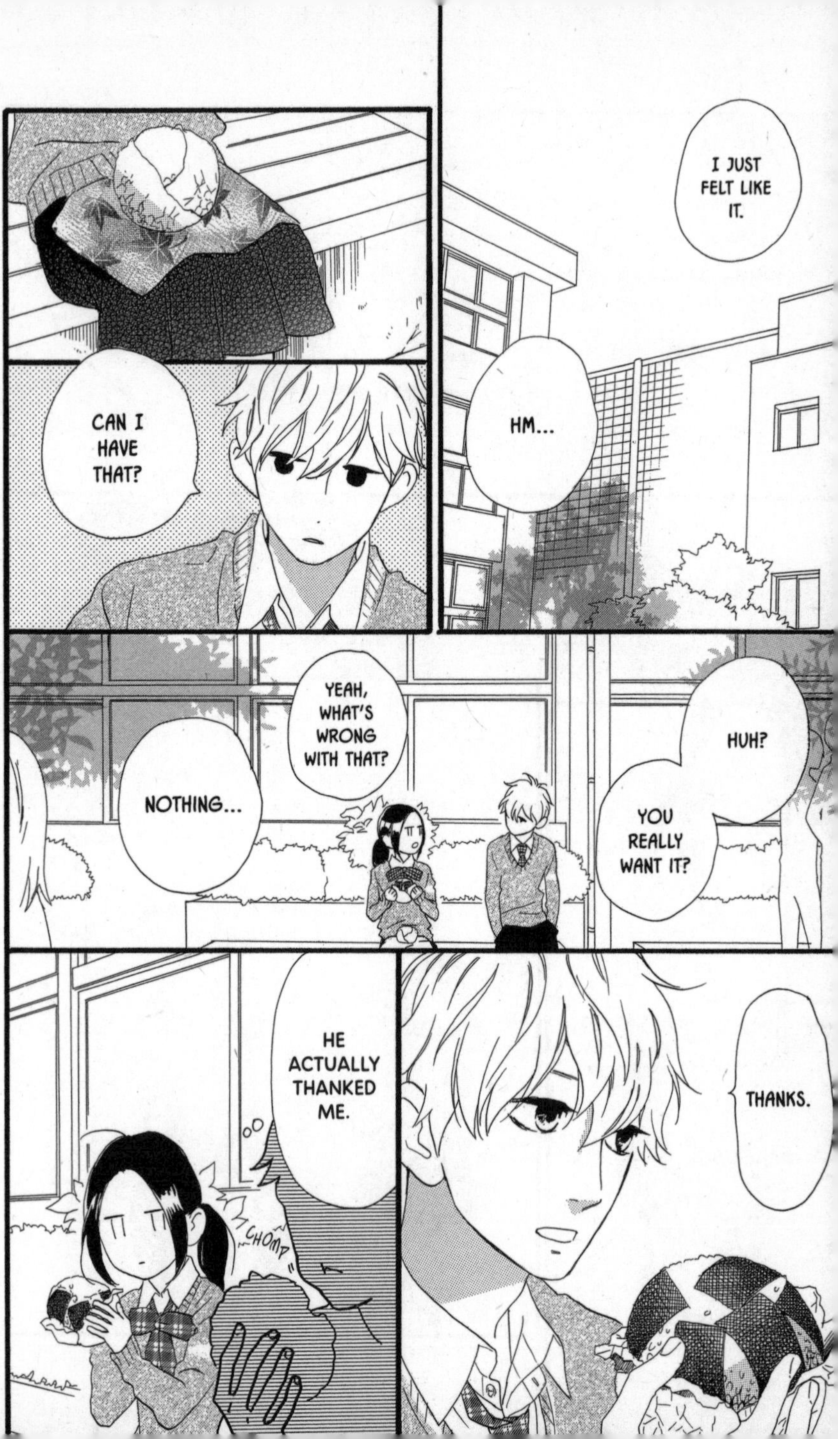
I JUST FELT LIKE IT.
HM...
CAN I HAVE THAT?
HUH?
YOU REALLY WANT IT?
YEAH, WHAT'S WRONG WITH THAT?
NOTHING...
THANKS.
HE ACTUALLY THANKED ME.
CHOMP

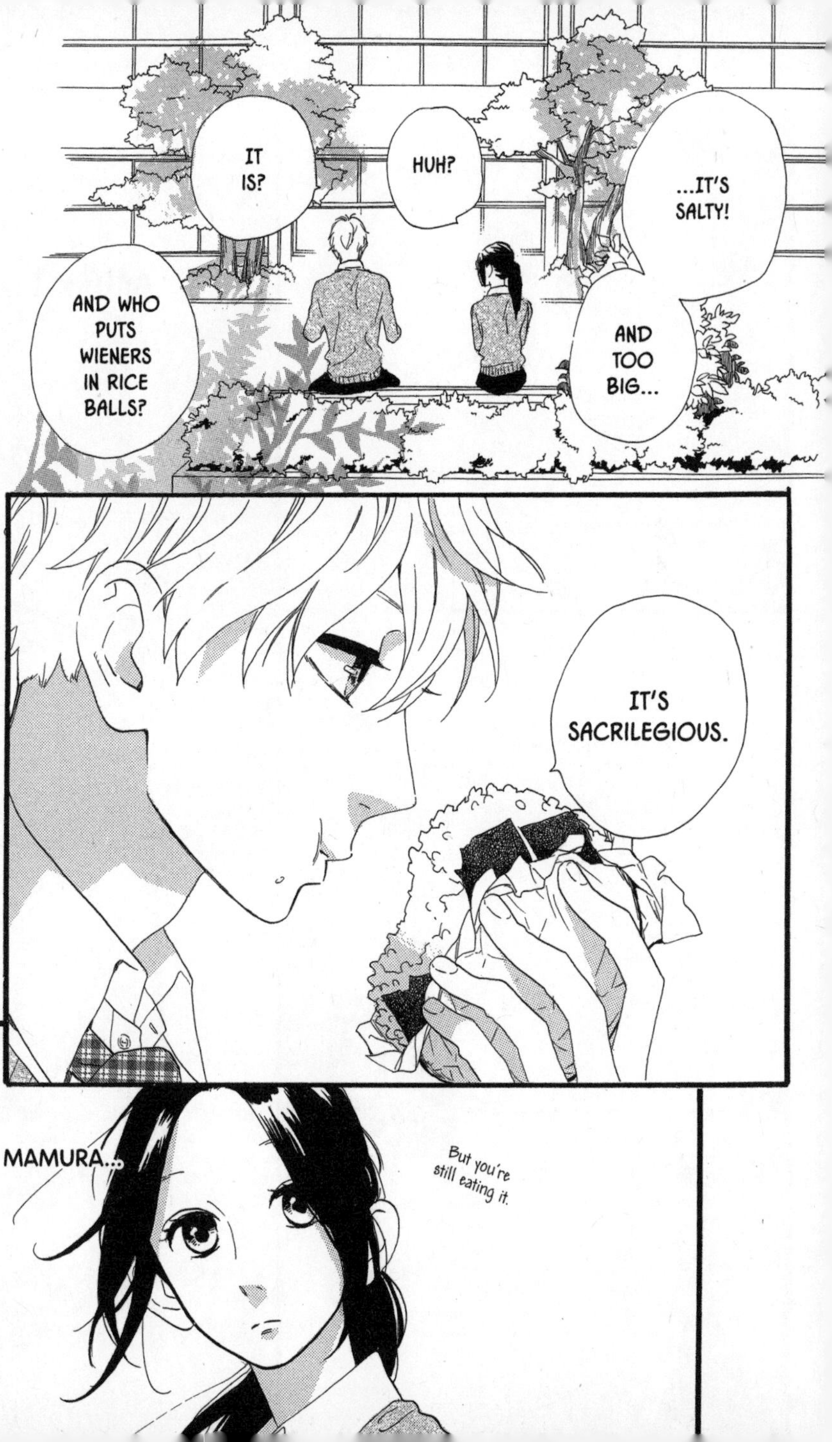
...IT'S SALTY!
AND TOO BIG...
HUH?
IT IS?
AND WHO PUTS WIENERS IN RICE BALLS?
IT'S SACRILEGIOUS.
But you're still eating it.
MAMURA...

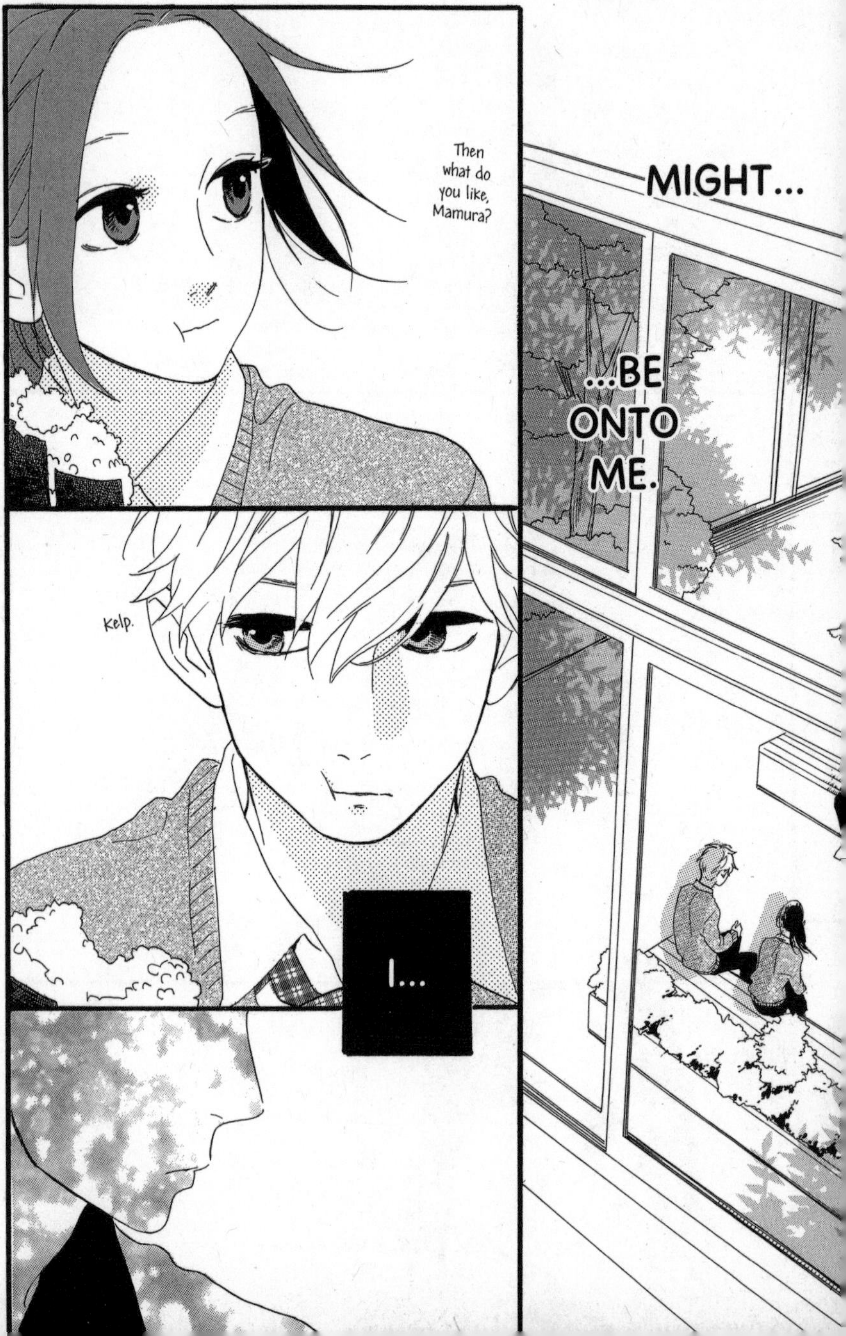
MIGHT...
...BE ONTO ME.
Then what do you like, Mamura?
Kelp.
I...

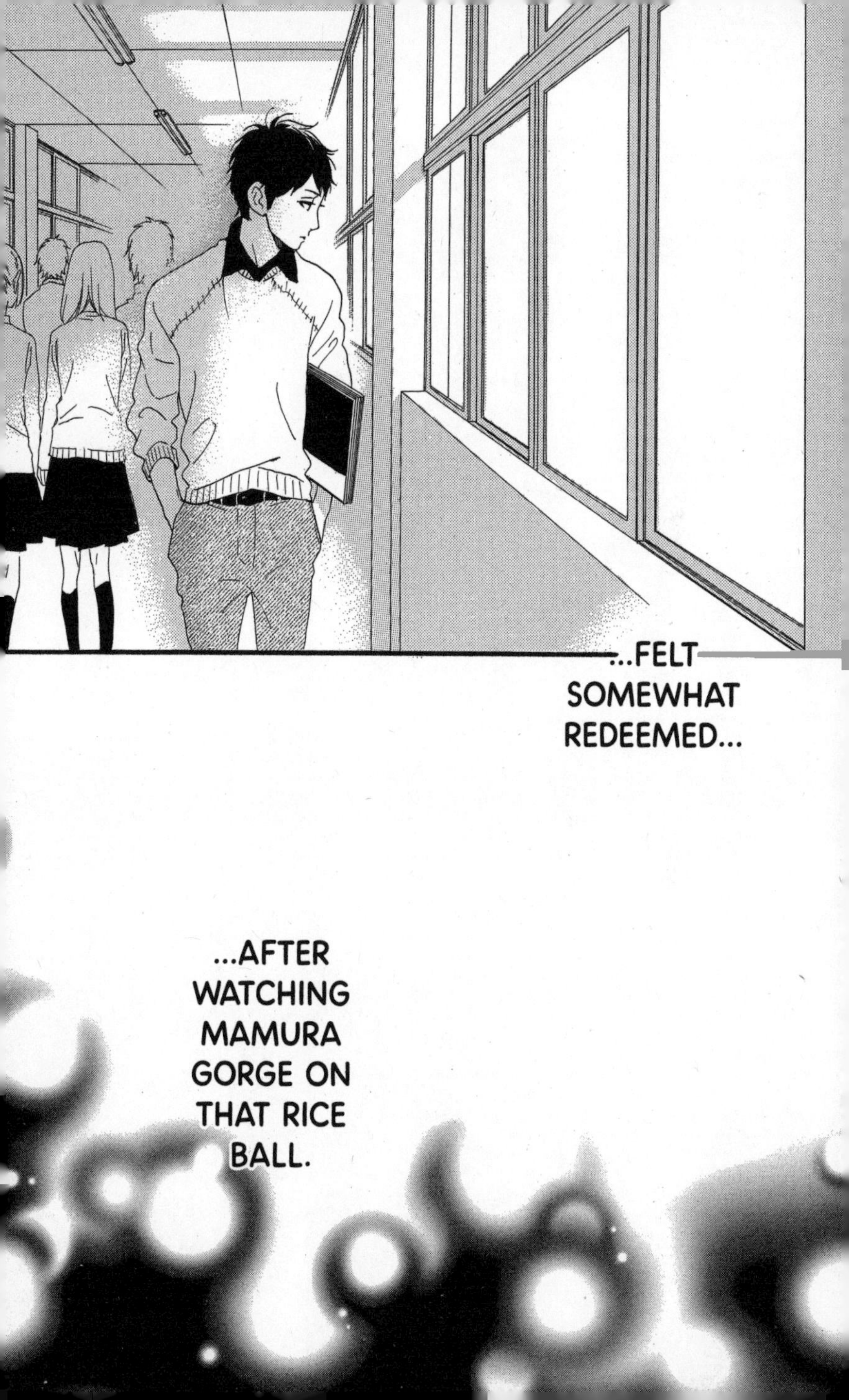
...FELT SOMEWHAT REDEEMED...
...AFTER WATCHING MAMURA GORGE ON THAT RICE BALL.

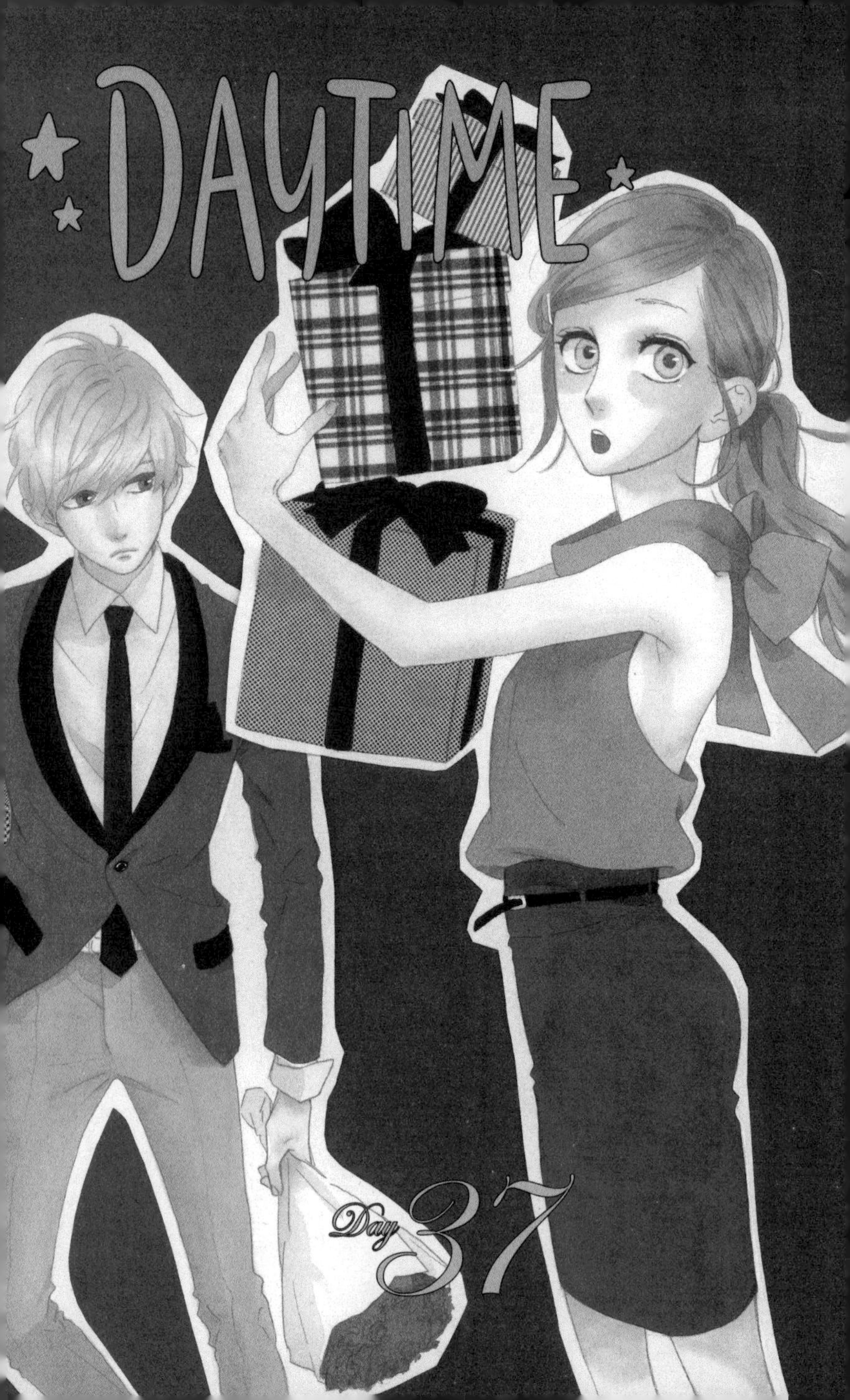
DAYTIME
Day 37

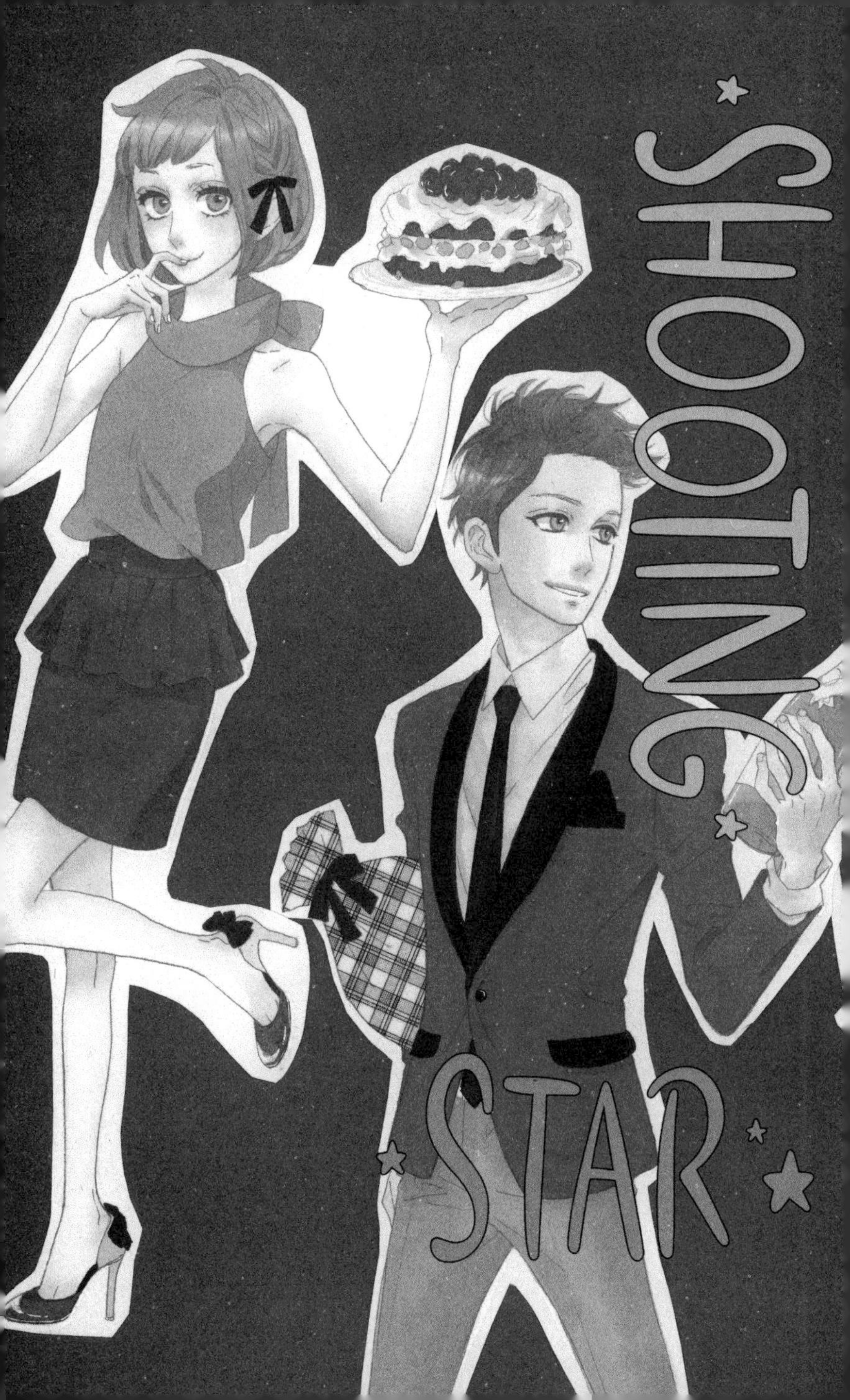
SHOOTING
STAR

By the way...

I took a trip to London the other day! Sachie Noborio, one of my assistants, mentioned that she wanted to see James McAvoy onstage. So I went with her and another assistant. ♪
I must say:

London's the best!!!

It was a very busy time for us, but we managed to rearrange our schedules to make the trip, and it was totally worth it.
I had no idea it was such a wonderful place!! Everything we saw was glamorous. The towns were pretty, and everyone was so kind!!
There was just one thing that stood out.

The faces of both the men and the women were far above average.

What a shock it was to see my face in the mirror.

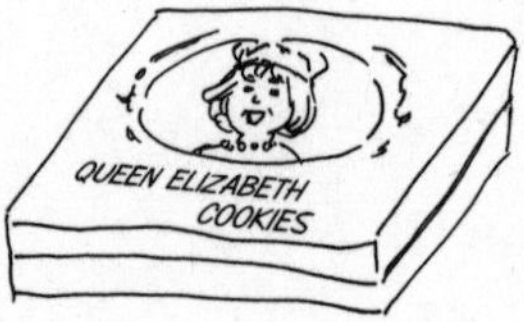
QUEEN ELIZABETH
COOKIES

← I bought these cookies for the editorial staff.

Noborio bought the same thing for the *Betsucomi* magazine staff.

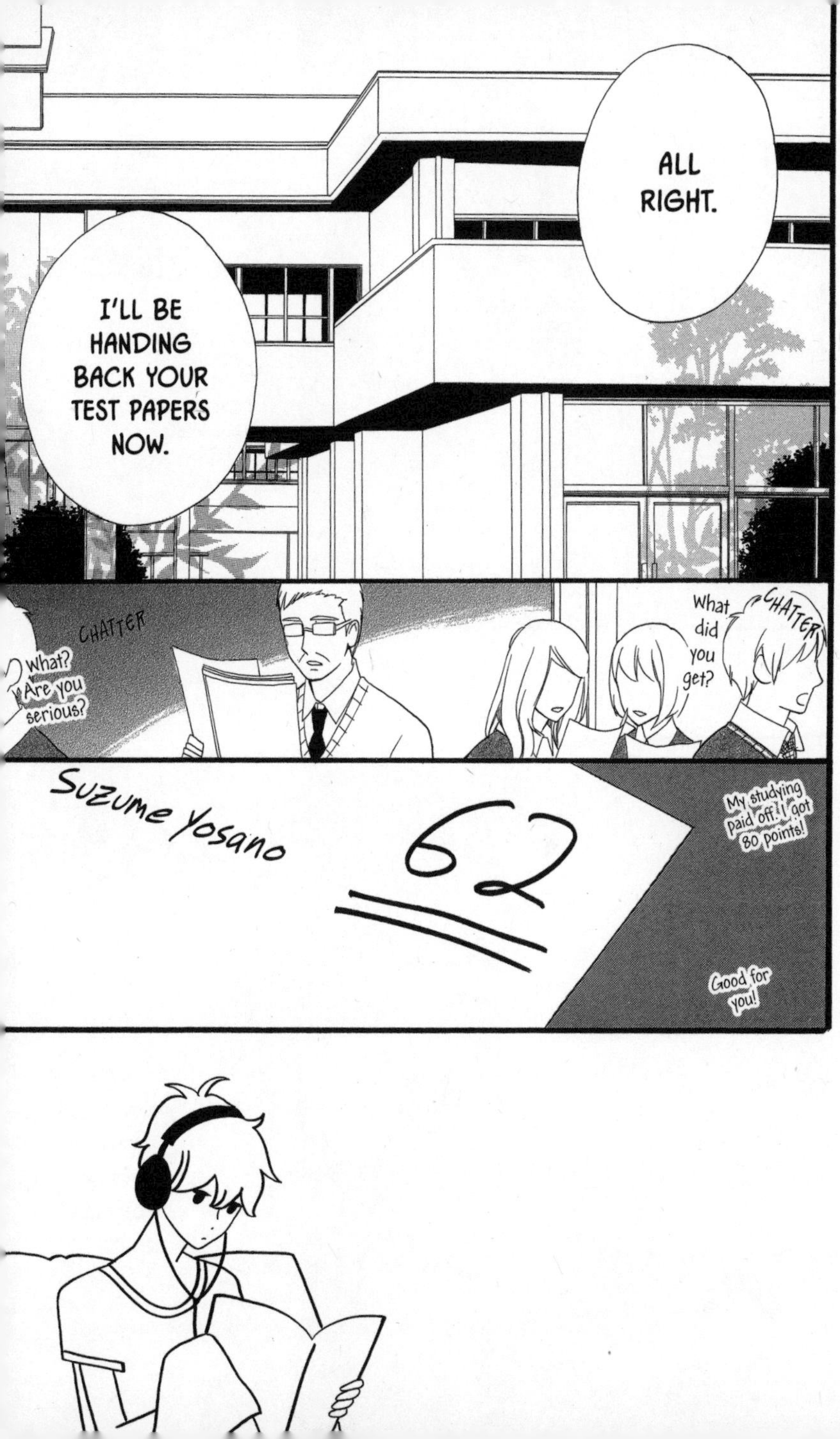
ALL RIGHT.
I'LL BE HANDING BACK YOUR TEST PAPERS NOW.
CHATTER
What did you get?
CHATTER
What? Are you serious?
My studying paid off! I got 80 points!
Good for you!
Suzume Yosano
62

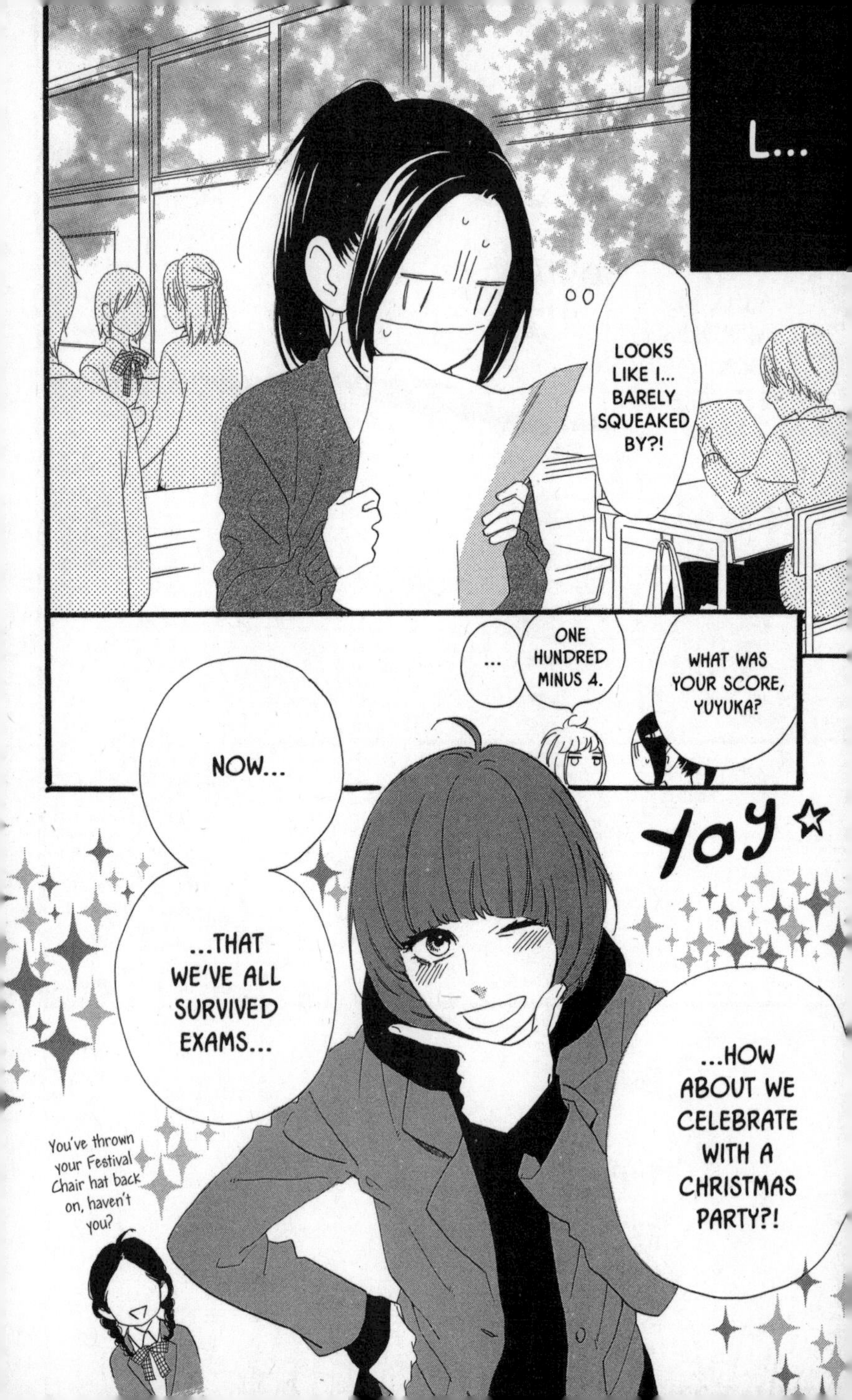
L...
LOOKS LIKE I... BARELY SQUEAKED BY?!
WHAT WAS YOUR SCORE, YUYUKA?
ONE HUNDRED MINUS 4.
...
Yay☆
NOW...
...THAT WE'VE ALL SURVIVED EXAMS...
...HOW ABOUT WE CELEBRATE WITH A CHRISTMAS PARTY?!
You've thrown your Festival Chair hat back on, haven't you?

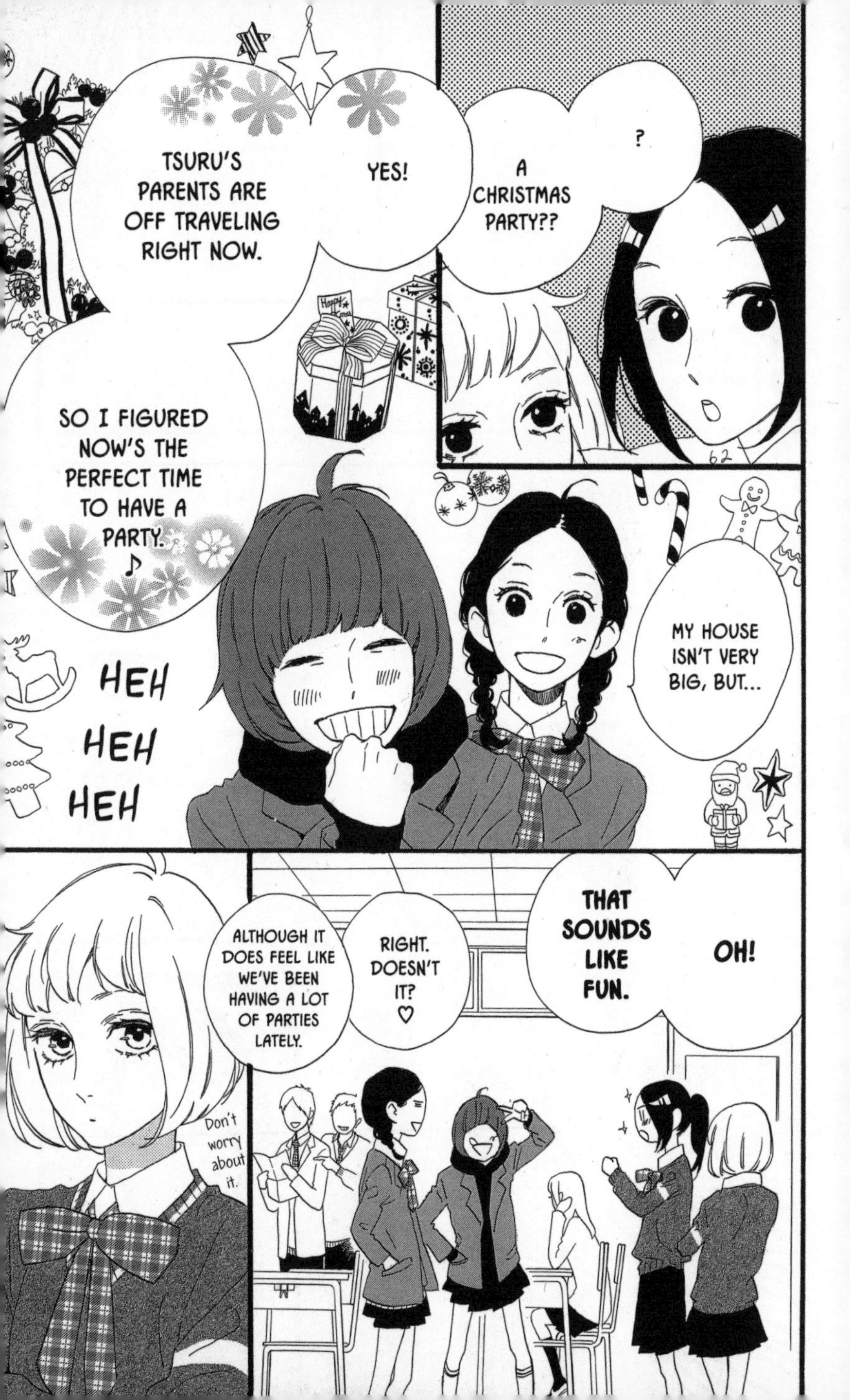
?
A CHRISTMAS PARTY??
YES!
TSURU'S PARENTS ARE OFF TRAVELING RIGHT NOW.
SO I FIGURED NOW'S THE PERFECT TIME TO HAVE A PARTY. ♪
MY HOUSE ISN'T VERY BIG, BUT...
HEH HEH HEH
OH!
THAT SOUNDS LIKE FUN.
RIGHT. DOESN'T IT? ♡
ALTHOUGH IT DOES FEEL LIKE WE'VE BEEN HAVING A LOT OF PARTIES LATELY.
Don't worry about it.

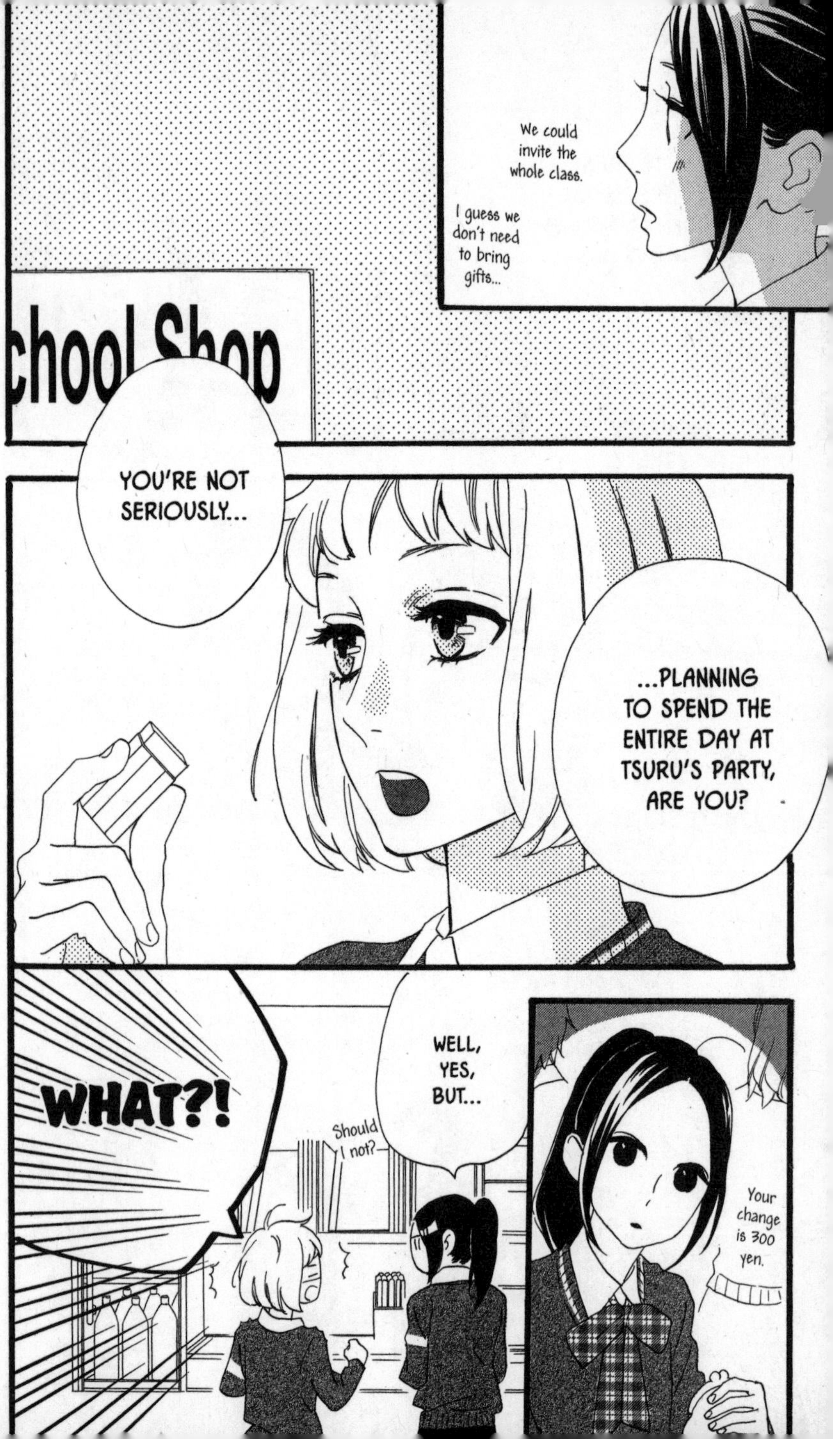

We could invite the whole class.
I guess we don't need to bring gifts...
chool Shop
YOU'RE NOT SERIOUSLY...
...PLANNING TO SPEND THE ENTIRE DAY AT TSURU'S PARTY, ARE YOU?
Your change is 300 yen.
WELL, YES, BUT...
Should I not?
WHAT?!

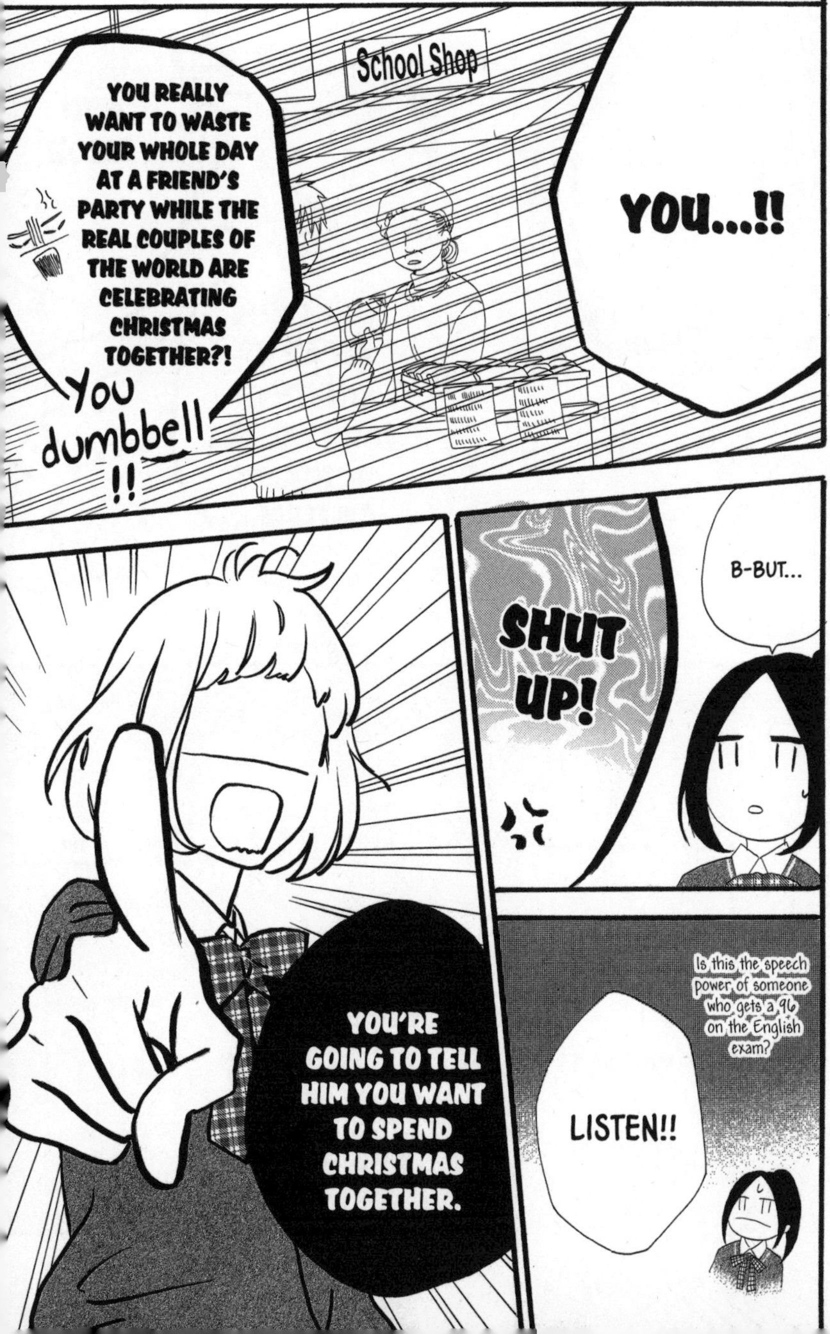
YOU...!!
School Shop
YOU REALLY WANT TO WASTE YOUR WHOLE DAY AT A FRIEND'S PARTY WHILE THE REAL COUPLES OF THE WORLD ARE CELEBRATING CHRISTMAS TOGETHER?!
You dumbbell !!
B-BUT...
SHUT UP!
Is this the speech power of someone who gets a 96 on the English exam?
LISTEN!!
YOU'RE GOING TO TELL HIM YOU WANT TO SPEND CHRISTMAS TOGETHER.

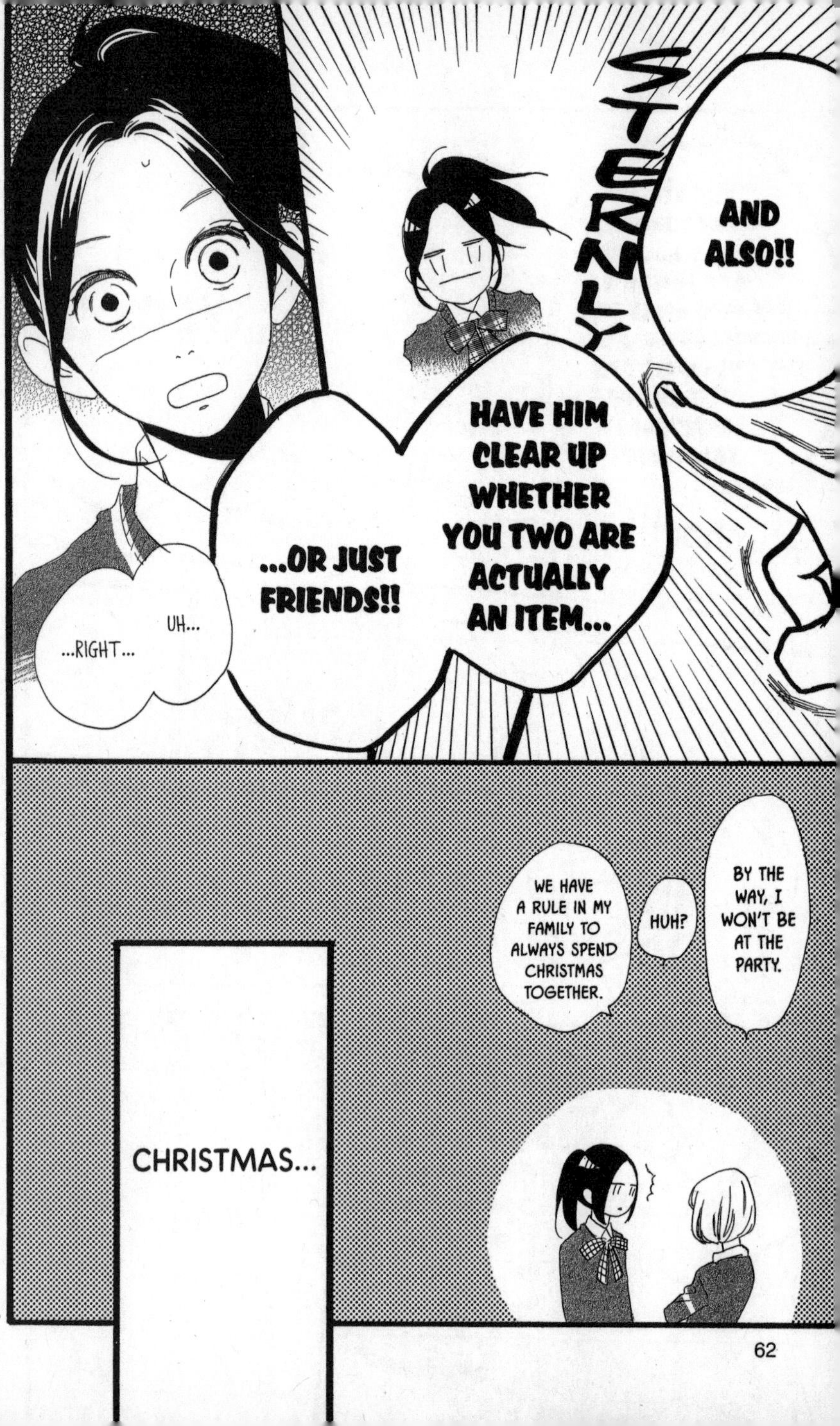
AND ALSO!!
STERNLY
HAVE HIM CLEAR UP WHETHER YOU TWO ARE ACTUALLY AN ITEM...
...OR JUST FRIENDS!!
UH...
...RIGHT...
BY THE WAY, I WON'T BE AT THE PARTY.
HUH?
WE HAVE A RULE IN MY FAMILY TO ALWAYS SPEND CHRISTMAS TOGETHER.
CHRISTMAS...

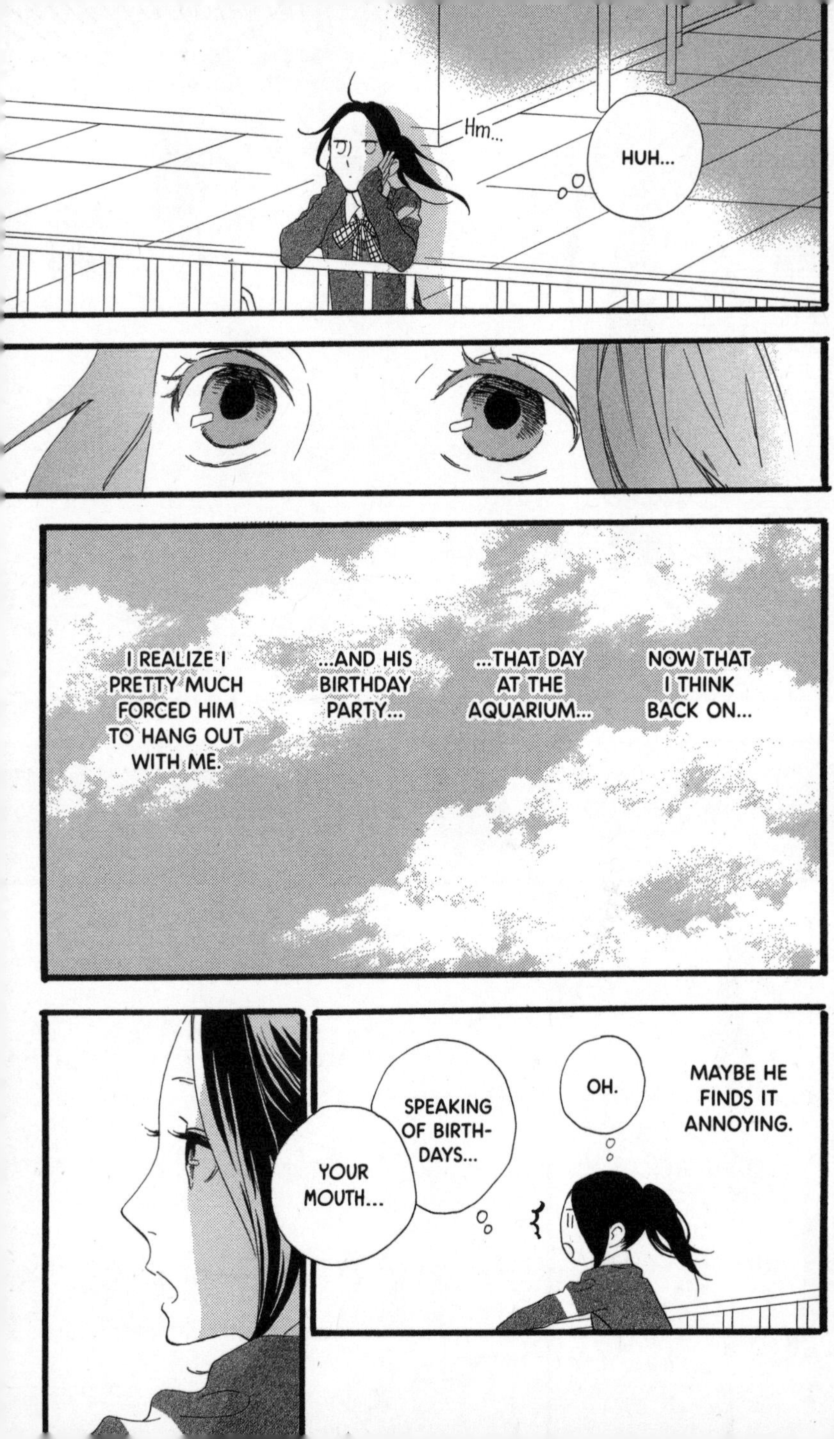
HUH...
Hm...
NOW THAT I THINK BACK ON...
...THAT DAY AT THE AQUARIUM...
...AND HIS BIRTHDAY PARTY...
I REALIZE I PRETTY MUCH FORCED HIM TO HANG OUT WITH ME.
MAYBE HE FINDS IT ANNOYING.
OH.
SPEAKING OF BIRTH-DAYS...
YOUR MOUTH...

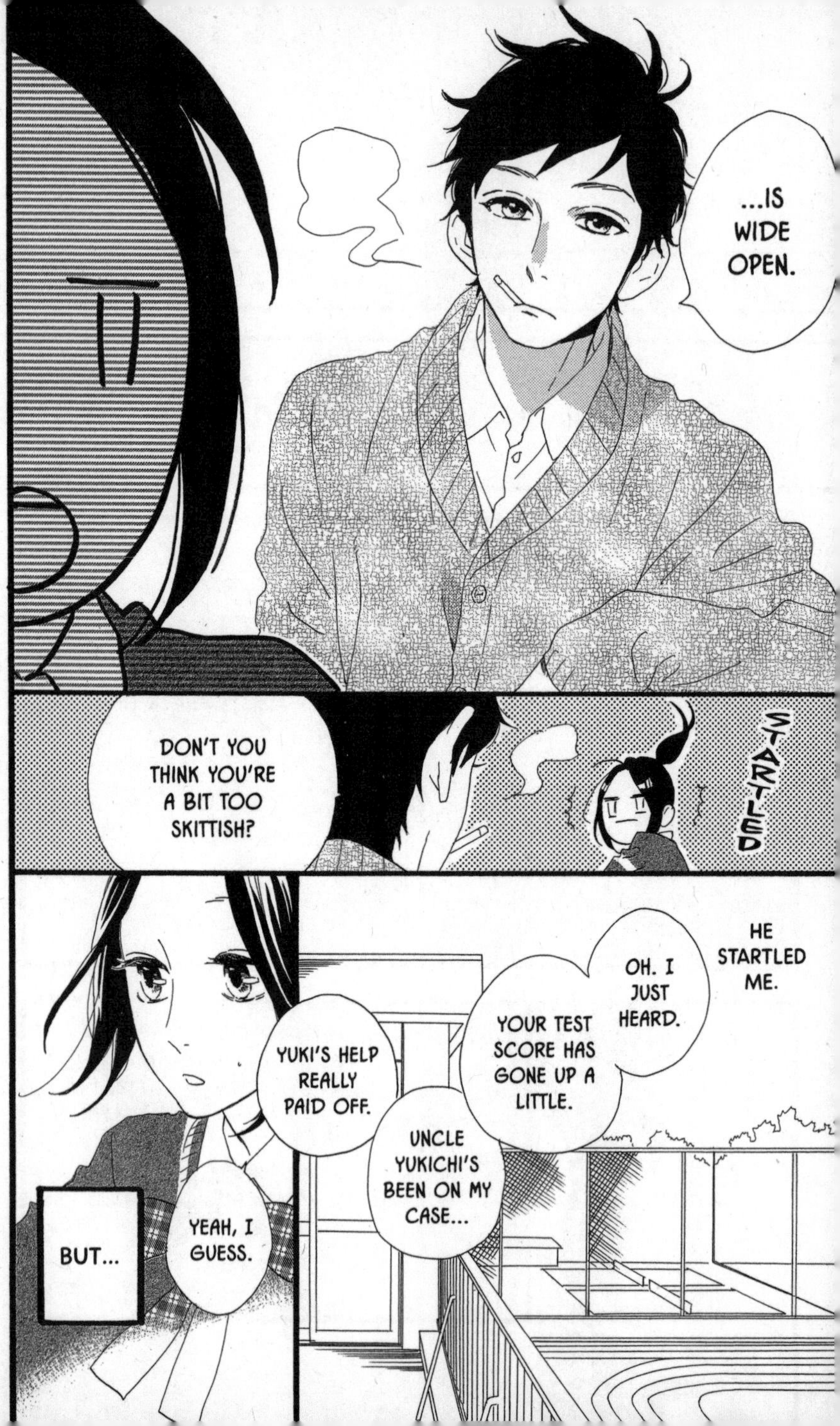

...IS WIDE OPEN.
STARTLED
DON'T YOU THINK YOU'RE A BIT TOO SKITTISH?
HE STARTLED ME.
OH. I JUST HEARD.
YOUR TEST SCORE HAS GONE UP A LITTLE.
UNCLE YUKICHI'S BEEN ON MY CASE...
YUKI'S HELP REALLY PAID OFF.
YEAH, I GUESS.
BUT...

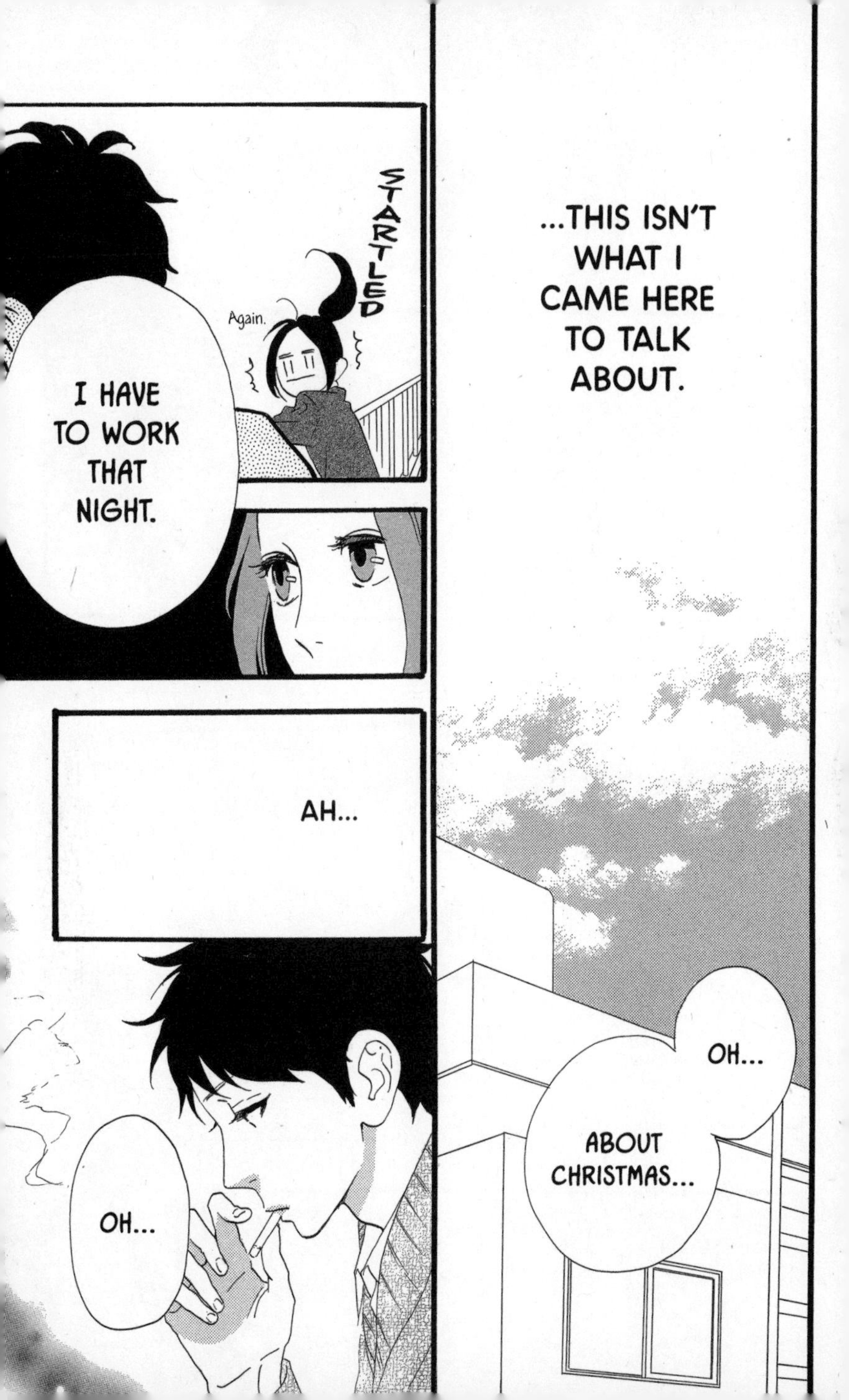
...THIS ISN'T WHAT I CAME HERE TO TALK ABOUT.
OH... ABOUT CHRISTMAS...
STARTLED
Again.
I HAVE TO WORK THAT NIGHT.
AH...
OH...

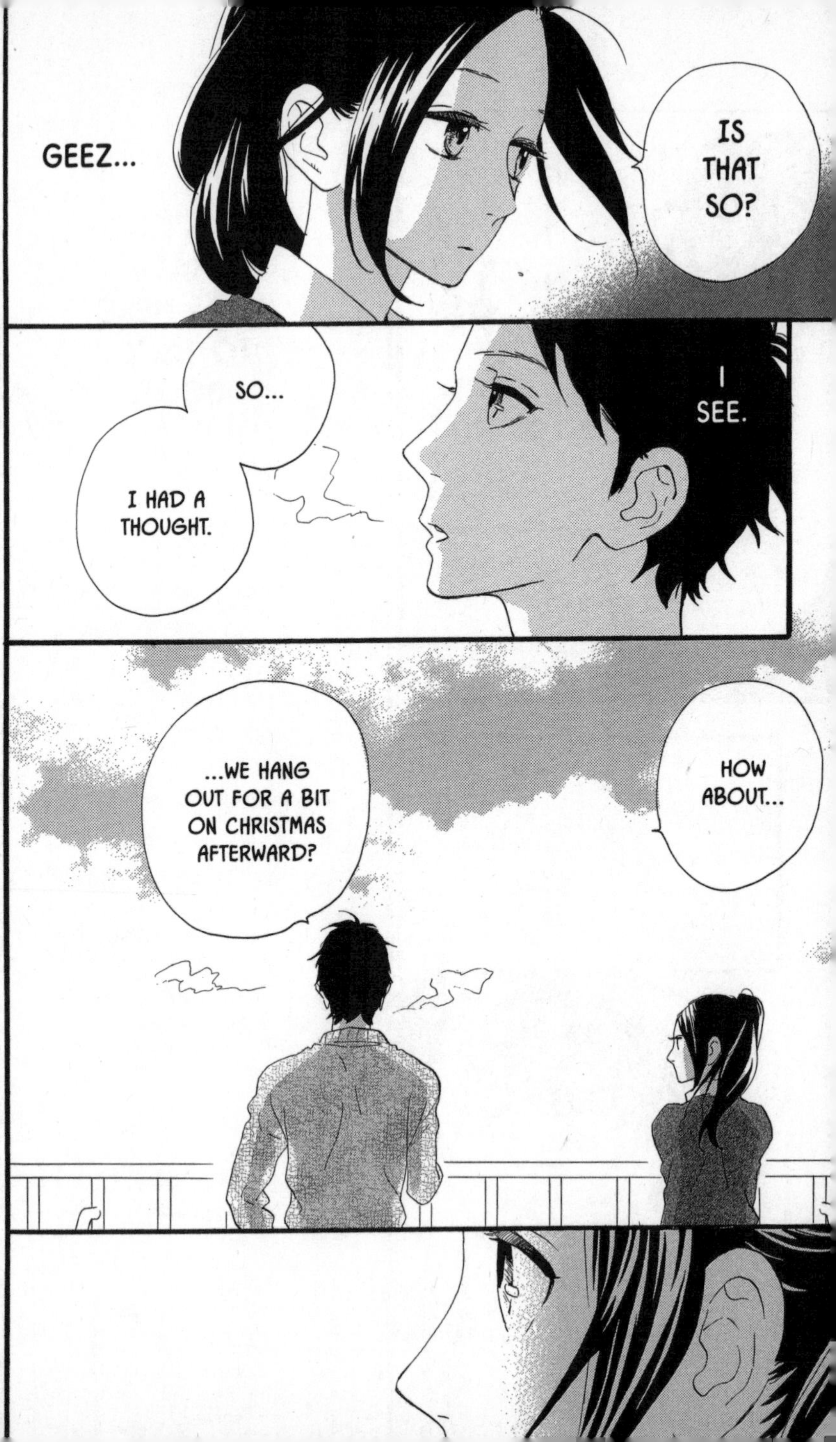
IS THAT SO?
GEEZ...
I SEE.
SO...
I HAD A THOUGHT.
HOW ABOUT...
...WE HANG OUT FOR A BIT ON CHRISTMAS AFTERWARD?

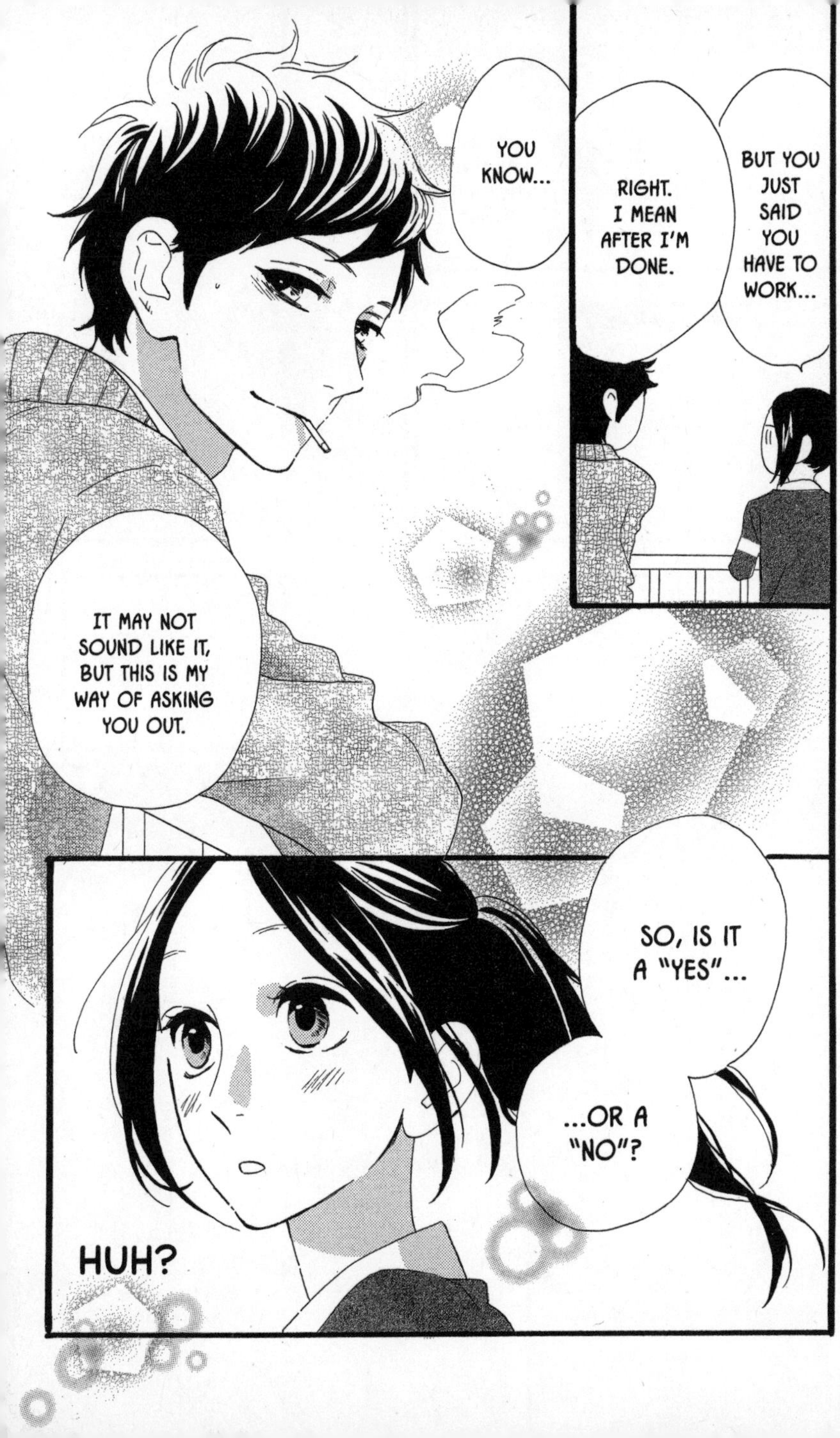
BUT YOU JUST SAID YOU HAVE TO WORK...
RIGHT. I MEAN AFTER I'M DONE.
YOU KNOW...
IT MAY NOT SOUND LIKE IT, BUT THIS IS MY WAY OF ASKING YOU OUT.
SO, IS IT A "YES"...
...OR A "NO"?
HUH?

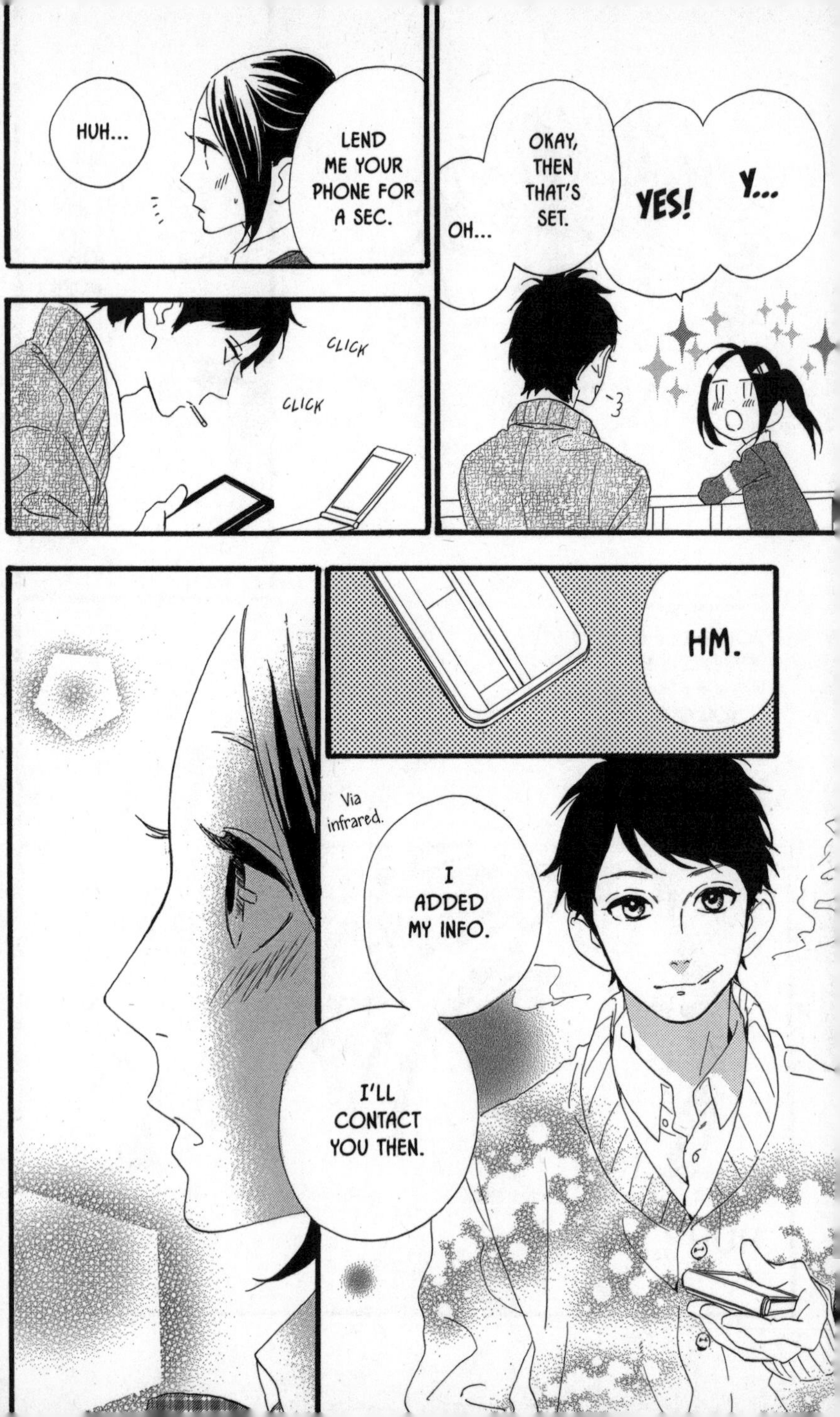
Y...
YES!
OKAY, THEN THAT'S SET.
OH...
LEND ME YOUR PHONE FOR A SEC.
HUH...
CLICK
CLICK
HM.
Via infrared.
I ADDED MY INFO.
I'LL CONTACT YOU THEN.

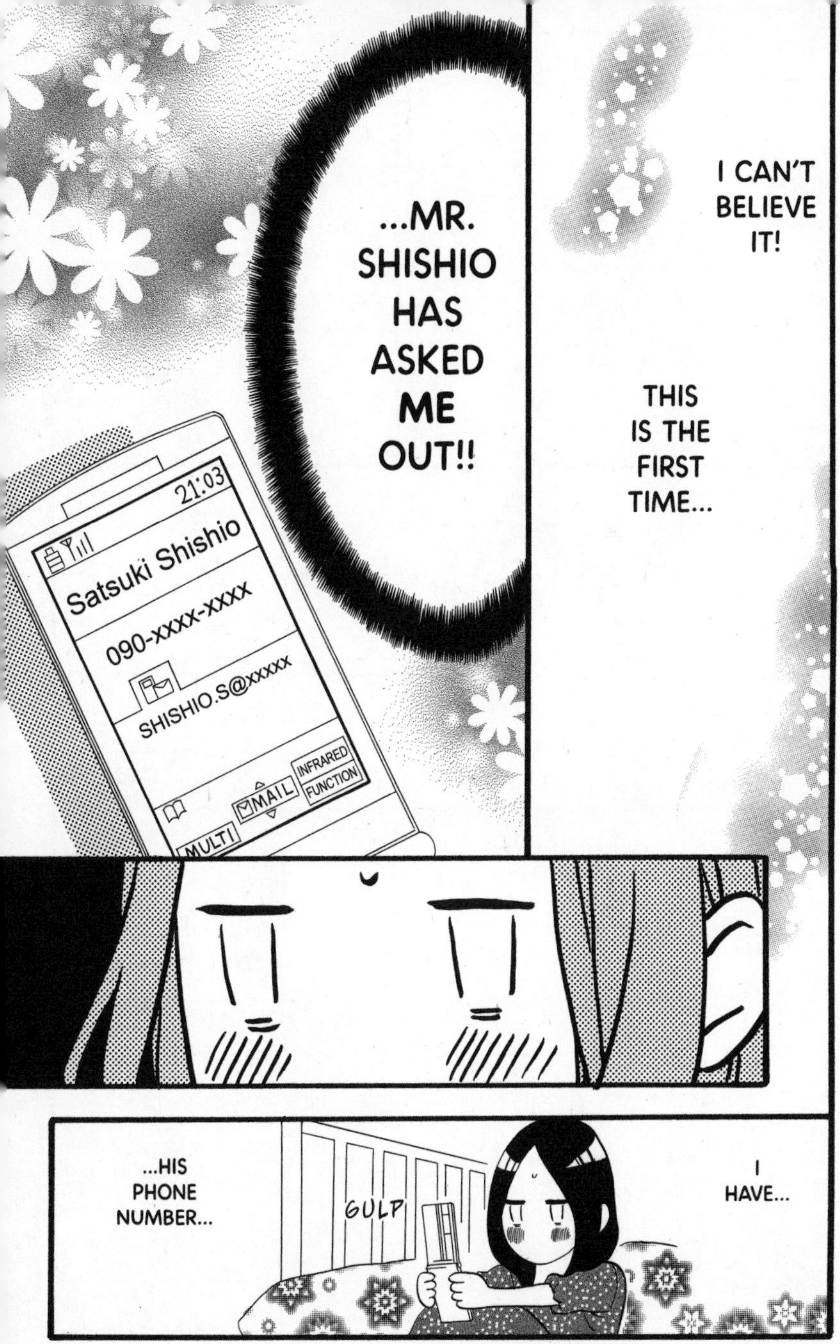
I CAN'T BELIEVE IT!
THIS IS THE FIRST TIME...
...MR. SHISHIO HAS ASKED **ME** OUT!!
21:03
Satsuki Shishio
090-XXXX-XXXX
SHISHIO.S@XXXXX
INFRARED
FUNCTION
MAIL
MULTI
I HAVE...
...HIS PHONE NUMBER...
GULP

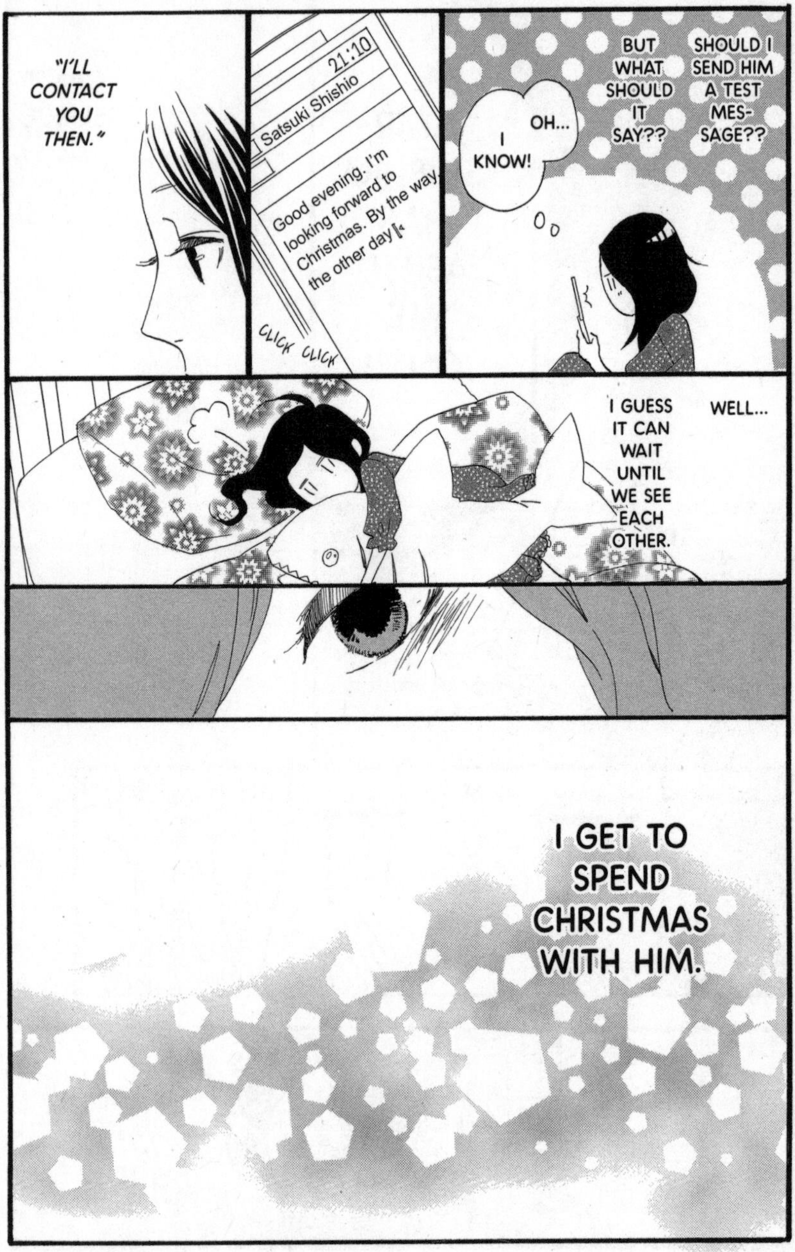
SHOULD I SEND HIM A TEST MES-SAGE??
BUT WHAT SHOULD IT SAY??
OH... I KNOW!
21:10
Satsuki Shishio
Good evening. I'm looking forward to Christmas. By the way, the other day
CLICK CLICK
"I'LL CONTACT YOU THEN."
WELL...
I GUESS IT CAN WAIT UNTIL WE SEE EACH OTHER.
I GET TO SPEND CHRISTMAS WITH HIM.

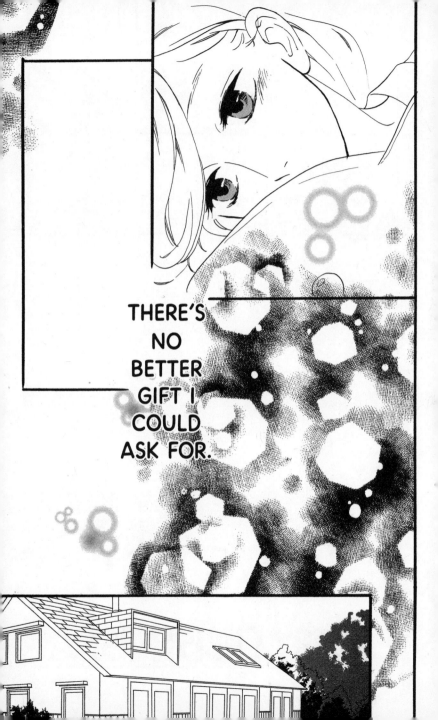

THERE'S NO BETTER GIFT I COULD ASK FOR.

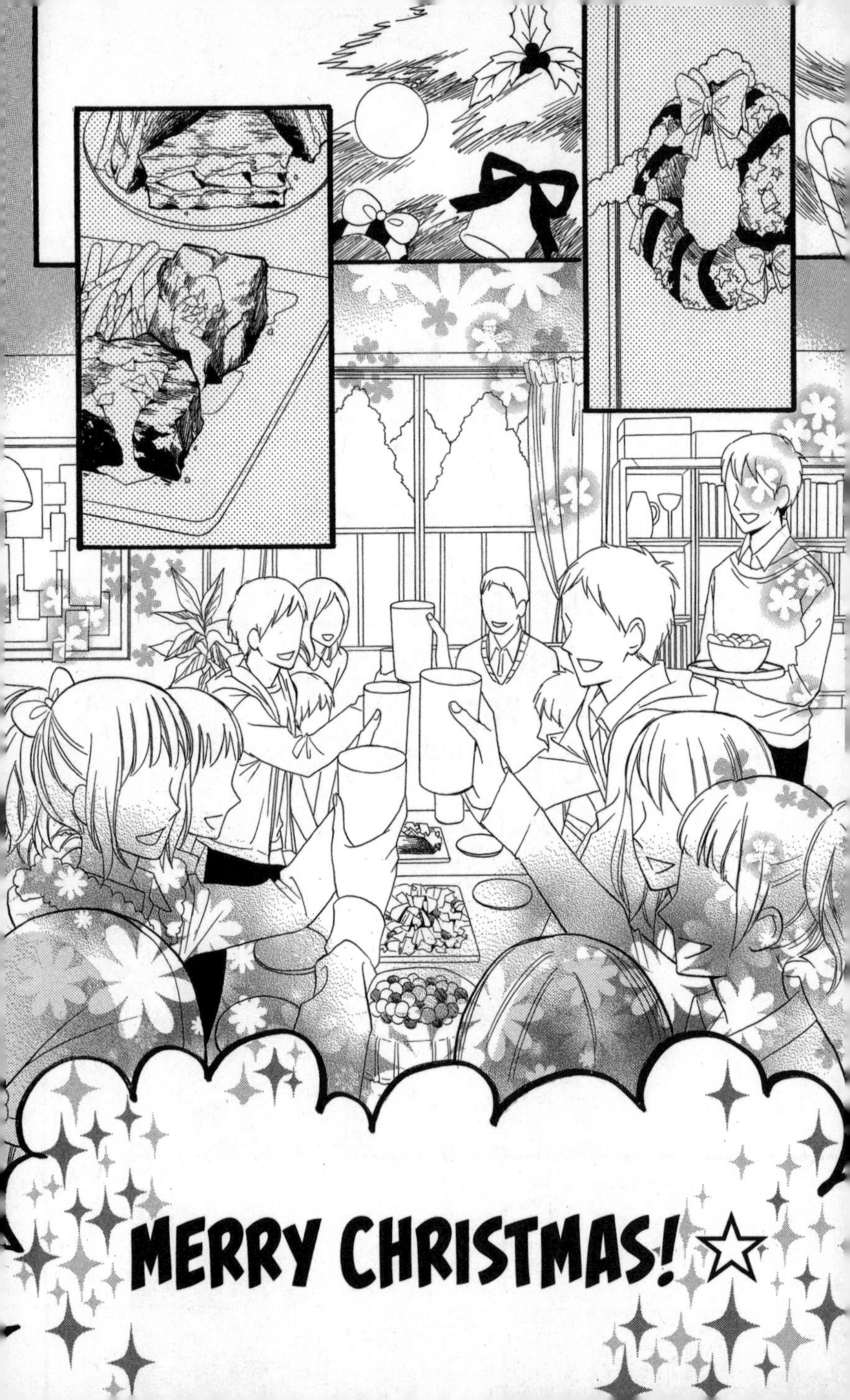
MERRY CHRISTMAS! ☆

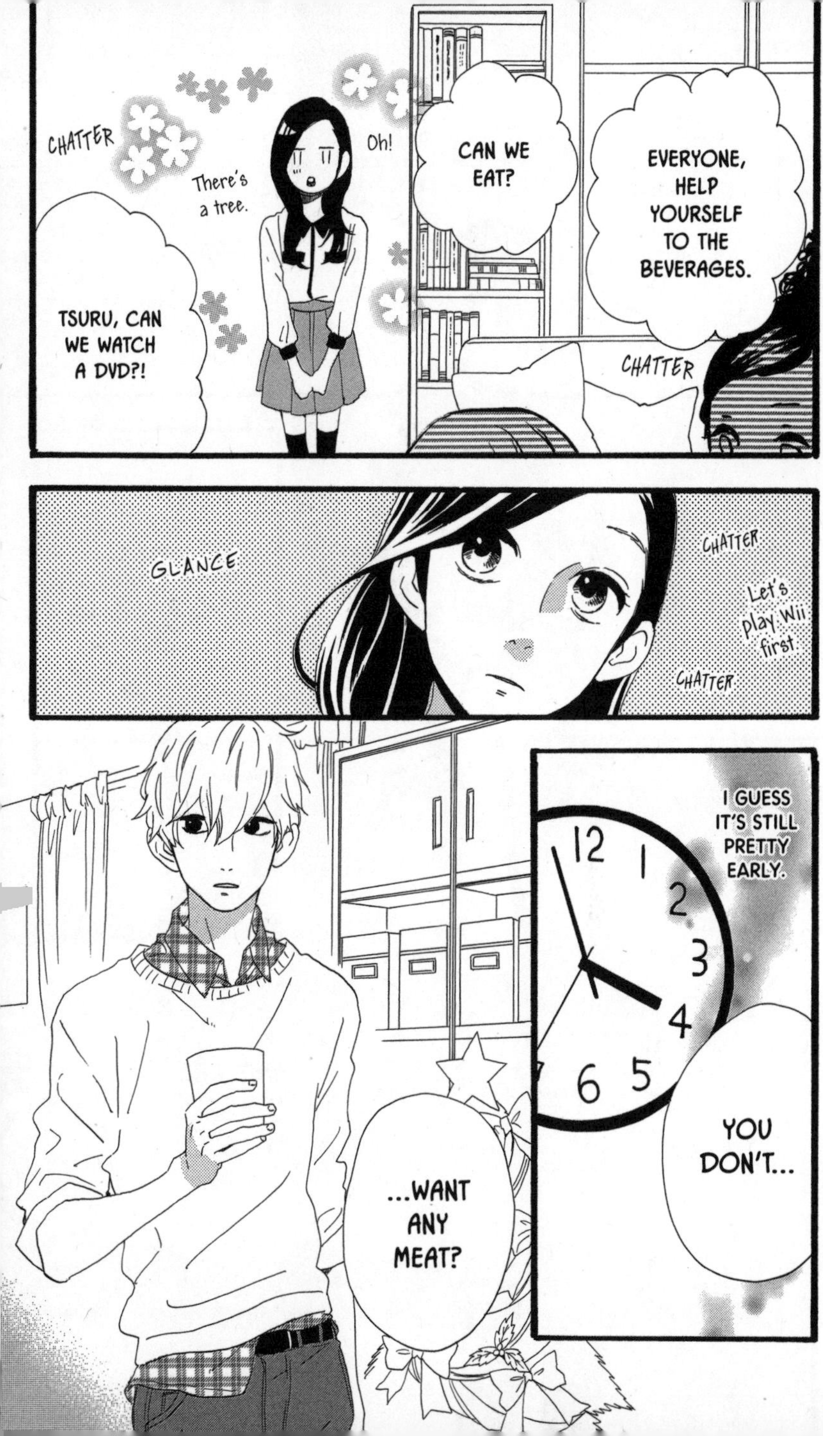
EVERYONE, HELP YOURSELF TO THE BEVERAGES.
CAN WE EAT?
CHATTER
Oh!
There's a tree.
CHATTER
TSURU, CAN WE WATCH A DVD?!
CHATTER
Let's play Wii first.
CHATTER
GLANCE
I GUESS IT'S STILL PRETTY EARLY.
YOU DON'T...
...WANT ANY MEAT?

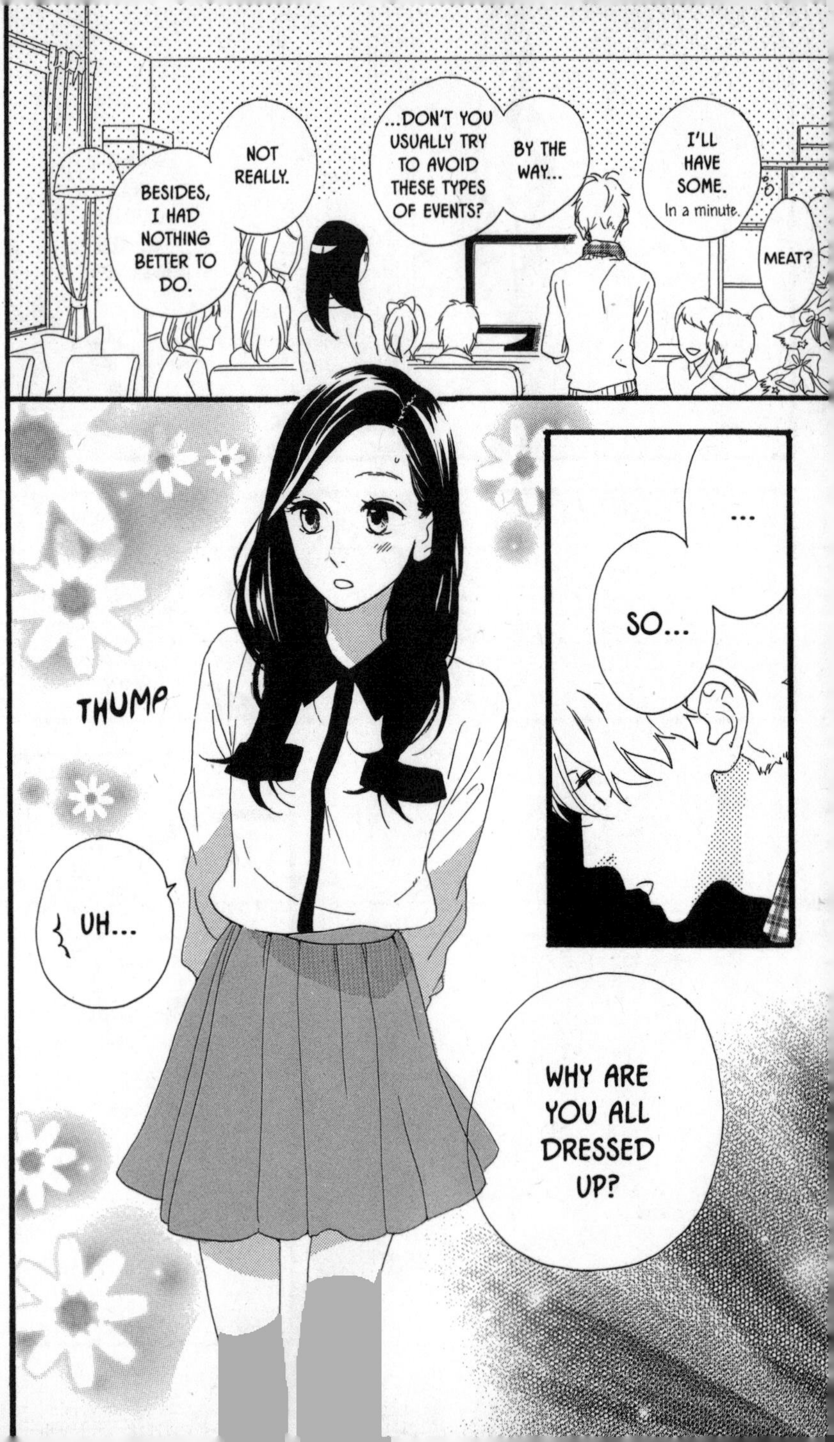
MEAT?
I'LL HAVE SOME. In a minute.
BY THE WAY...
...DON'T YOU USUALLY TRY TO AVOID THESE TYPES OF EVENTS?
NOT REALLY.
BESIDES, I HAD NOTHING BETTER TO DO.
...
SO...
WHY ARE YOU ALL DRESSED UP?
THUMP
UH...

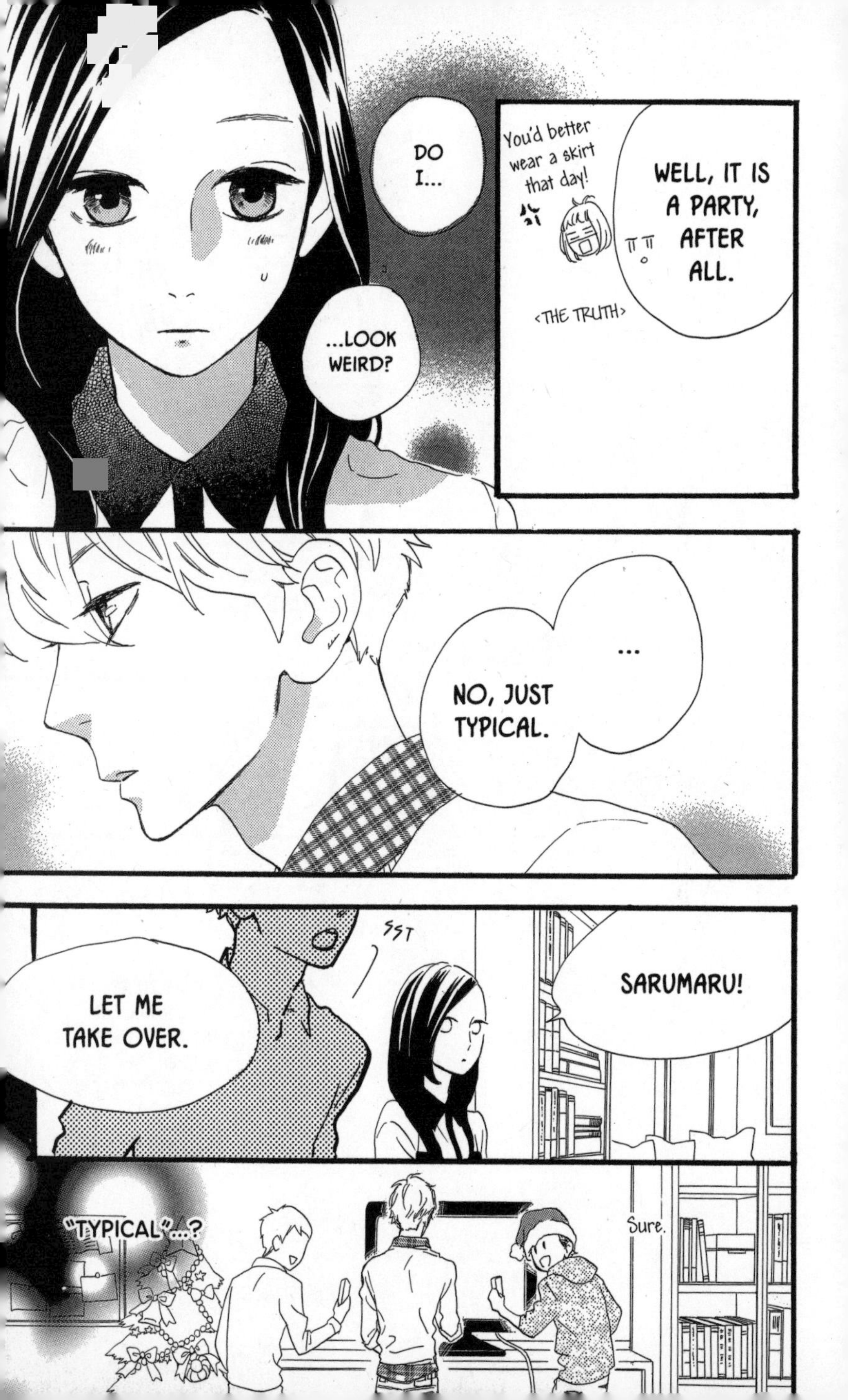

WELL, IT IS A PARTY, AFTER ALL.
You'd better wear a skirt that day!
<THE TRUTH>
DO I...
...LOOK WEIRD?
...
NO, JUST TYPICAL.
SARUMARU!
SST
LET ME TAKE OVER.
Sure.
"TYPICAL"...?

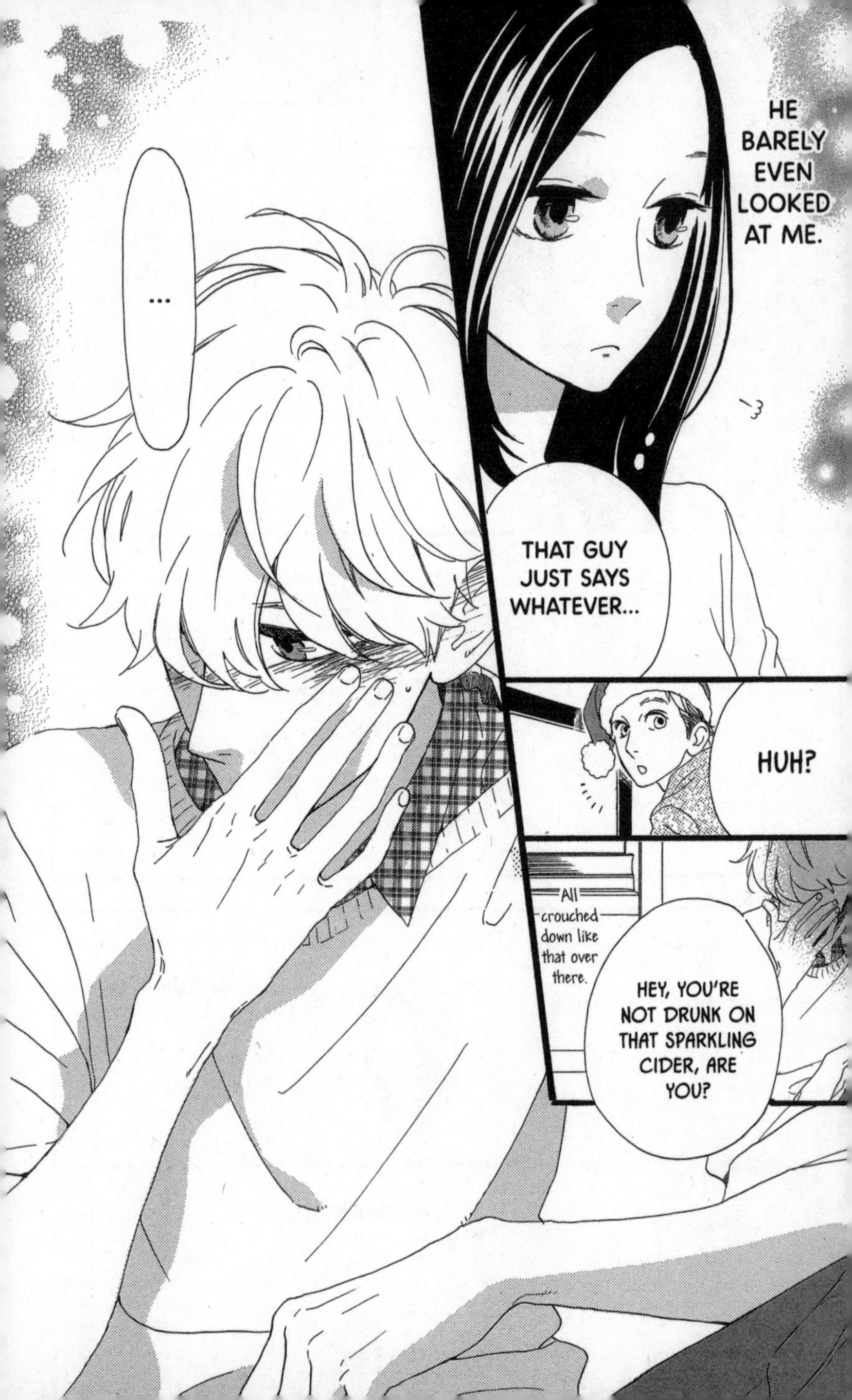
HE BARELY EVEN LOOKED AT ME.
THAT GUY JUST SAYS WHATEVER...
HUH?
HEY, YOU'RE NOT DRUNK ON THAT SPARKLING CIDER, ARE YOU?
All crouched down like that over there.
...

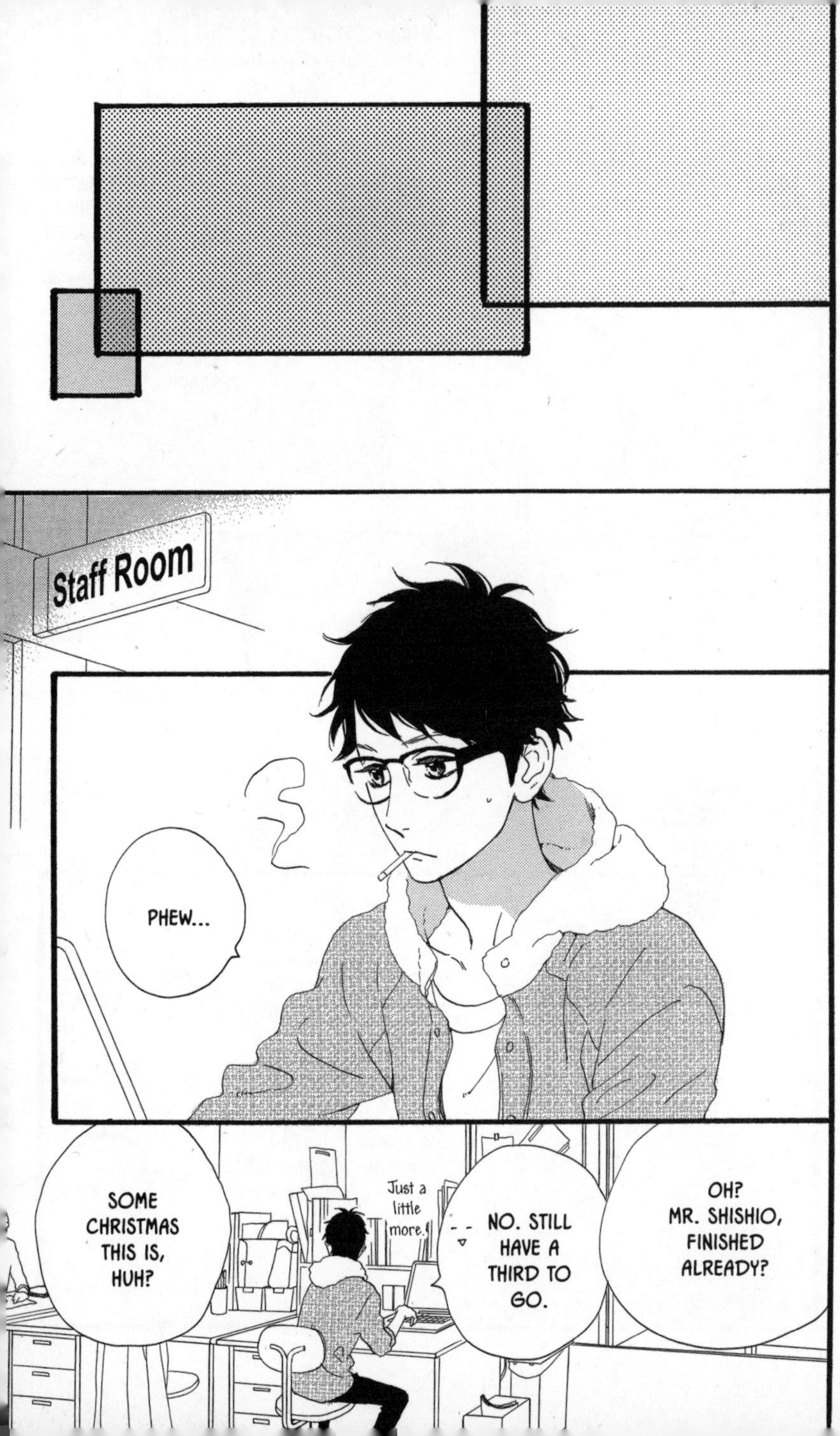
Staff Room
PHEW...
OH? MR. SHISHIO, FINISHED ALREADY?
NO. STILL HAVE A THIRD TO GO.
Just a little more.
SOME CHRISTMAS THIS IS, HUH?

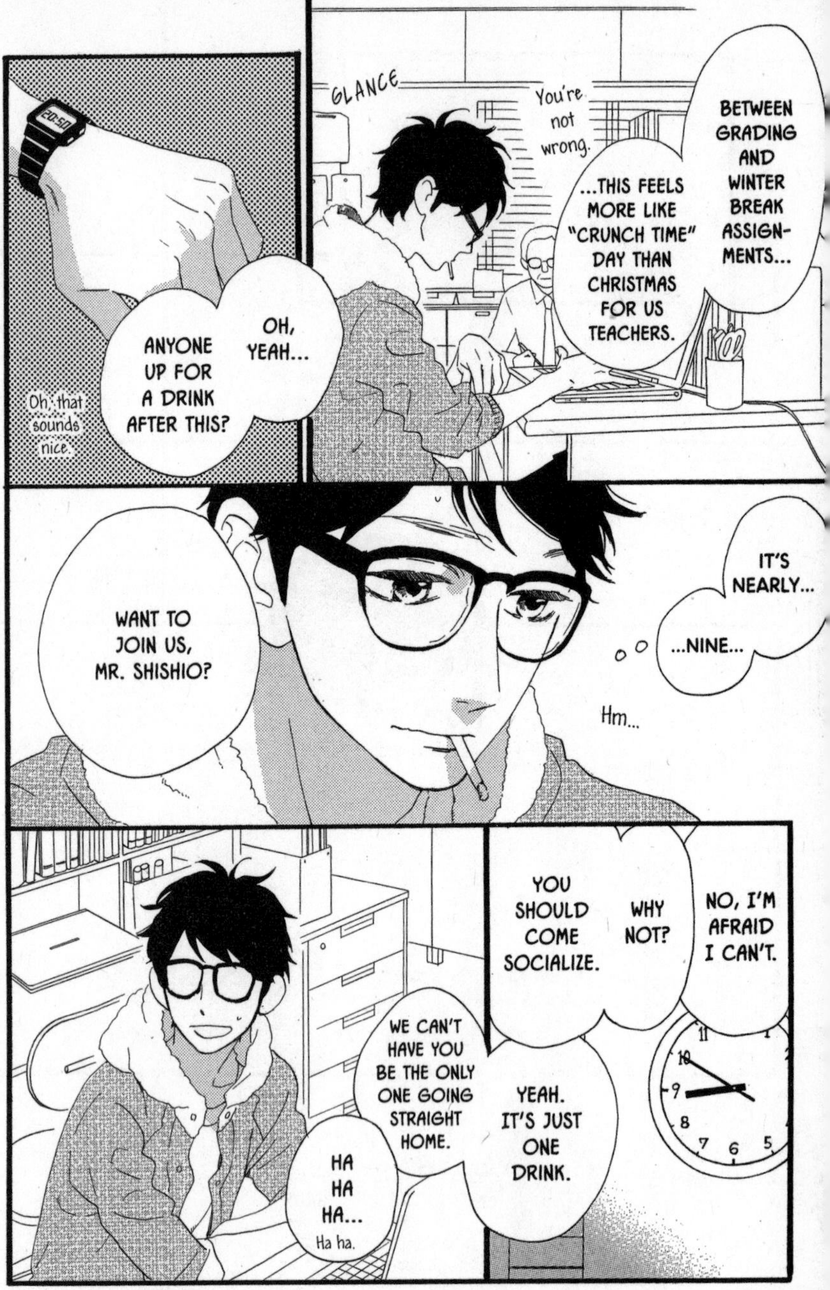
BETWEEN GRADING AND WINTER BREAK ASSIGNMENTS...
...THIS FEELS MORE LIKE "CRUNCH TIME" DAY THAN CHRISTMAS FOR US TEACHERS.
You're not wrong.
GLANCE
OH, YEAH...
ANYONE UP FOR A DRINK AFTER THIS?
Oh, that sounds nice.
IT'S NEARLY...
...NINE...
Hm...
WANT TO JOIN US, MR. SHISHIO?
NO, I'M AFRAID I CAN'T.
WHY NOT?
YOU SHOULD COME SOCIALIZE.
YEAH. IT'S JUST ONE DRINK.
WE CAN'T HAVE YOU BE THE ONLY ONE GOING STRAIGHT HOME.
HA HA HA...
Ha ha.

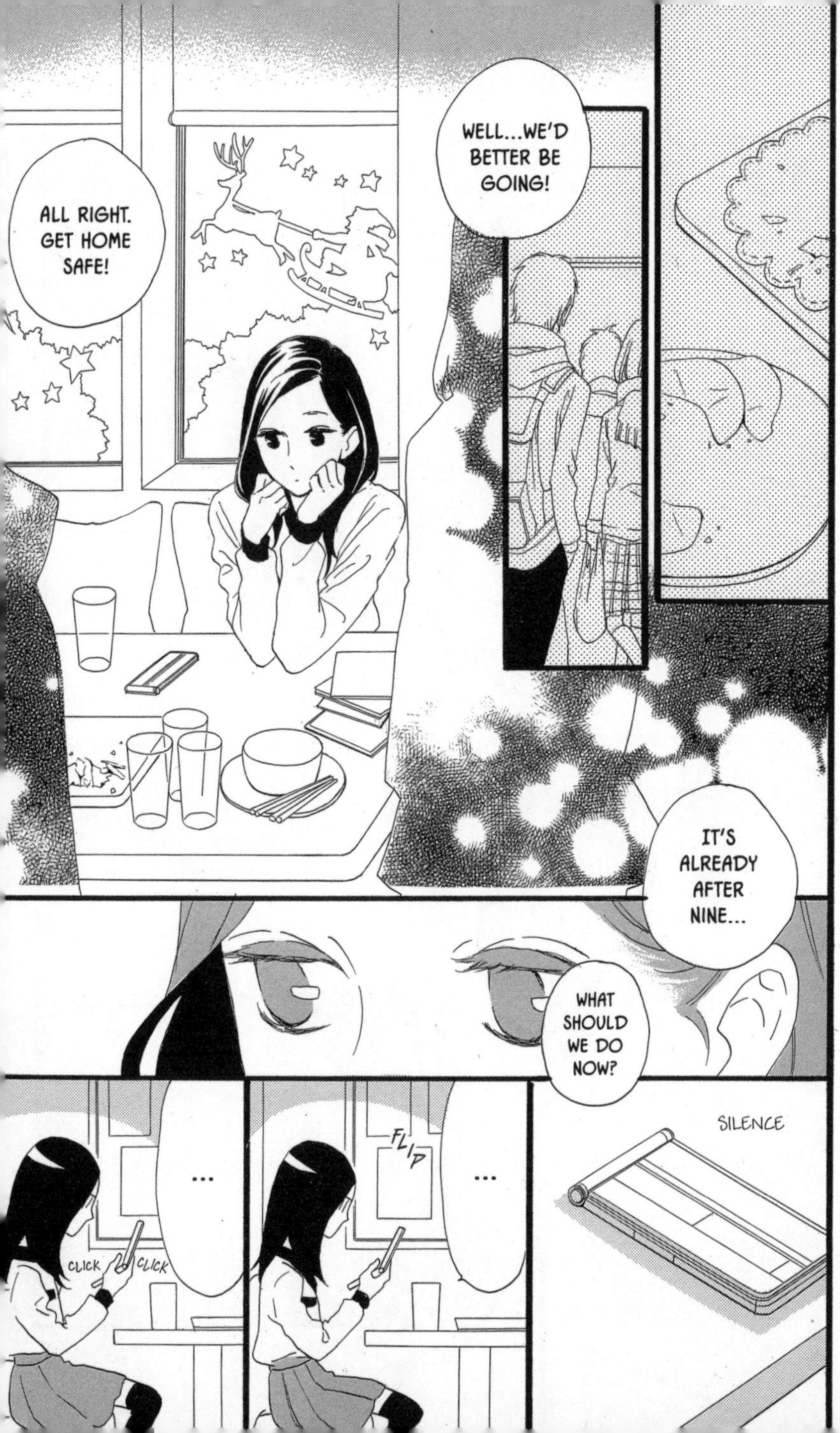
WELL...WE'D BETTER BE GOING!
ALL RIGHT. GET HOME SAFE!
IT'S ALREADY AFTER NINE...
WHAT SHOULD WE DO NOW?
SILENCE
FLIP
...
CLICK
CLICK
...

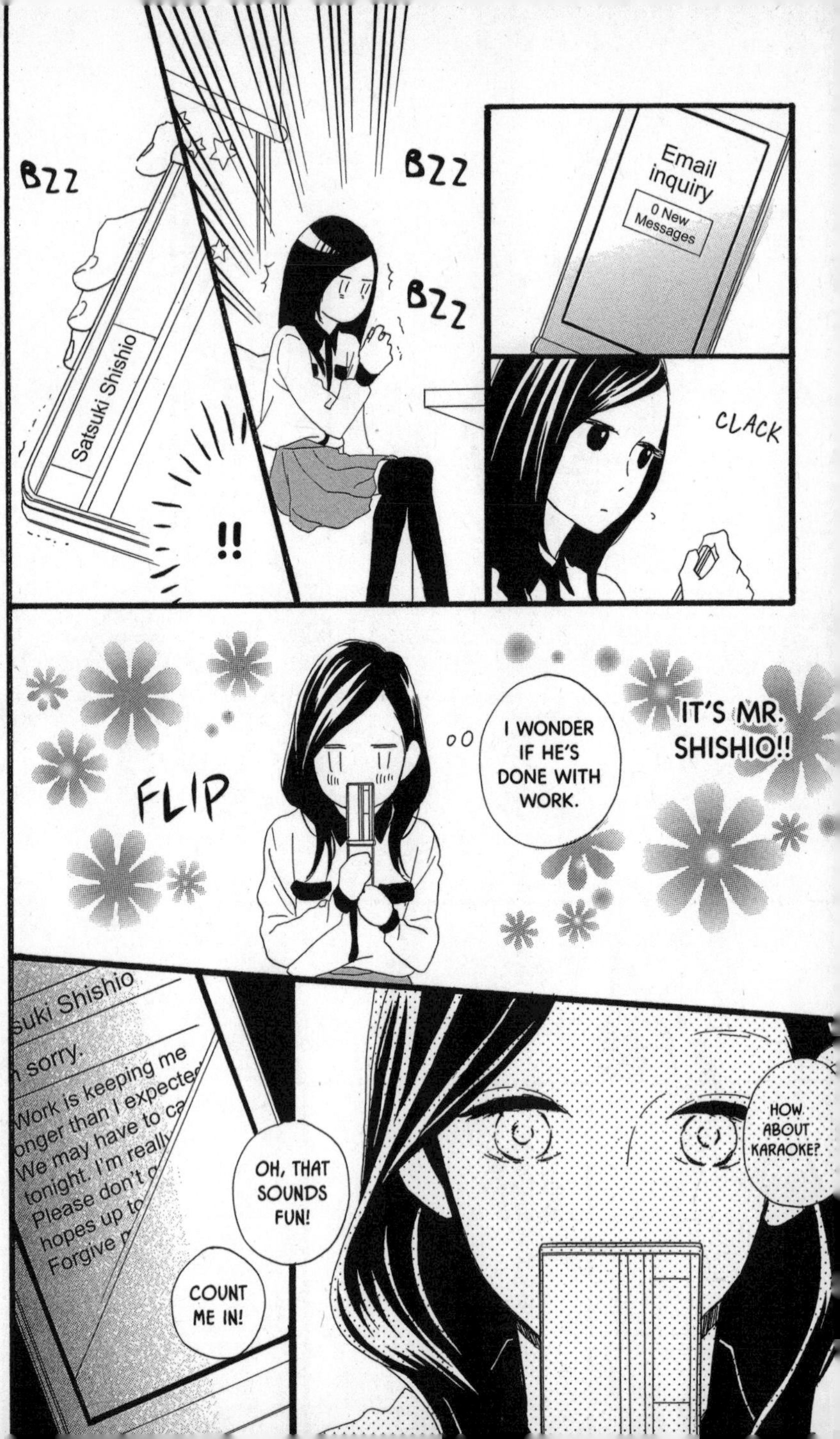
Email inquiry
0 New Messages
CLACK
BZZ
BZZ
BZZ
Satsuki Shishio
!!
IT'S MR. SHISHIO!!
I WONDER IF HE'S DONE WITH WORK.
FLIP
HOW ABOUT KARAOKE?
OH, THAT SOUNDS FUN!
COUNT ME IN!
suki Shishio
n sorry.
Work is keeping me
onger than I expecte
We may have to ca
tonight. I'm really
Please don't g
hopes up to
Forgive

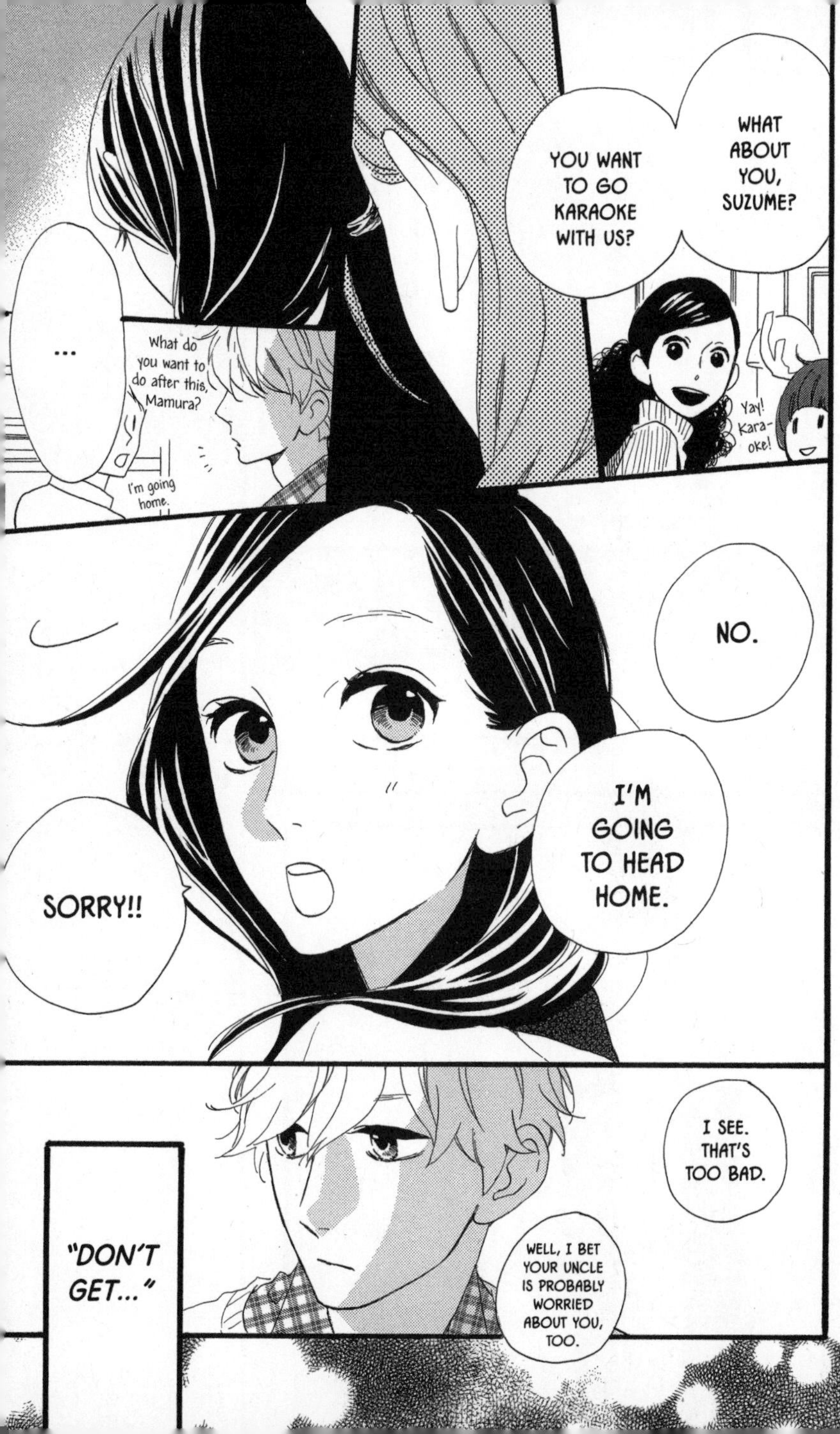
WHAT ABOUT YOU, SUZUME?
YOU WANT TO GO KARAOKE WITH US?
Yay! Kara-oke!
What do you want to do after this, Mamura?
I'm going home.
...
NO.
I'M GOING TO HEAD HOME.
SORRY!!
I SEE. THAT'S TOO BAD.
WELL, I BET YOUR UNCLE IS PROBABLY WORRIED ABOUT YOU, TOO.
"DON'T GET..."

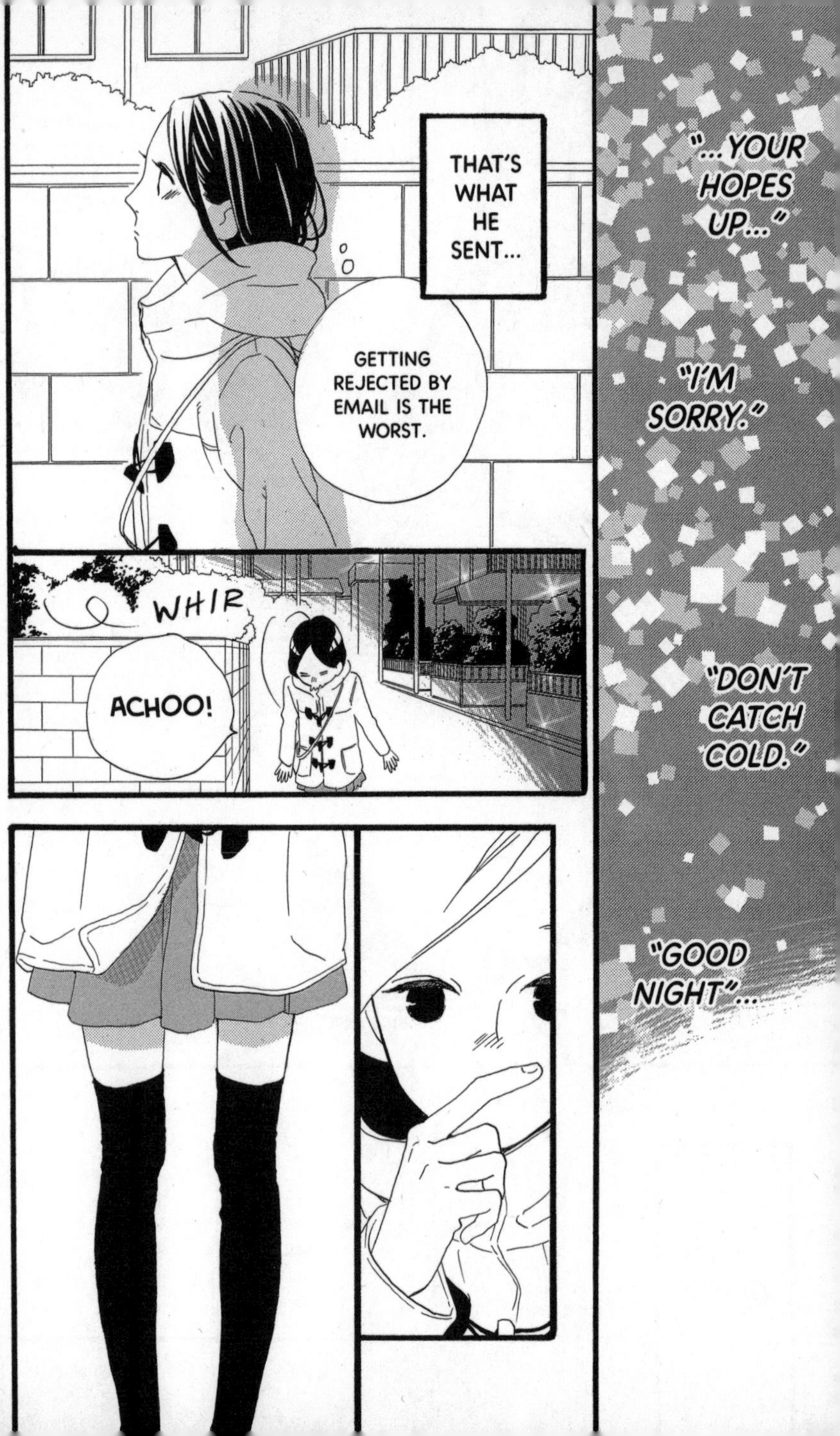
"...YOUR HOPES UP..."
"I'M SORRY."
"DON'T CATCH COLD."
"GOOD NIGHT"...
THAT'S WHAT HE SENT...
GETTING REJECTED BY EMAIL IS THE WORST.
WHIR
ACHOO!

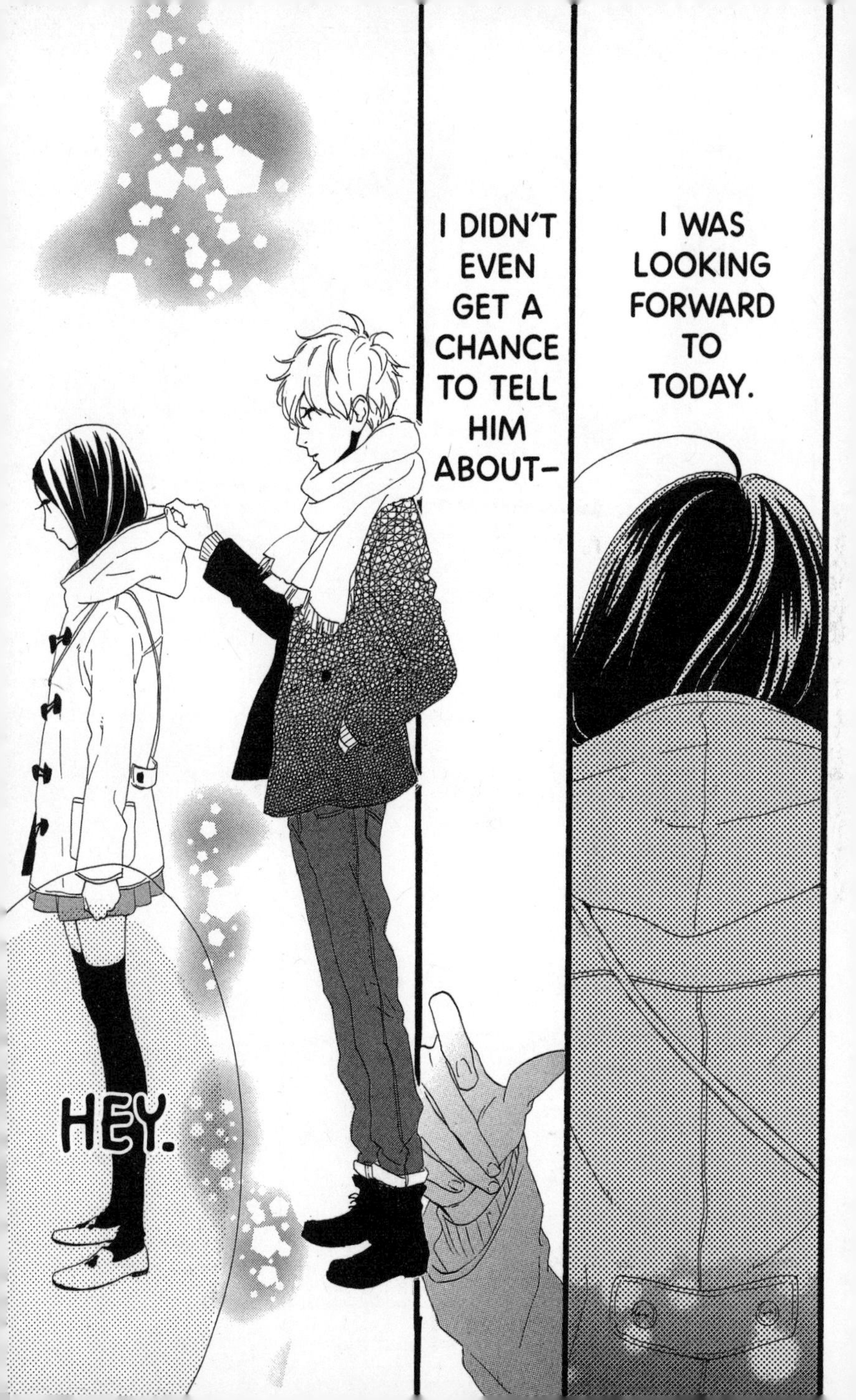
I WAS LOOKING FORWARD TO TODAY.
I DIDN'T EVEN GET A CHANCE TO TELL HIM ABOUT–
HEY.

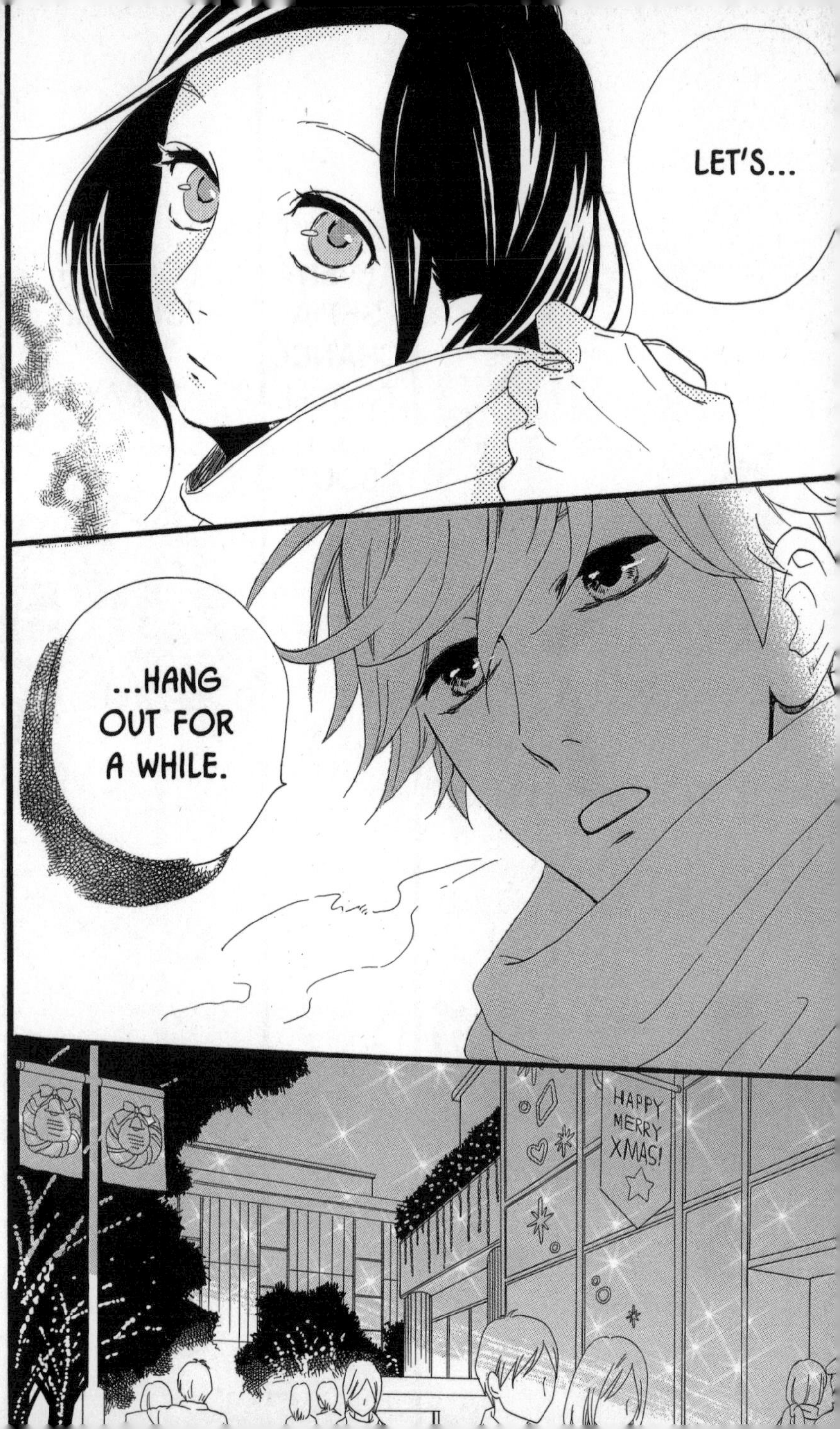
LET'S...
...HANG OUT FOR A WHILE.
HAPPY MERRY XMAS!

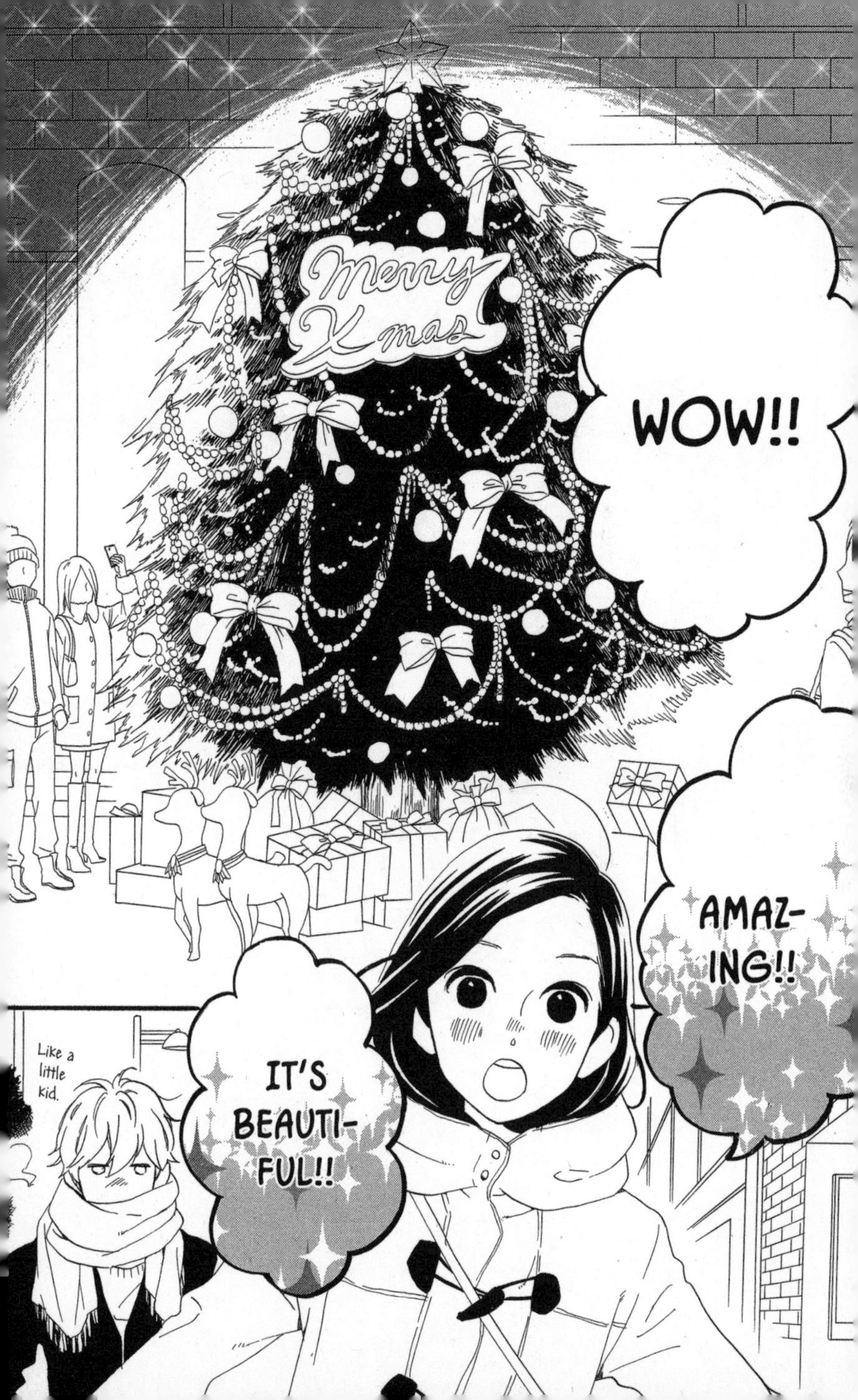
Merry X-mas
WOW!!
AMAZ-ING!!
IT'S BEAUTI-FUL!!
Like a little kid.

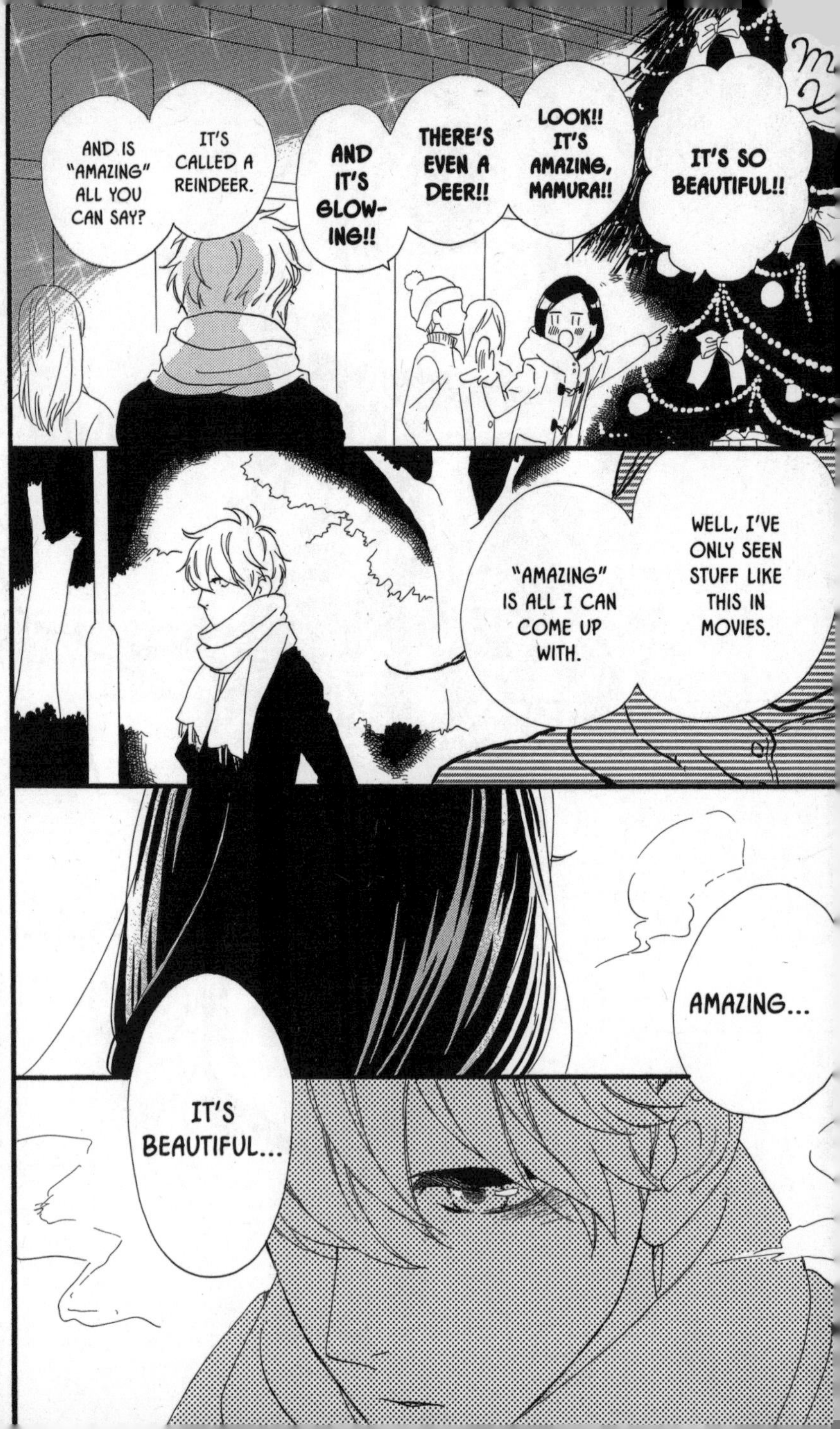
IT'S SO BEAUTIFUL!!
LOOK!! IT'S AMAZING, MAMURA!!
THERE'S EVEN A DEER!!
AND IT'S GLOWING!!
IT'S CALLED A REINDEER.
AND IS "AMAZING" ALL YOU CAN SAY?
WELL, I'VE ONLY SEEN STUFF LIKE THIS IN MOVIES.
"AMAZING" IS ALL I CAN COME UP WITH.
AMAZING...
IT'S BEAUTIFUL...

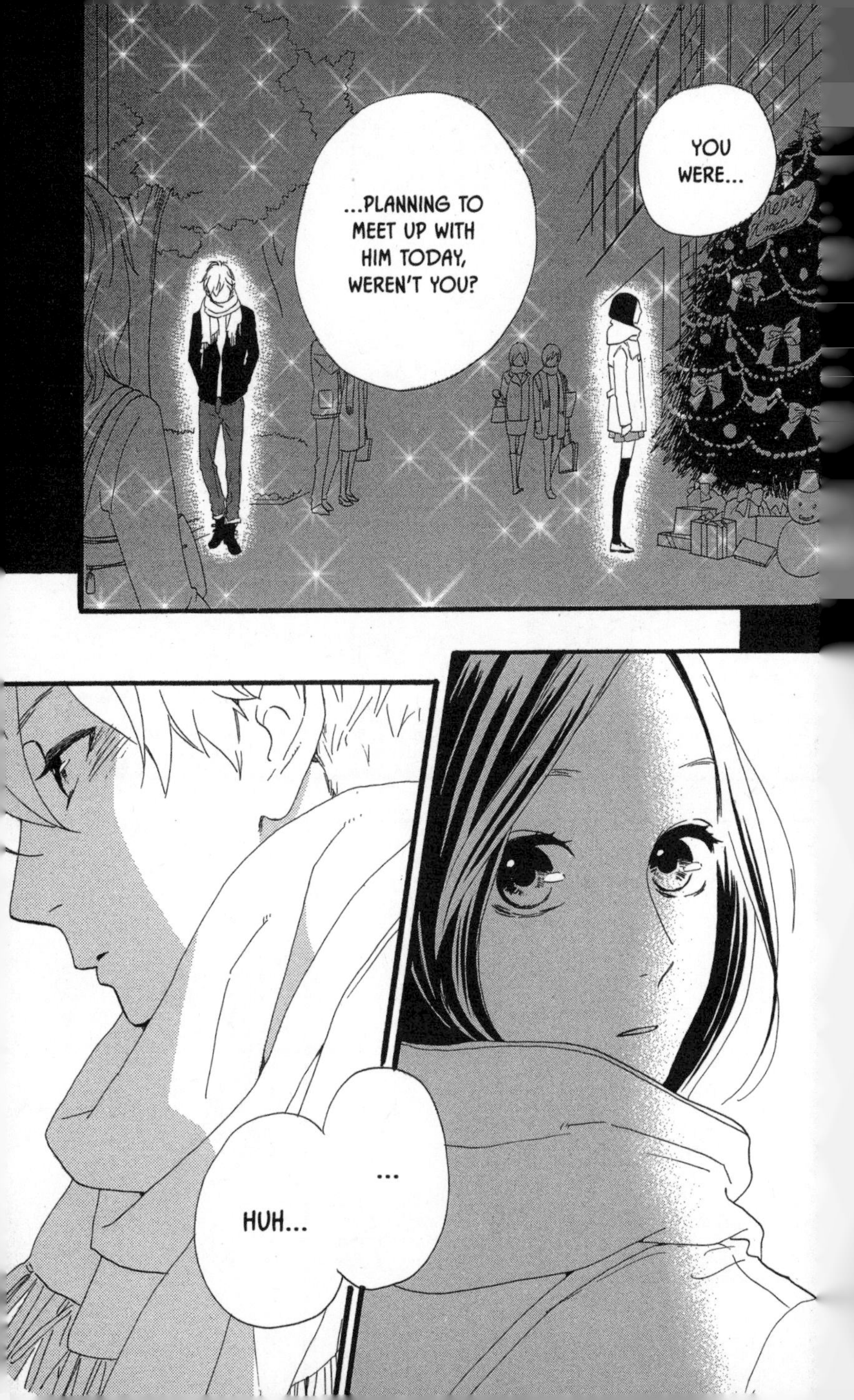
YOU WERE...
...PLANNING TO MEET UP WITH HIM TODAY, WEREN'T YOU?
... HUH...

UH...

OH.

I KINDA...

...HAVE AN EYE...

...FOR THESE THINGS.

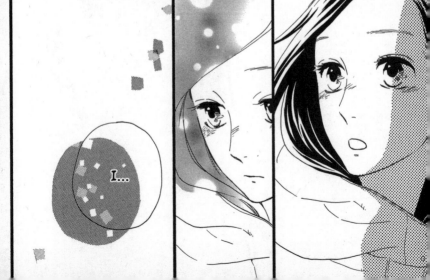

I...

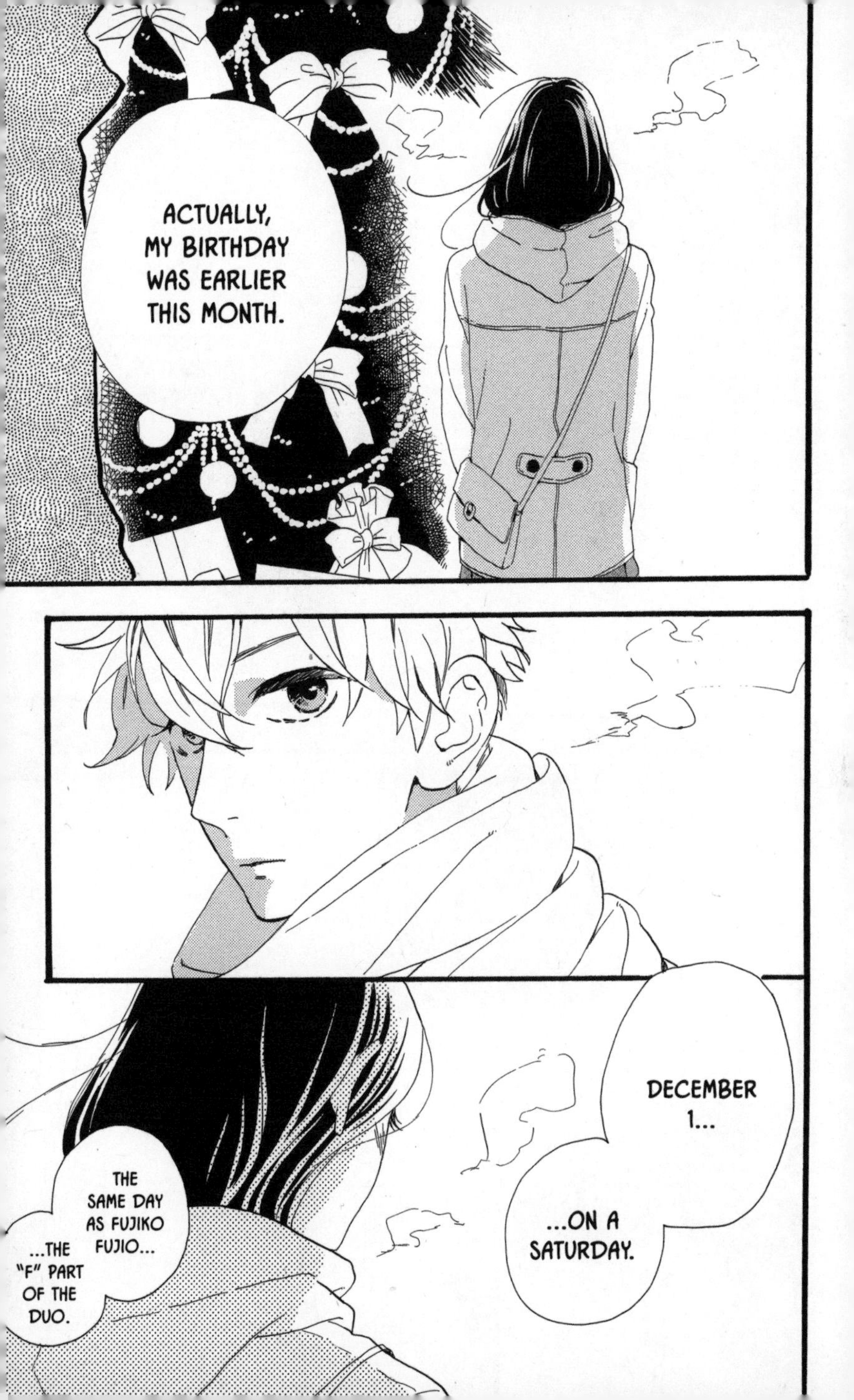
ACTUALLY, MY BIRTHDAY WAS EARLIER THIS MONTH.
DECEMBER 1...
...ON A SATURDAY.
THE SAME DAY AS FUJIKO FUJIO...
...THE "F" PART OF THE DUO.

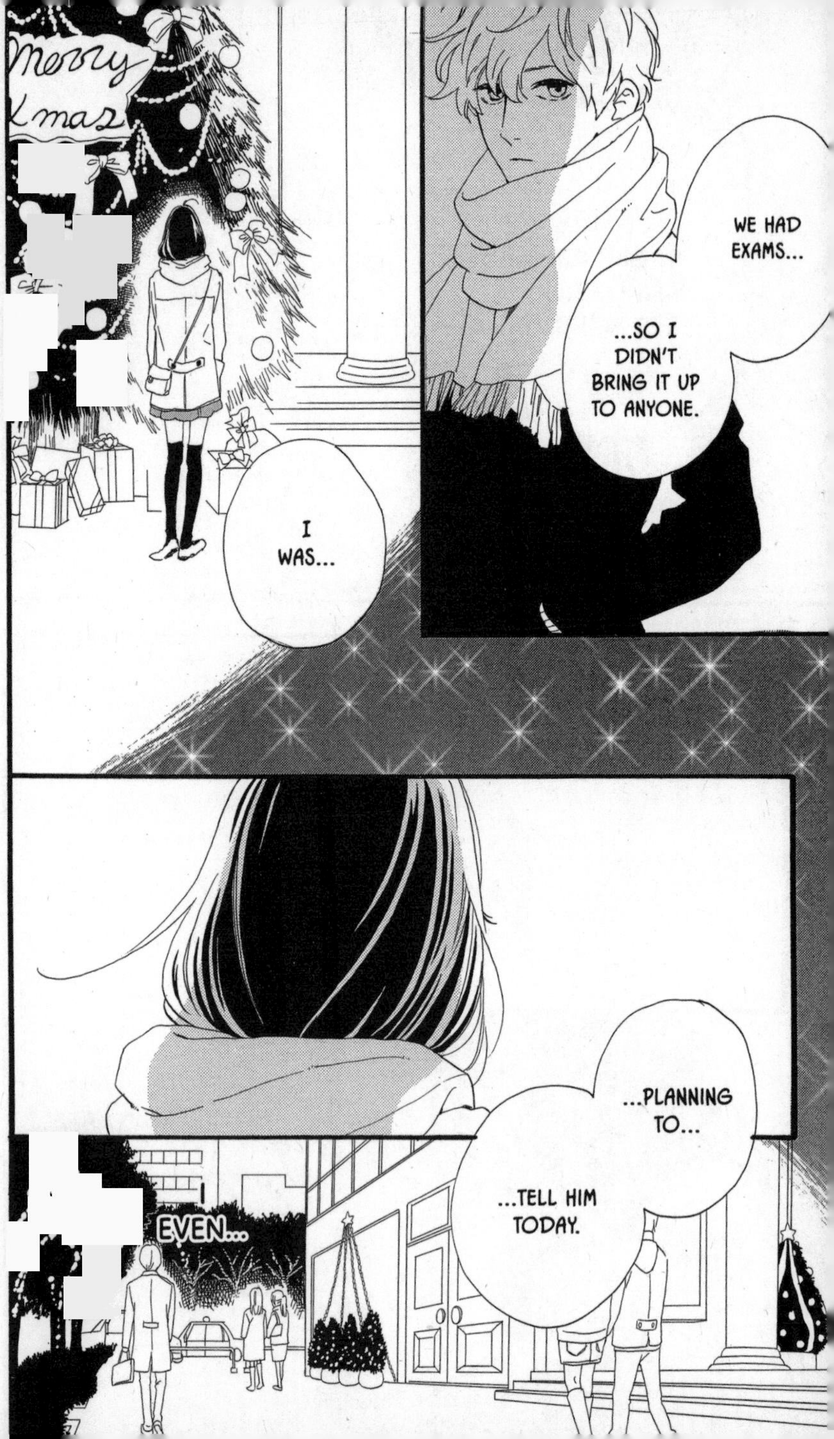
Merry Xmas
WE HAD EXAMS...
...SO I DIDN'T BRING IT UP TO ANYONE.
I WAS...
...PLANNING TO...
...TELL HIM TODAY.
EVEN...

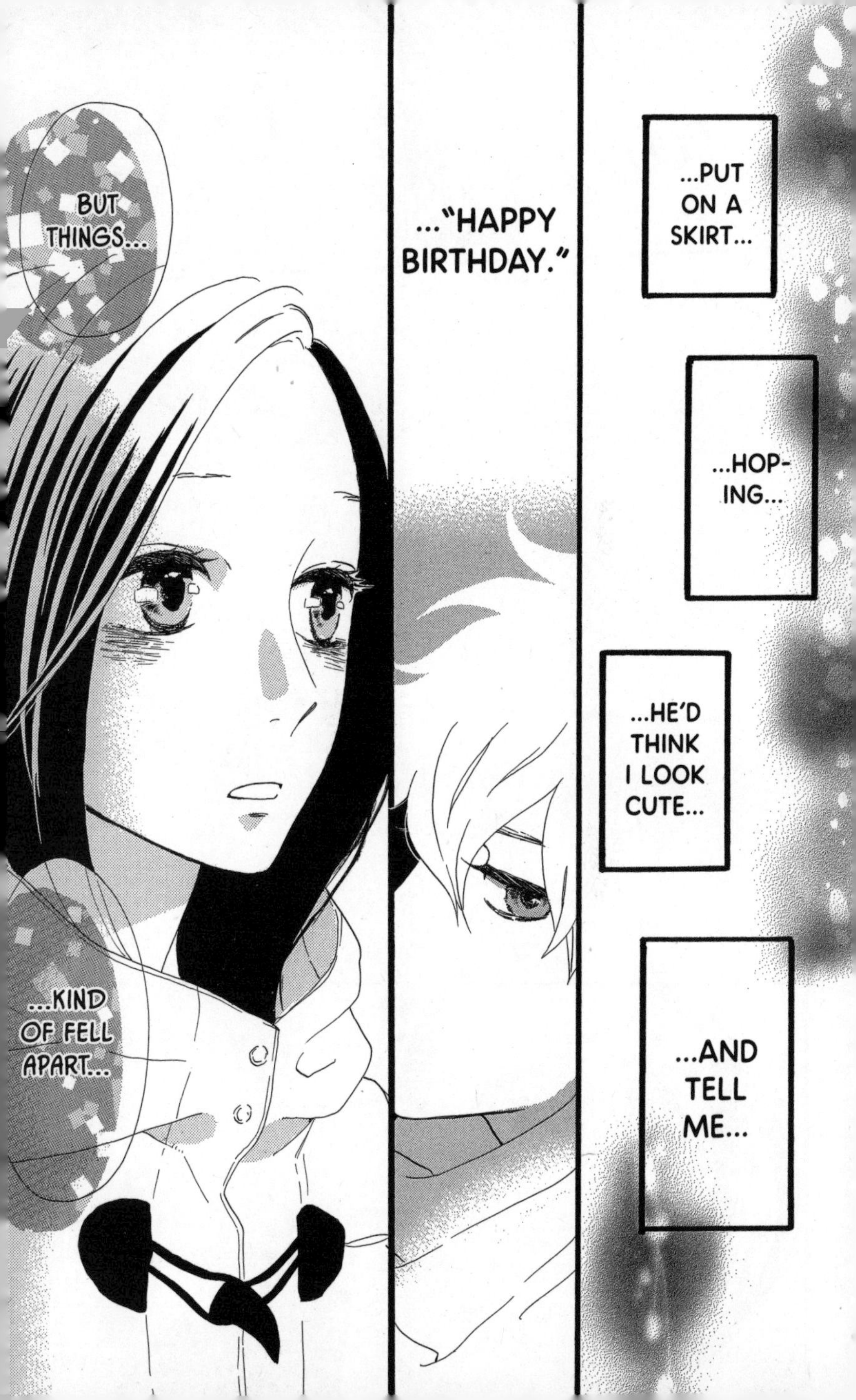
...PUT ON A SKIRT...
...HOP-ING...
...HE'D THINK I LOOK CUTE...
...AND TELL ME...
..."HAPPY BIRTHDAY."
BUT THINGS...
...KIND OF FELL APART...

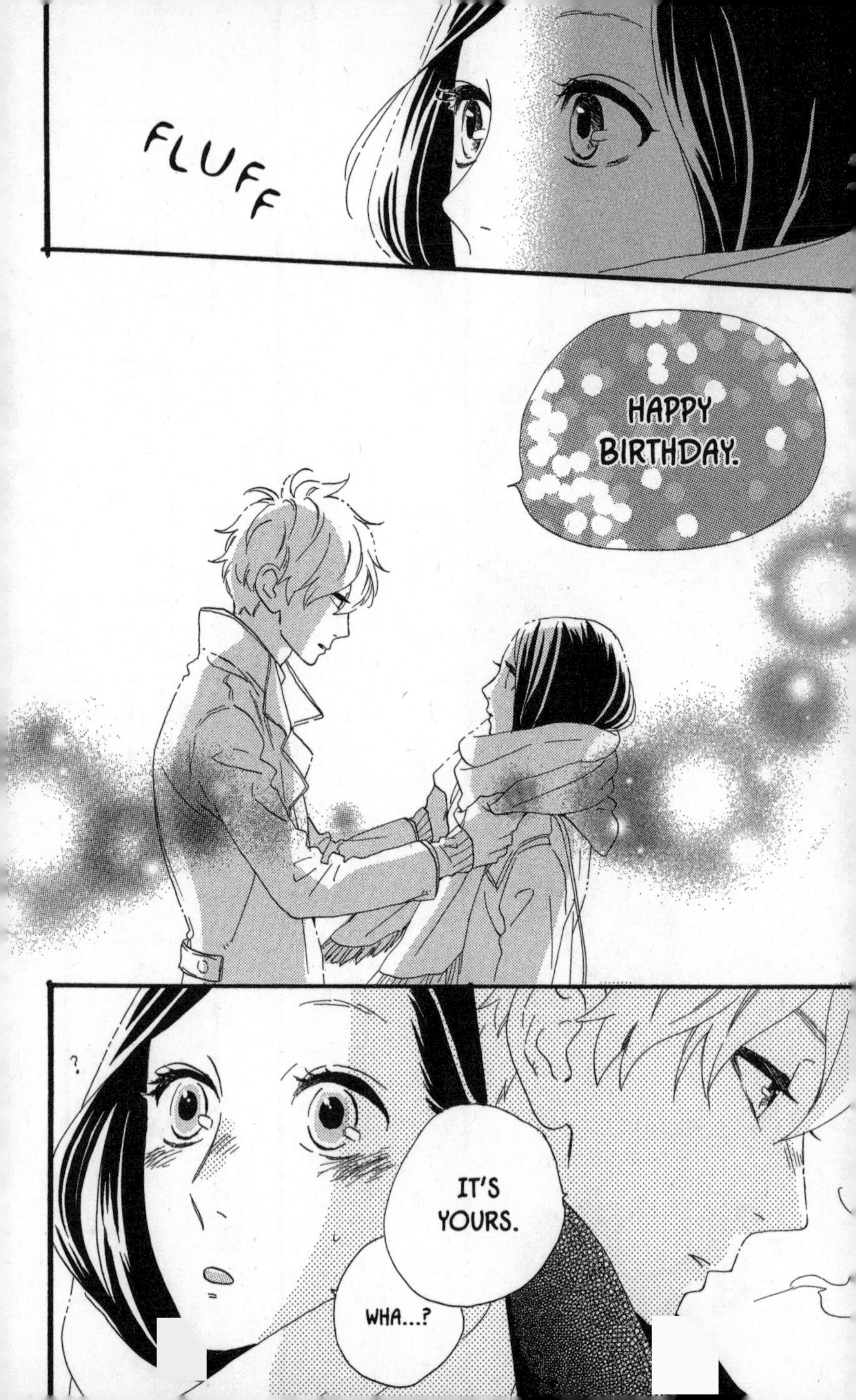
FLUFF
HAPPY BIRTHDAY.
?
IT'S YOURS.
WHA...?

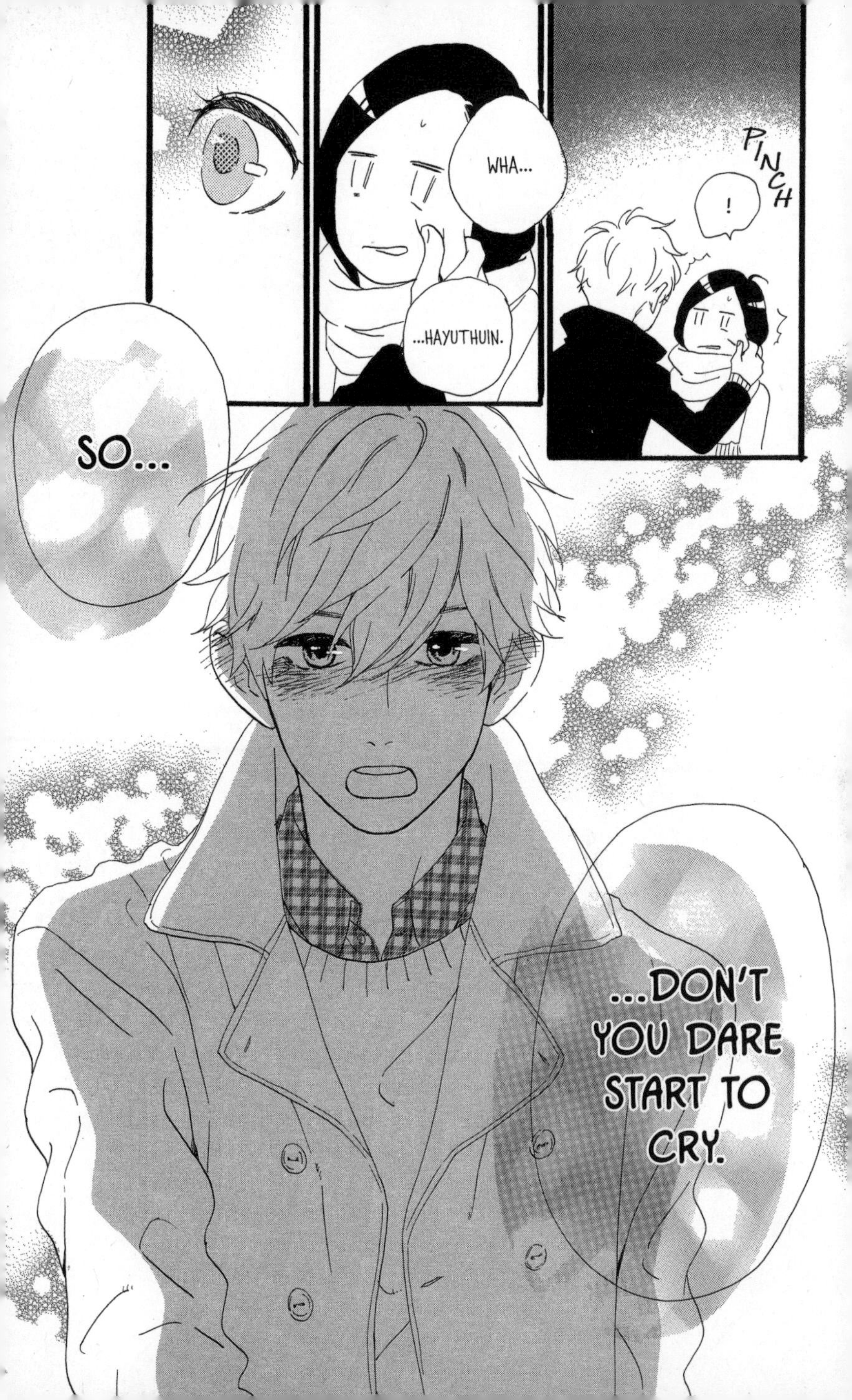
PINCH
!
WHA...
...HAYUTHUIN.
SO...
...DON'T YOU DARE START TO CRY.

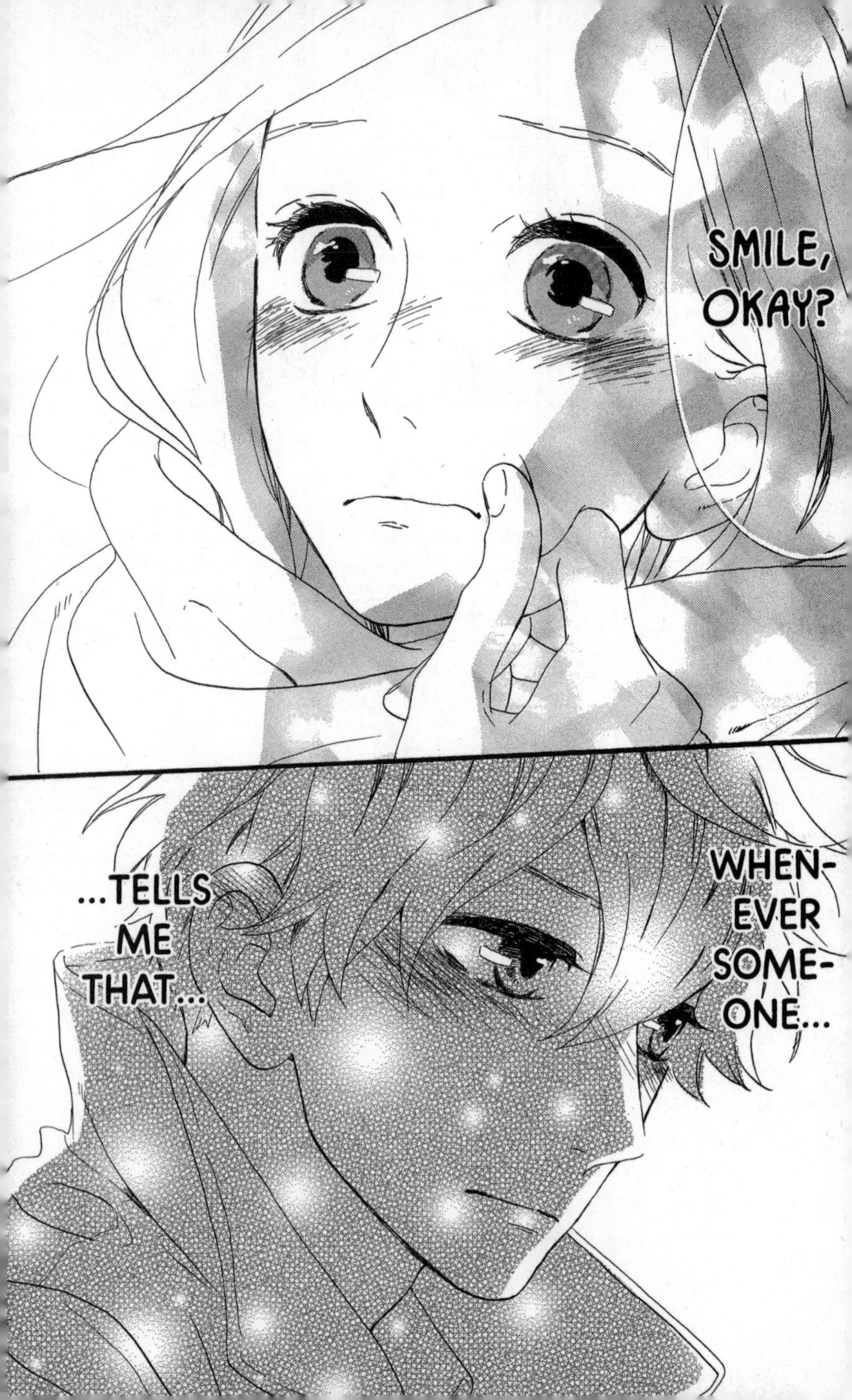
SMILE, OKAY?
WHEN-EVER SOME-ONE...
...TELLS ME THAT...

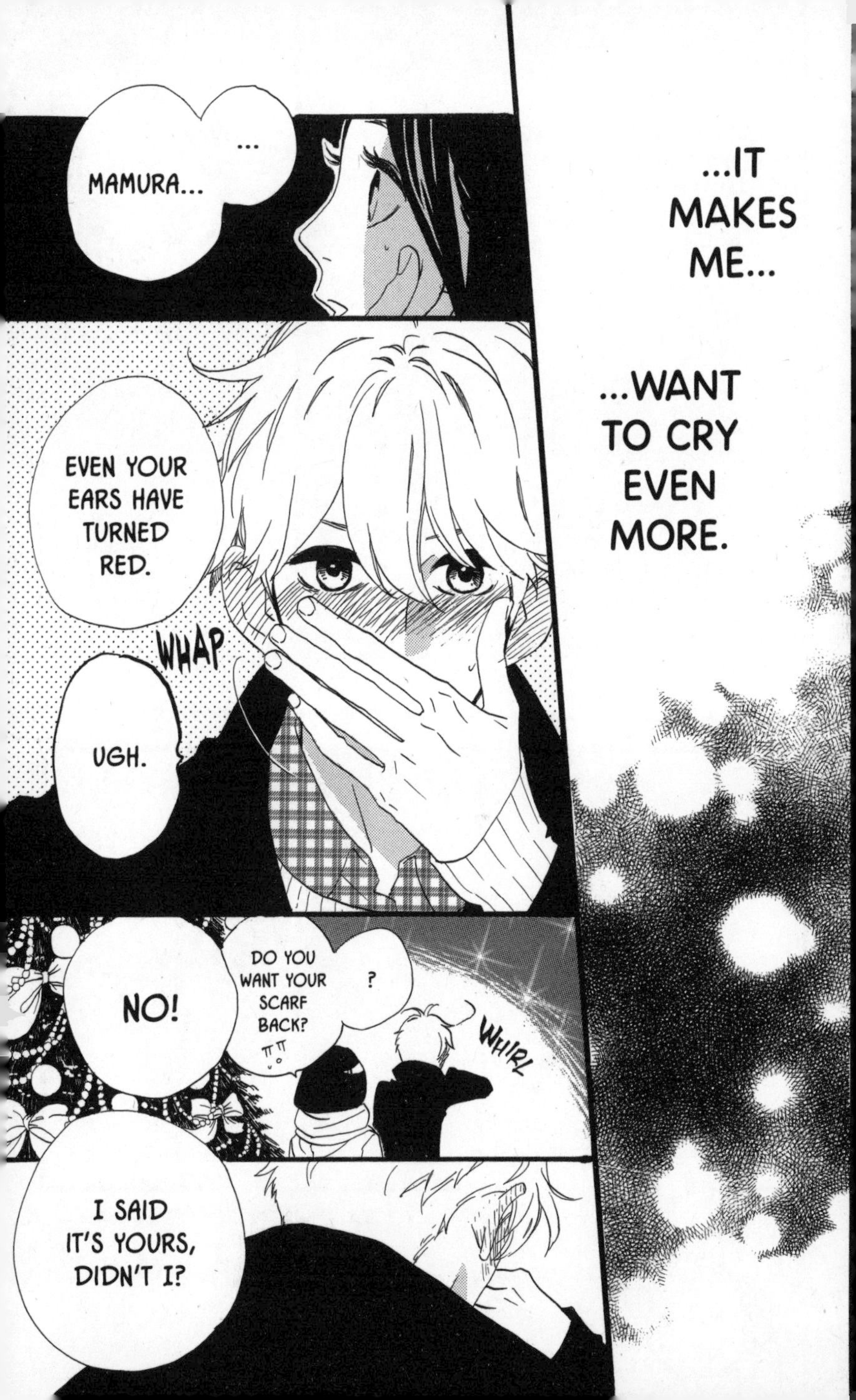
...IT MAKES ME...
...WANT TO CRY EVEN MORE.
...
MAMURA...
EVEN YOUR EARS HAVE TURNED RED.
WHAP
UGH.
WHIRL
?
DO YOU WANT YOUR SCARF BACK?
NO!
I SAID IT'S YOURS, DIDN'T I?

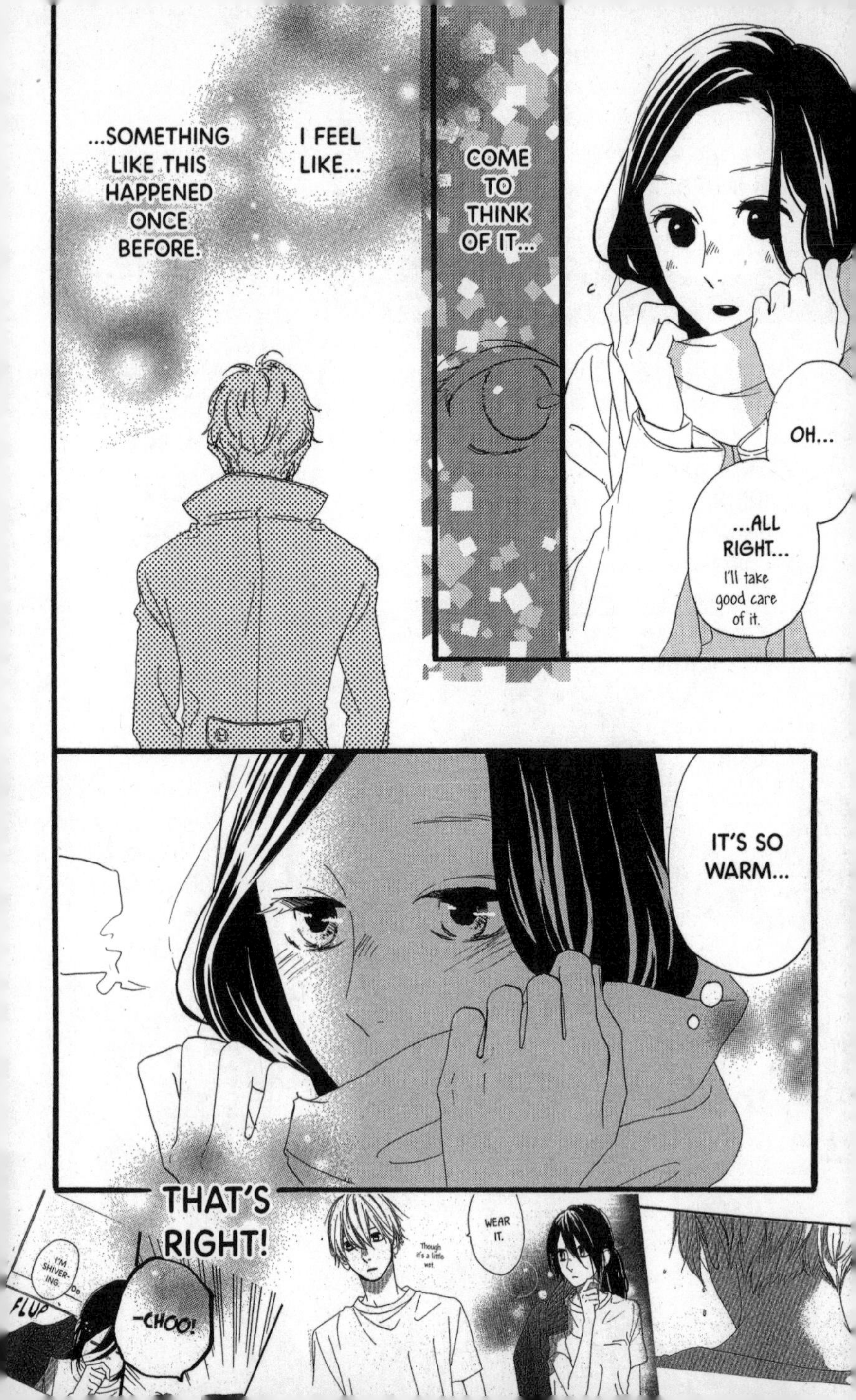
OH...
...ALL RIGHT... I'll take good care of it.
COME TO THINK OF IT...
I FEEL LIKE...
...SOMETHING LIKE THIS HAPPENED ONCE BEFORE.
IT'S SO WARM...
WEAR IT.
Though it's a little wet.
THAT'S RIGHT!
-CHOO!
I'M SHIVERING.
FLUP

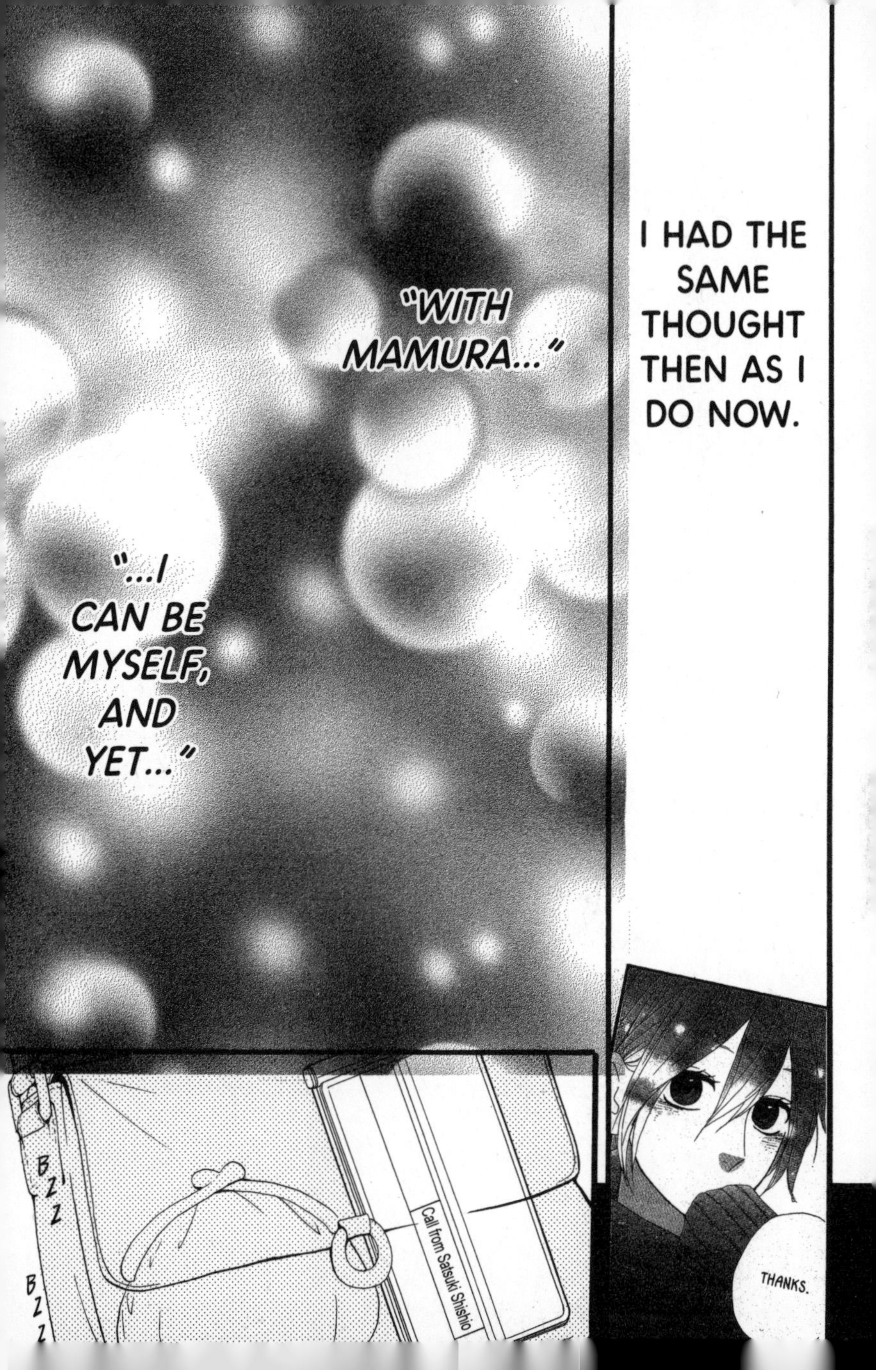
I HAD THE SAME THOUGHT THEN AS I DO NOW.
THANKS.
"WITH MAMURA..."
"...I CAN BE MYSELF, AND YET..."
BZZ
BZZ
Call from Satsuki Shishio

By the way... ②

McAvoy's performance was wonderful!!
It was at a very small theater, so the performers were only three meters away. The acting was so powerful!! I don't usually care much for plays, but I enjoyed this one very much!!

After the play, to justify traveling all that way to England, we decided to wait at the stage door for the actors to exit. After about 15 minutes, McAvoy appeared!! What?! That's pretty quick, isn't it?! And he began to sign autographs as though on a production line. Unfortunately, I didn't have any paper with me, so I couldn't get his autograph.

Our eyes met three or four times and his eyes seemed to be asking me, "Don't you want me to sign anything?" I'm sorry, McAvoy... After that, he took a picture with everyone, and then vanished like the wind...or so I thought. On our way home, I saw him using an ATM like a regular guy. He seems like a guy who likes to move at his own pace.

He had dark circles under his eyes.

McAvoy

If you want an autograph, please line up on this side. Please don't stand in the street; it's dangerous.

McAvoy guided his fans like a security guard.

He seems awfully tired...

After all, he had been onstage for three hours...

Me

Ms. Noborio

Assistant

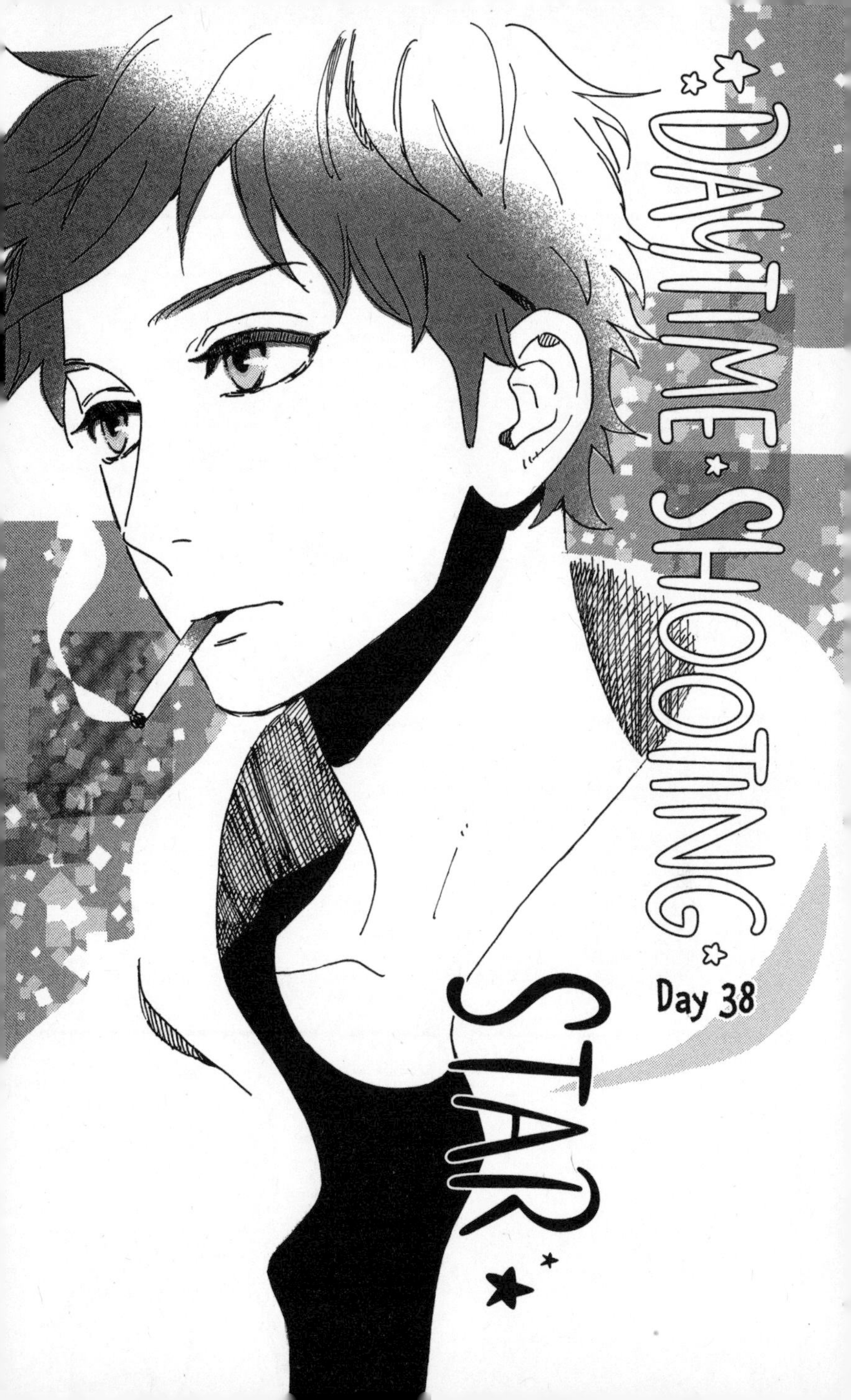
DAYTIME SHOOTING STAR
Day 38

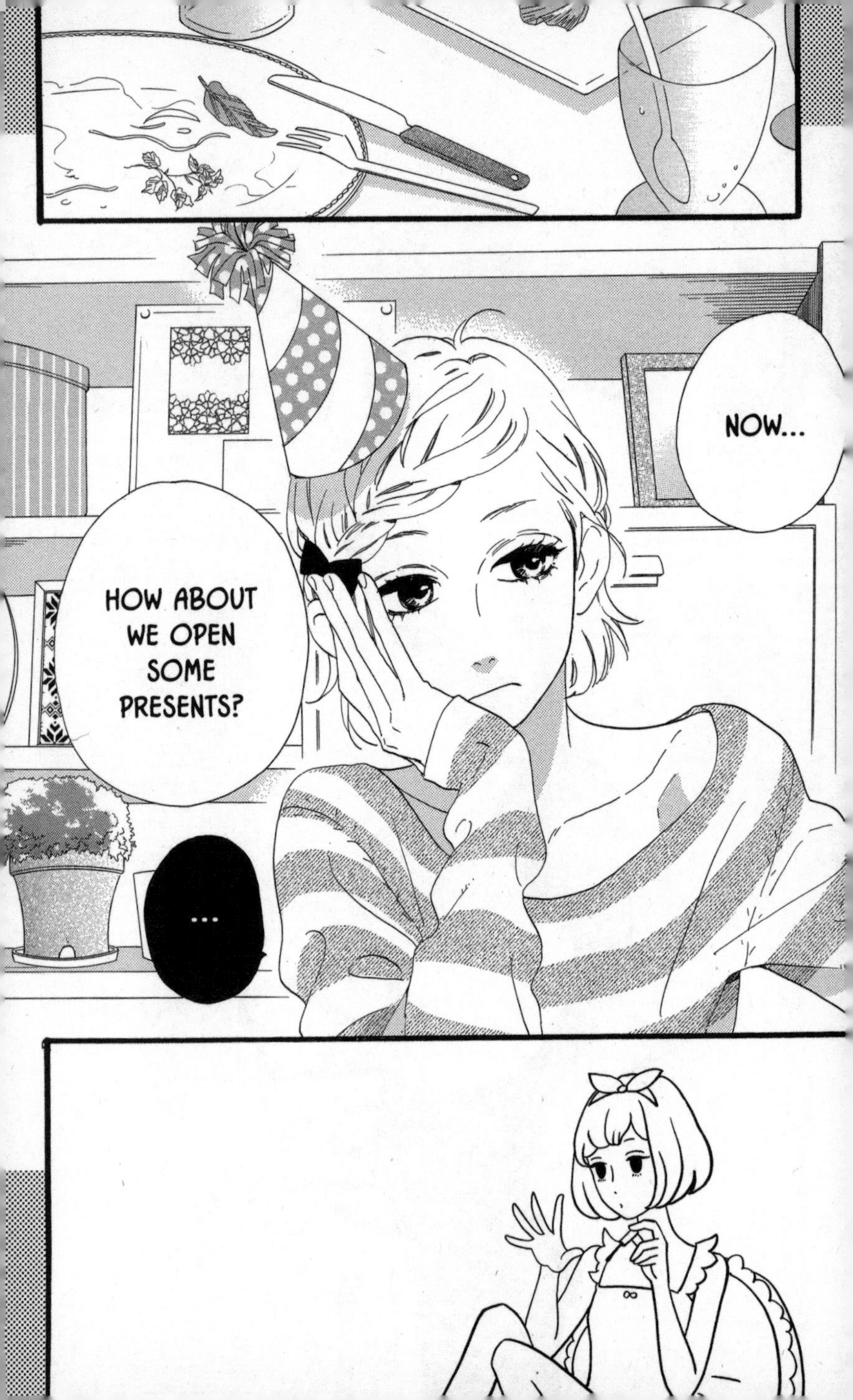
NOW...
HOW ABOUT WE OPEN SOME PRESENTS?
...

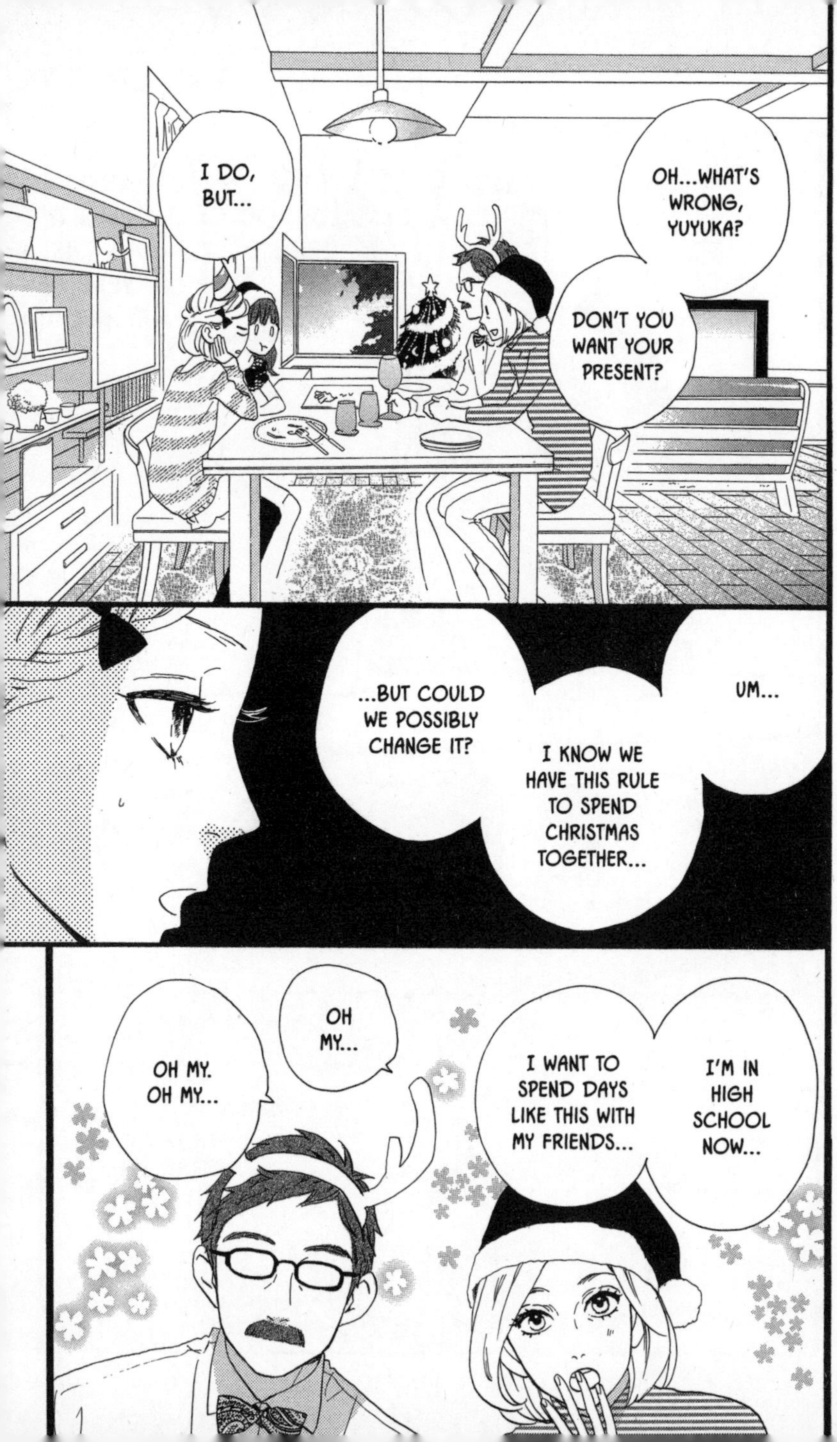
OH...WHAT'S WRONG, YUYUKA?
DON'T YOU WANT YOUR PRESENT?
I DO, BUT...
UM...
I KNOW WE HAVE THIS RULE TO SPEND CHRISTMAS TOGETHER...
...BUT COULD WE POSSIBLY CHANGE IT?
I'M IN HIGH SCHOOL NOW...
I WANT TO SPEND DAYS LIKE THIS WITH MY FRIENDS...
OH MY...
OH MY. OH MY...

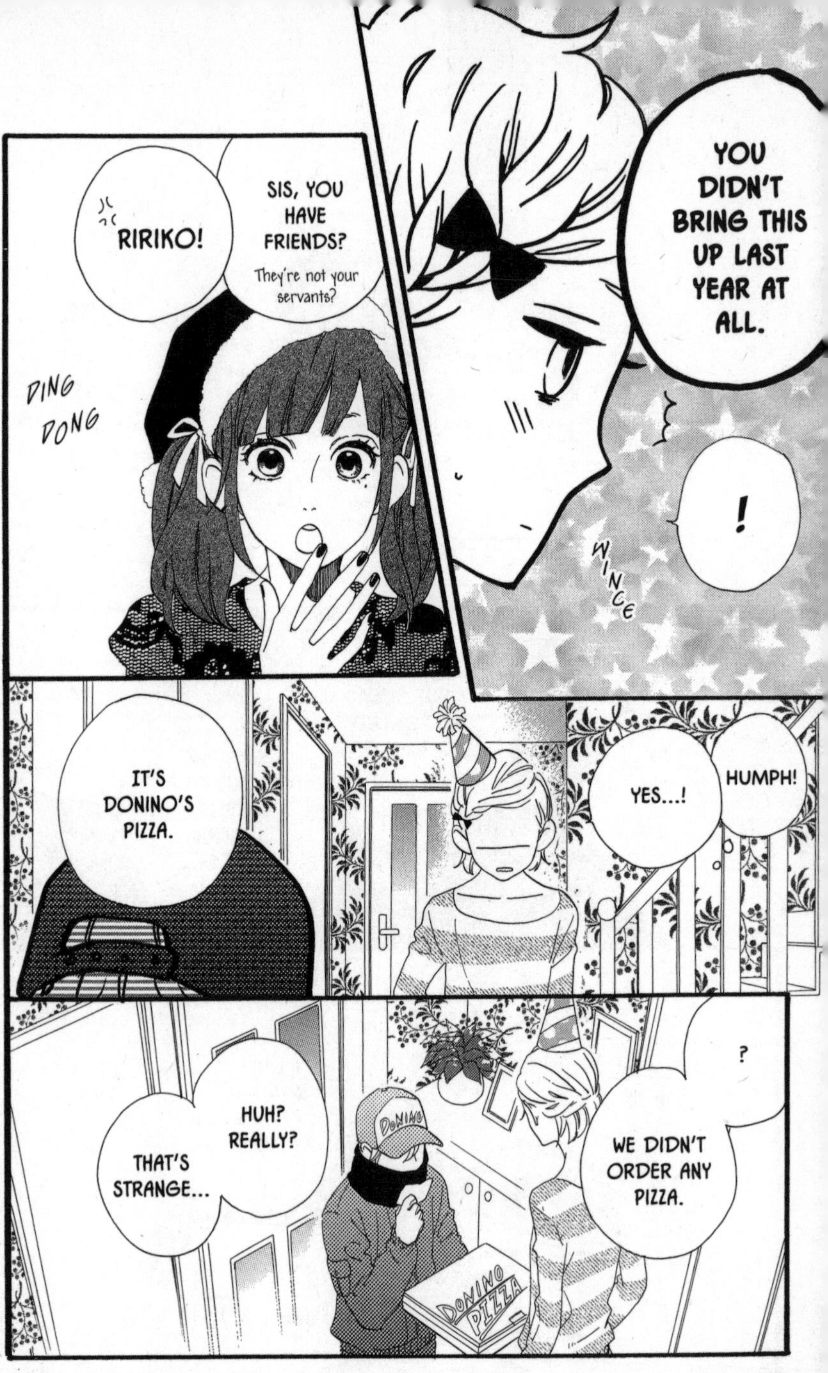
YOU DIDN'T BRING THIS UP LAST YEAR AT ALL.
!
WINCE
SIS, YOU HAVE FRIENDS?
They're not your servants?
RIRIKO!
DING DONG
HUMPH!
YES...!
IT'S DONINO'S PIZZA.
?
WE DIDN'T ORDER ANY PIZZA.
HUH? REALLY?
THAT'S STRANGE...
DONINO
DONINO PIZZA

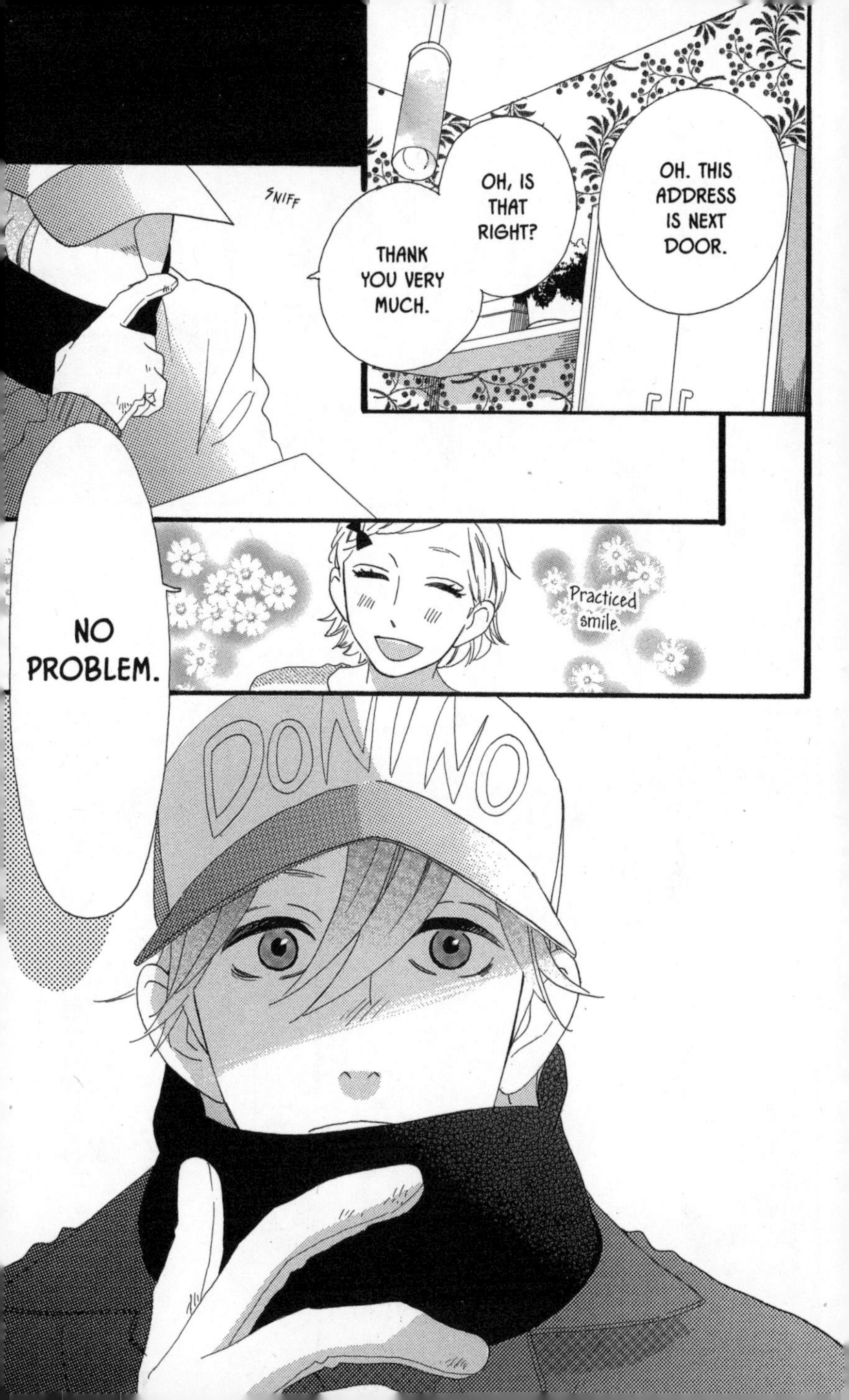
OH. THIS ADDRESS IS NEXT DOOR.
OH, IS THAT RIGHT?
THANK YOU VERY MUCH.
SNIFF
Practiced smile.
NO PROBLEM.

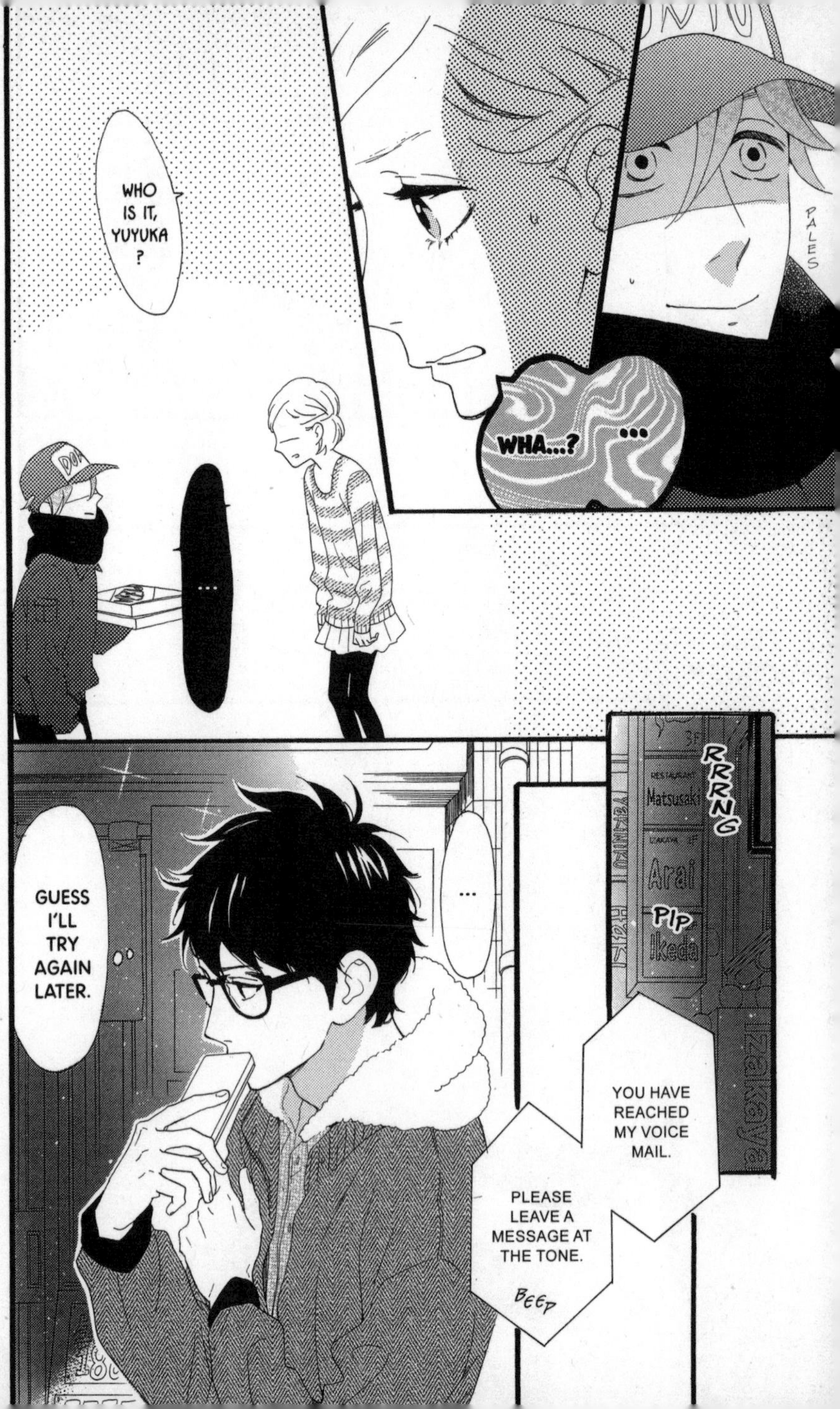
PALES
WHA...?
...
WHO IS IT, YUYUKA?
...
3F
RESTAURANT
Matsusaki
Arai
Ikeda
RRRNG
PIP
YOU HAVE REACHED MY VOICE MAIL.
PLEASE LEAVE A MESSAGE AT THE TONE.
BEEP
...
GUESS I'LL TRY AGAIN LATER.

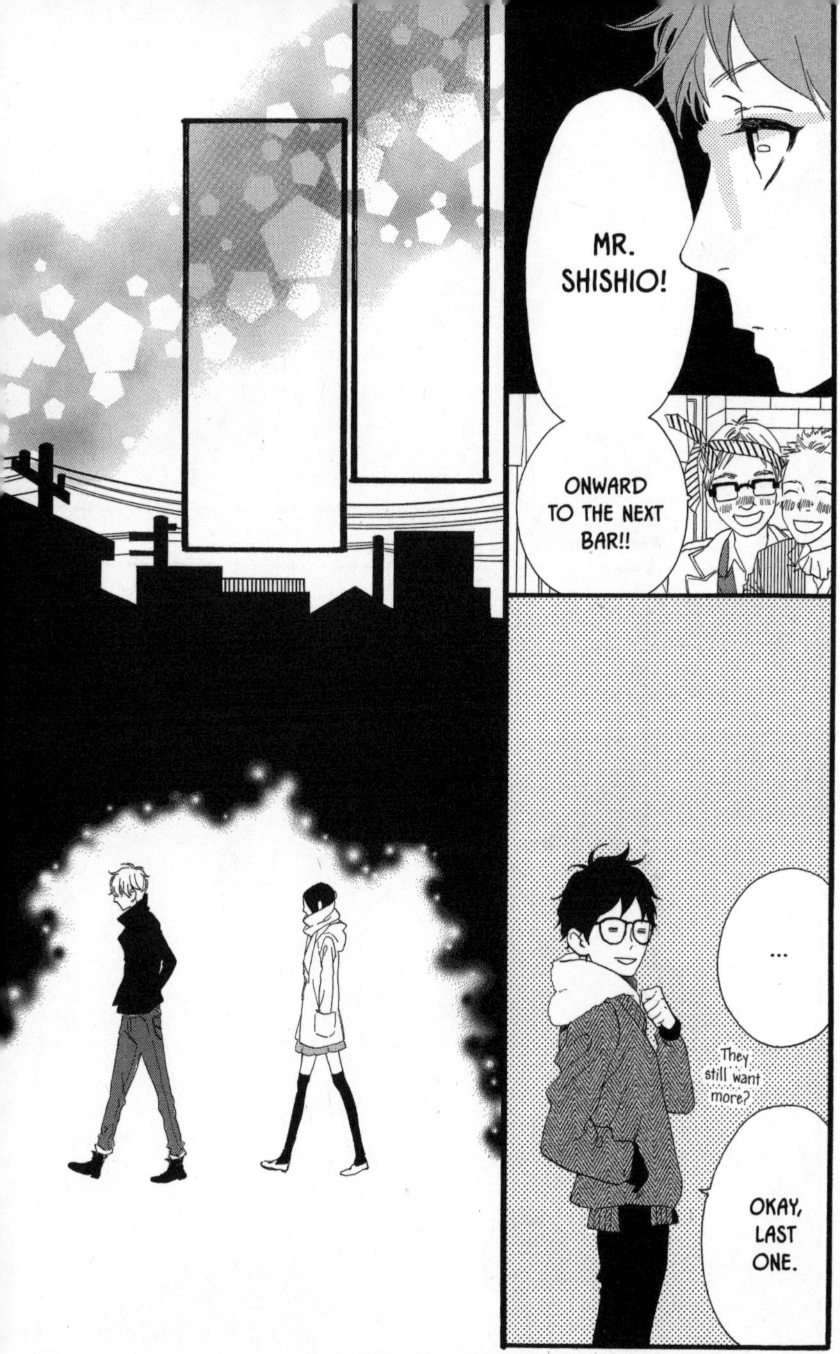
MR. SHISHIO!
ONWARD TO THE NEXT BAR!!
...
They still want more?
OKAY, LAST ONE.

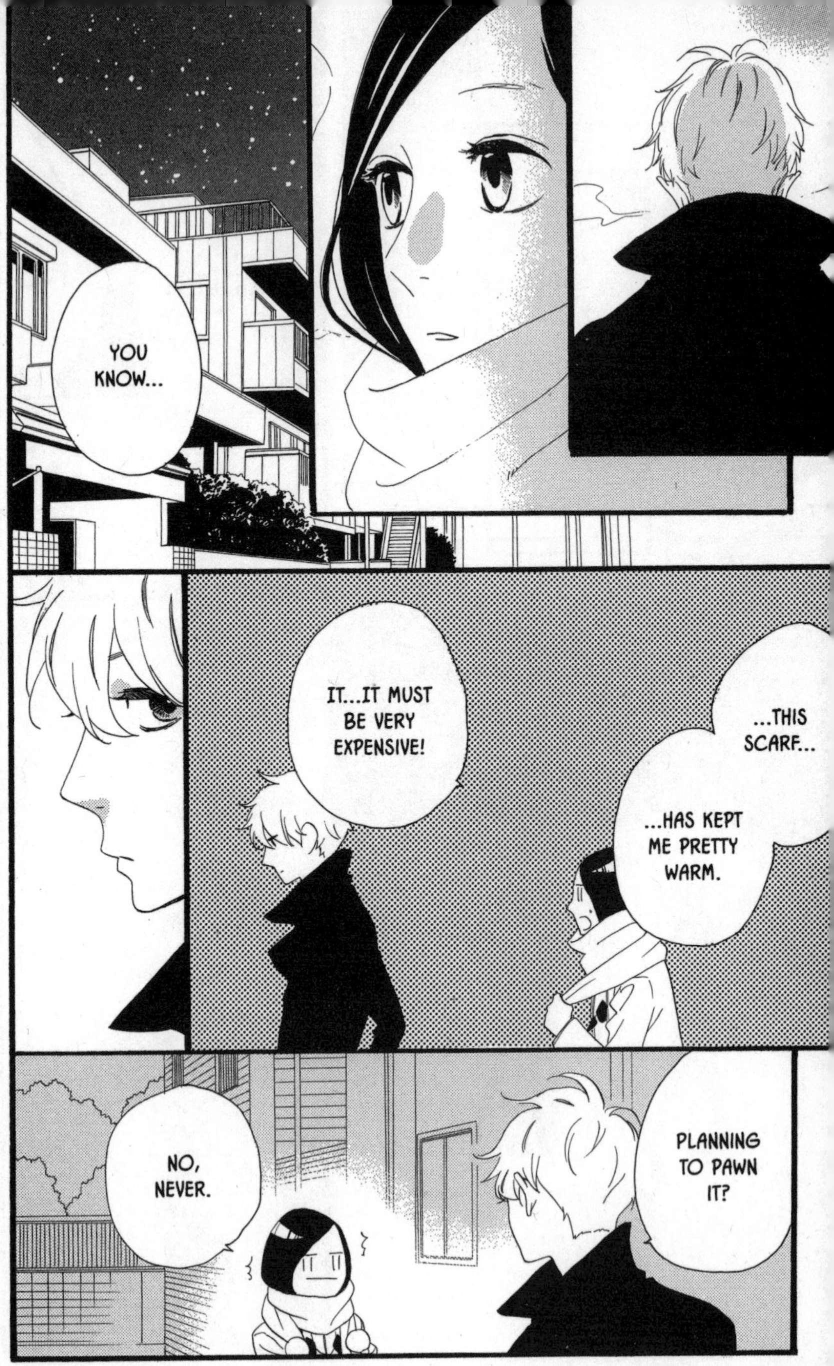
YOU KNOW...
...THIS SCARF...
...HAS KEPT ME PRETTY WARM.
IT...IT MUST BE VERY EXPENSIVE!
PLANNING TO PAWN IT?
NO, NEVER.

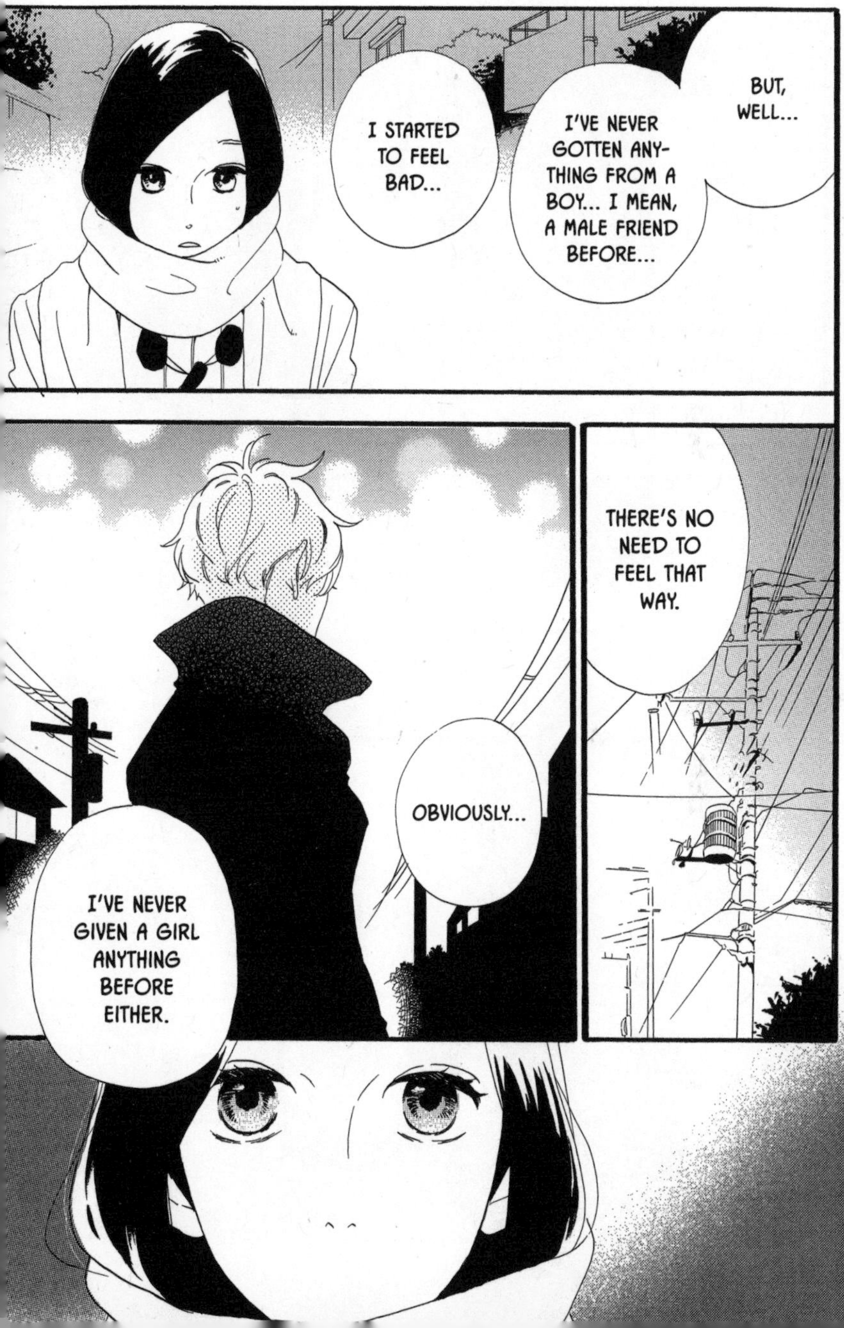
BUT, WELL...
I'VE NEVER GOTTEN ANYTHING FROM A BOY... I MEAN, A MALE FRIEND BEFORE...
I STARTED TO FEEL BAD...
THERE'S NO NEED TO FEEL THAT WAY.
OBVIOUSLY...
I'VE NEVER GIVEN A GIRL ANYTHING BEFORE EITHER.

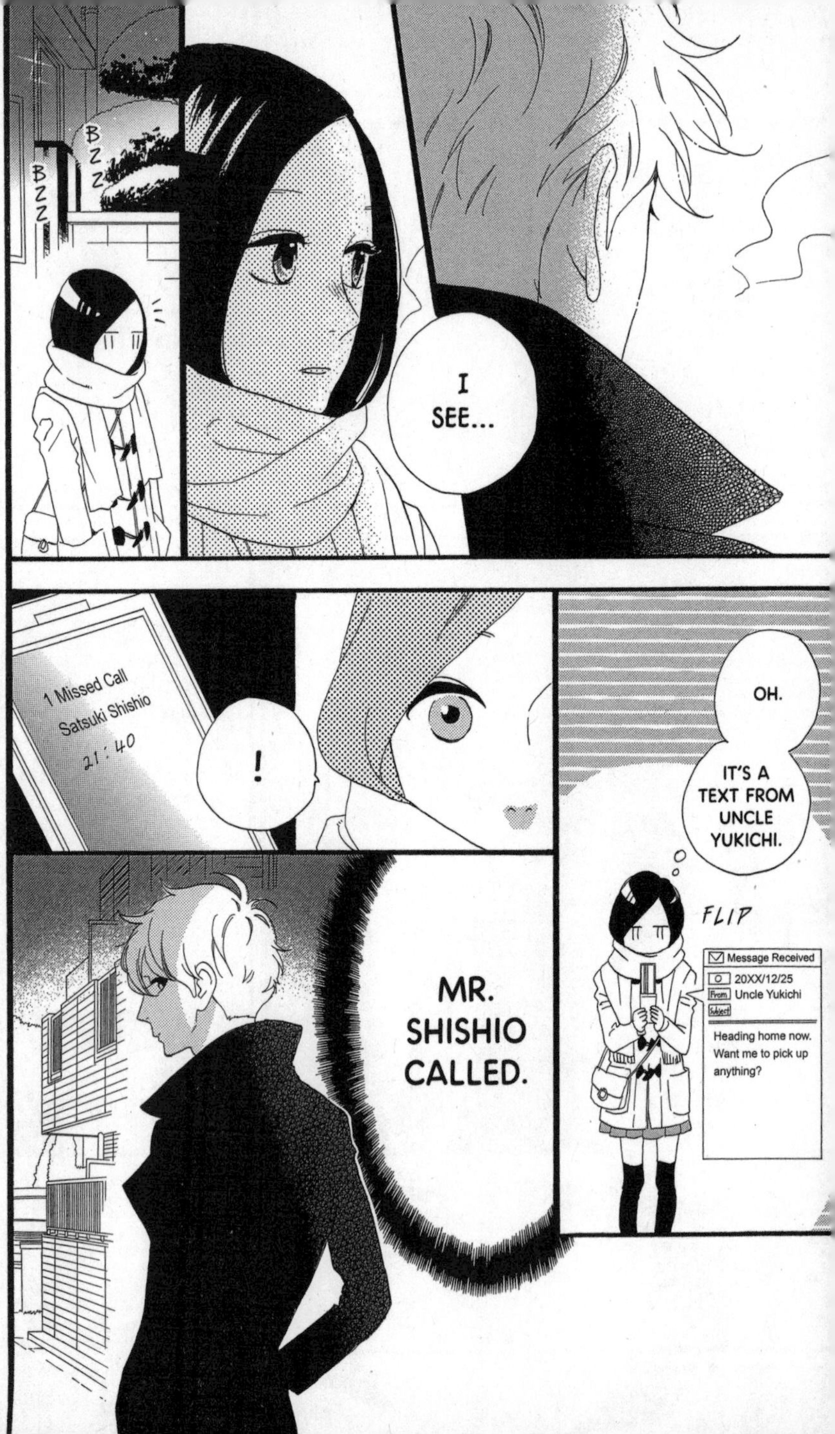

I SEE...
BZZ
BZZ
OH.
IT'S A TEXT FROM UNCLE YUKICHI.
FLIP
Message Received
20XX/12/25
From Uncle Yukichi
Subject
Heading home now. Want me to pick up anything?
!
1 Missed Call
Satsuki Shishio
21:40
MR. SHISHIO CALLED.

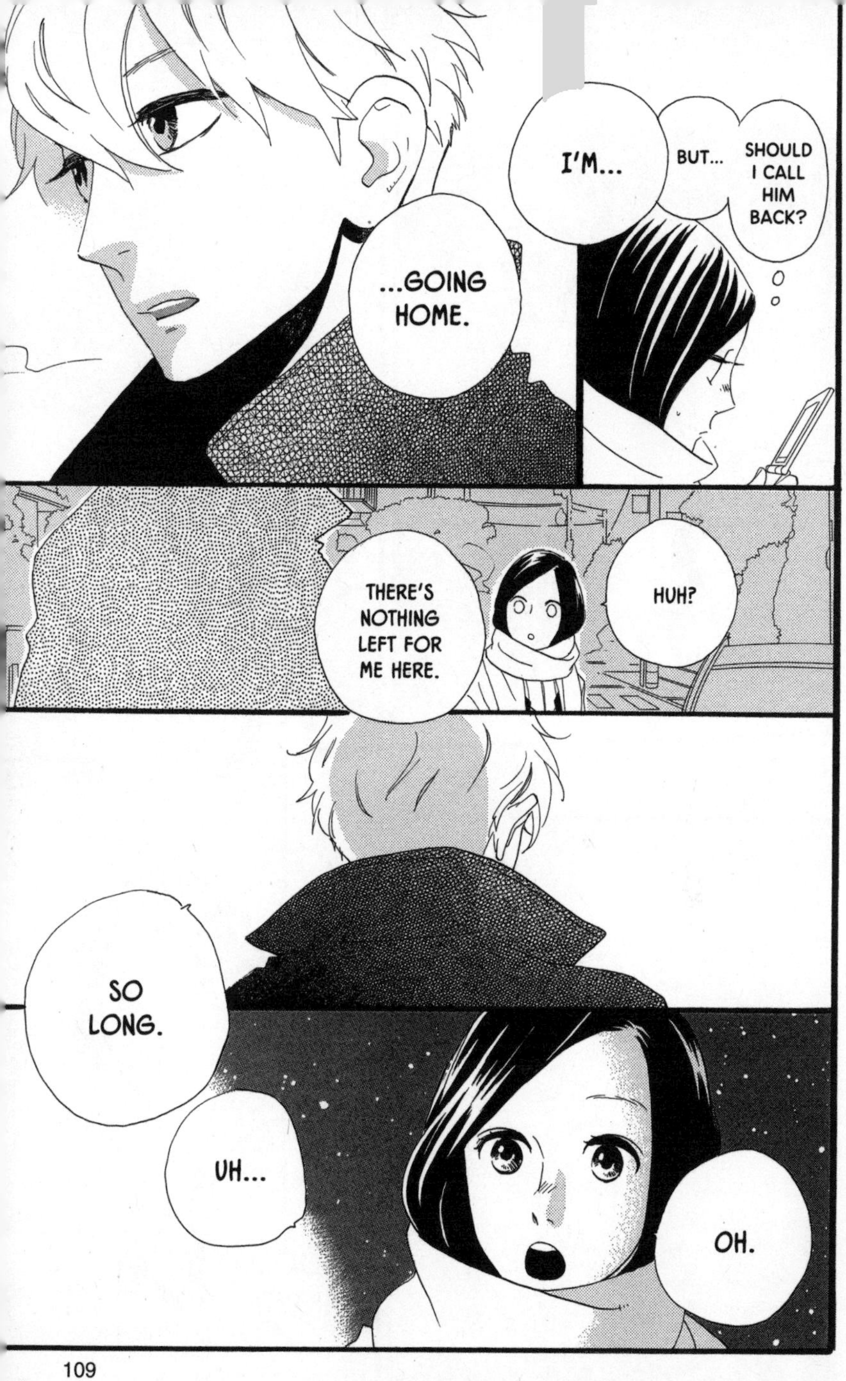
SHOULD I CALL HIM BACK?
BUT...
I'M...
...GOING HOME.
HUH?
THERE'S NOTHING LEFT FOR ME HERE.
SO LONG.
OH.
UH...

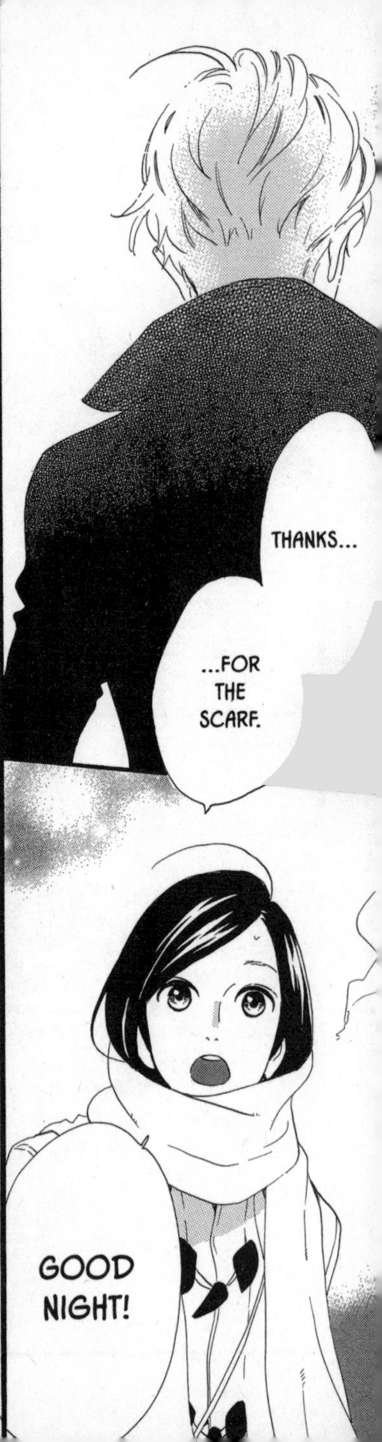
THANKS...
...FOR THE SCARF.
GOOD NIGHT!

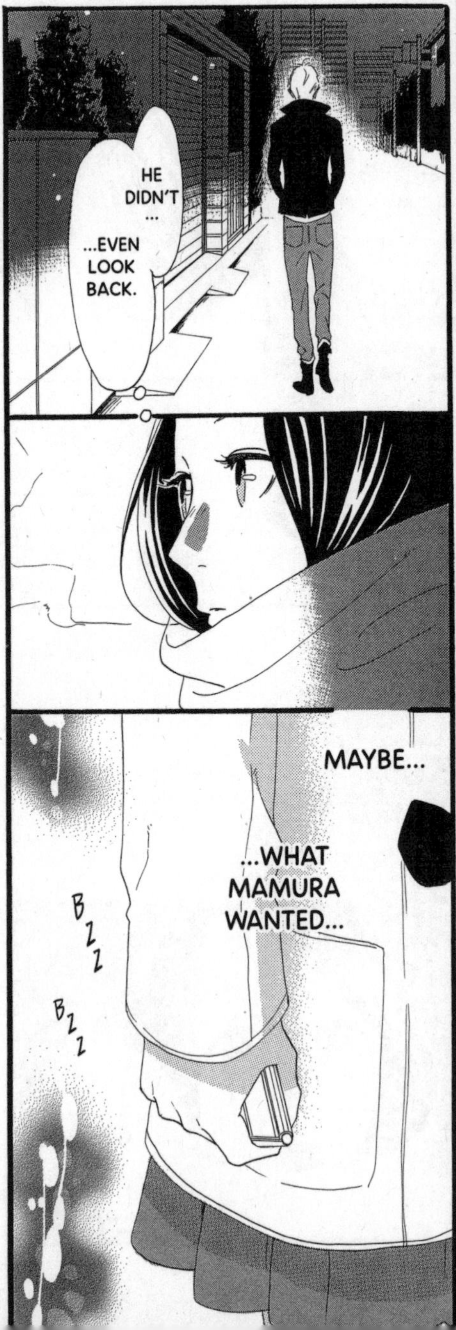
HE DIDN'T ...
...EVEN LOOK BACK.
MAYBE...
...WHAT MAMURA WANTED...
BZZ
BZZ

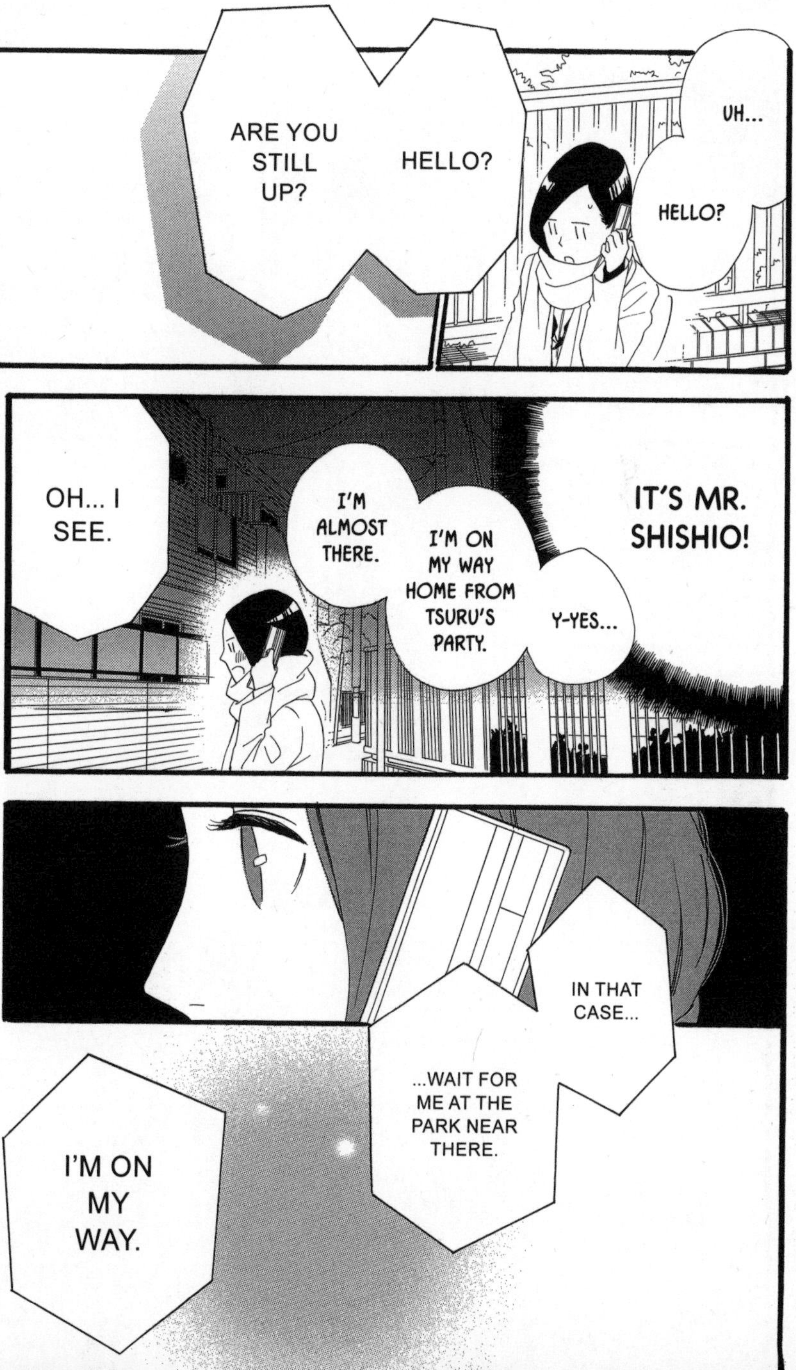
UH...
HELLO?
HELLO?
ARE YOU STILL UP?
IT'S MR. SHISHIO!
Y-YES...
I'M ON MY WAY HOME FROM TSURU'S PARTY.
I'M ALMOST THERE.
OH... I SEE.
IN THAT CASE...
...WAIT FOR ME AT THE PARK NEAR THERE.
I'M ON MY WAY.

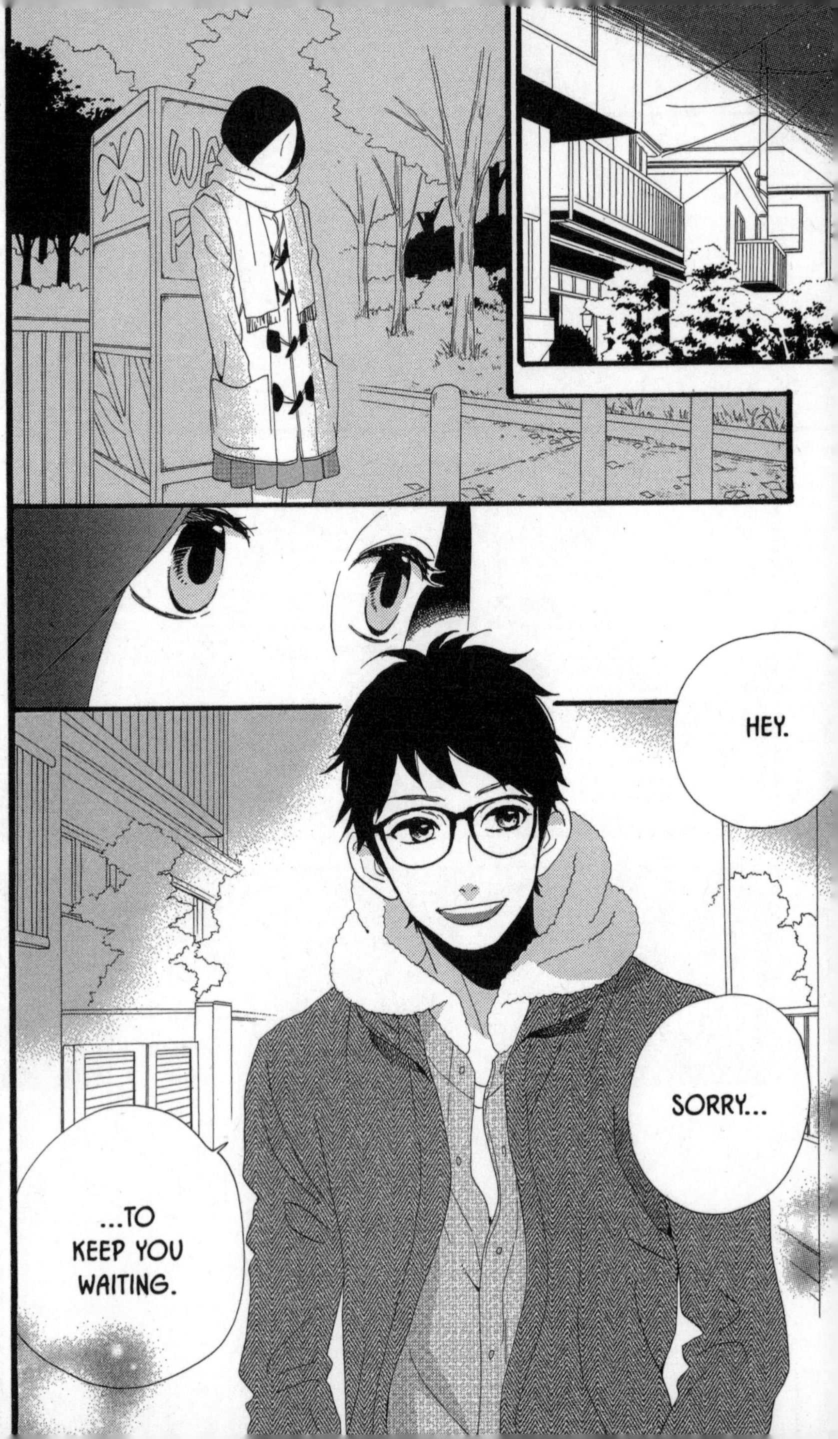
HEY.
SORRY...
...TO KEEP YOU WAITING.

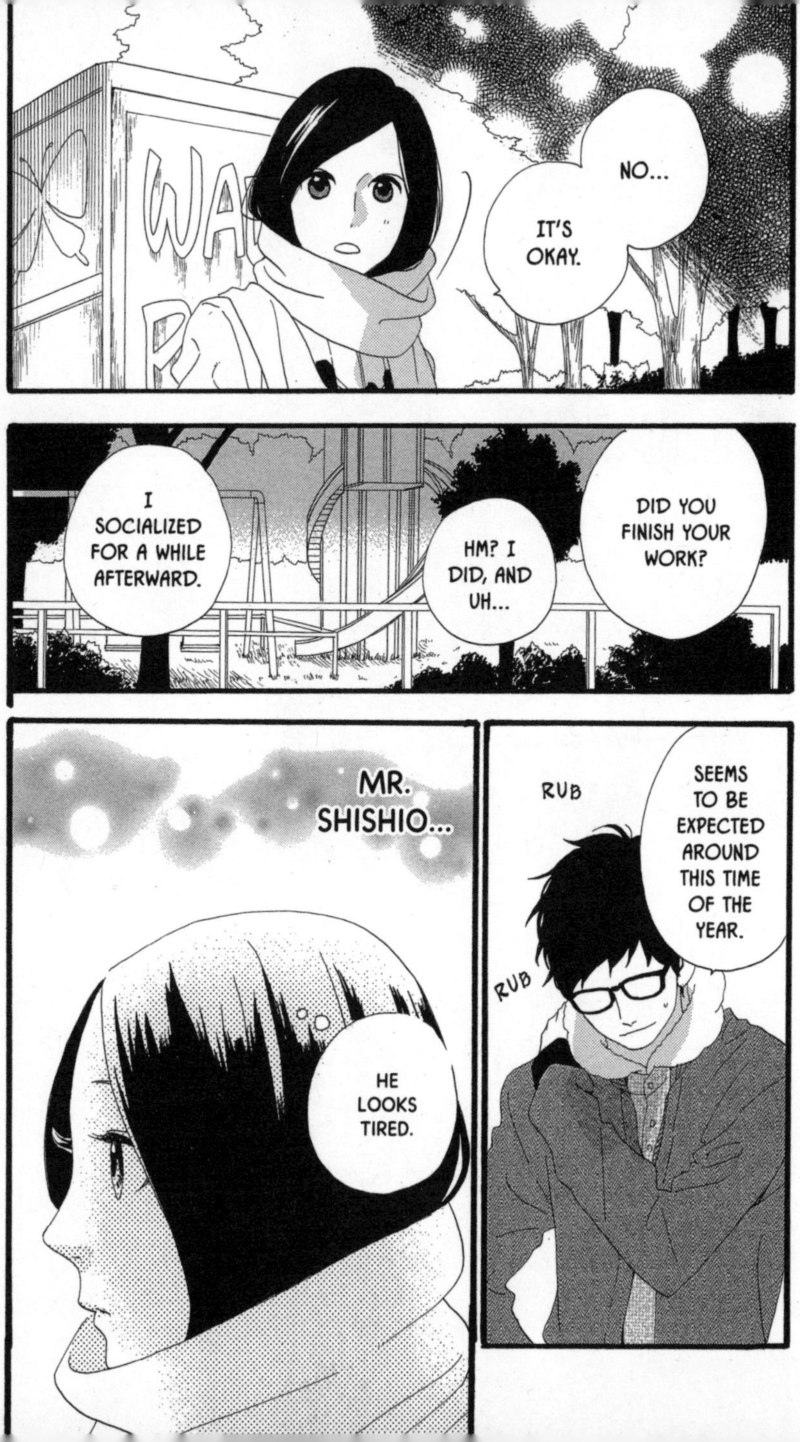
NO...
IT'S OKAY.
DID YOU FINISH YOUR WORK?
HM? I DID, AND UH...
I SOCIALIZED FOR A WHILE AFTERWARD.
SEEMS TO BE EXPECTED AROUND THIS TIME OF THE YEAR.
RUB
RUB
MR. SHISHIO...
HE LOOKS TIRED.

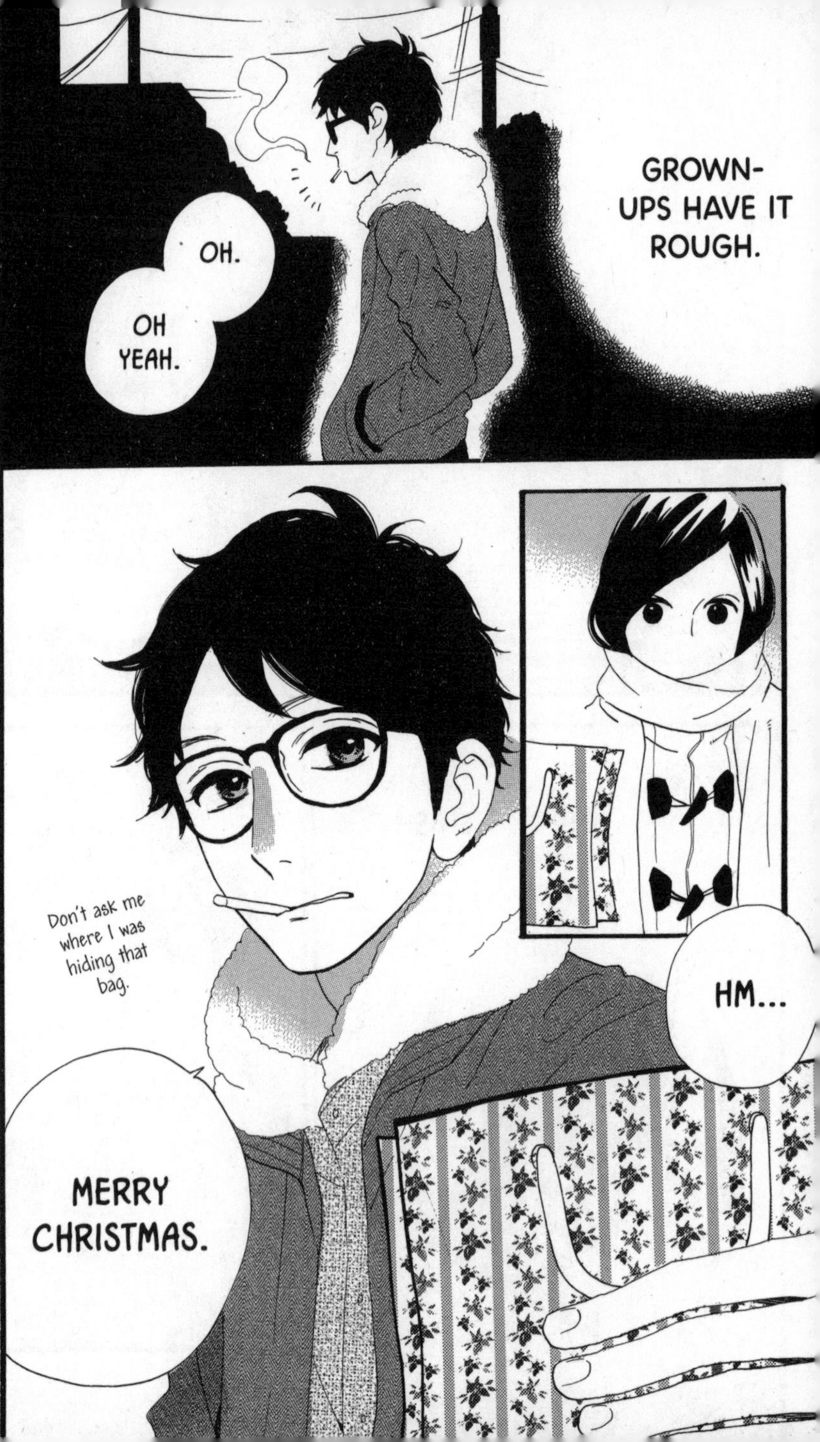
GROWN-UPS HAVE IT ROUGH.
OH.
OH YEAH.
HM...
Don't ask me where I was hiding that bag.
MERRY CHRISTMAS.

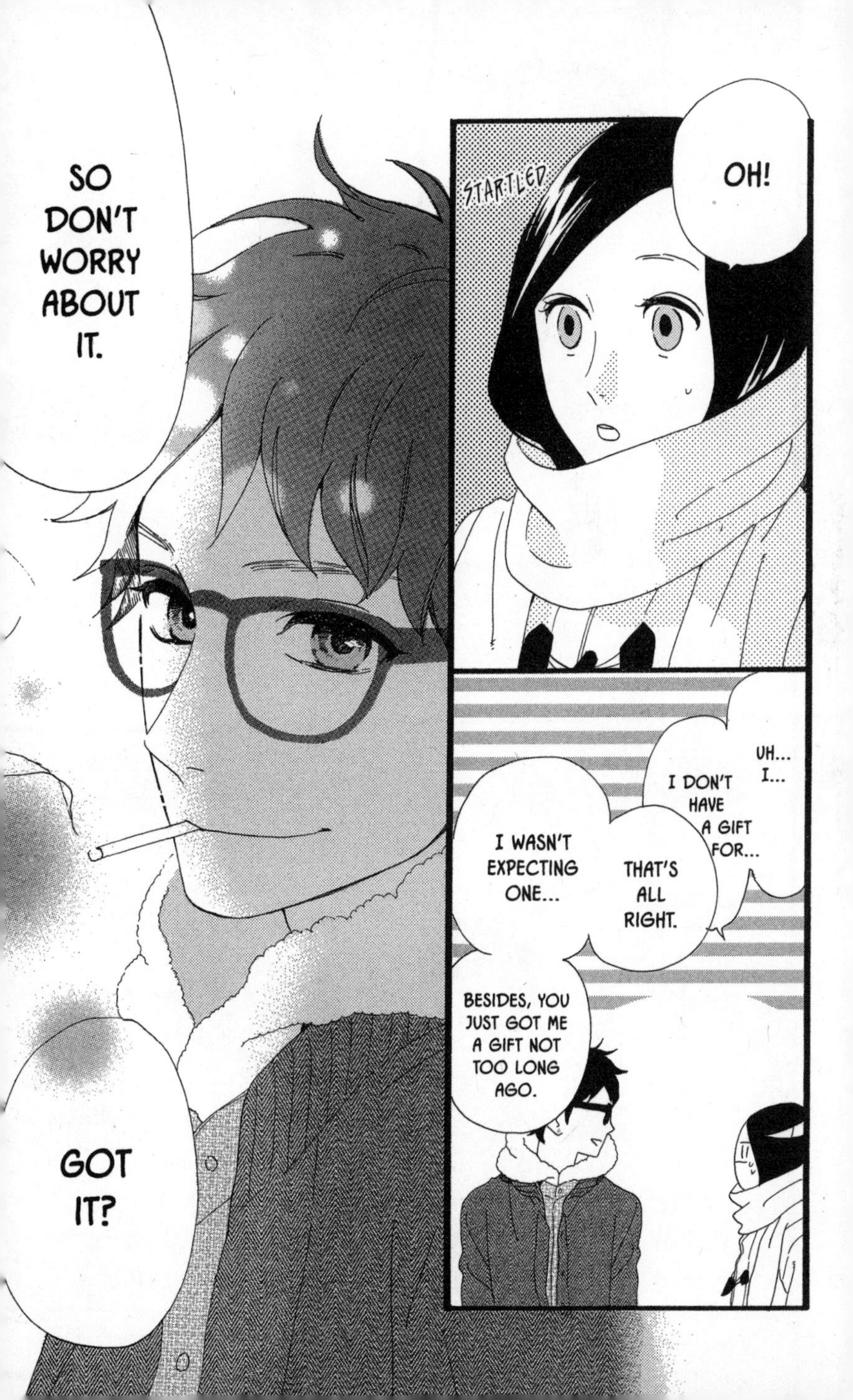
OH!
STARTLED
UH... I... I DON'T HAVE A GIFT FOR...
THAT'S ALL RIGHT.
I WASN'T EXPECTING ONE...
BESIDES, YOU JUST GOT ME A GIFT NOT TOO LONG AGO.
SO DON'T WORRY ABOUT IT.
GOT IT?

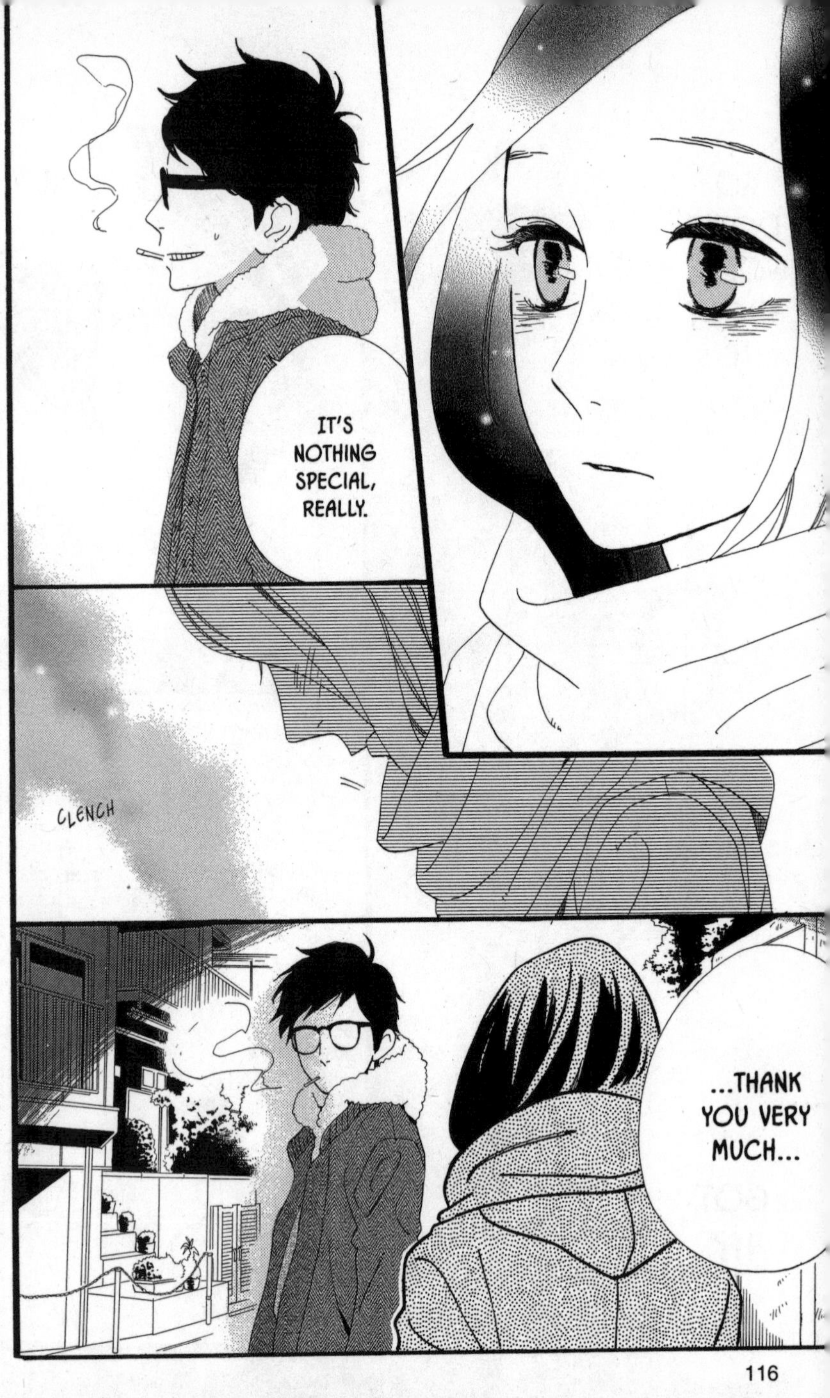
IT'S NOTHING SPECIAL, REALLY.
CLENCH
...THANK YOU VERY MUCH...

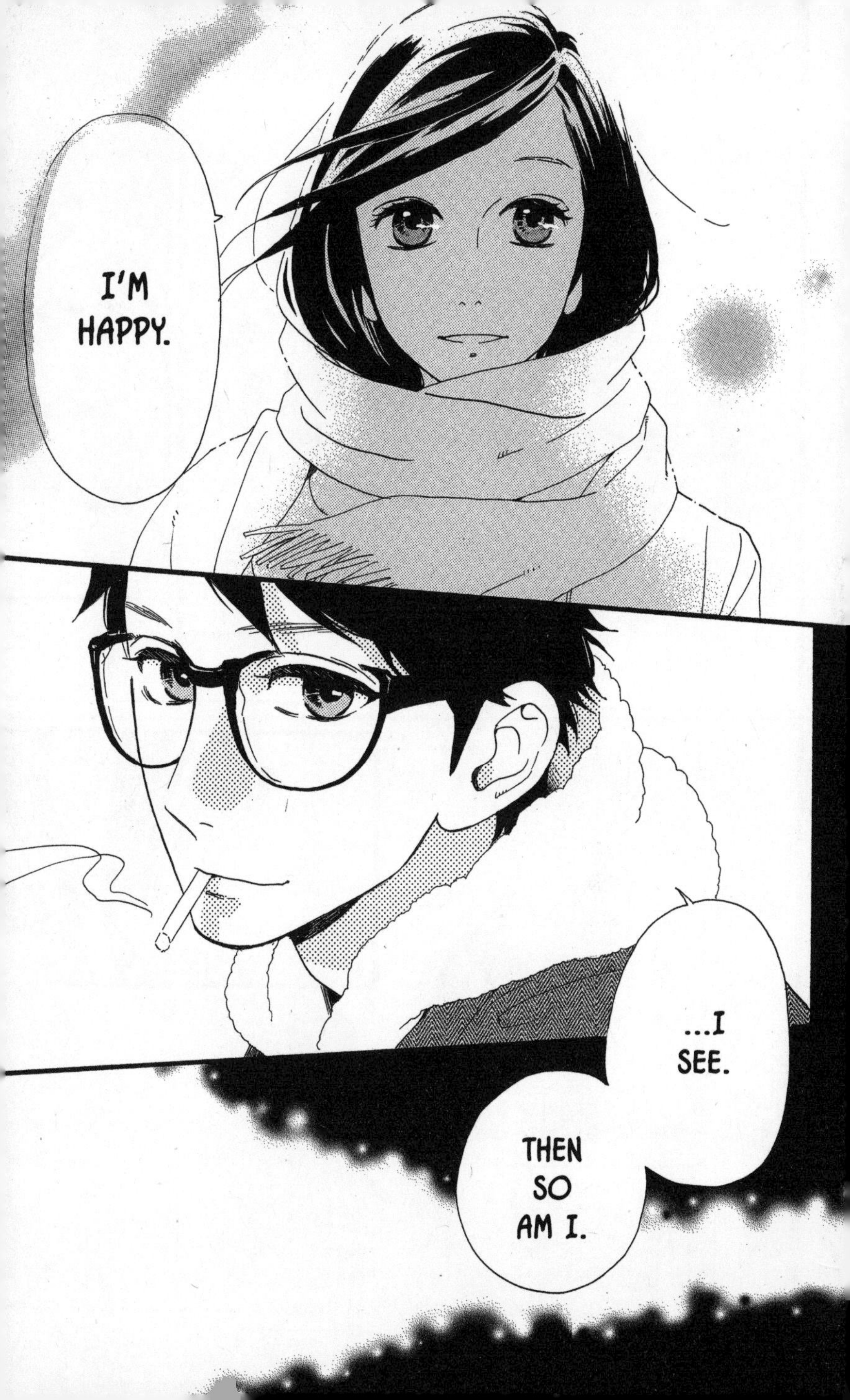
I'M HAPPY.
...I SEE.
THEN SO AM I.

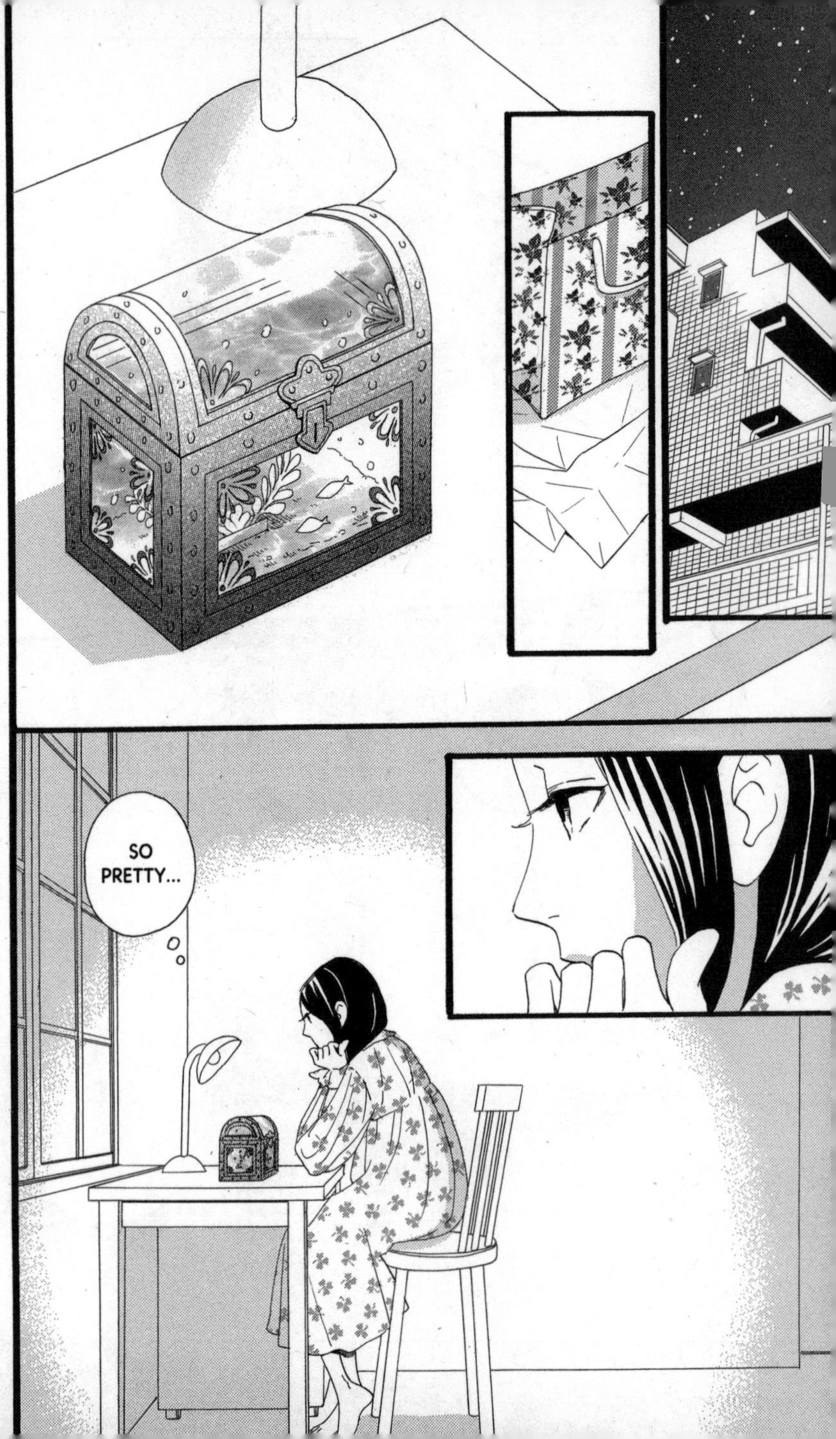
SO PRETTY...

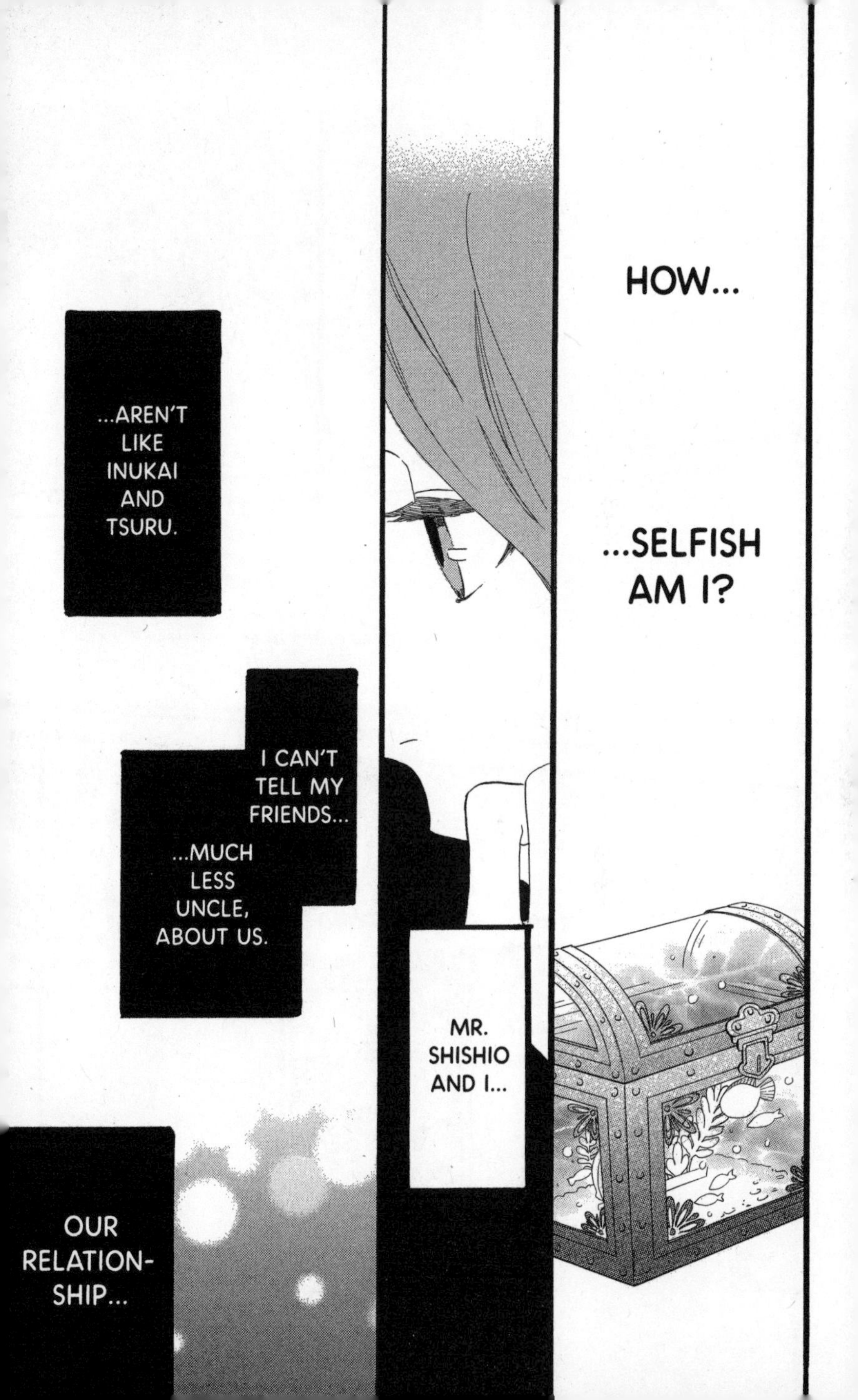
HOW...
...SELFISH AM I?
MR. SHISHIO AND I...
...AREN'T LIKE INUKAI AND TSURU.
I CAN'T TELL MY FRIENDS...
...MUCH LESS UNCLE, ABOUT US.
OUR RELATION-SHIP...

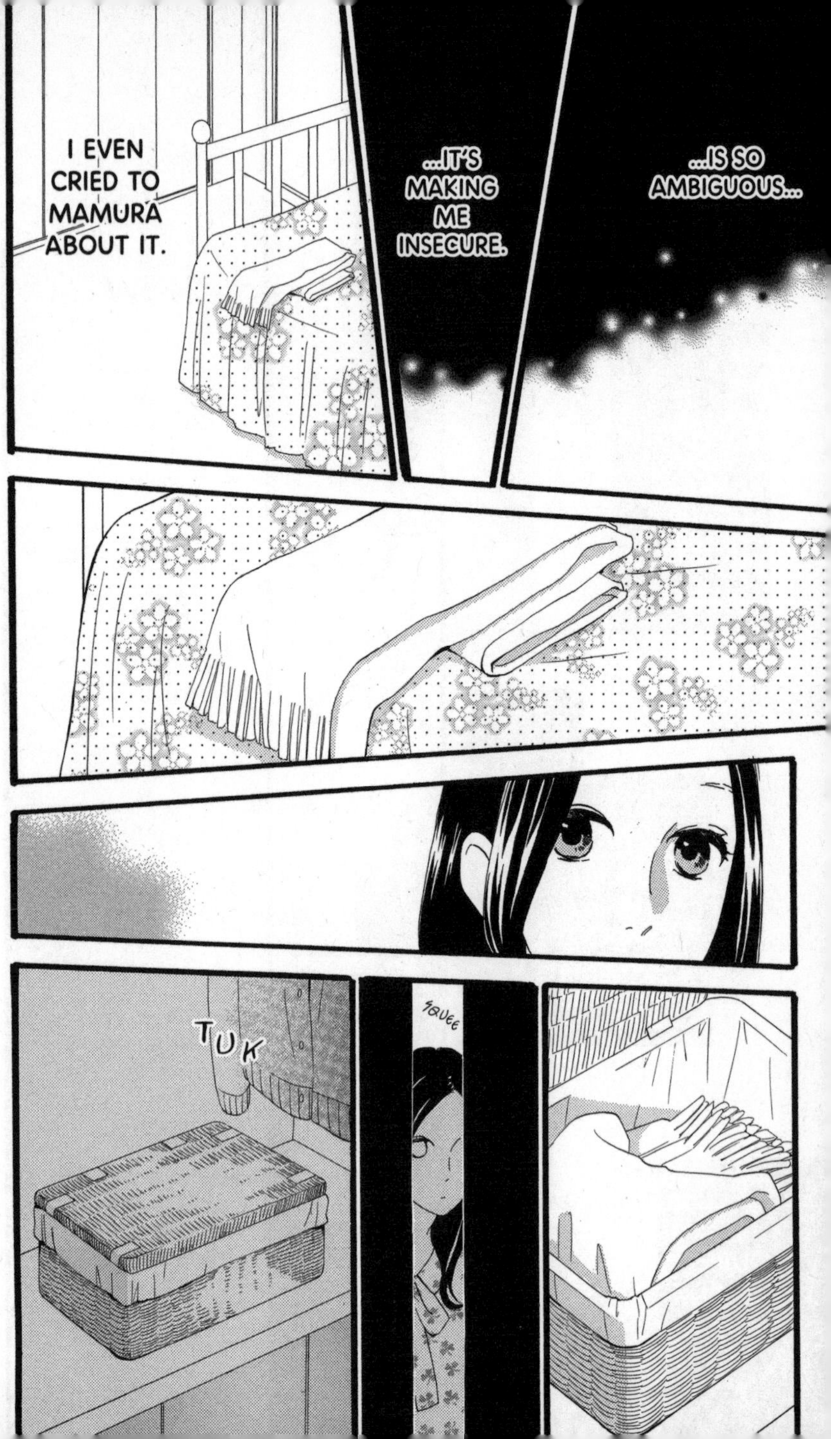
...IS SO AMBIGUOUS...
...IT'S MAKING ME INSECURE.
I EVEN CRIED TO MAMURA ABOUT IT.
SQUEE
TUK

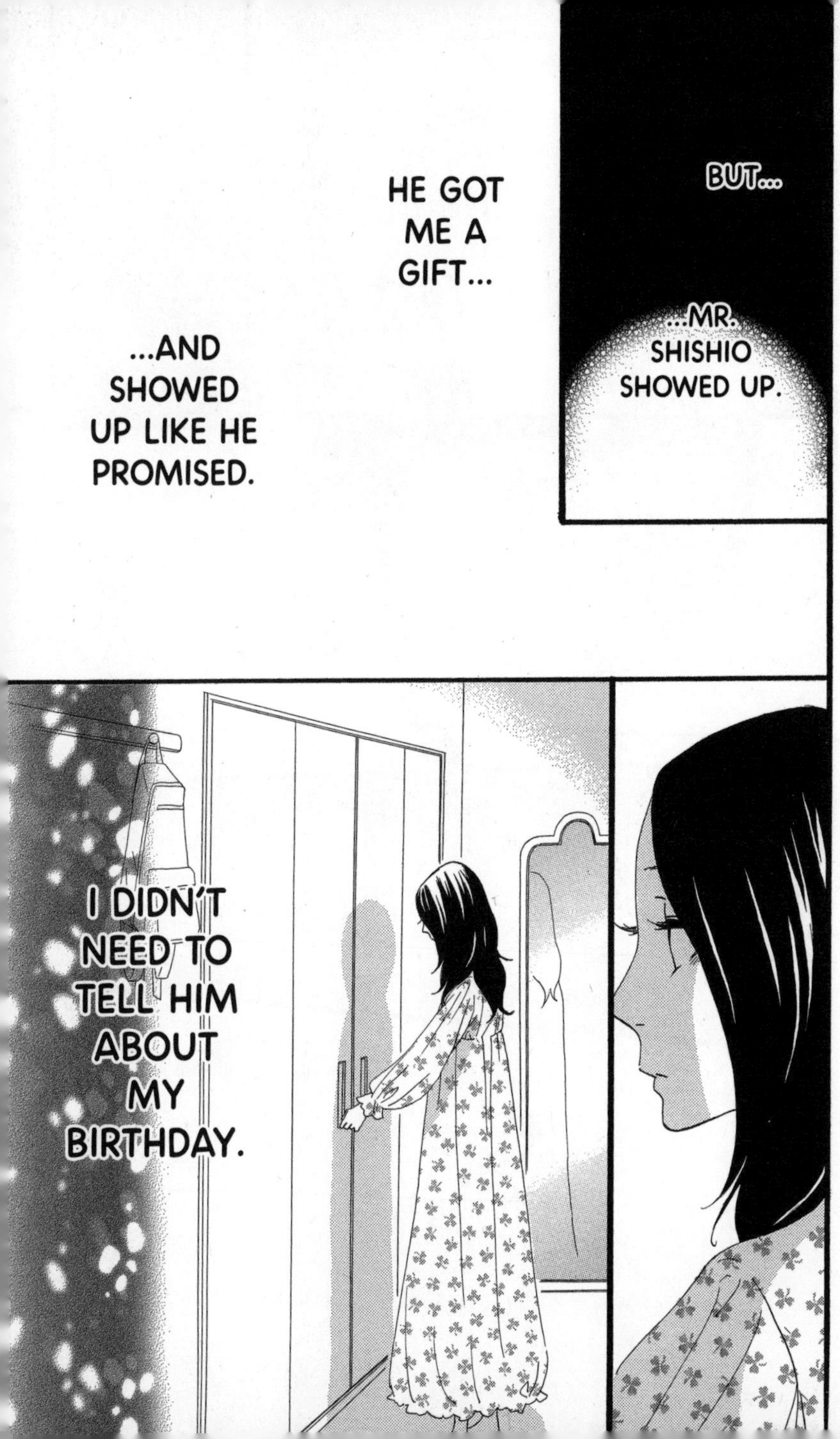
BUT...
...MR. SHISHIO SHOWED UP.
HE GOT ME A GIFT...
...AND SHOWED UP LIKE HE PROMISED.
I DIDN'T NEED TO TELL HIM ABOUT MY BIRTHDAY.

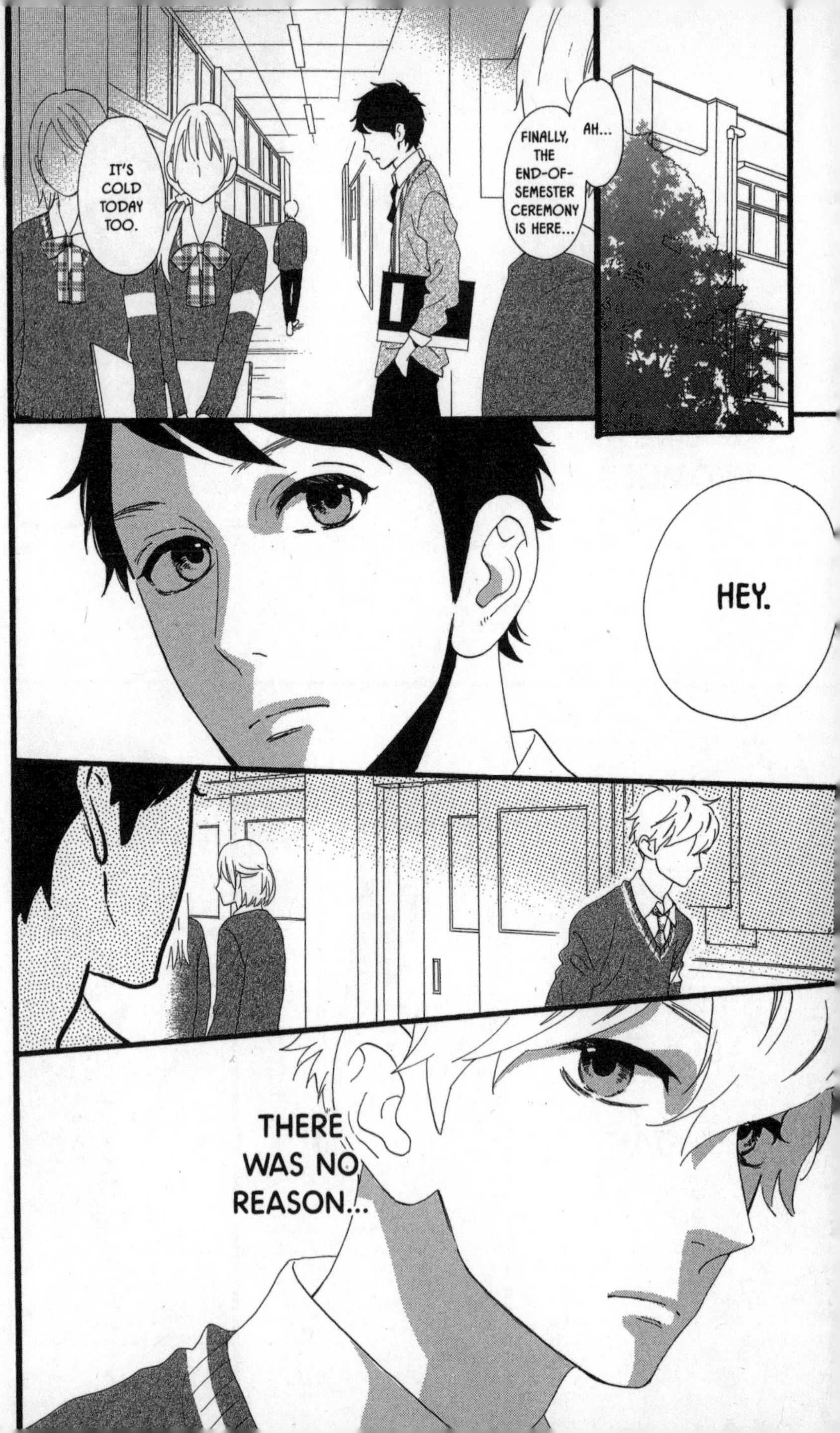
AH...
FINALLY, THE END-OF-SEMESTER CEREMONY IS HERE...
IT'S COLD TODAY TOO.
HEY.
THERE WAS NO REASON...

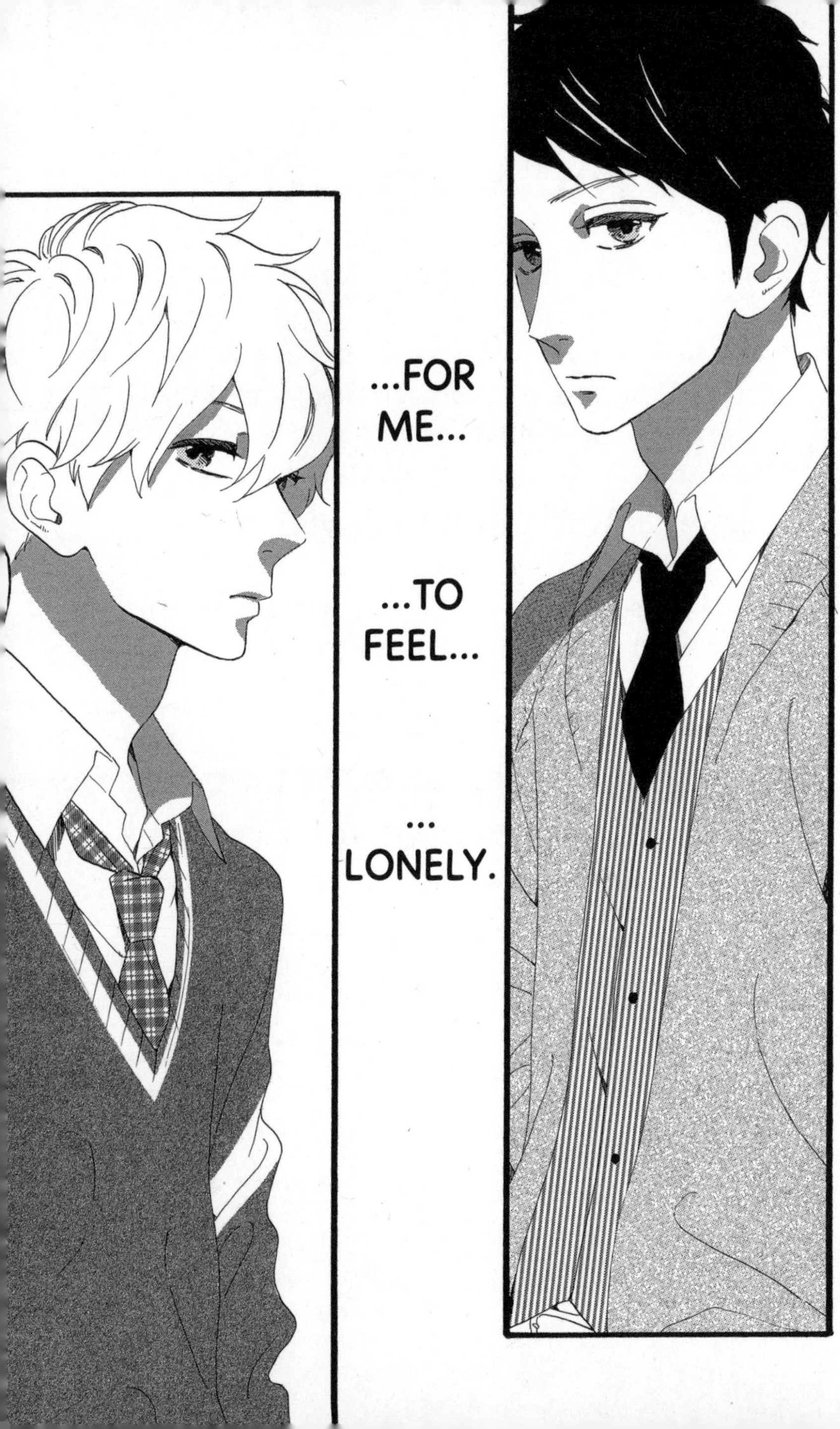
...FOR ME...
...TO FEEL...
...LONELY.

By the way... ③

A miracle happened just before McAvoy's play...

Our excitement grew as the start of the play drew near. Suddenly, my eye caught sight of someone who sat down a little to our right in the row in front of us. He looked very familiar, so I took a good look and realized,

why... that's Jude Law!!!

For a second, I thought my eyes were playing tricks on me after seeing so many beautiful people there, but I swear it was Jude Law. (It seems he had come to see the play with his friends.) He was so handsome that we couldn't stop giggling. And we were all certain **our plane would crash on our return flight** since we'd used up all our luck for the year in England.

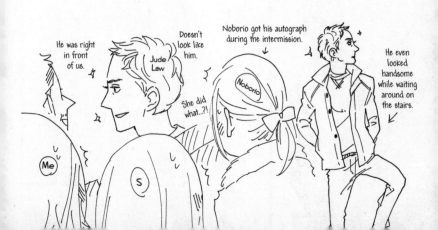

He even looked handsome while waiting around on the stairs.
Noborio got his autograph during the intermission.
Noborio
She did what...?!
Doesn't look like him.
Jude Law
S
He was right in front of us.
Me

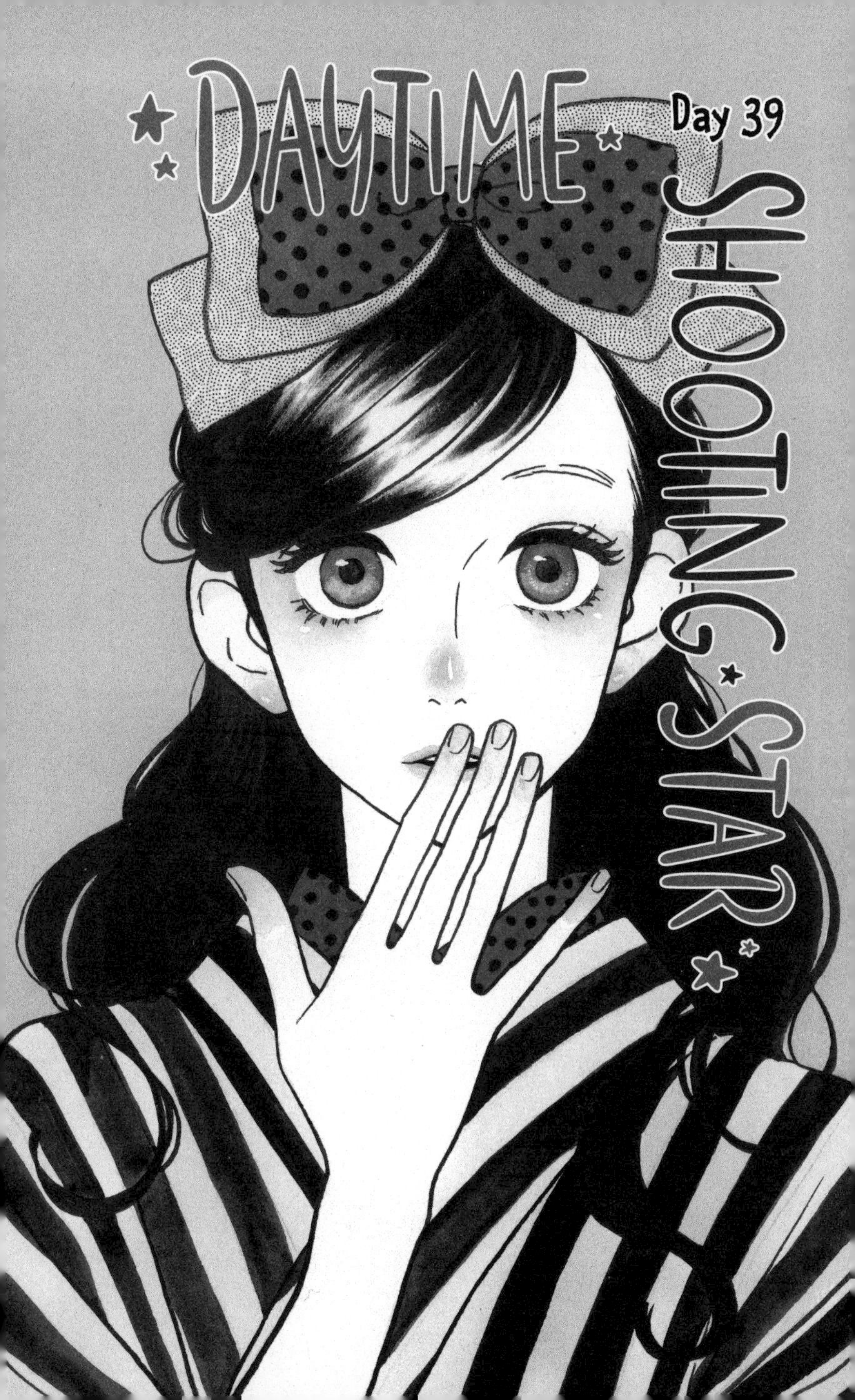
DAYTIME
SHOOTING STAR
Day 39

DAYTIME SHOOTING STAR

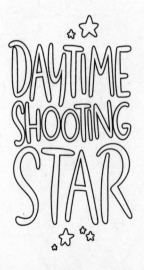

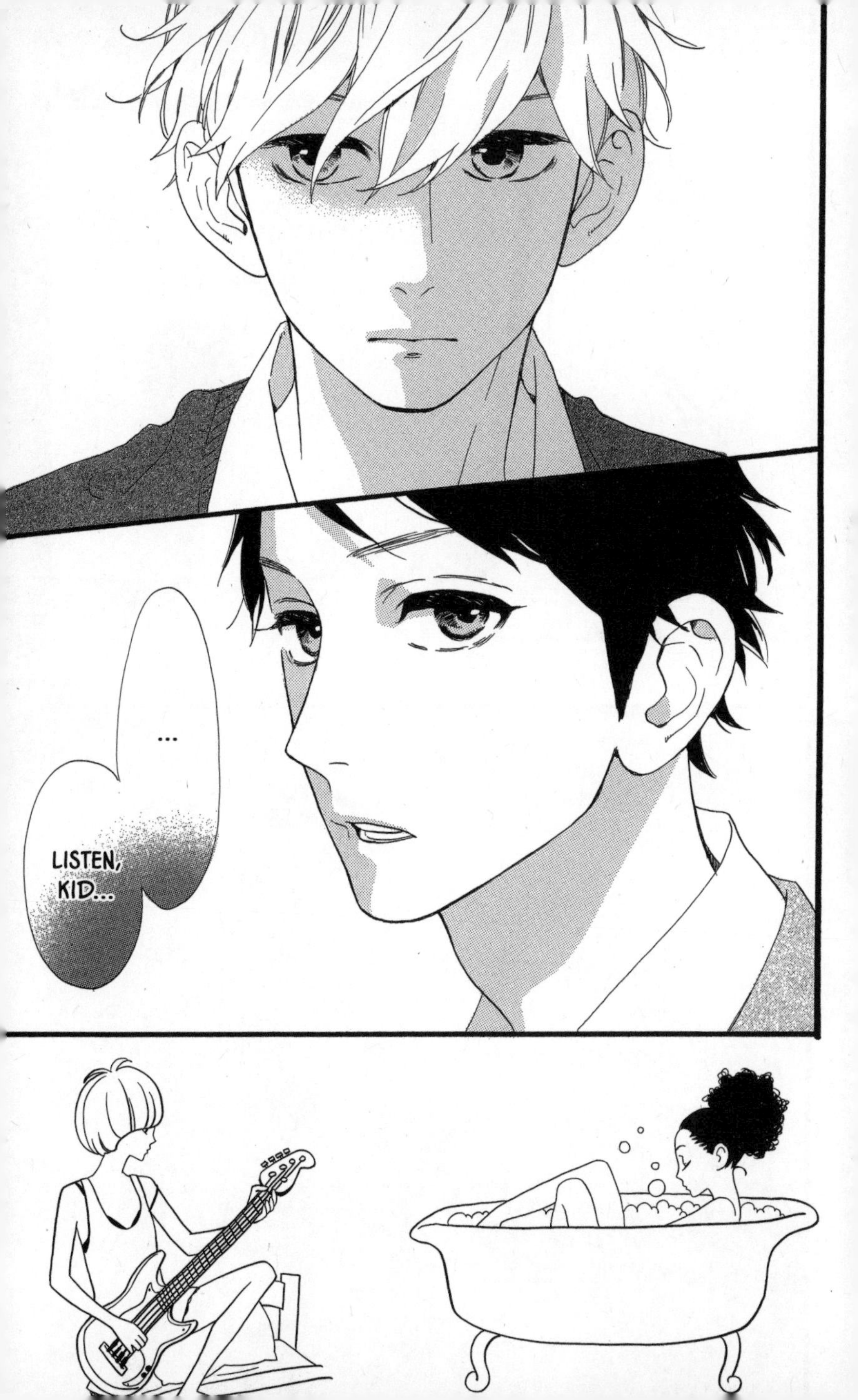
...
LISTEN, KID...

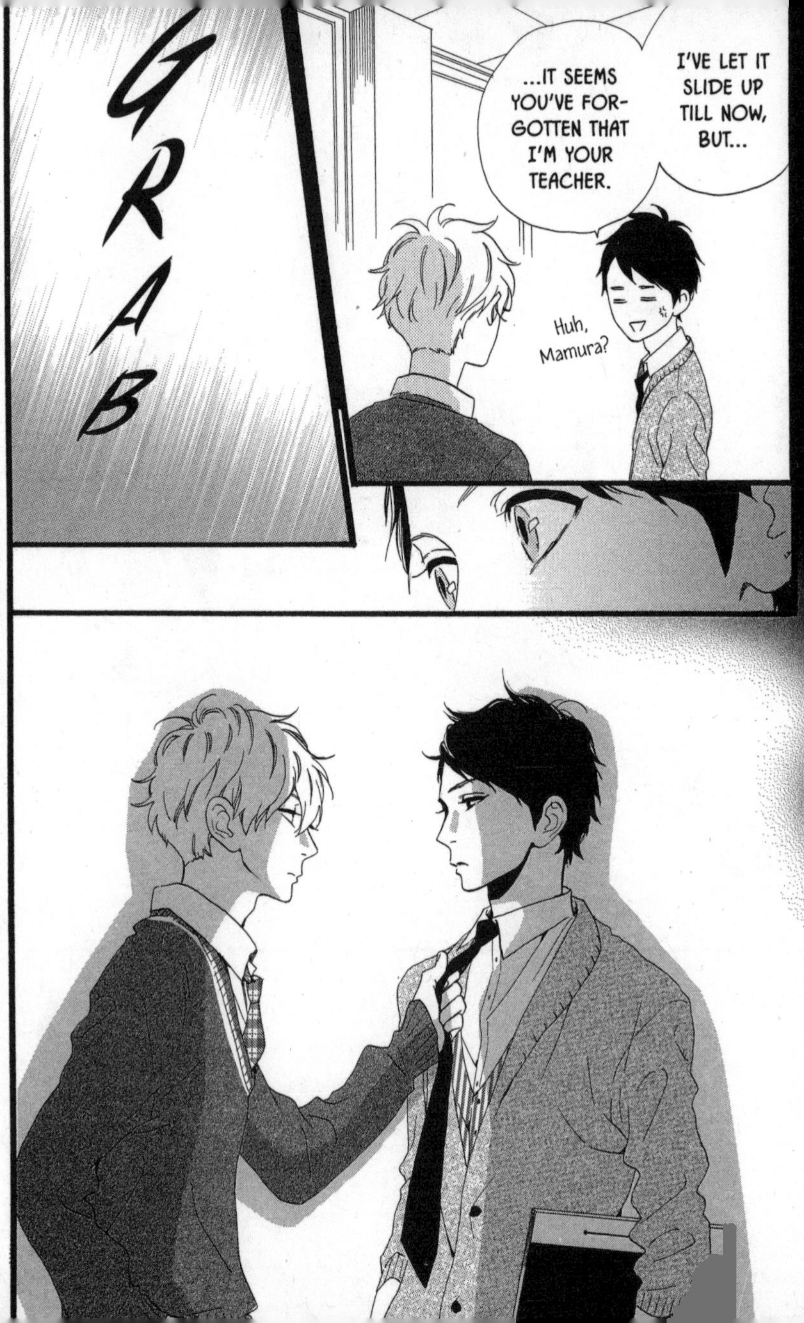
I'VE LET IT SLIDE UP TILL NOW, BUT...
...IT SEEMS YOU'VE FOR-GOTTEN THAT I'M YOUR TEACHER.
Huh, Mamura?
GRAB

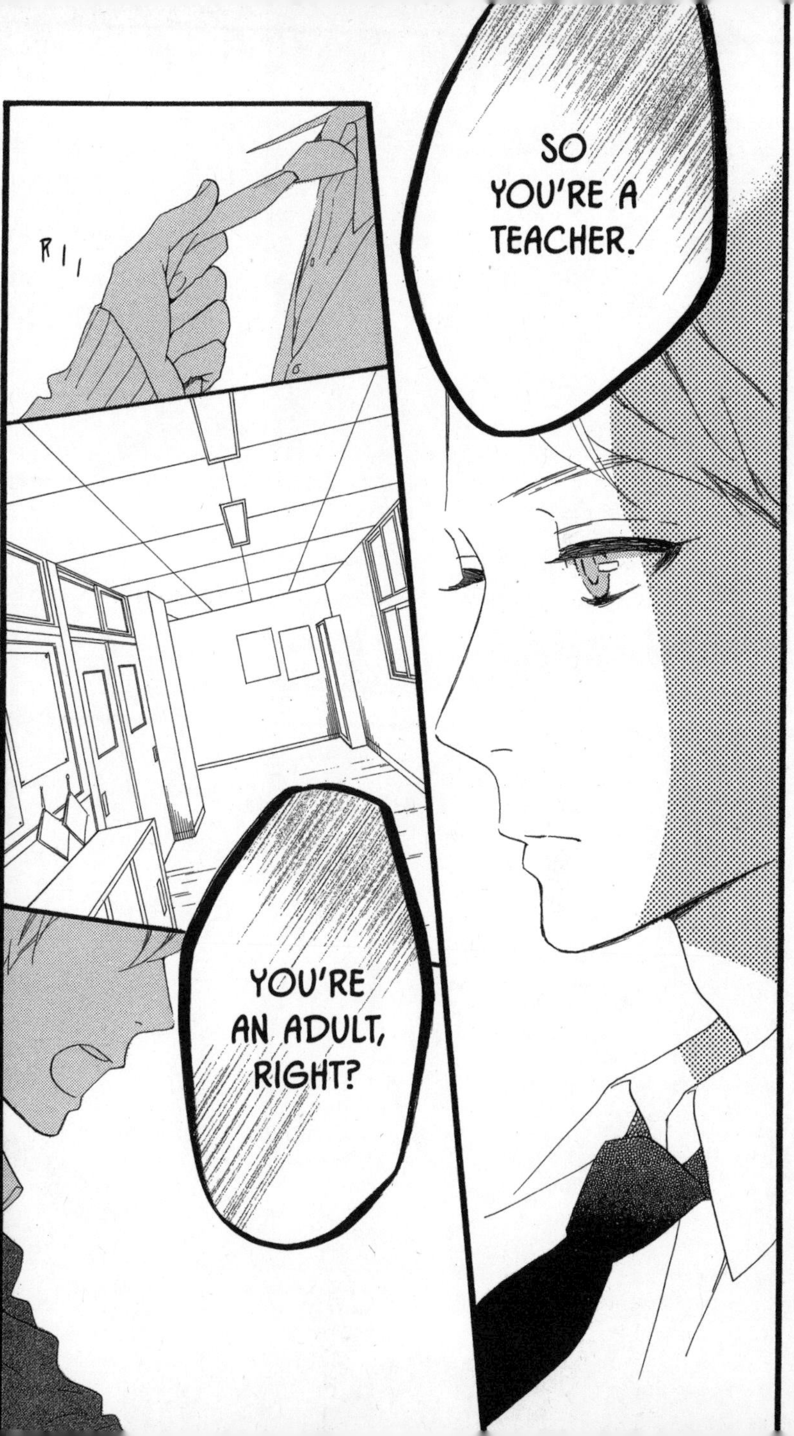
SO YOU'RE A TEACHER.
RII
YOU'RE AN ADULT, RIGHT?

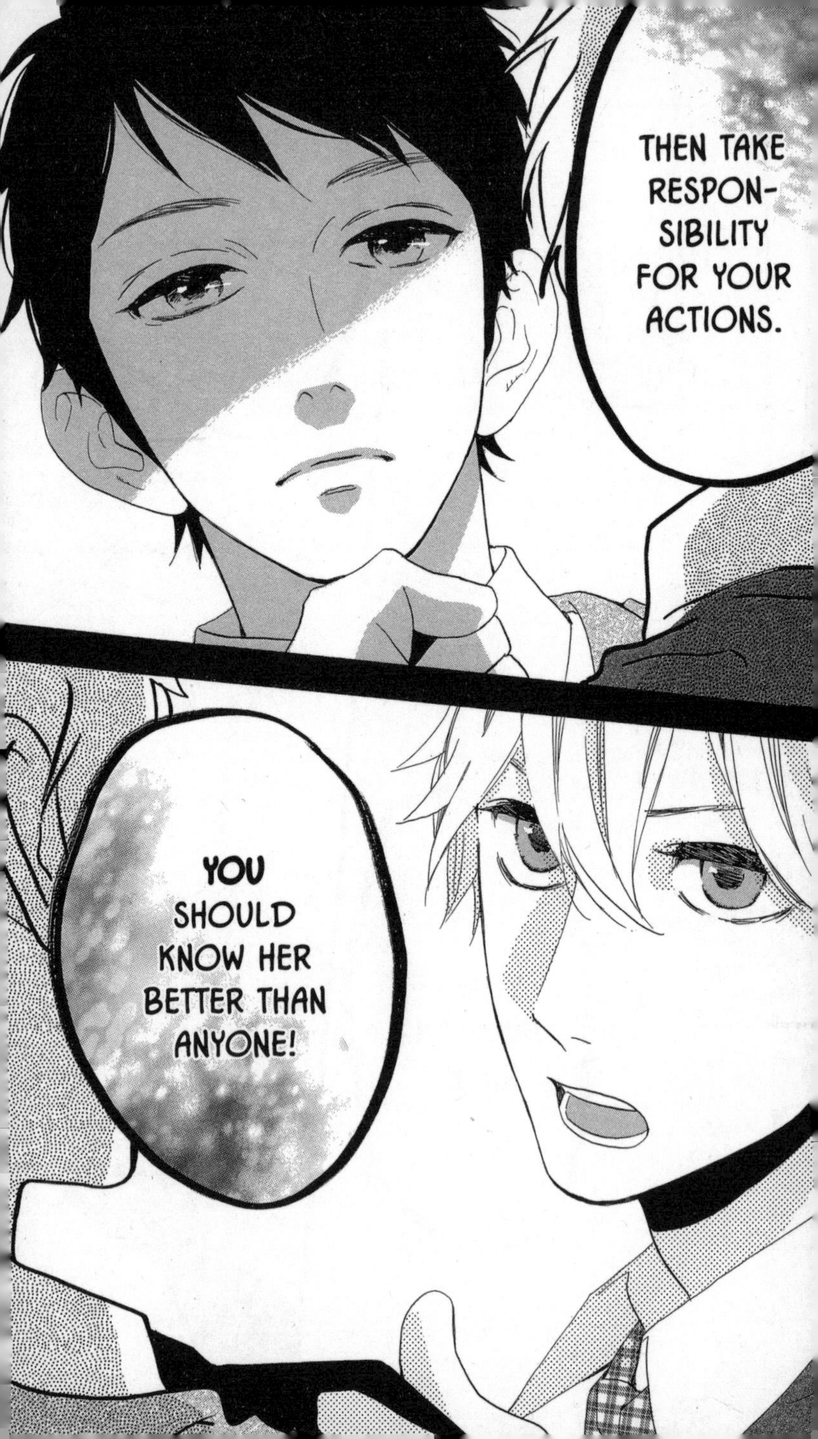
THEN TAKE RESPON-SIBILITY FOR YOUR ACTIONS.
YOU SHOULD KNOW HER BETTER THAN ANYONE!

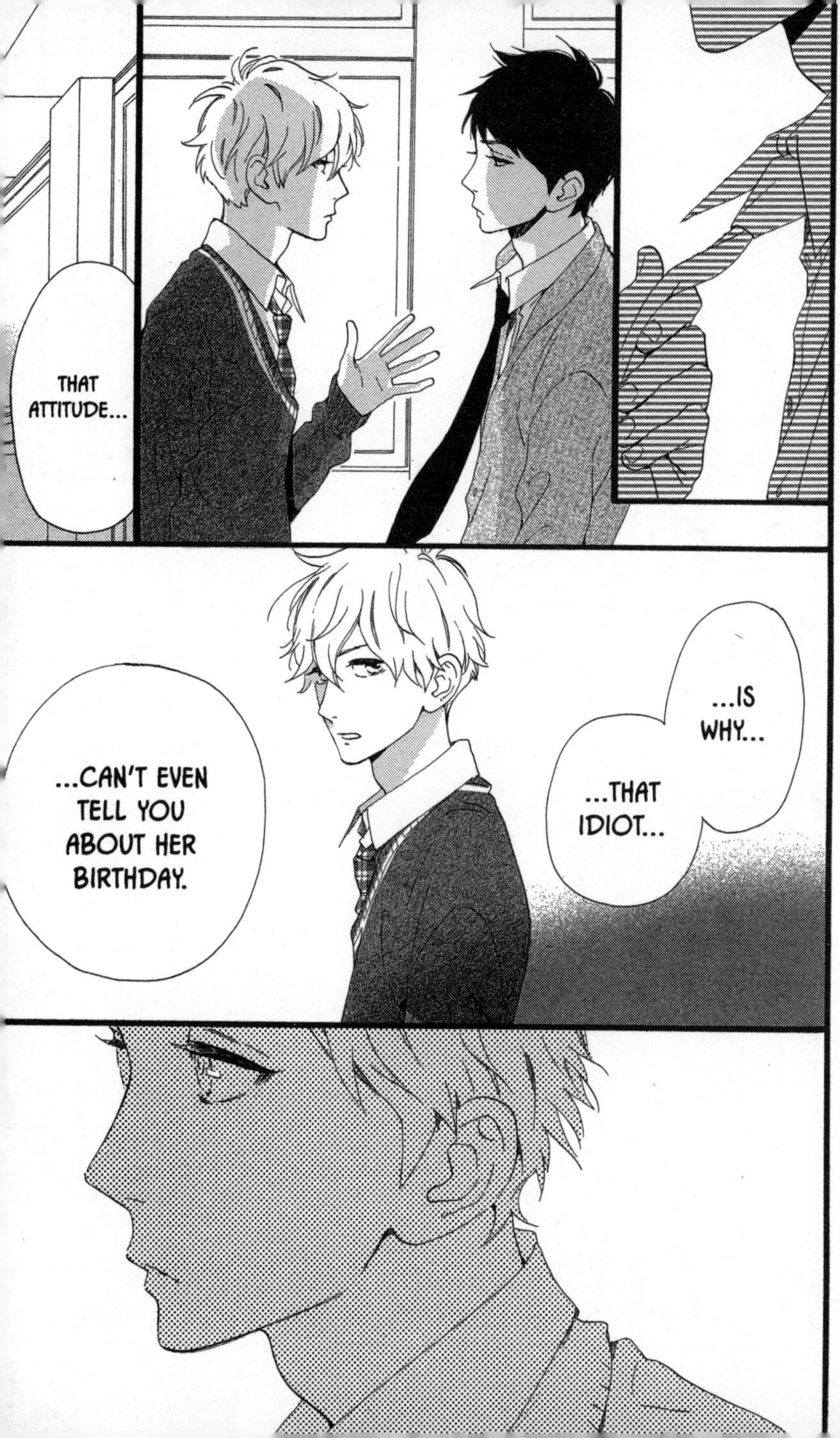
THAT ATTITUDE...
...IS WHY...
...THAT IDIOT...
...CAN'T EVEN TELL YOU ABOUT HER BIRTHDAY.

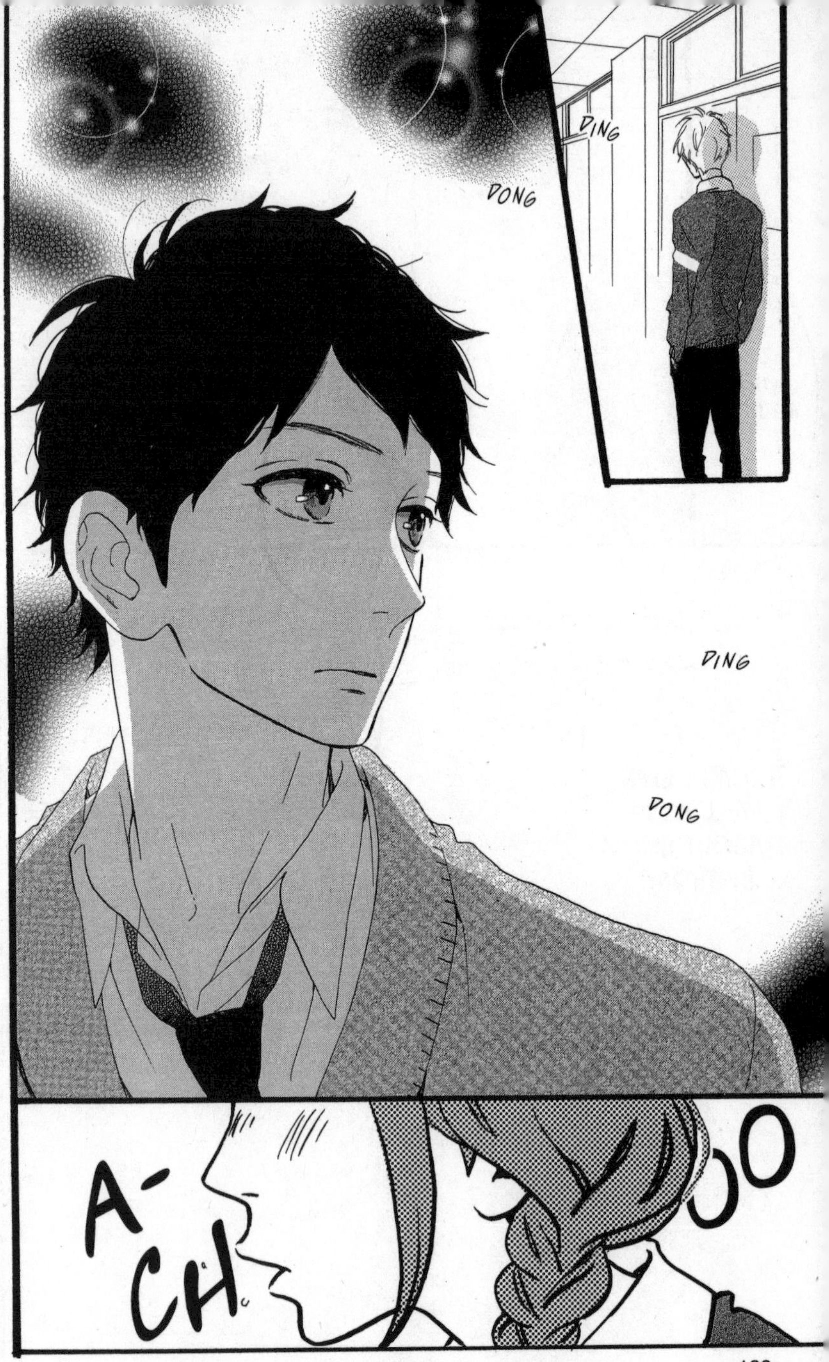
DING
DONG
DING
DONG
A-CHOO

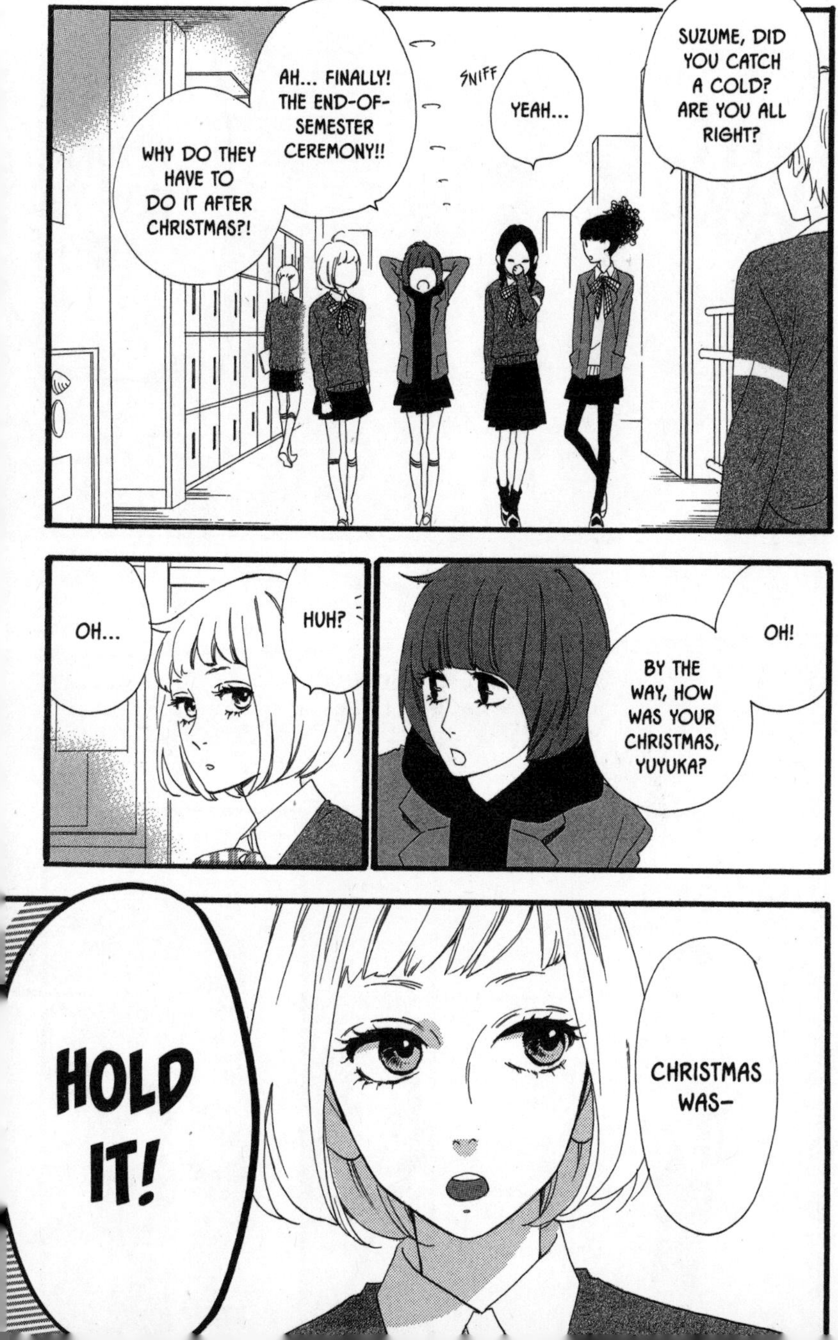
SUZUME, DID YOU CATCH A COLD? ARE YOU ALL RIGHT?
SNIFF
YEAH...
AH... FINALLY! THE END-OF-SEMESTER CEREMONY!!
WHY DO THEY HAVE TO DO IT AFTER CHRISTMAS?!
OH!
BY THE WAY, HOW WAS YOUR CHRISTMAS, YUYUKA?
HUH?
OH...
CHRISTMAS WAS–
HOLD IT!

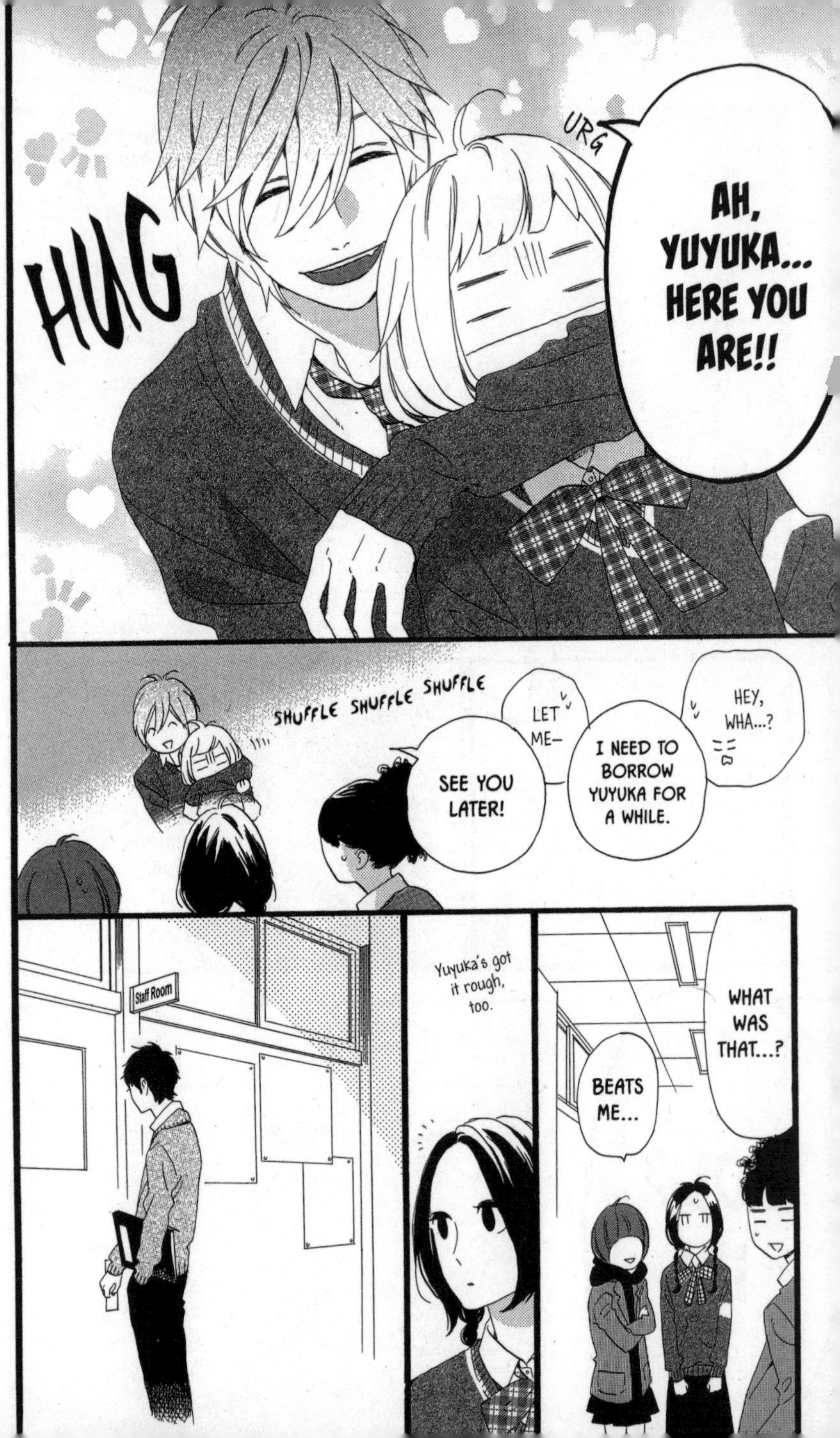
URG
AH, YUYUKA... HERE YOU ARE!!
HUG
HEY, WHA...?
I NEED TO BORROW YUYUKA FOR A WHILE.
LET ME—
SEE YOU LATER!
SHUFFLE SHUFFLE SHUFFLE
WHAT WAS THAT...?
BEATS ME...
Yuyuka's got it rough, too.
Staff Room

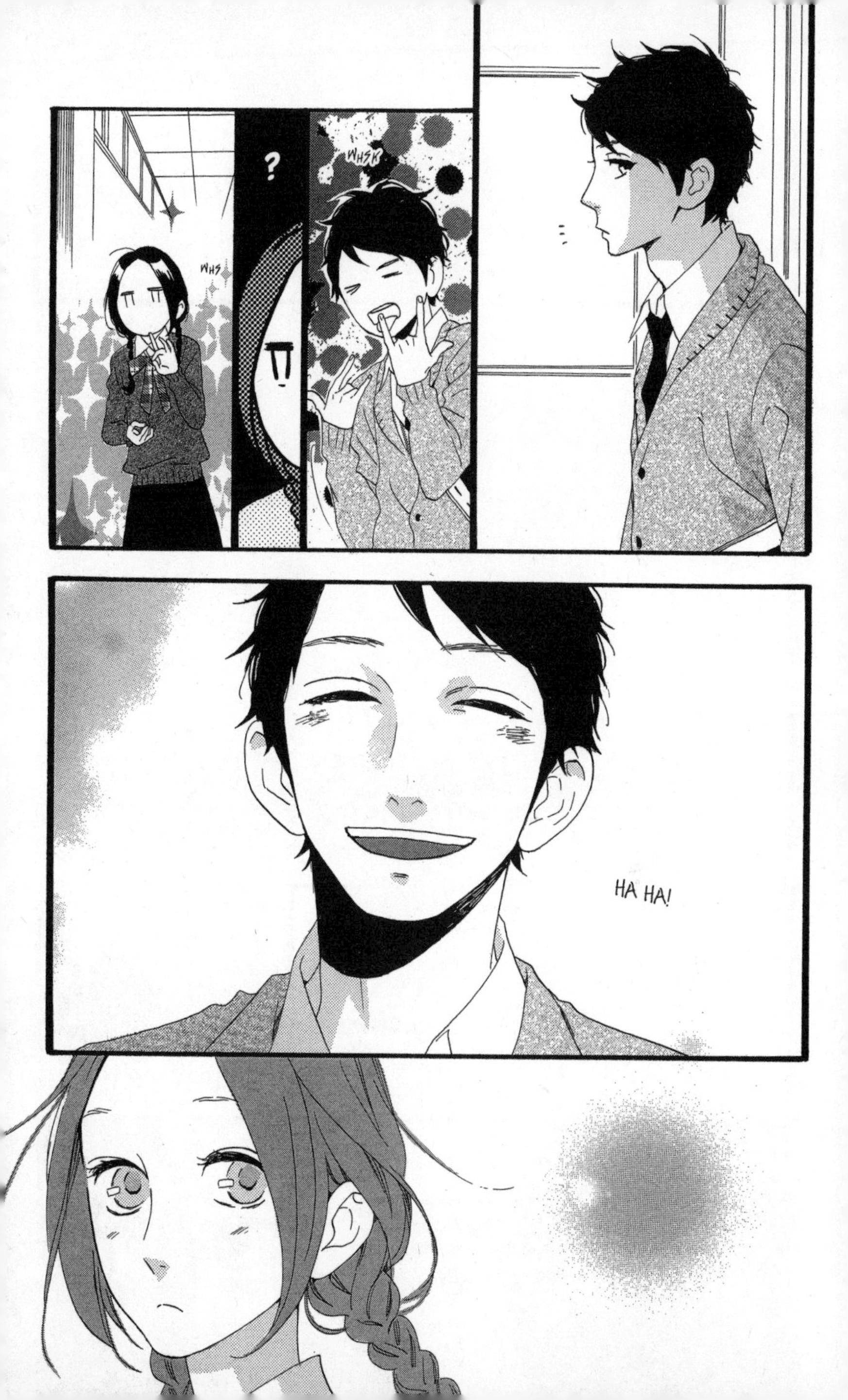

WHSK
?
WHS
HA HA!

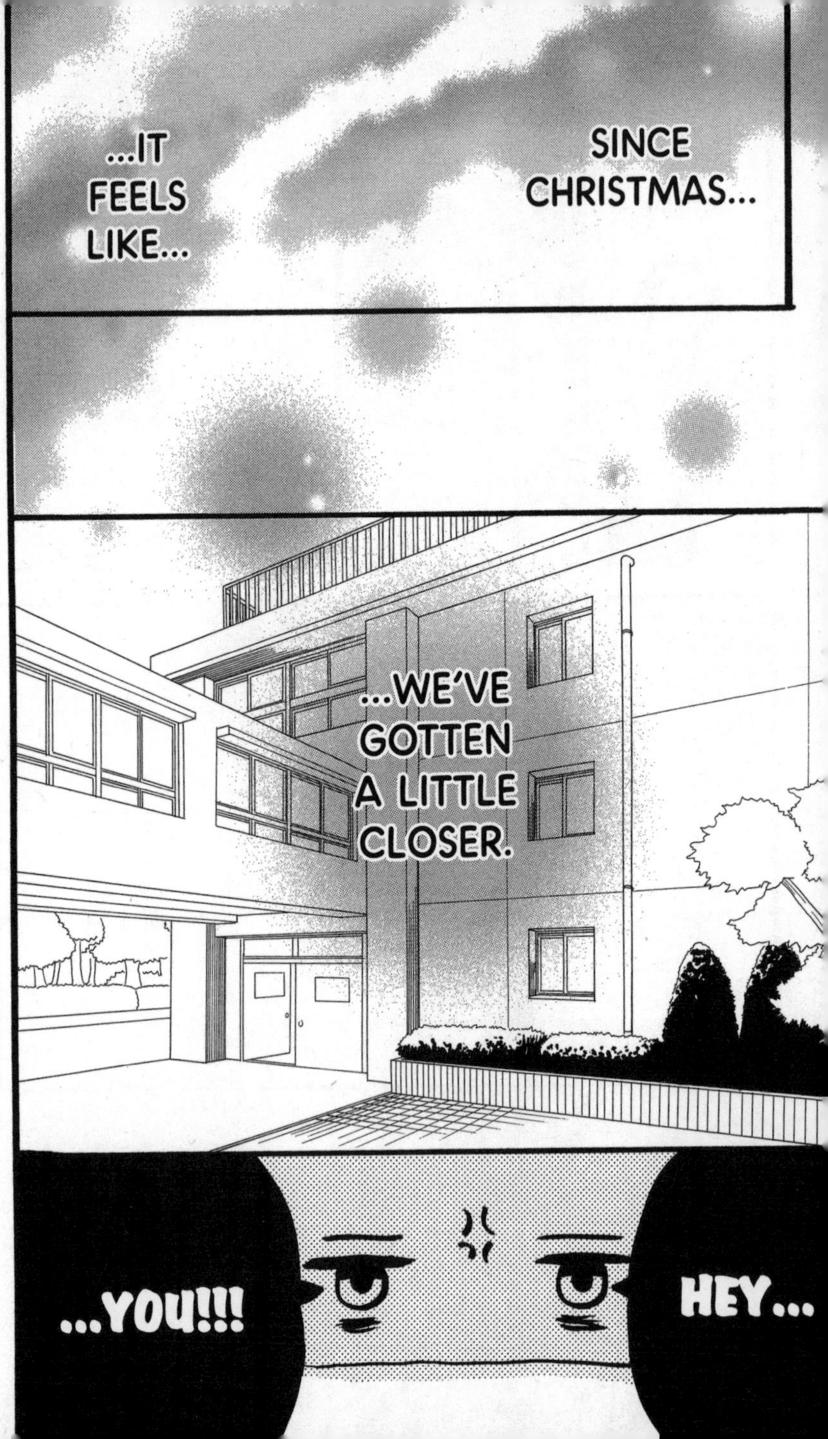
SINCE CHRISTMAS...
...IT FEELS LIKE...
...WE'VE GOTTEN A LITTLE CLOSER.
HEY...
...YOU!!!

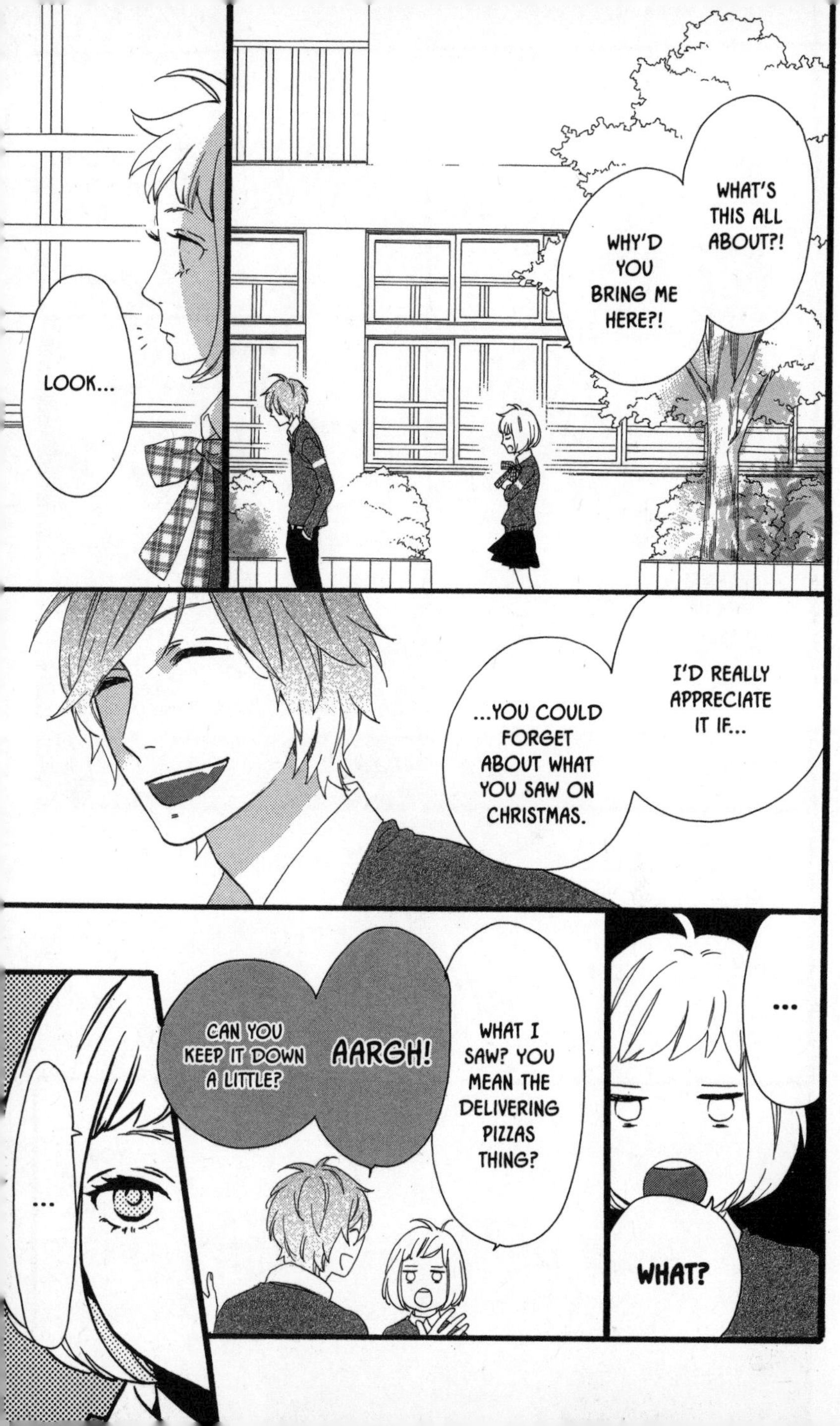
WHAT'S THIS ALL ABOUT?!
WHY'D YOU BRING ME HERE?!
LOOK...
I'D REALLY APPRECIATE IT IF...
...YOU COULD FORGET ABOUT WHAT YOU SAW ON CHRISTMAS.
...
WHAT?
WHAT I SAW? YOU MEAN THE DELIVERING PIZZAS THING?
AARGH!
CAN YOU KEEP IT DOWN A LITTLE?
...

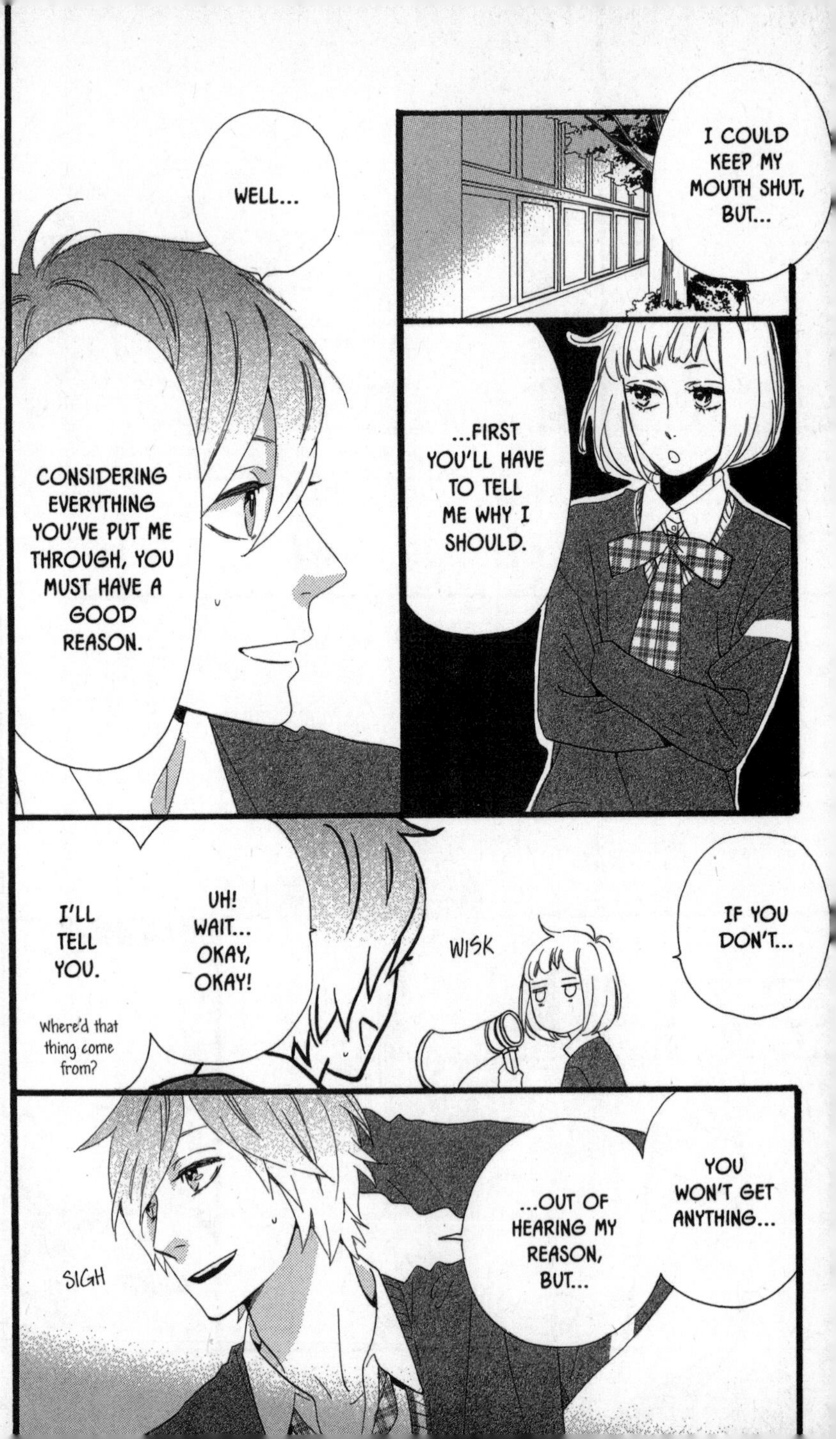
I COULD KEEP MY MOUTH SHUT, BUT...
...FIRST YOU'LL HAVE TO TELL ME WHY I SHOULD.
WELL...
CONSIDERING EVERYTHING YOU'VE PUT ME THROUGH, YOU MUST HAVE A GOOD REASON.
IF YOU DON'T...
WISK
UH! WAIT... OKAY, OKAY!
I'LL TELL YOU.
Where'd that thing come from?
YOU WON'T GET ANYTHING...
...OUT OF HEARING MY REASON, BUT...
SIGH

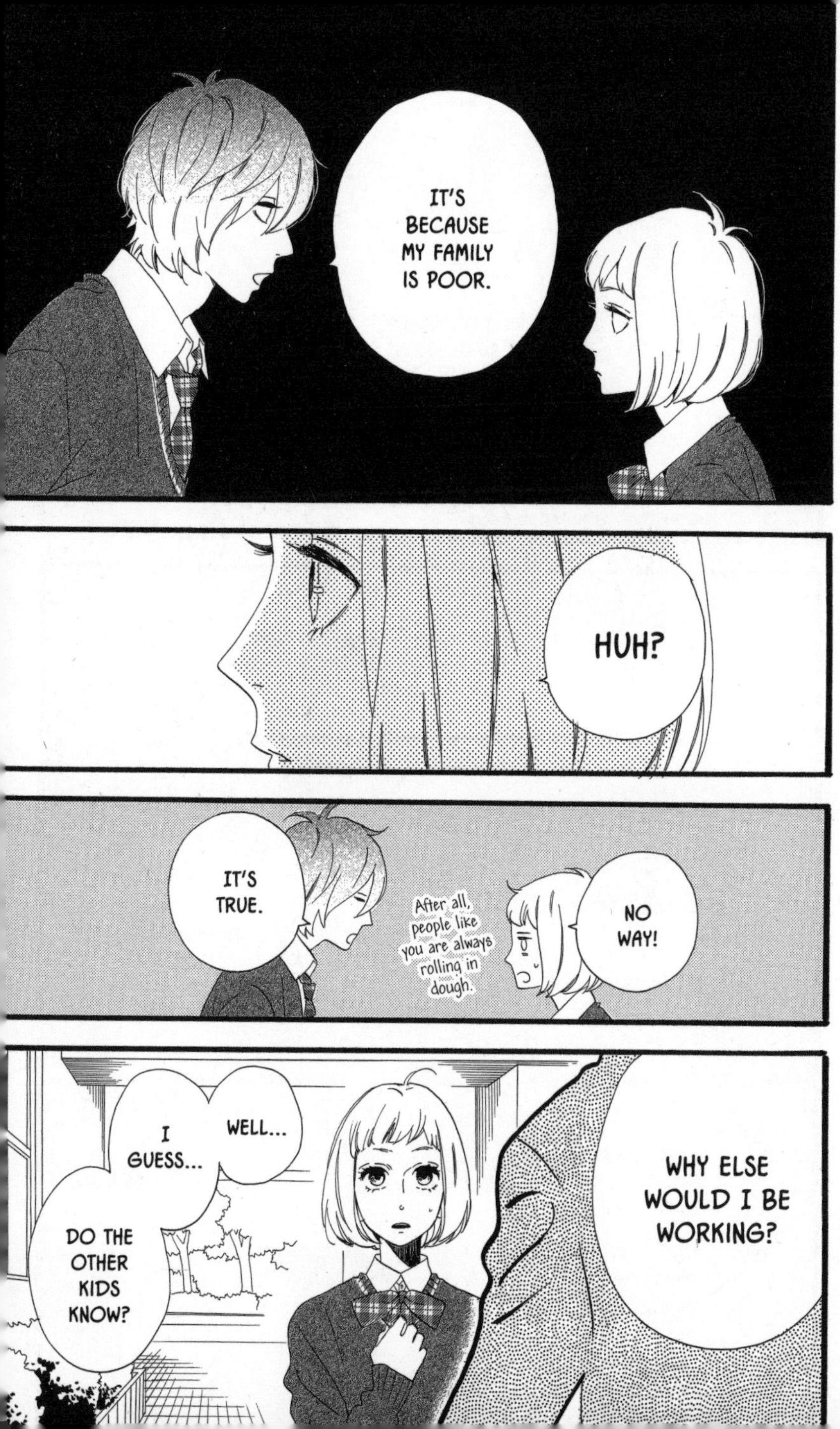
IT'S BECAUSE MY FAMILY IS POOR.
HUH?
NO WAY!
After all, people like you are always rolling in dough.
IT'S TRUE.
WHY ELSE WOULD I BE WORKING?
WELL...
I GUESS...
DO THE OTHER KIDS KNOW?

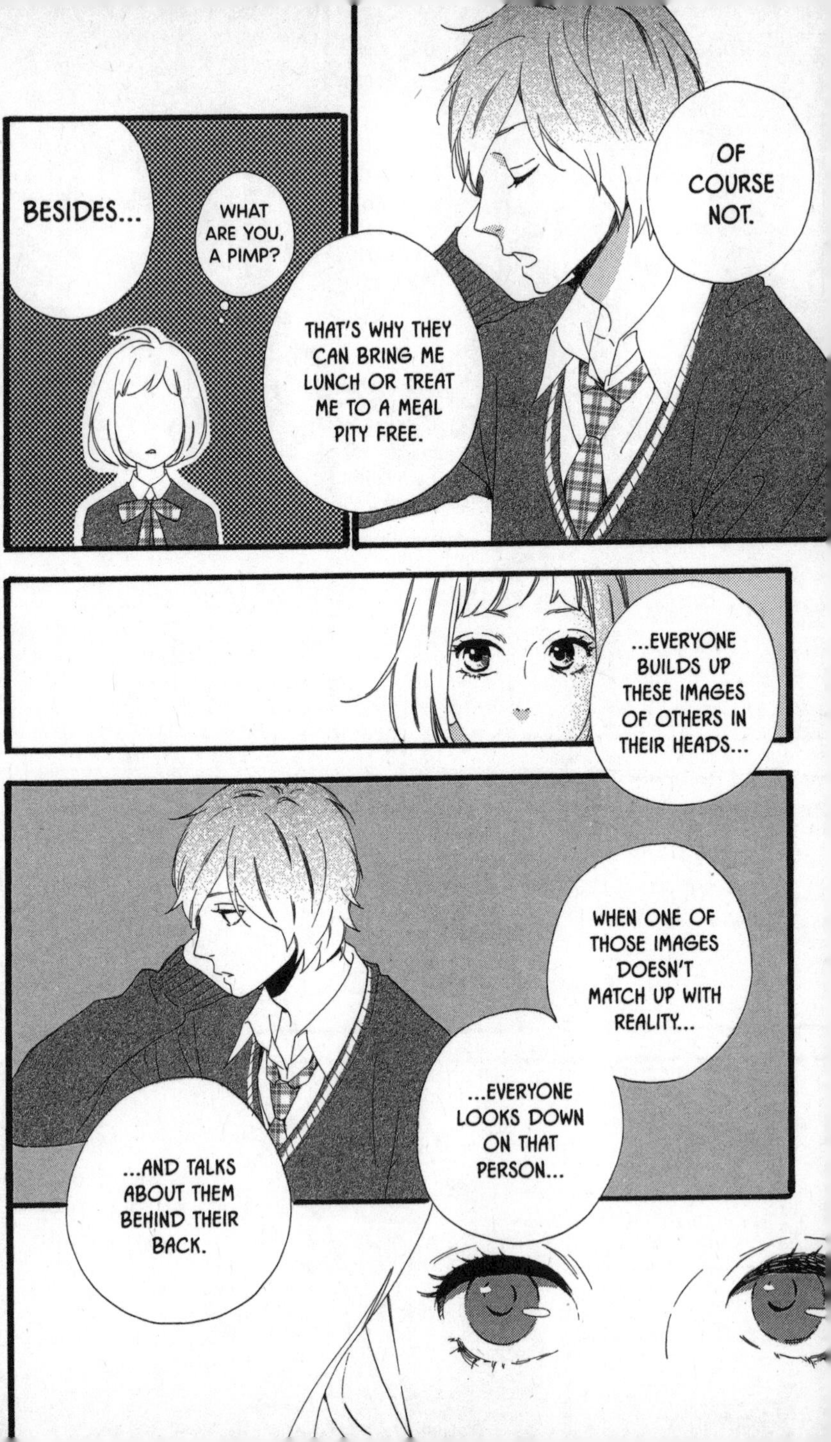
OF COURSE NOT.
THAT'S WHY THEY CAN BRING ME LUNCH OR TREAT ME TO A MEAL PITY FREE.
WHAT ARE YOU, A PIMP?
BESIDES...
...EVERYONE BUILDS UP THESE IMAGES OF OTHERS IN THEIR HEADS...
WHEN ONE OF THOSE IMAGES DOESN'T MATCH UP WITH REALITY...
...EVERYONE LOOKS DOWN ON THAT PERSON...
...AND TALKS ABOUT THEM BEHIND THEIR BACK.

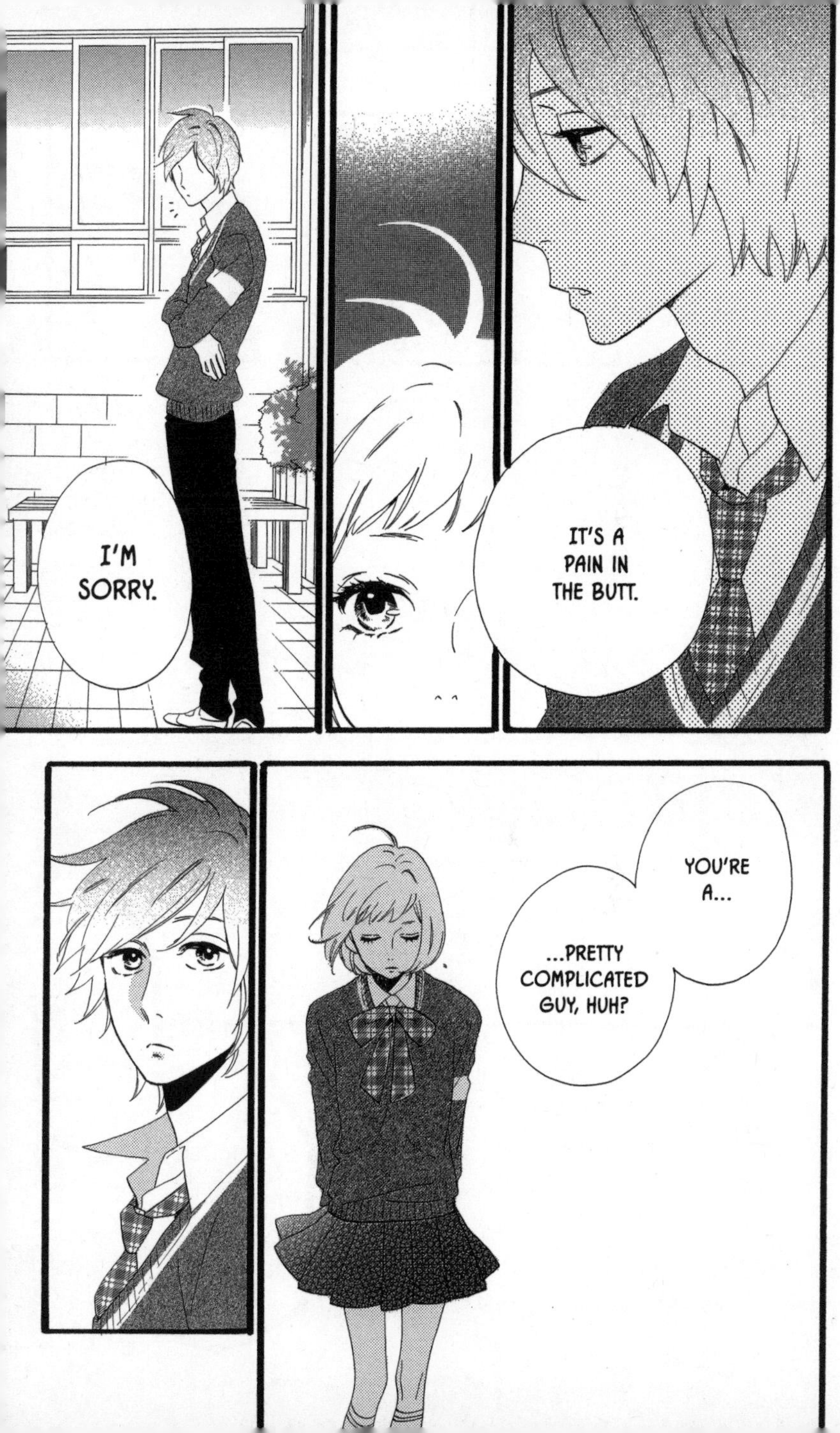
IT'S A PAIN IN THE BUTT.
I'M SORRY.
YOU'RE A...
...PRETTY COMPLICATED GUY, HUH?

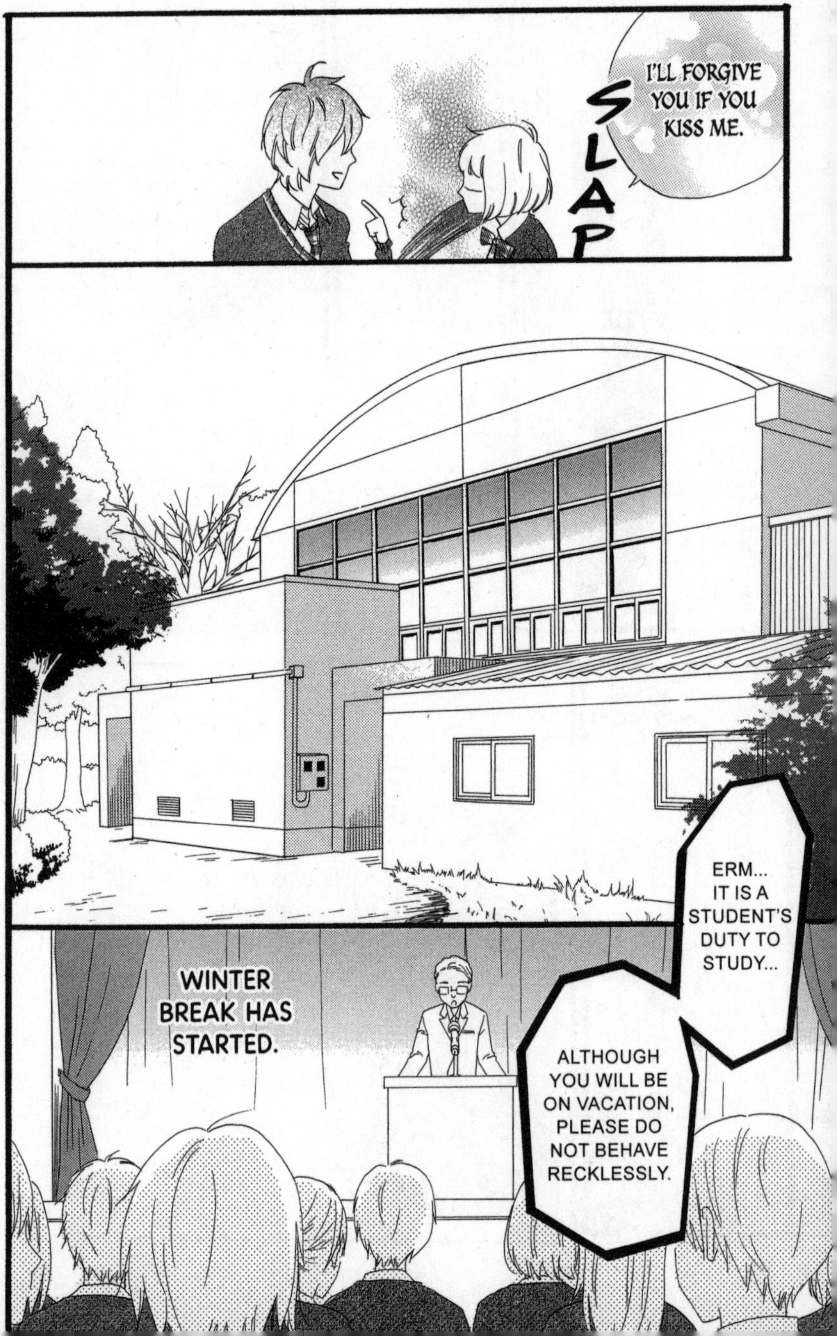
I'LL FORGIVE YOU IF YOU KISS ME.
SLAP
ERM... IT IS A STUDENT'S DUTY TO STUDY...
ALTHOUGH YOU WILL BE ON VACATION, PLEASE DO NOT BEHAVE RECKLESSLY.
WINTER BREAK HAS STARTED.

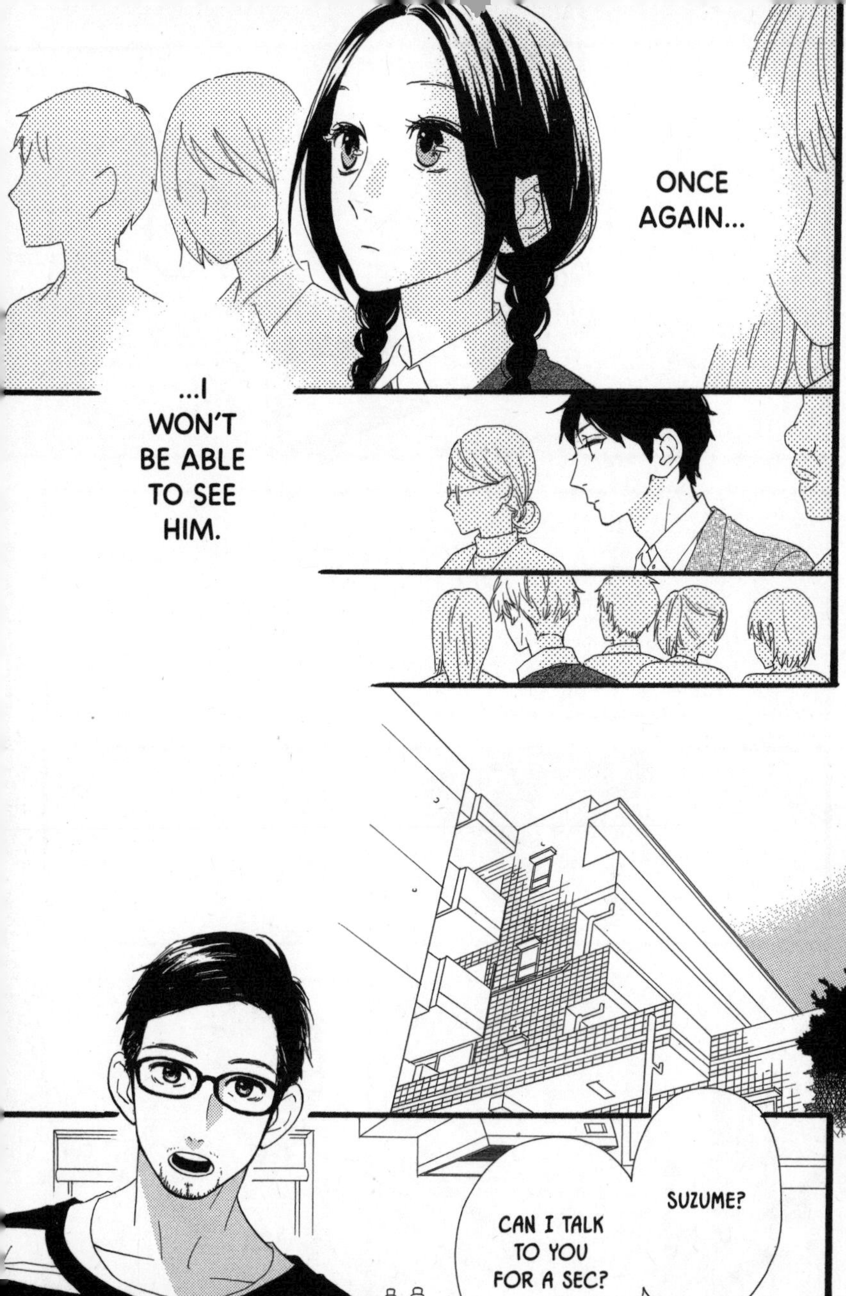
ONCE AGAIN...
...I WON'T BE ABLE TO SEE HIM.
SUZUME?
CAN I TALK TO YOU FOR A SEC?

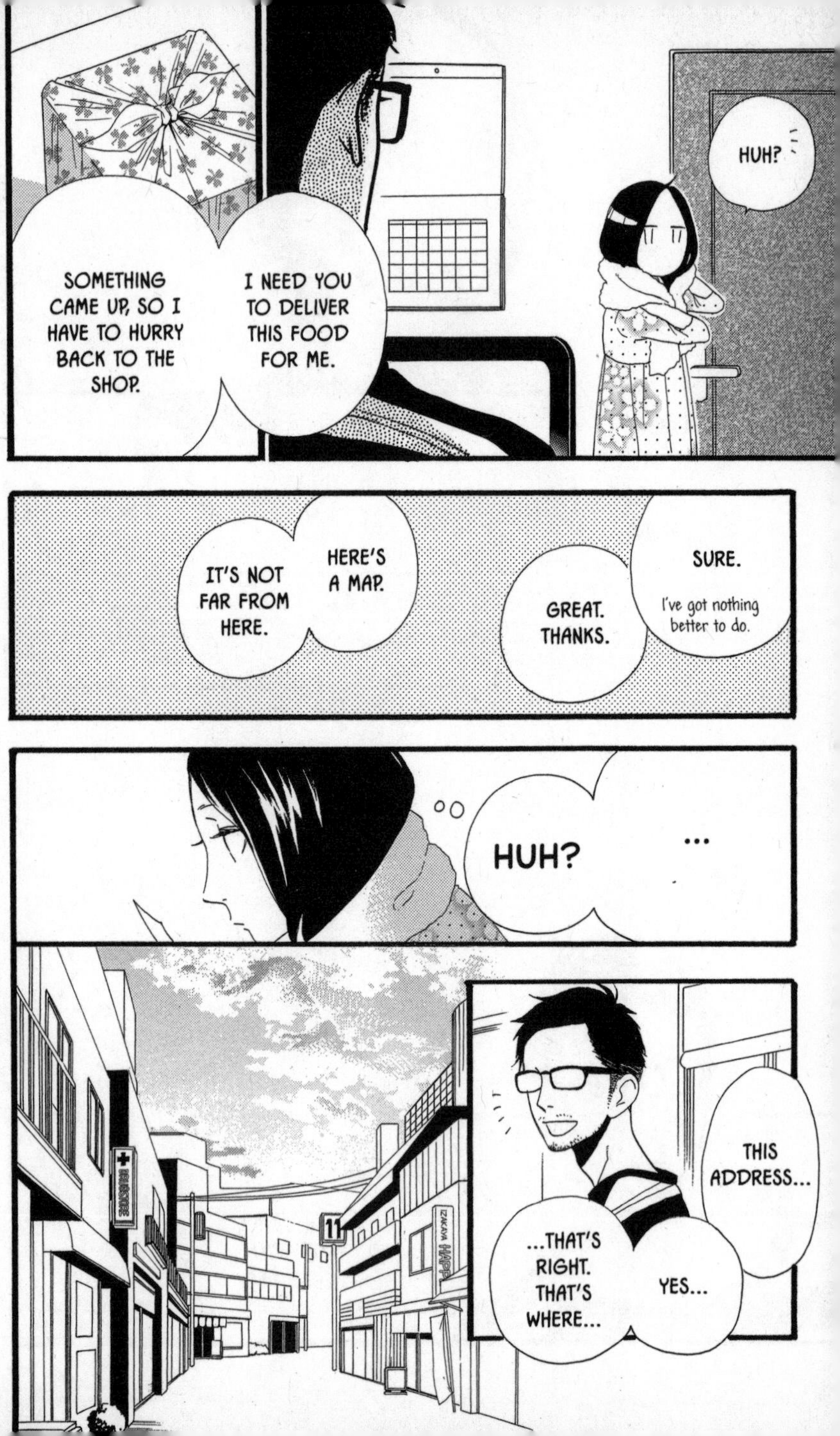
HUH?
I NEED YOU TO DELIVER THIS FOOD FOR ME.
SOMETHING CAME UP, SO I HAVE TO HURRY BACK TO THE SHOP.
SURE.
I've got nothing better to do.
GREAT. THANKS.
HERE'S A MAP.
IT'S NOT FAR FROM HERE.
...
HUH?
THIS ADDRESS...
YES...
...THAT'S RIGHT. THAT'S WHERE...

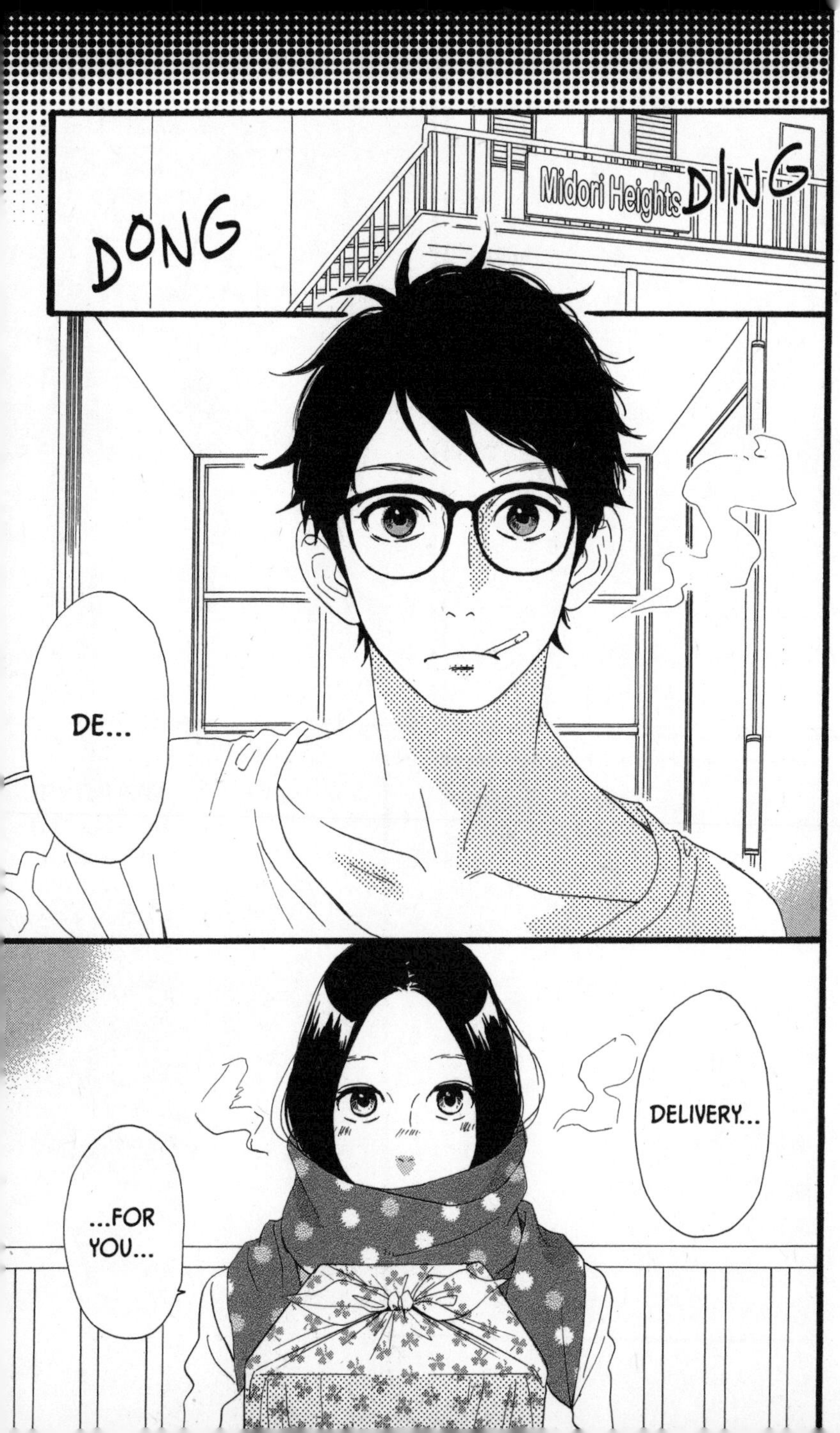

Midori Heights
DING
DONG
DE...
DELIVERY...
...FOR YOU...

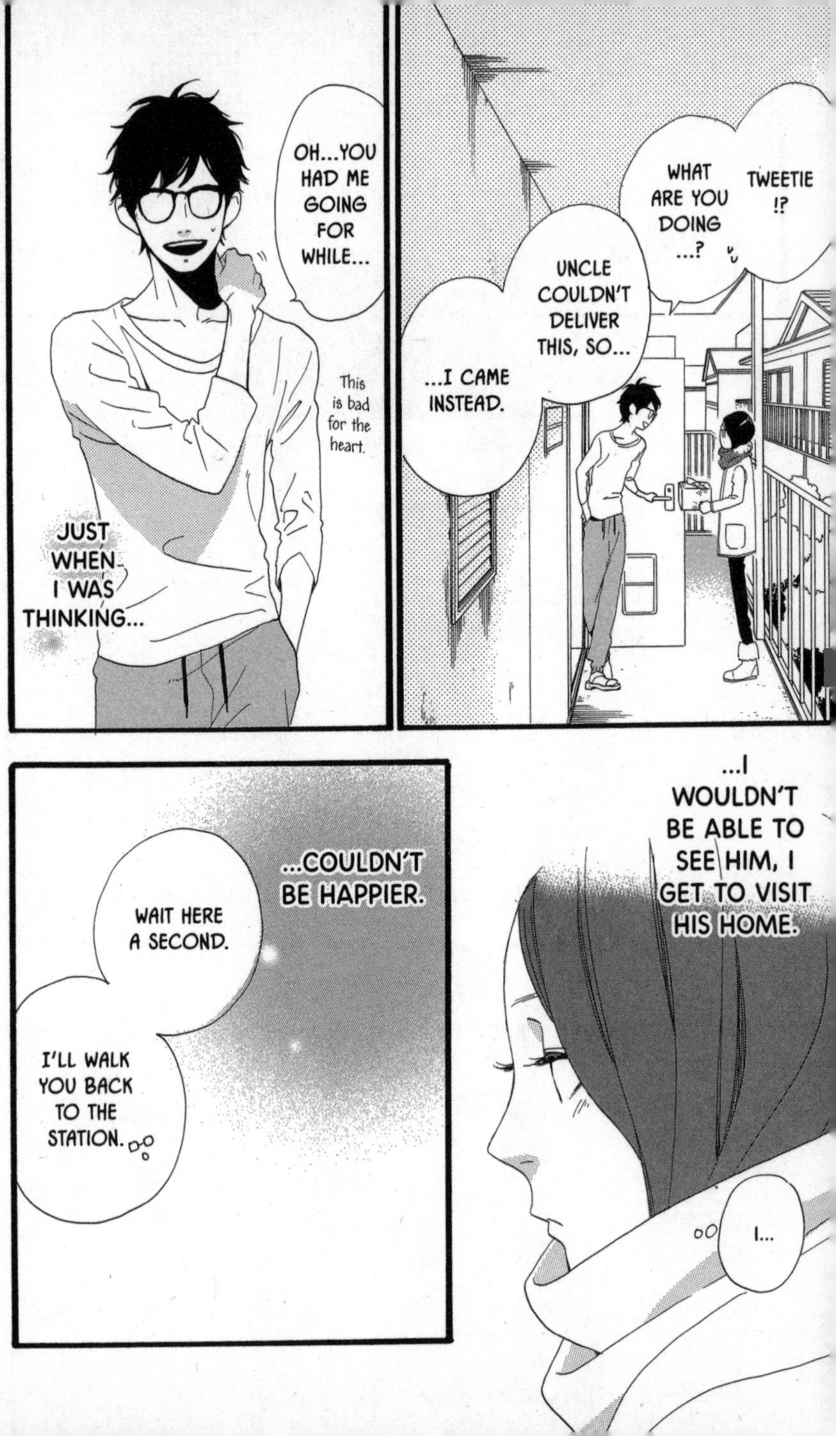
TWEETIE !?
WHAT ARE YOU DOING ...?
UNCLE COULDN'T DELIVER THIS, SO...
...I CAME INSTEAD.
OH...YOU HAD ME GOING FOR WHILE...
This is bad for the heart.
JUST WHEN I WAS THINKING...
...I WOULDN'T BE ABLE TO SEE HIM, I GET TO VISIT HIS HOME.
I...
...COULDN'T BE HAPPIER.
WAIT HERE A SECOND.
I'LL WALK YOU BACK TO THE STATION.

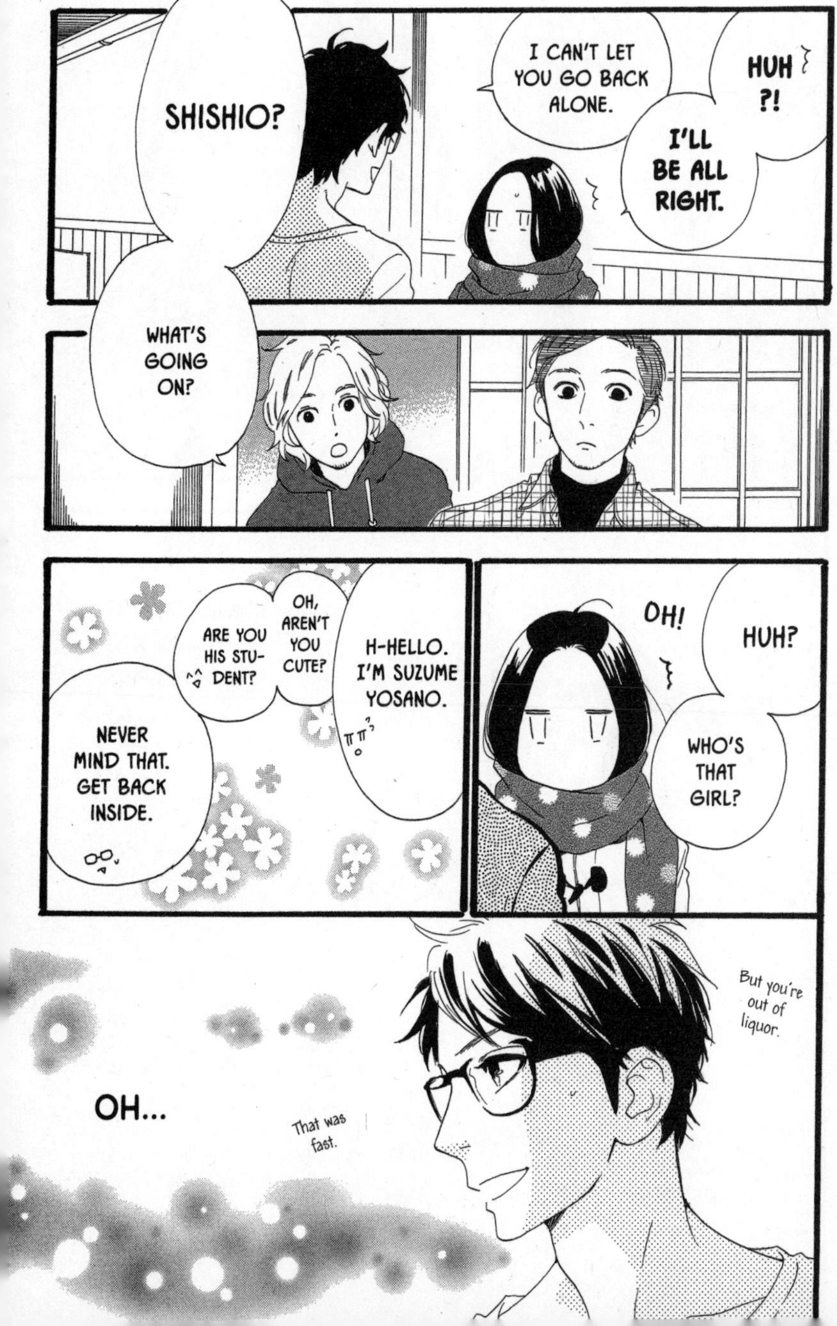
HUH ?!
I CAN'T LET YOU GO BACK ALONE.
I'LL BE ALL RIGHT.
SHISHIO?
WHAT'S GOING ON?
HUH?
OH!
WHO'S THAT GIRL?
H-HELLO. I'M SUZUME YOSANO.
OH, AREN'T YOU CUTE?
ARE YOU HIS STU-DENT?
NEVER MIND THAT. GET BACK INSIDE.
But you're out of liquor.
That was fast.
OH...

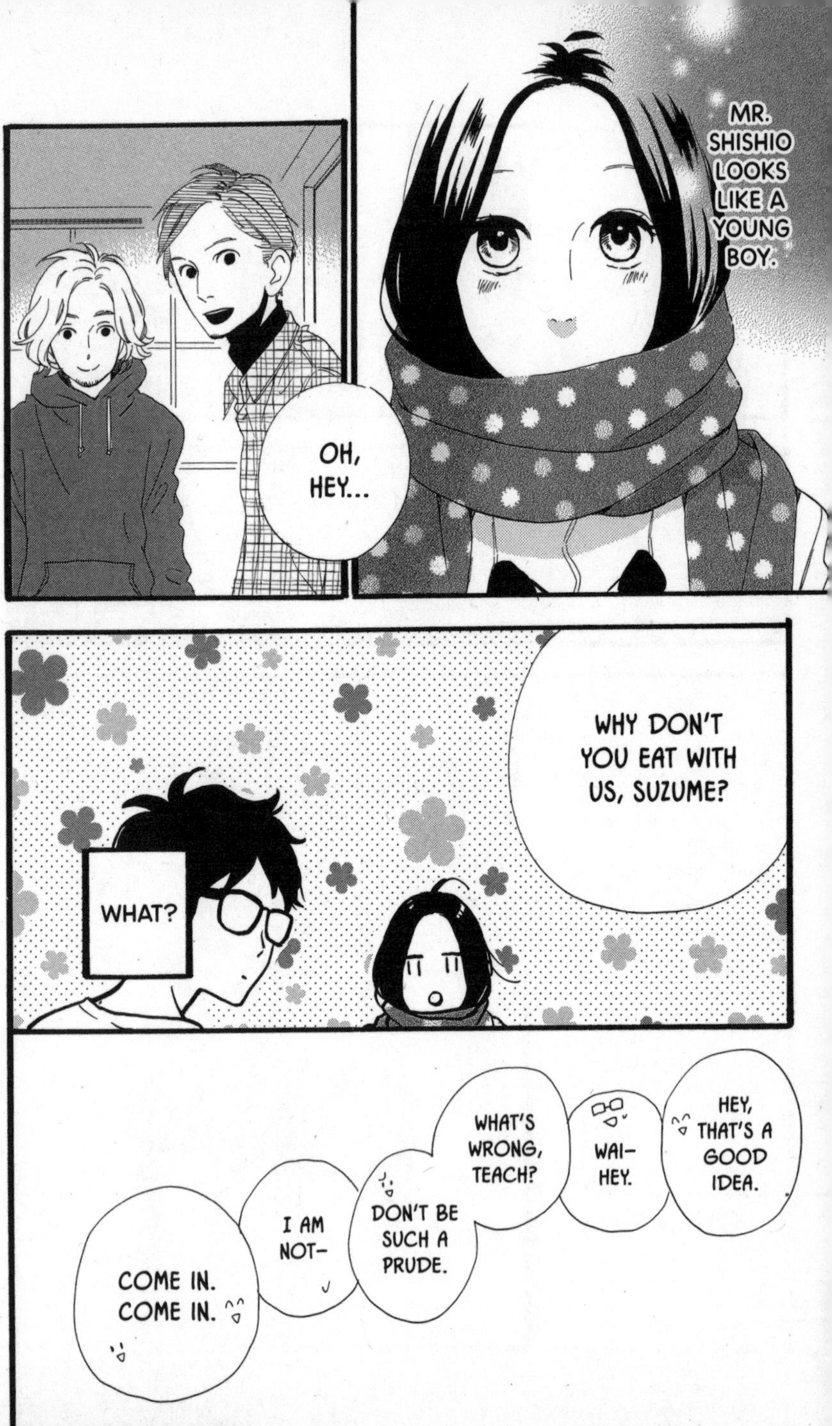
MR. SHISHIO LOOKS LIKE A YOUNG BOY.
OH, HEY...
WHY DON'T YOU EAT WITH US, SUZUME?
WHAT?
HEY, THAT'S A GOOD IDEA.
WAI- HEY.
WHAT'S WRONG, TEACH?
DON'T BE SUCH A PRUDE.
I AM NOT-
COME IN. COME IN.

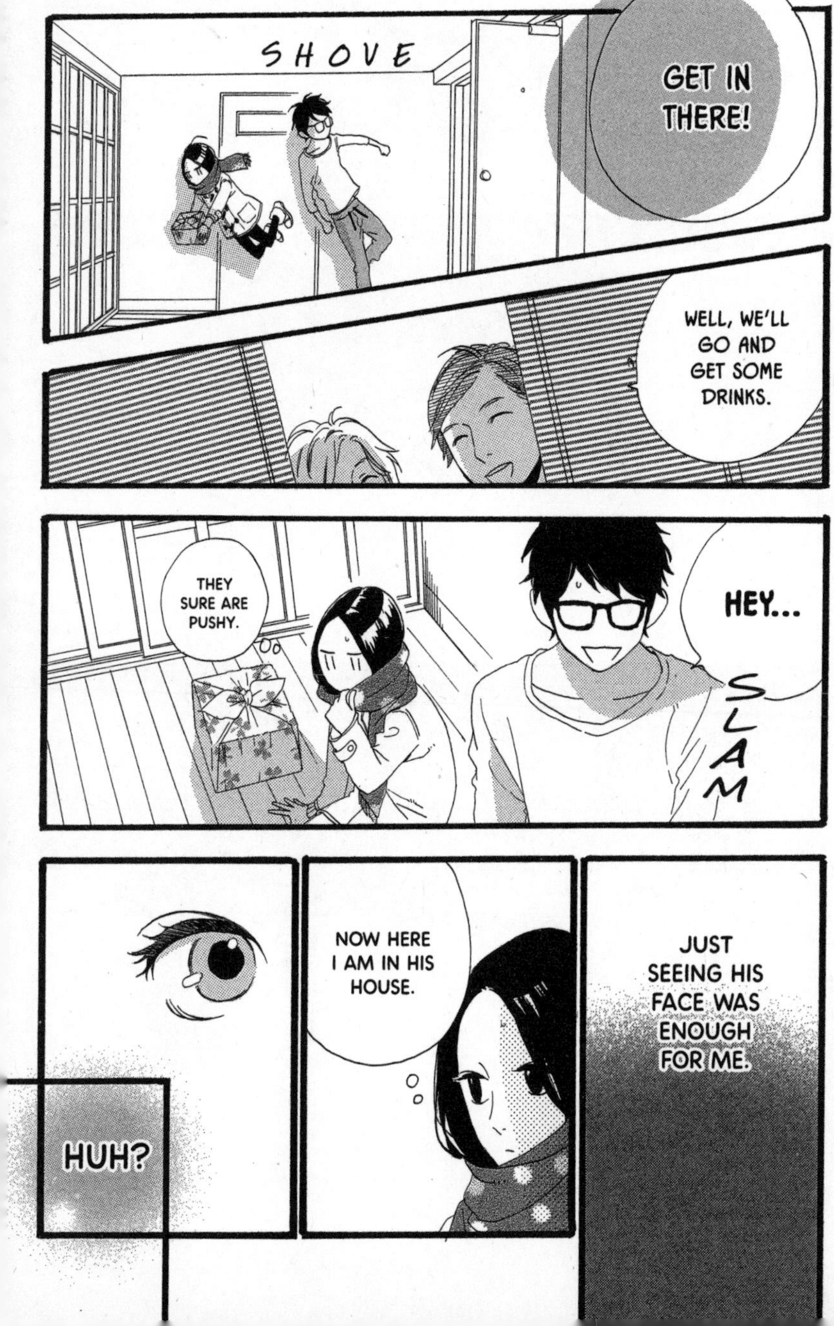
GET IN THERE!
SHOVE
WELL, WE'LL GO AND GET SOME DRINKS.
HEY...
SLAM
THEY SURE ARE PUSHY.
JUST SEEING HIS FACE WAS ENOUGH FOR ME.
NOW HERE I AM IN HIS HOUSE.
HUH?

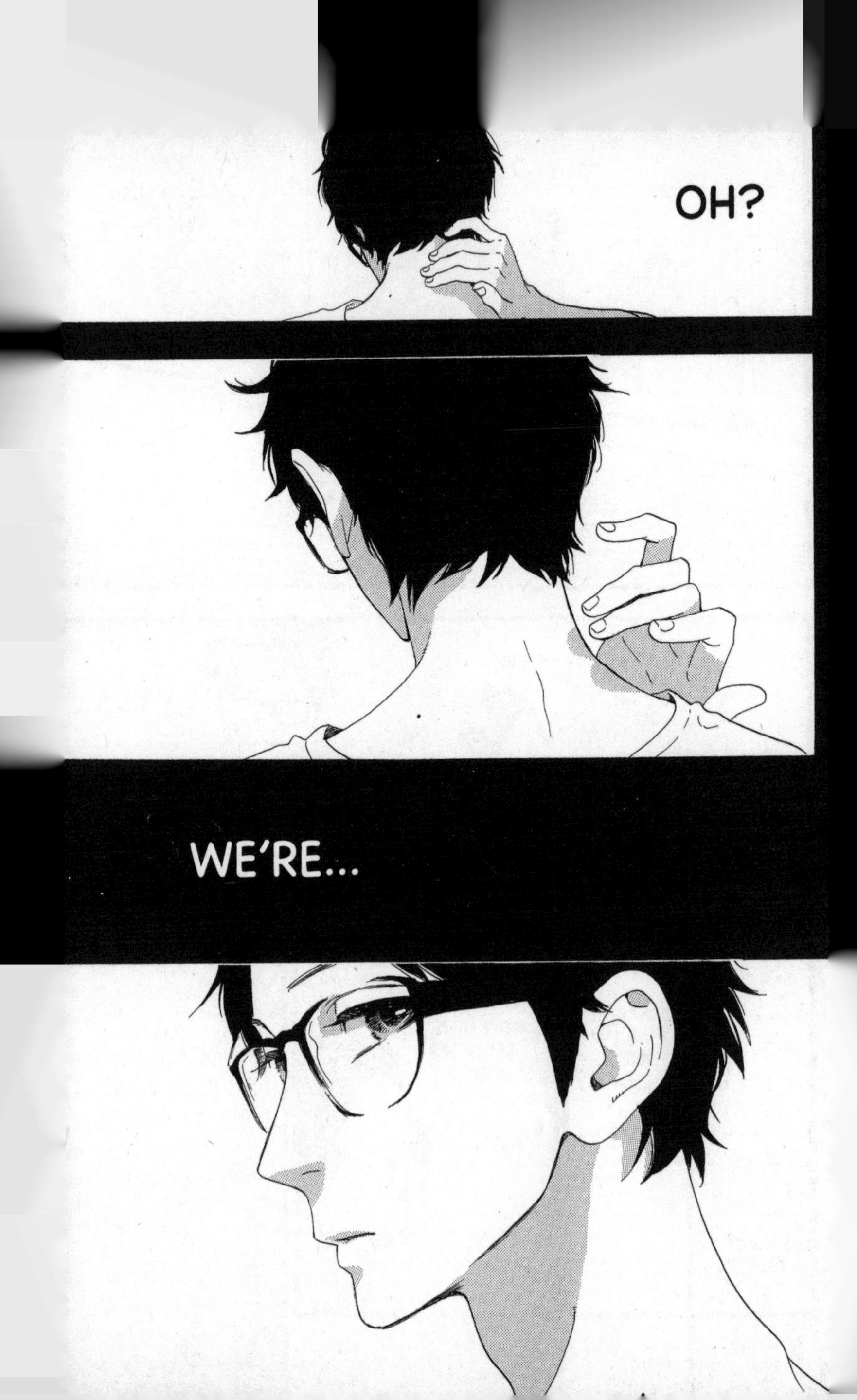
OH?
WE'RE...

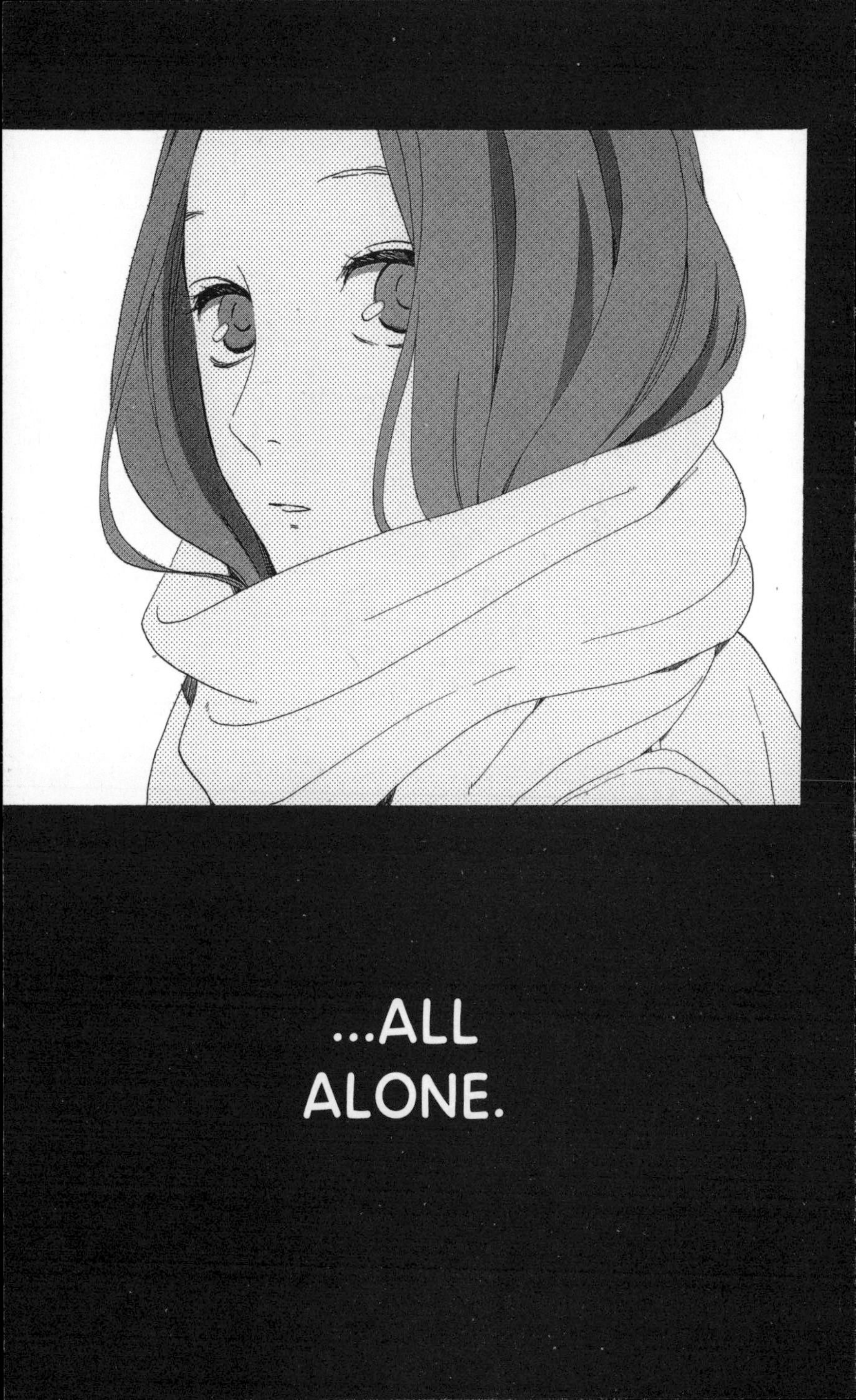
...ALL
ALONE.

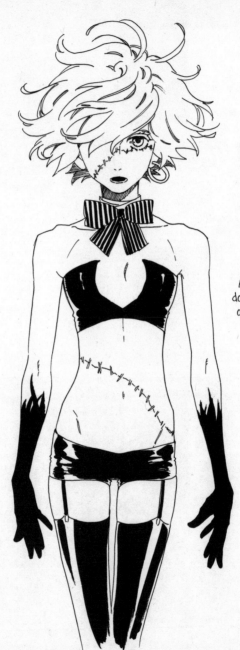

A random
doodle based
on a vague
concept.

The DAYTIME SHOOTING STAR

Chapter 40.

DAYTIME SHOOTING STAR

DAYTIME SHOOTING

STAR

Day 40

Mika Yamamori

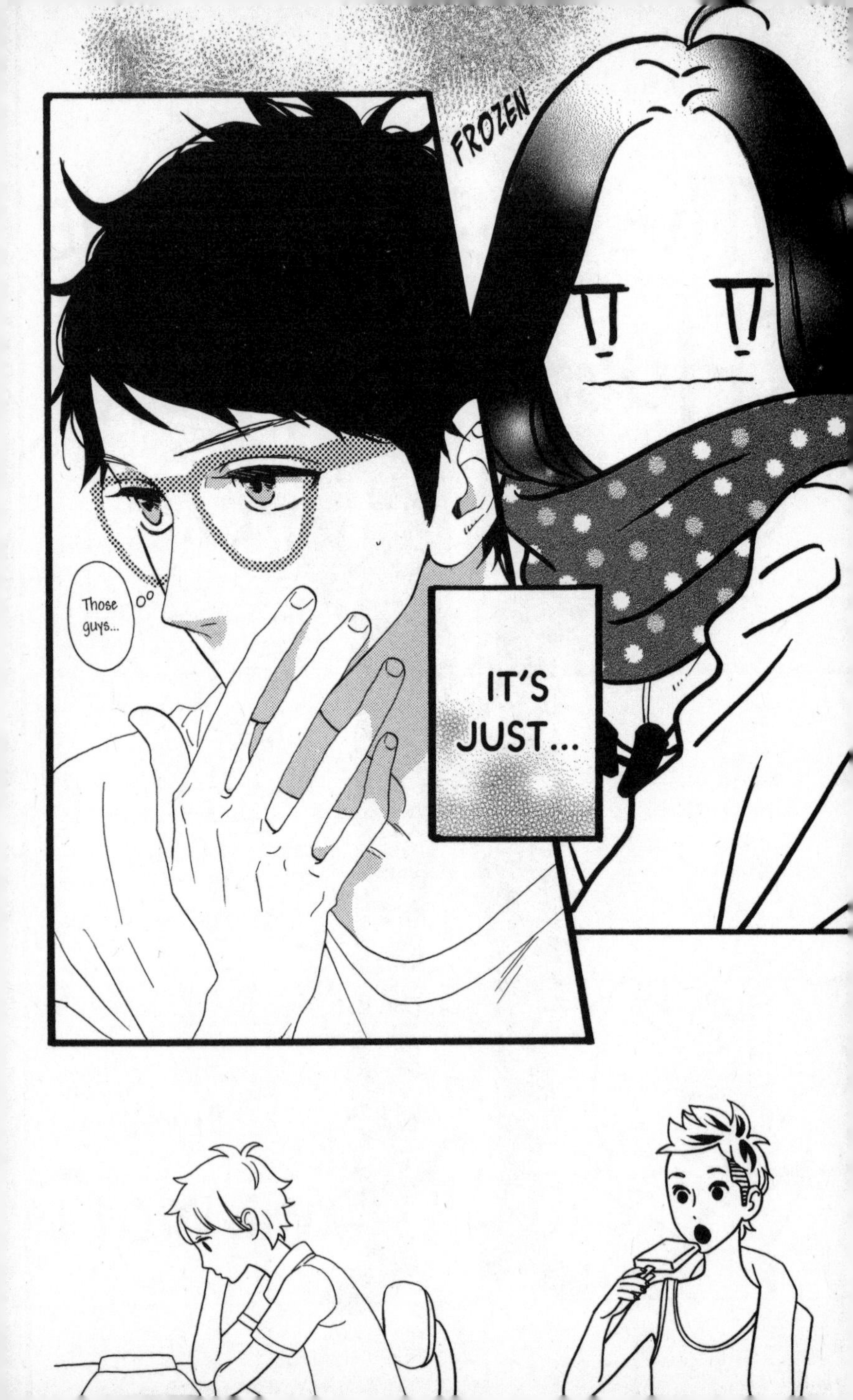
FROZEN
IT'S JUST...
Those guys...

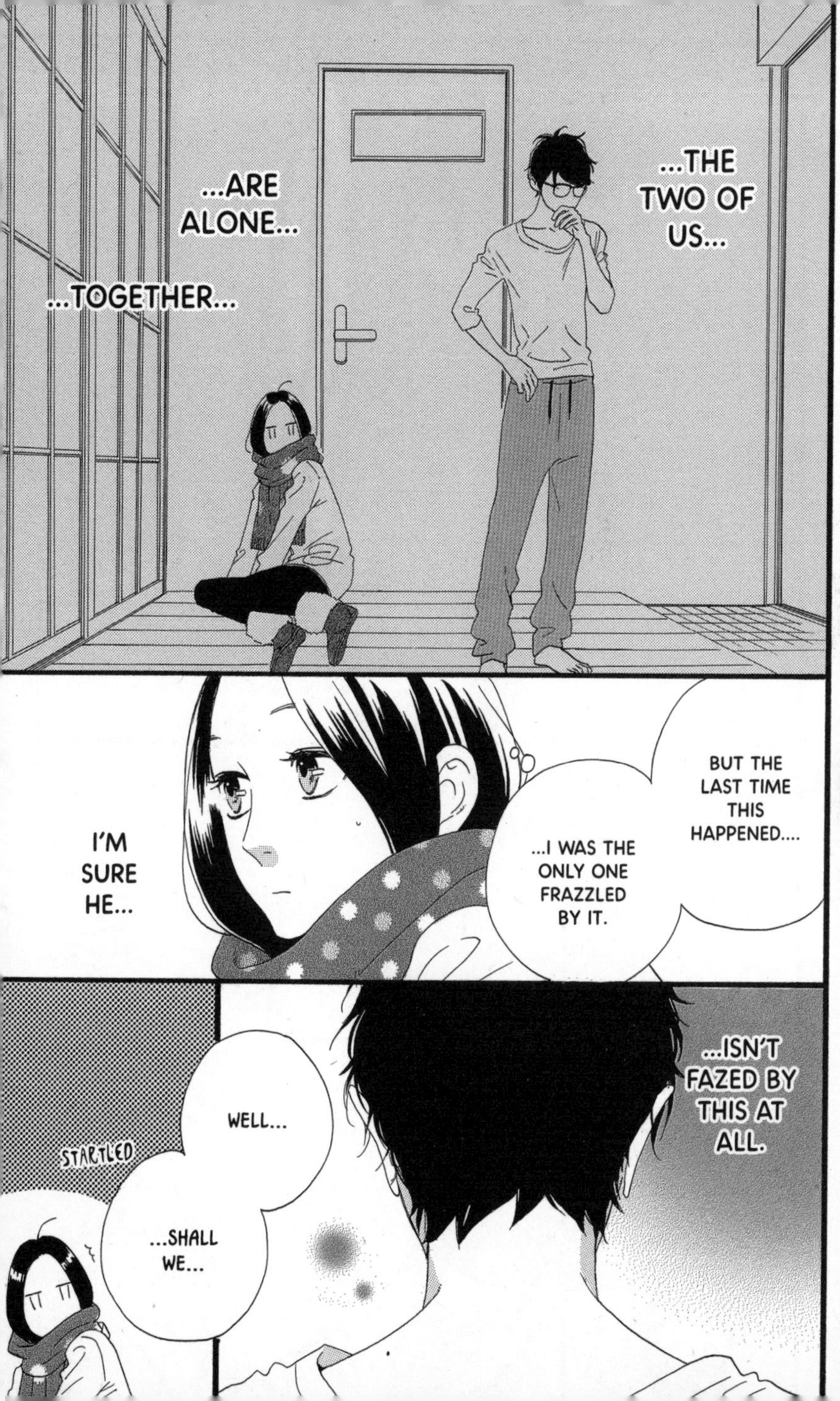
...THE TWO OF US...
...ARE ALONE...
...TOGETHER...
BUT THE LAST TIME THIS HAPPENED....
...I WAS THE ONLY ONE FRAZZLED BY IT.
I'M SURE HE...
...ISN'T FAZED BY THIS AT ALL.
WELL...
...SHALL WE...
STARTLED

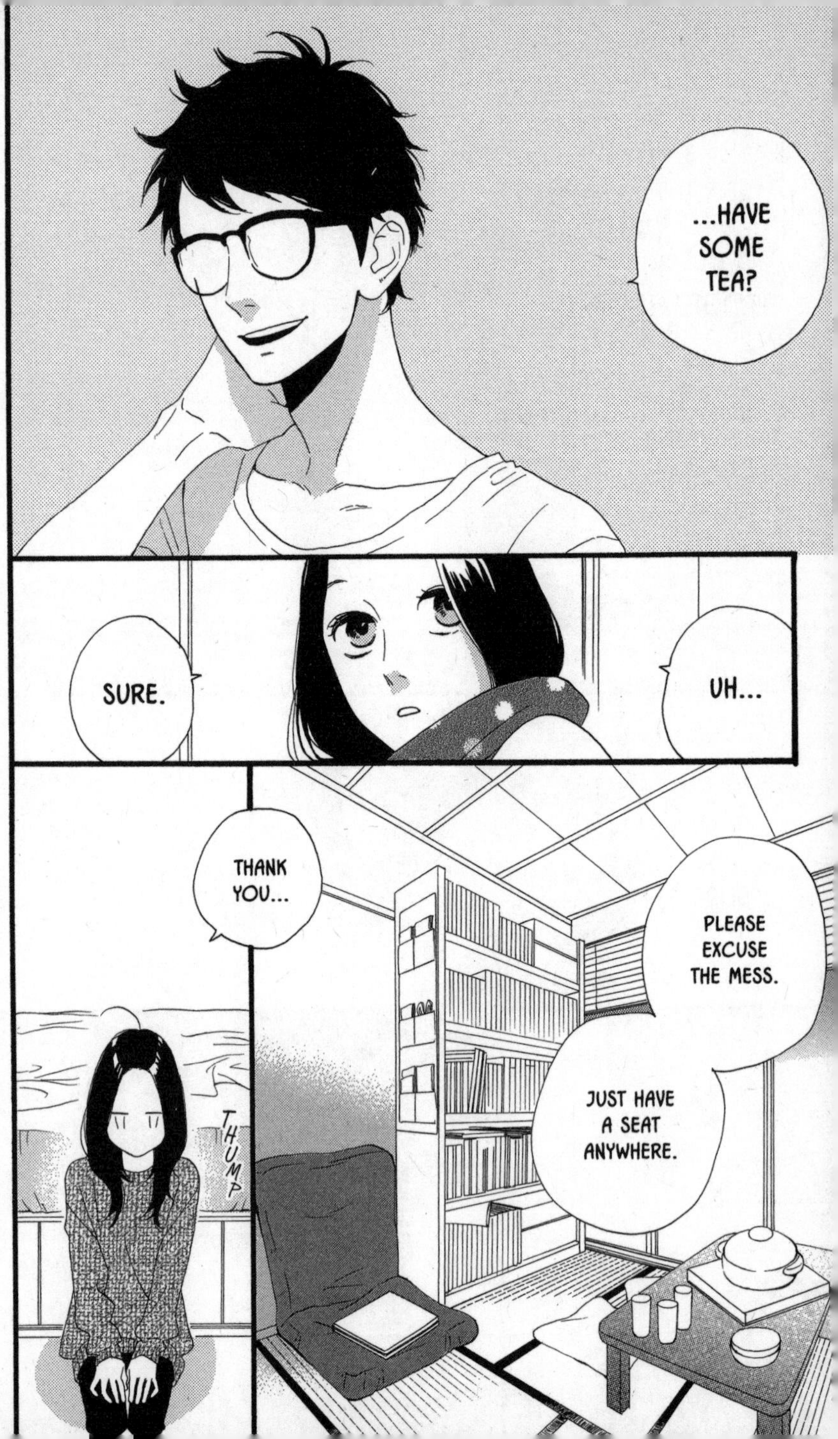
...HAVE SOME TEA?
UH...
SURE.
PLEASE EXCUSE THE MESS.
JUST HAVE A SEAT ANYWHERE.
THANK YOU...
THUMP

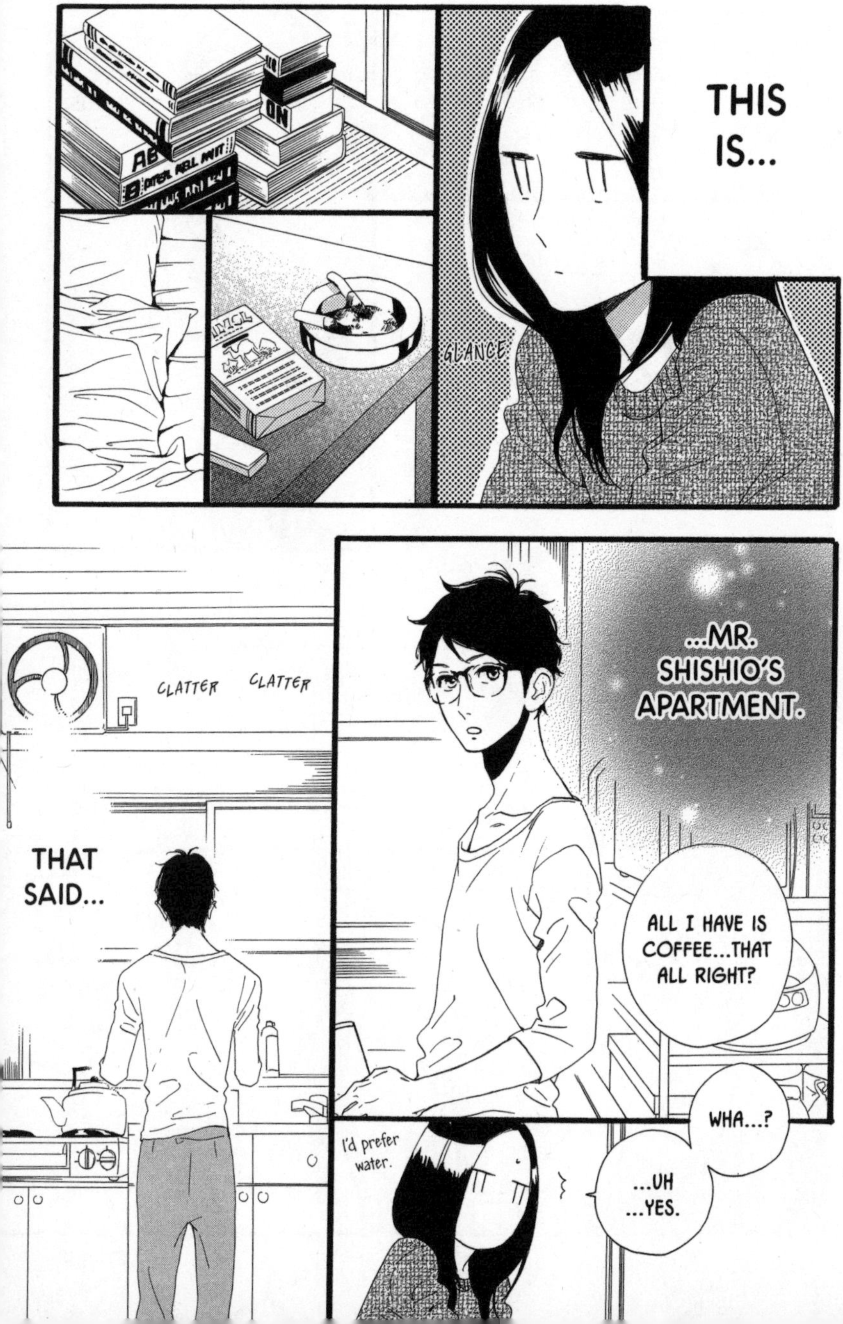
THIS IS...
GLANCE
...MR. SHISHIO'S APARTMENT.
ALL I HAVE IS COFFEE...THAT ALL RIGHT?
WHA...?
...UH ...YES.
I'd prefer water.
CLATTER CLATTER
THAT SAID...

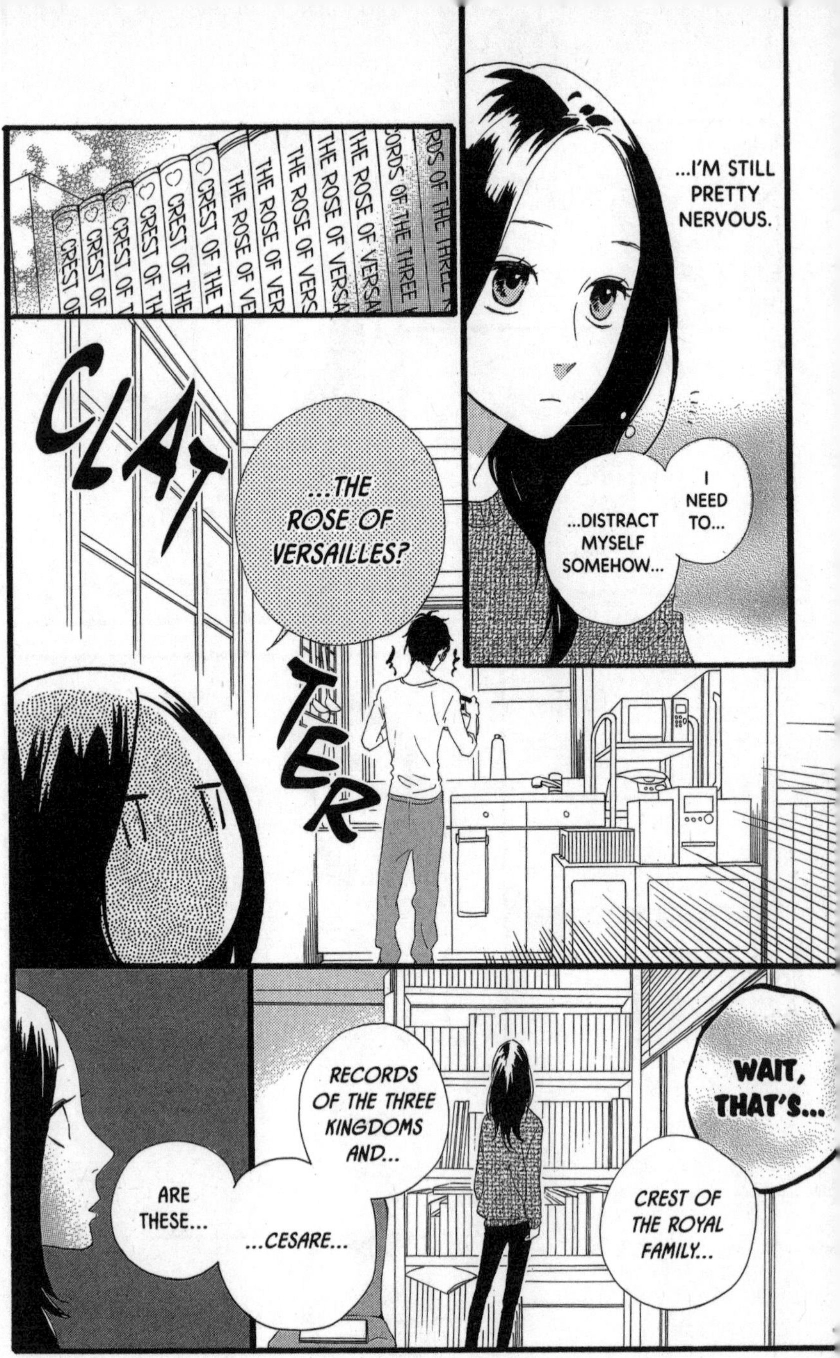
...I'M STILL PRETTY NERVOUS.
I NEED TO...
...DISTRACT MYSELF SOMEHOW...
CLATTER
...THE ROSE OF VERSAILLES?
WAIT, THAT'S...
CREST OF THE ROYAL FAMILY...
RECORDS OF THE THREE KINGDOMS AND...
...CESARE...
ARE THESE...

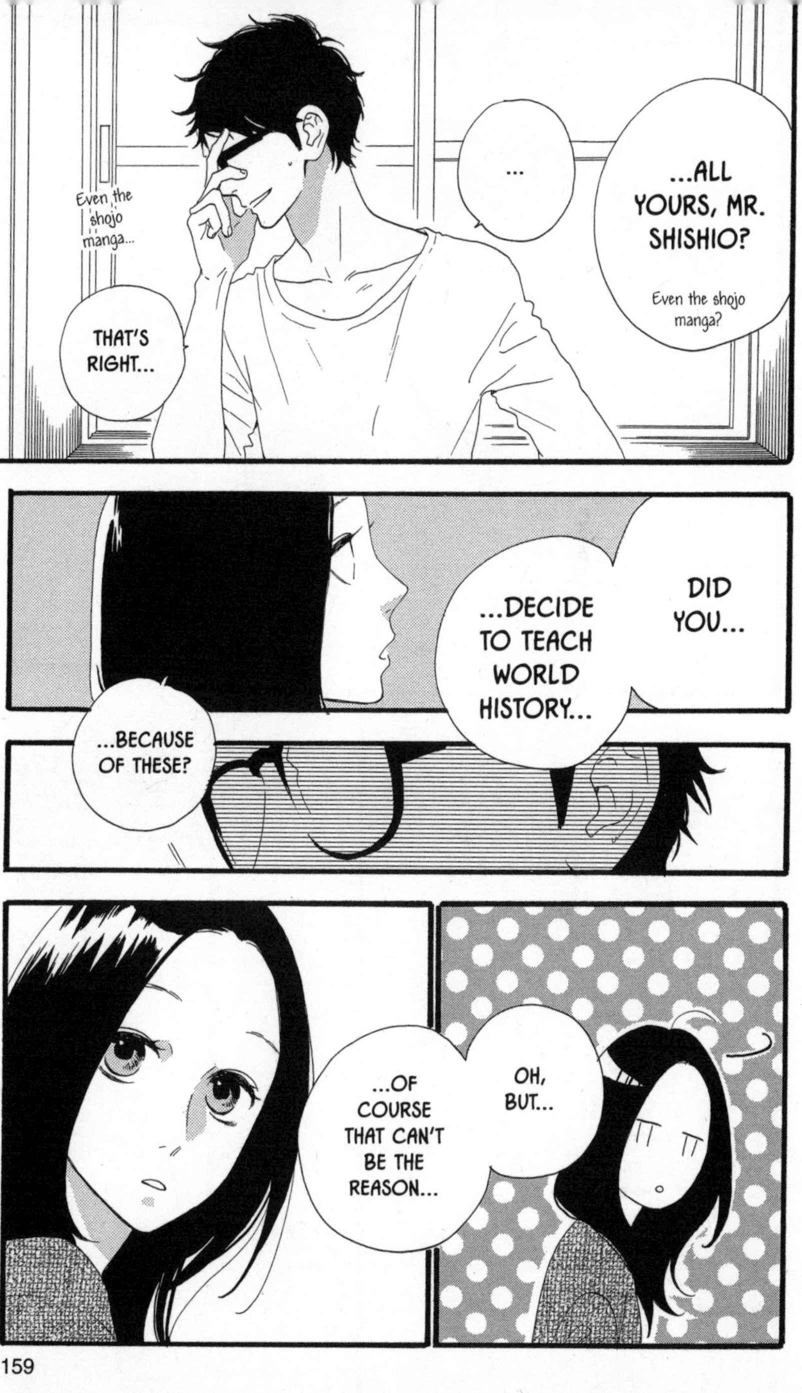

...ALL YOURS, MR. SHISHIO?
Even the shojo manga?
...
Even the shojo manga...
THAT'S RIGHT...
DID YOU...
...DECIDE TO TEACH WORLD HISTORY...
...BECAUSE OF THESE?
OH, BUT...
...OF COURSE THAT CAN'T BE THE REASON...

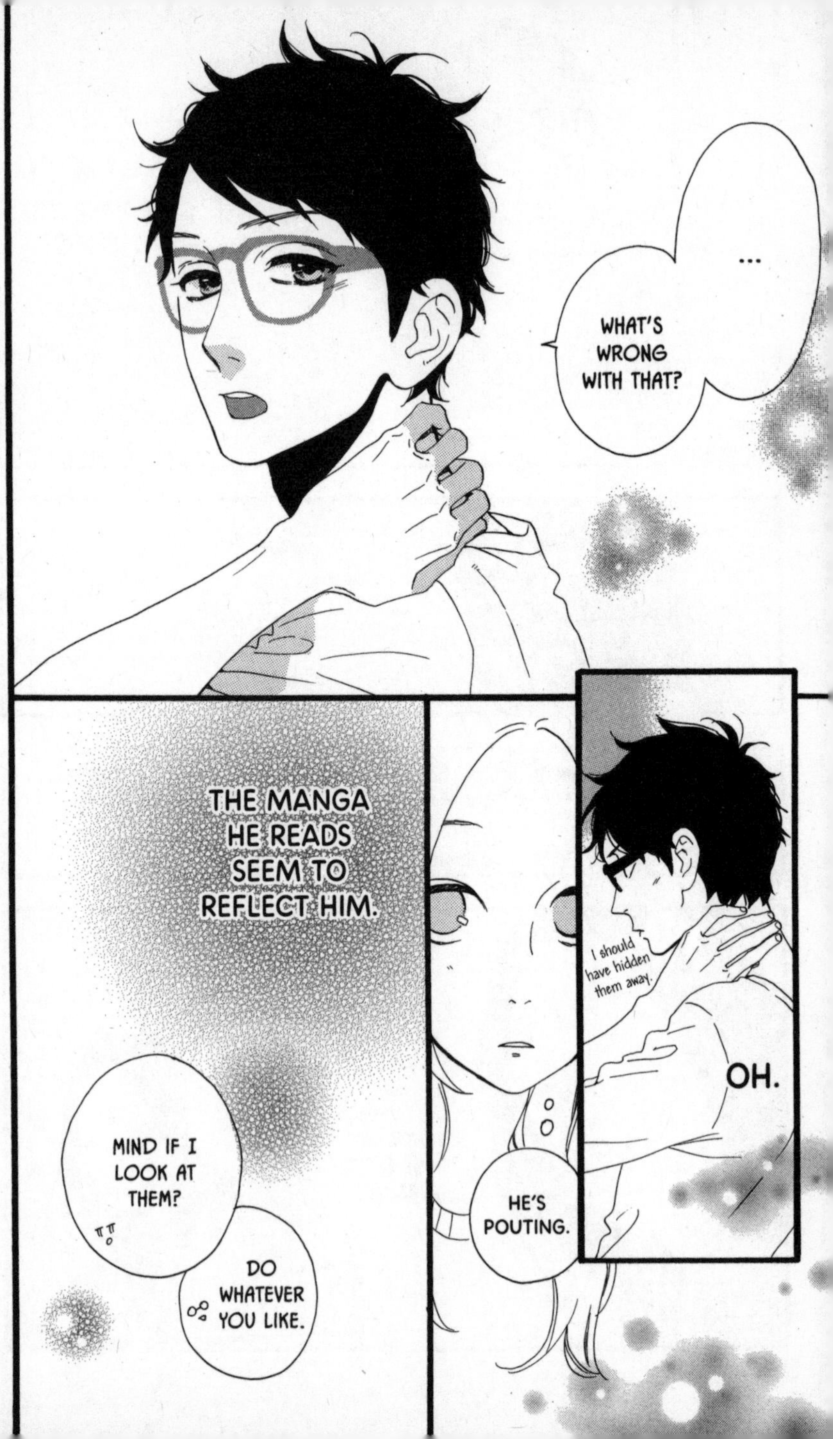
...
WHAT'S WRONG WITH THAT?
I should have hidden them away.
OH.
HE'S POUTING.
THE MANGA HE READS SEEM TO REFLECT HIM.
MIND IF I LOOK AT THEM?
DO WHATEVER YOU LIKE.

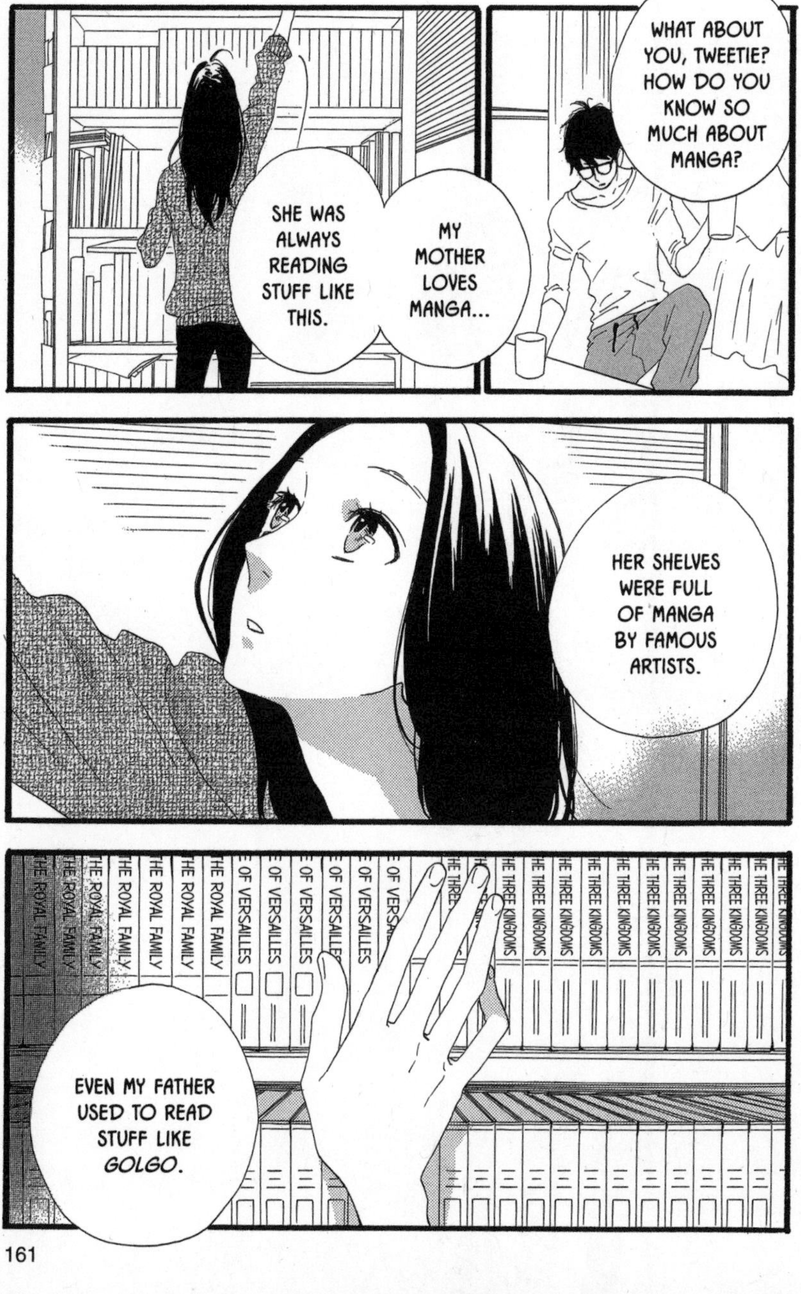
WHAT ABOUT YOU, TWEETIE? HOW DO YOU KNOW SO MUCH ABOUT MANGA?
MY MOTHER LOVES MANGA...
SHE WAS ALWAYS READING STUFF LIKE THIS.
HER SHELVES WERE FULL OF MANGA BY FAMOUS ARTISTS.
THE THREE KINGDOMS
OF VERSAILLES
THE ROYAL FAMILY
EVEN MY FATHER USED TO READ STUFF LIKE *GOLGO*.

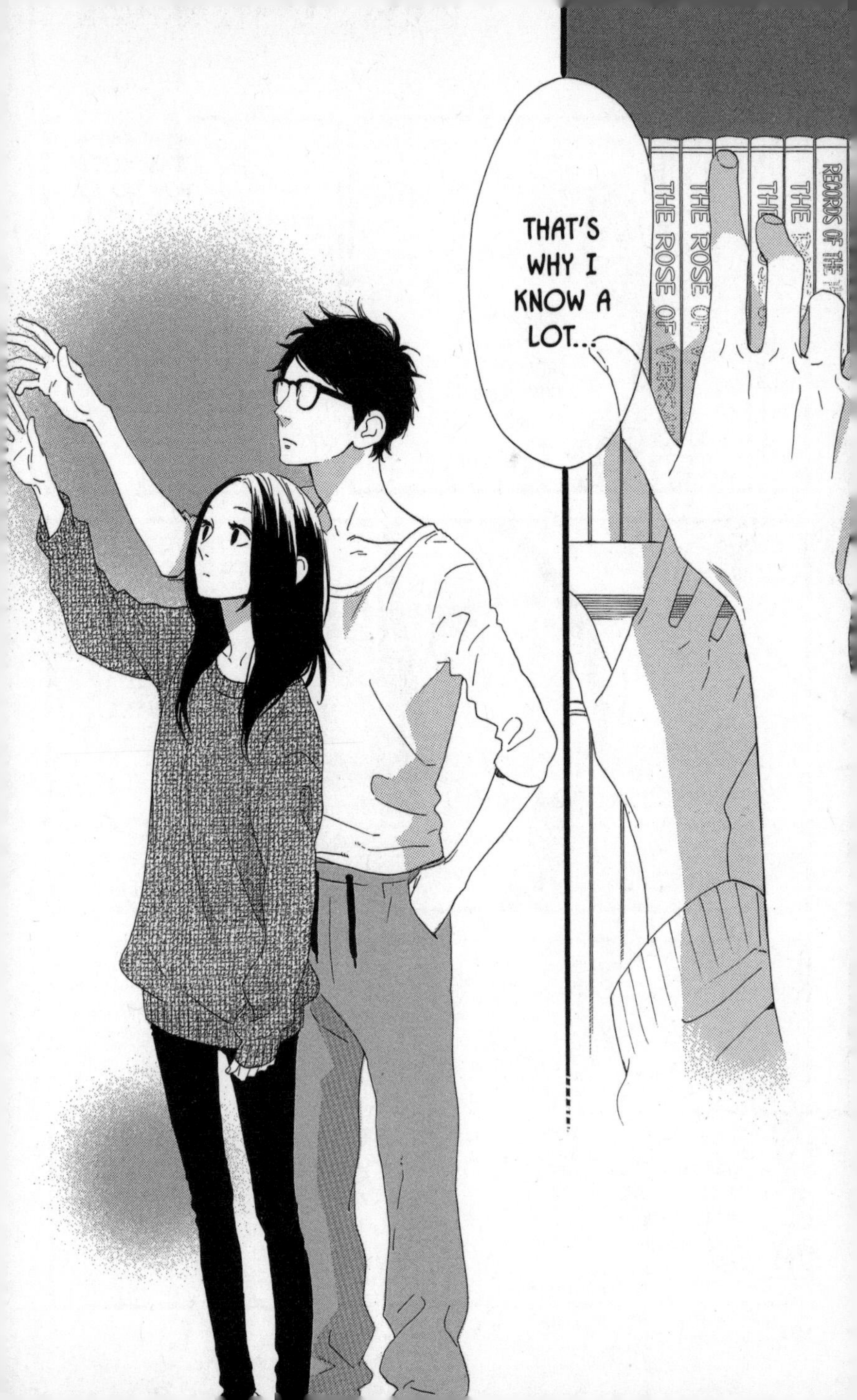
RECORDS OF THE
THE ROSE OF
THE ROSE OF
THAT'S WHY I KNOW A LOT...

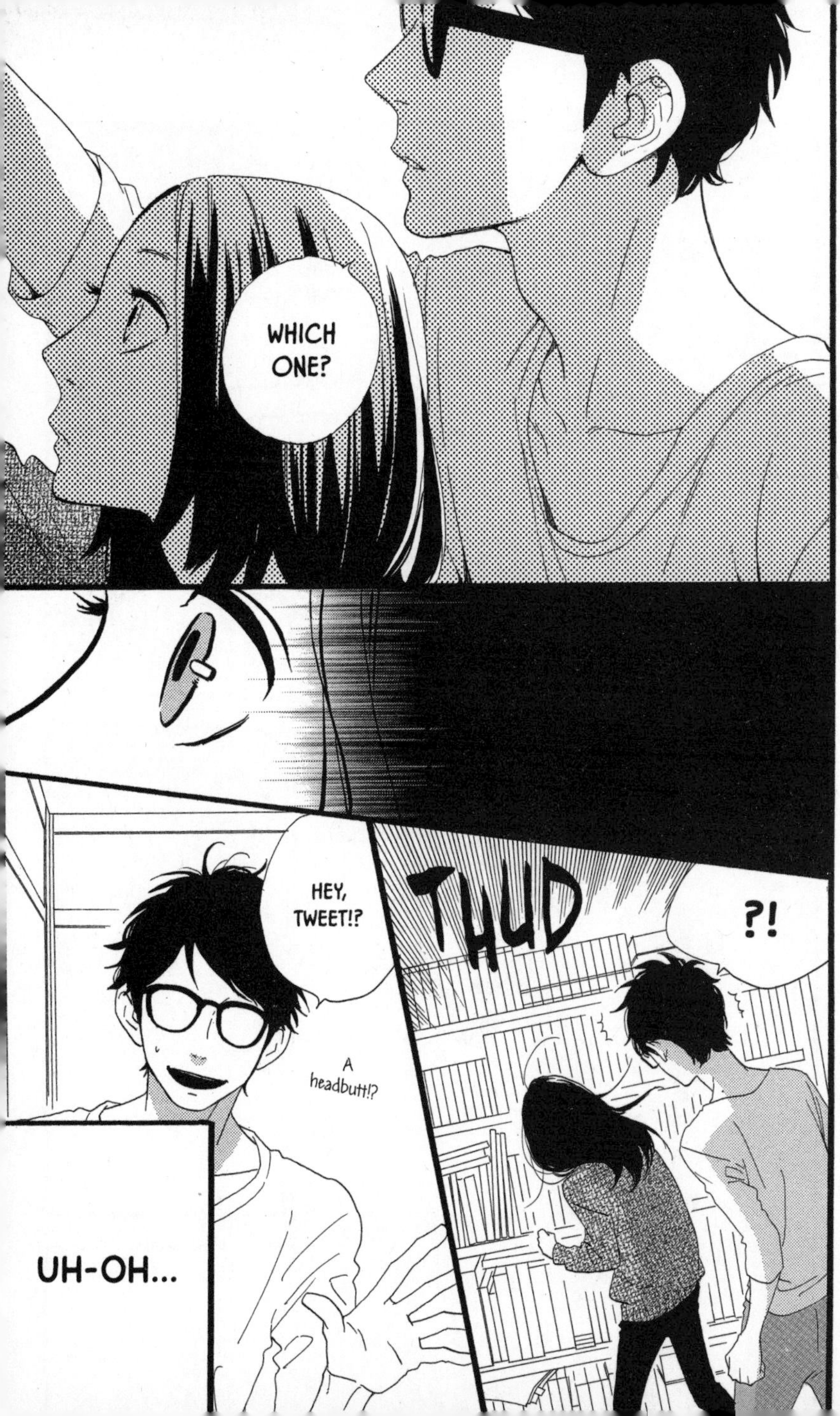
WHICH ONE?
?!
THUD
HEY, TWEET!?
A headbutt!?
UH-OH...

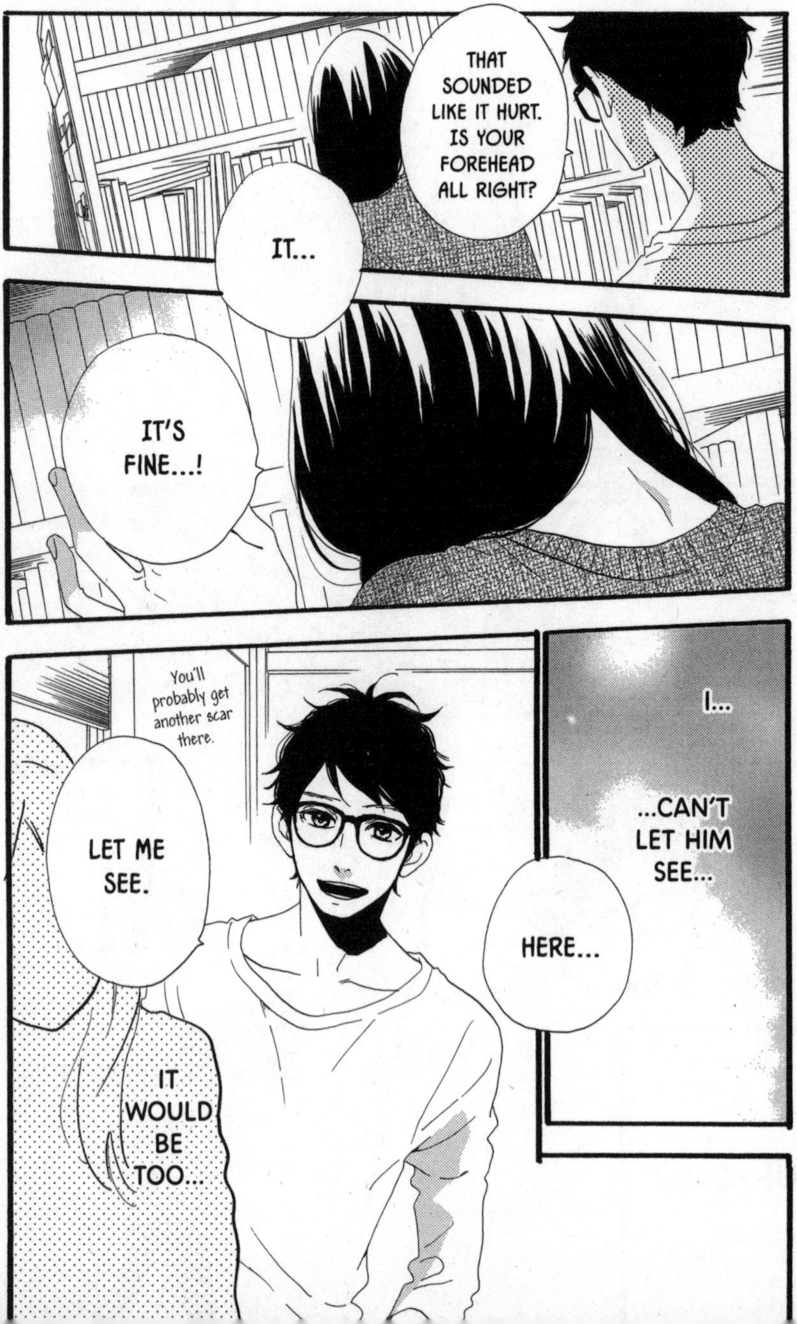
THAT SOUNDED LIKE IT HURT. IS YOUR FOREHEAD ALL RIGHT?
IT...
IT'S FINE...!
I...
...CAN'T LET HIM SEE...
You'll probably get another scar there.
LET ME SEE.
HERE...
IT WOULD BE TOO...

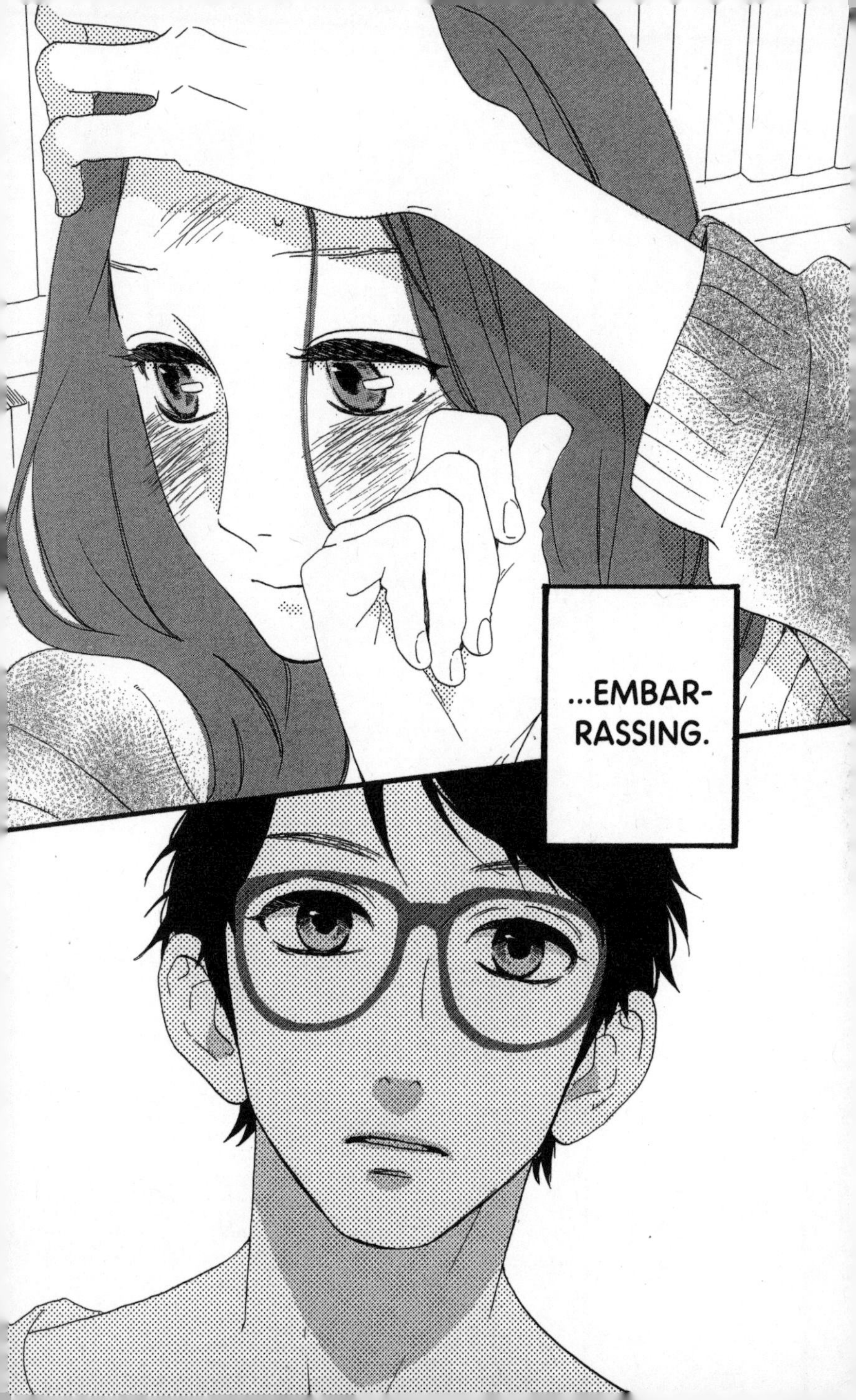
...EMBAR-
RASSING.

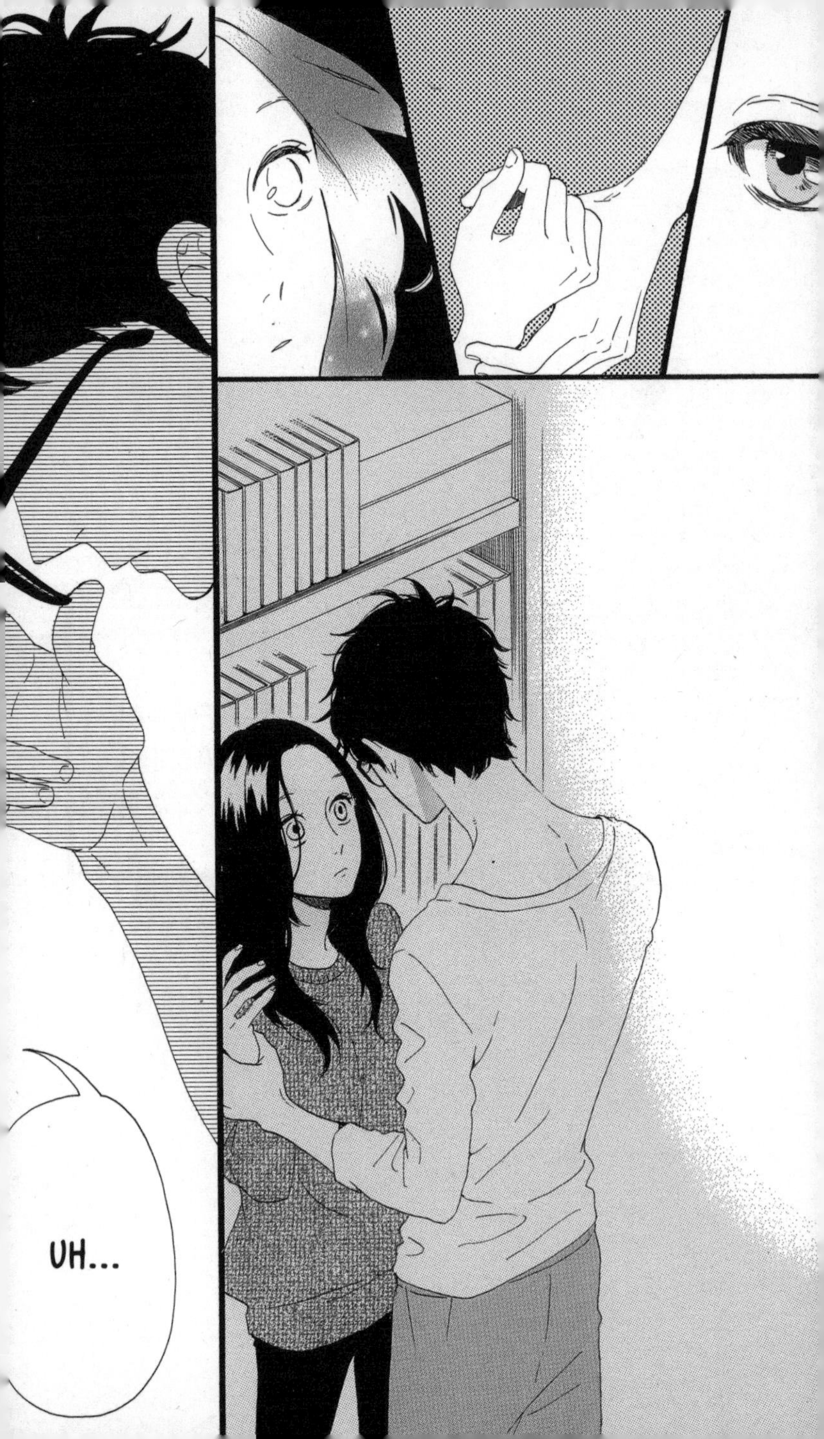
UH...

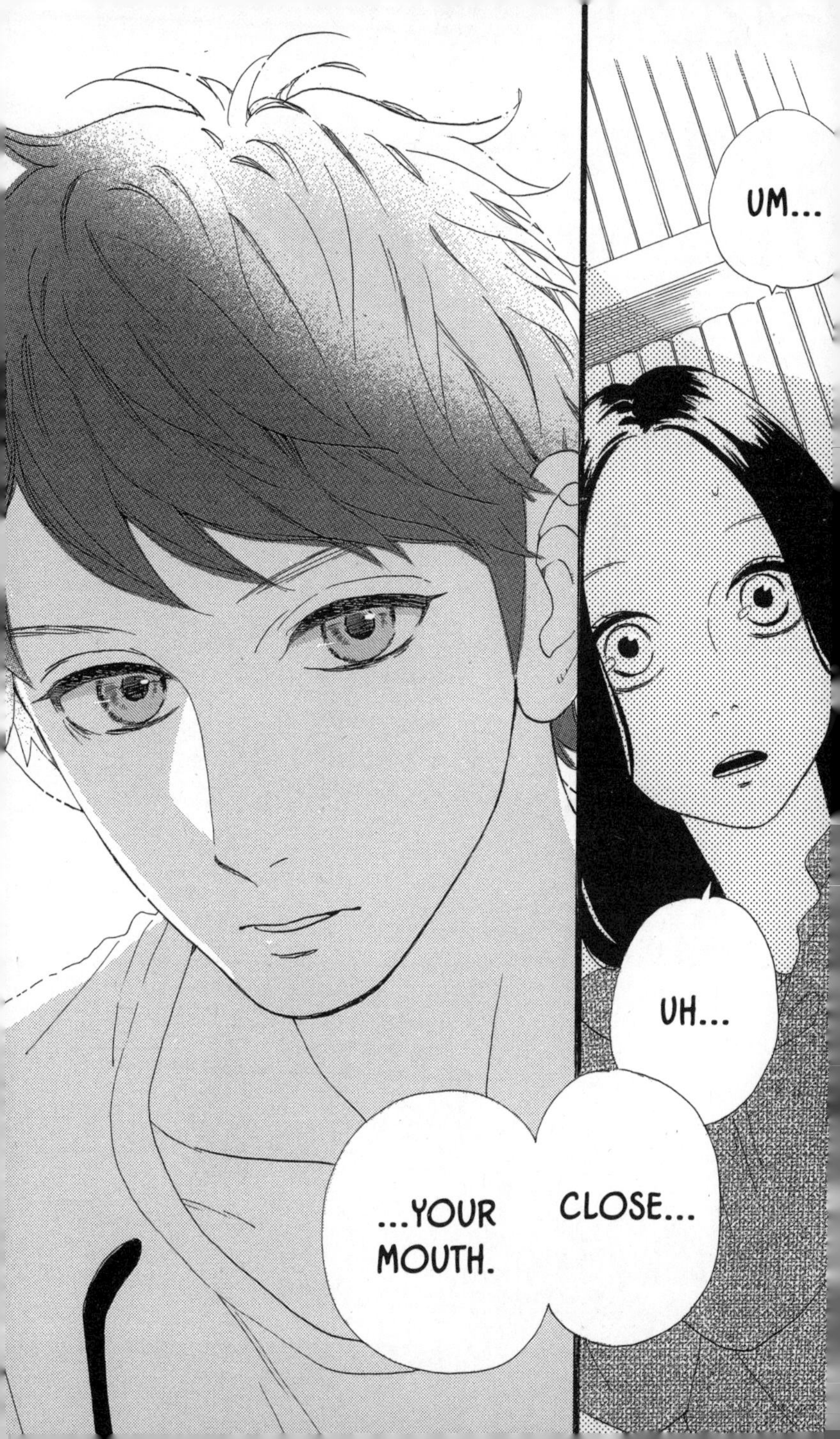
UM...
UH...
CLOSE...
...YOUR MOUTH.

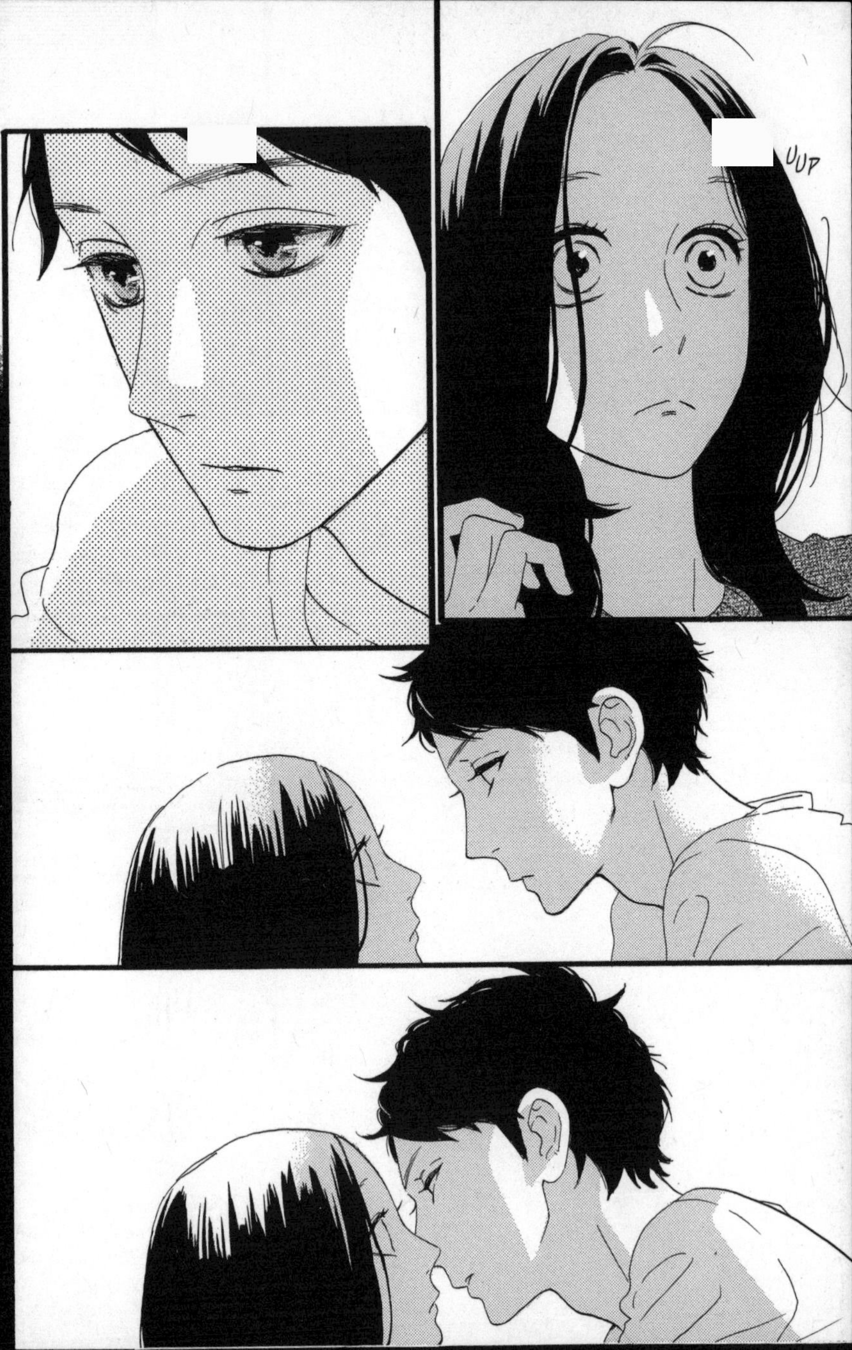
UUP

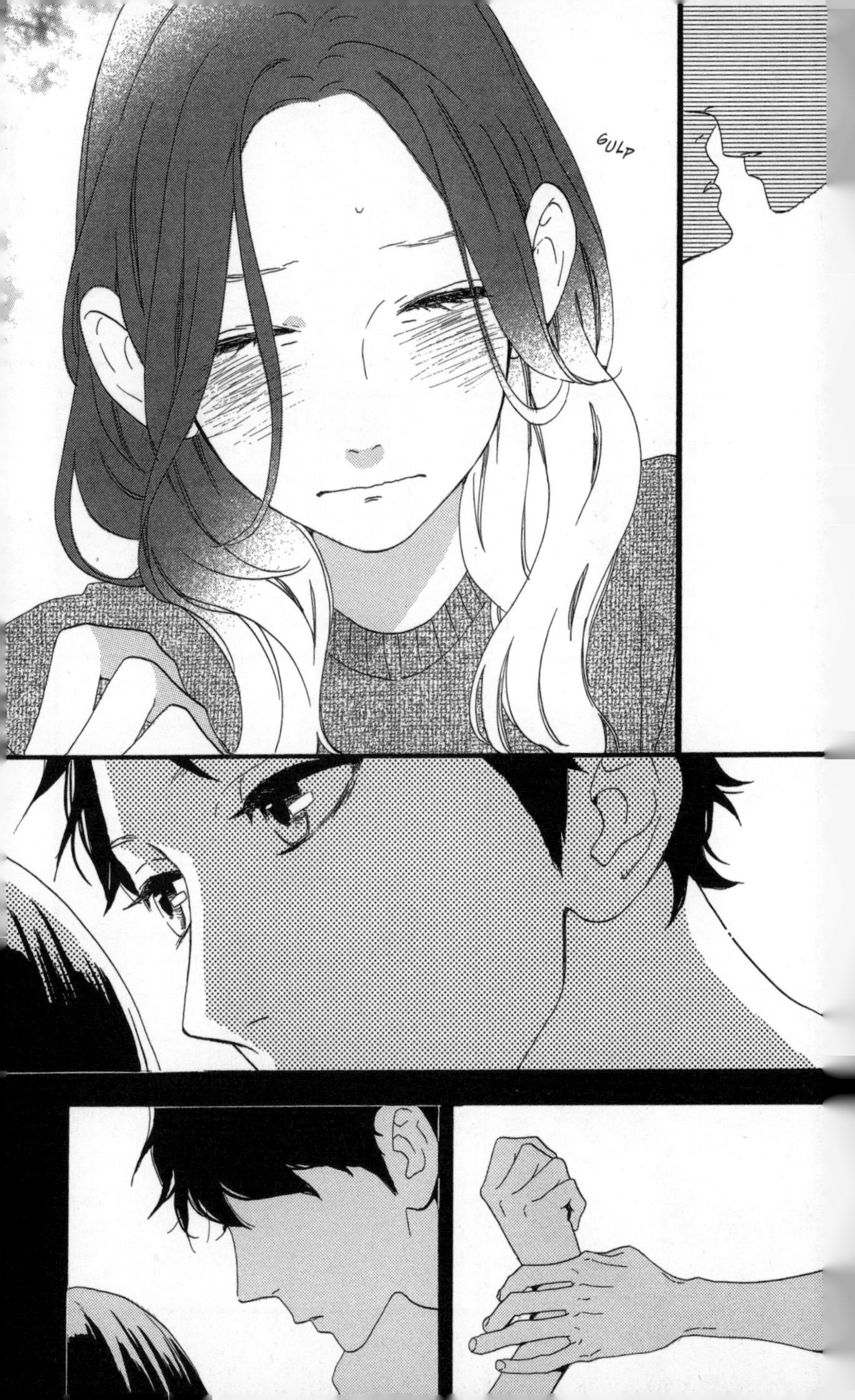
GULP

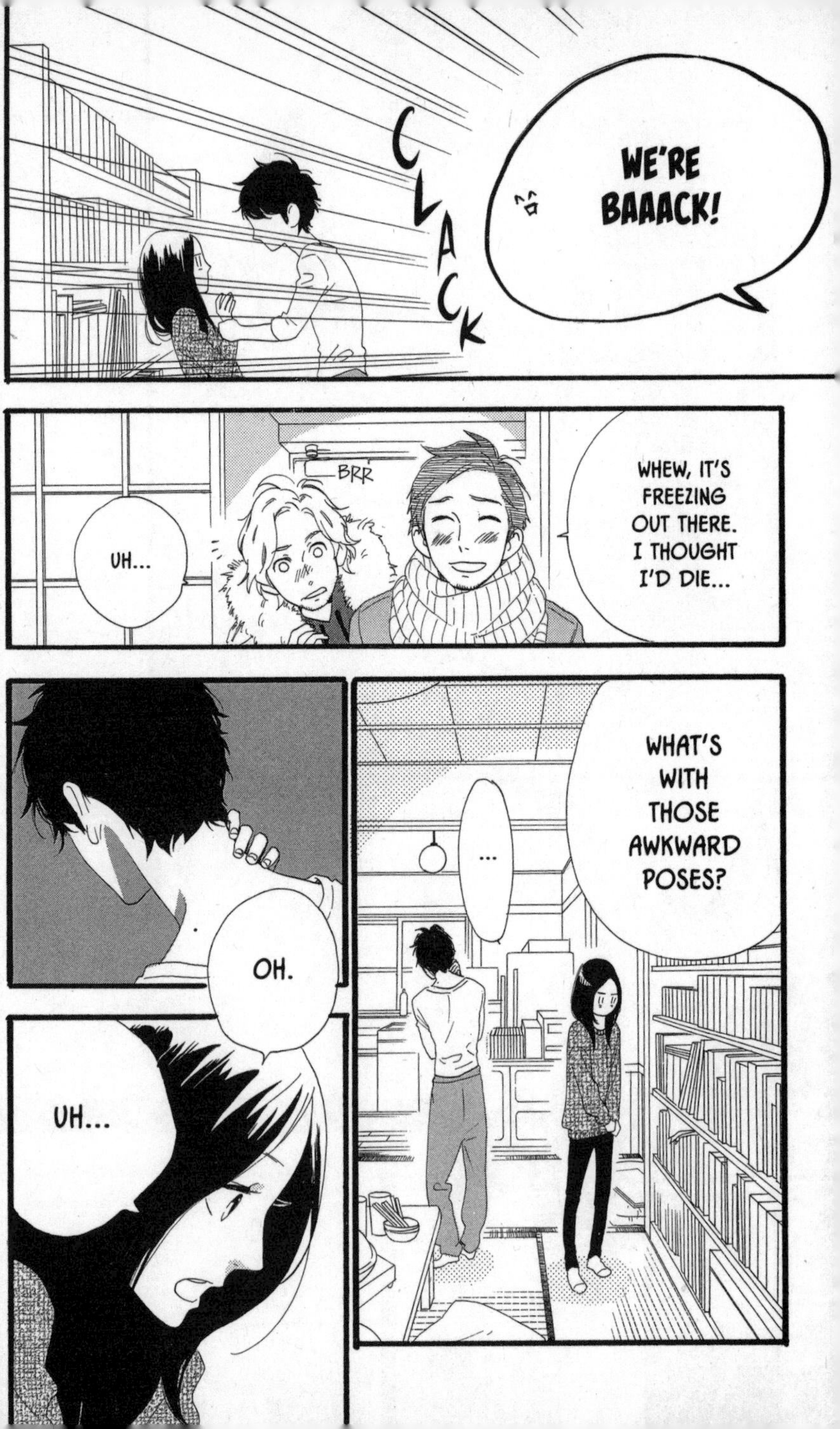
WE'RE BAAACK!
CLACK
WHEW, IT'S FREEZING OUT THERE. I THOUGHT I'D DIE...
BRR
UH...
WHAT'S WITH THOSE AWKWARD POSES?
...
OH.
UH...

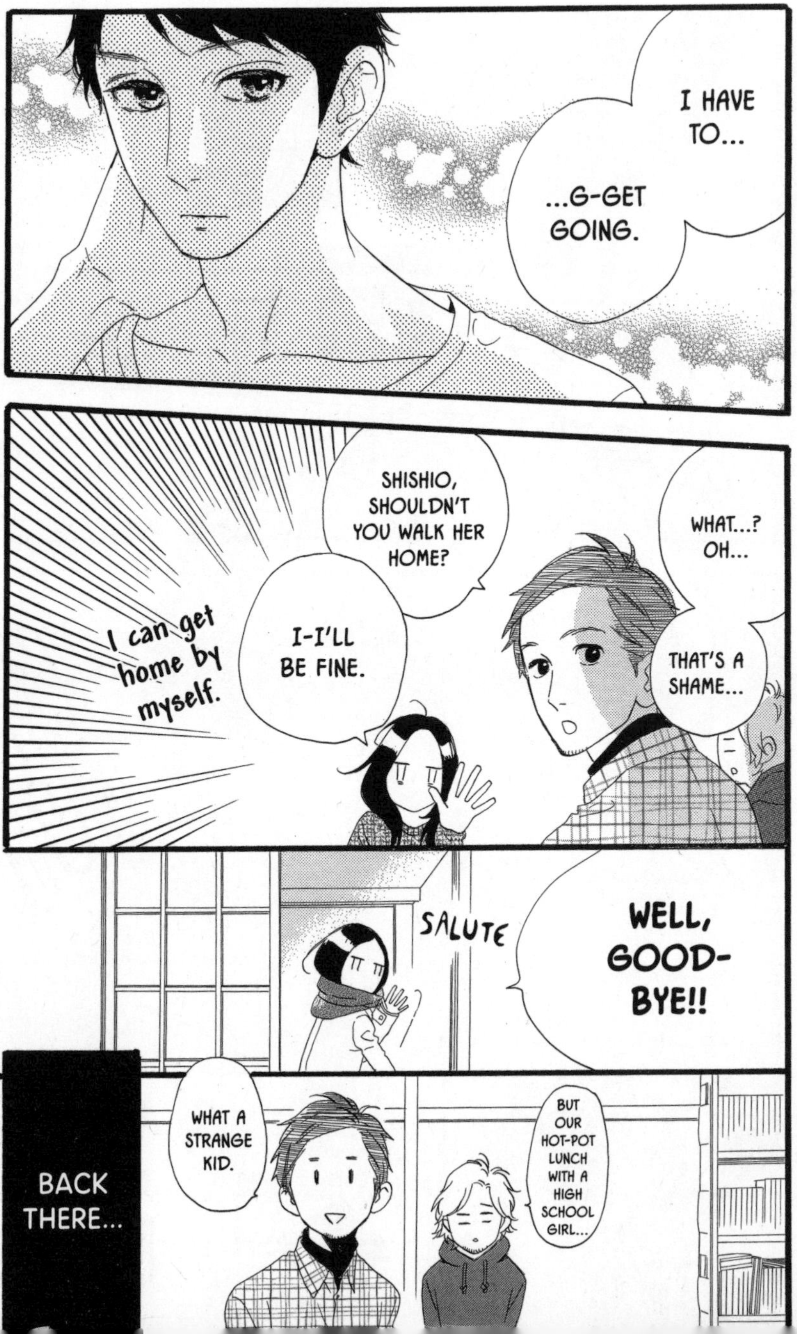
I HAVE TO...
...G-GET GOING.
WHAT...? OH...
SHISHIO, SHOULDN'T YOU WALK HER HOME?
THAT'S A SHAME...
I-I'LL BE FINE.
I can get home by myself.
WELL, GOOD-BYE!!
SALUTE
BUT OUR HOT-POT LUNCH WITH A HIGH SCHOOL GIRL...
WHAT A STRANGE KID.
BACK THERE...

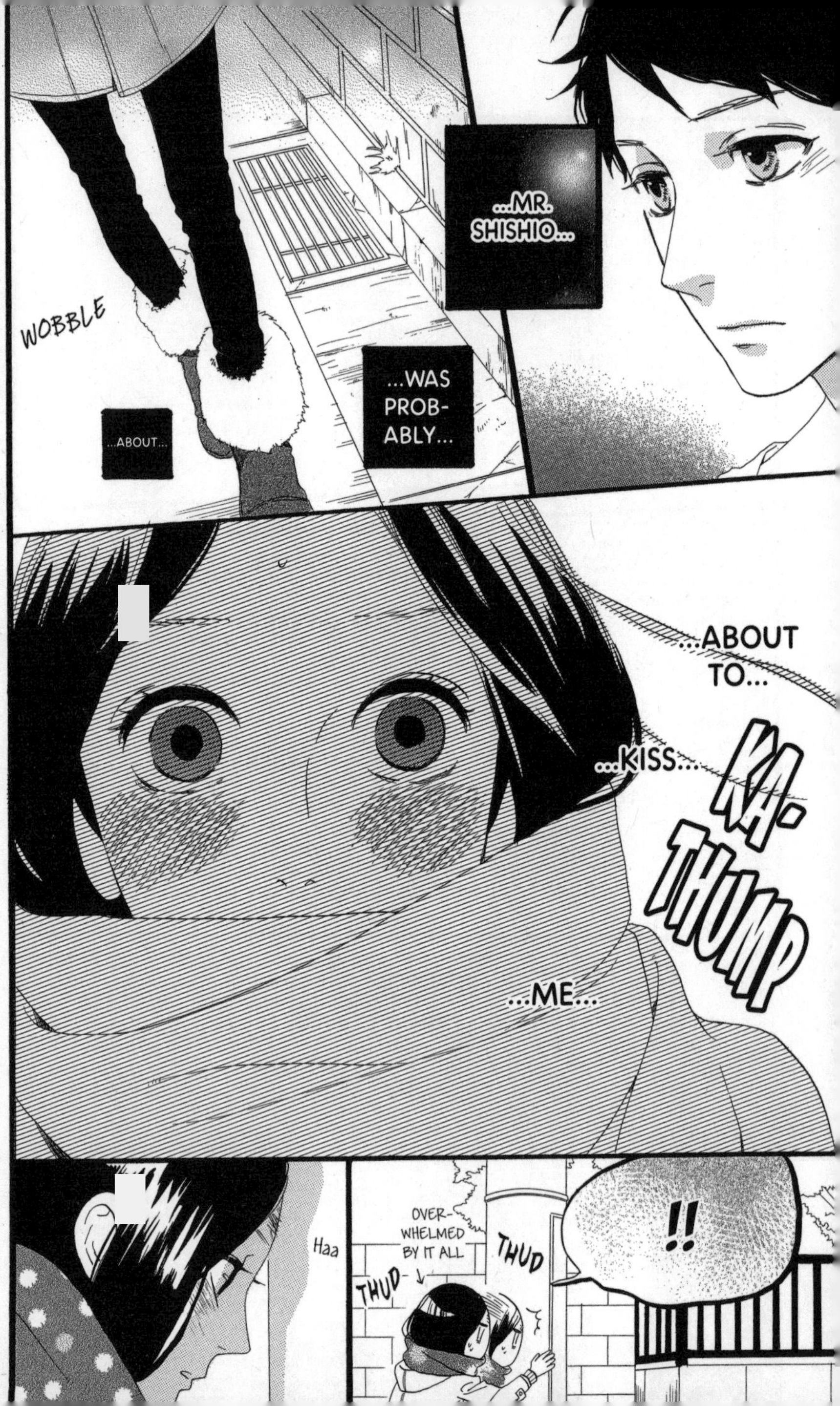
...MR. SHISHIO...
...WAS PROBABLY...
...ABOUT...
WOBBLE
...ABOUT TO...
...KISS...
KA-THUMP
...ME...
!!
THUD
OVER-WHELMED BY IT ALL
THUD-
Haa

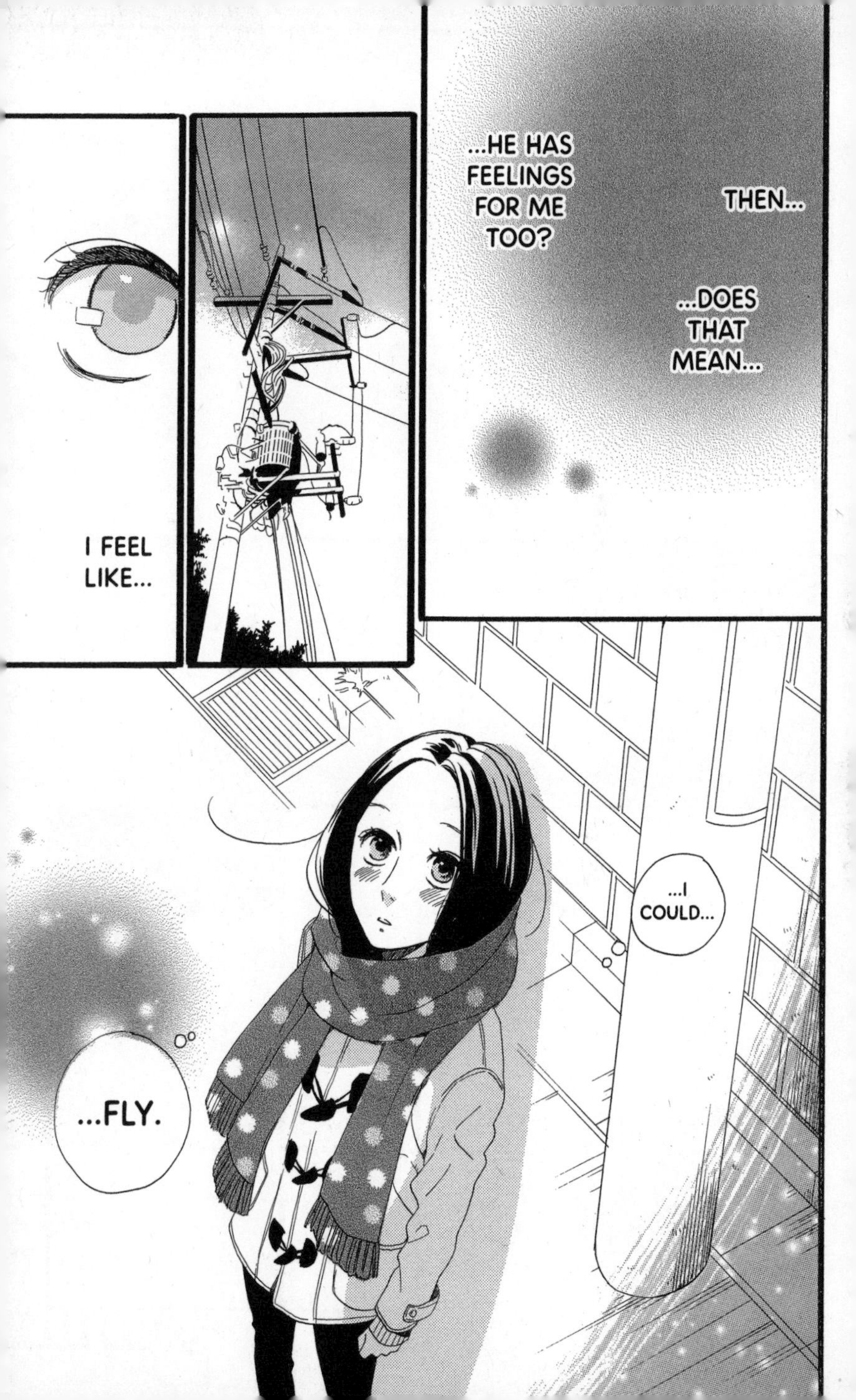
THEN...
...DOES THAT MEAN...
...HE HAS FEELINGS FOR ME TOO?
I FEEL LIKE...
...I COULD...
...FLY.

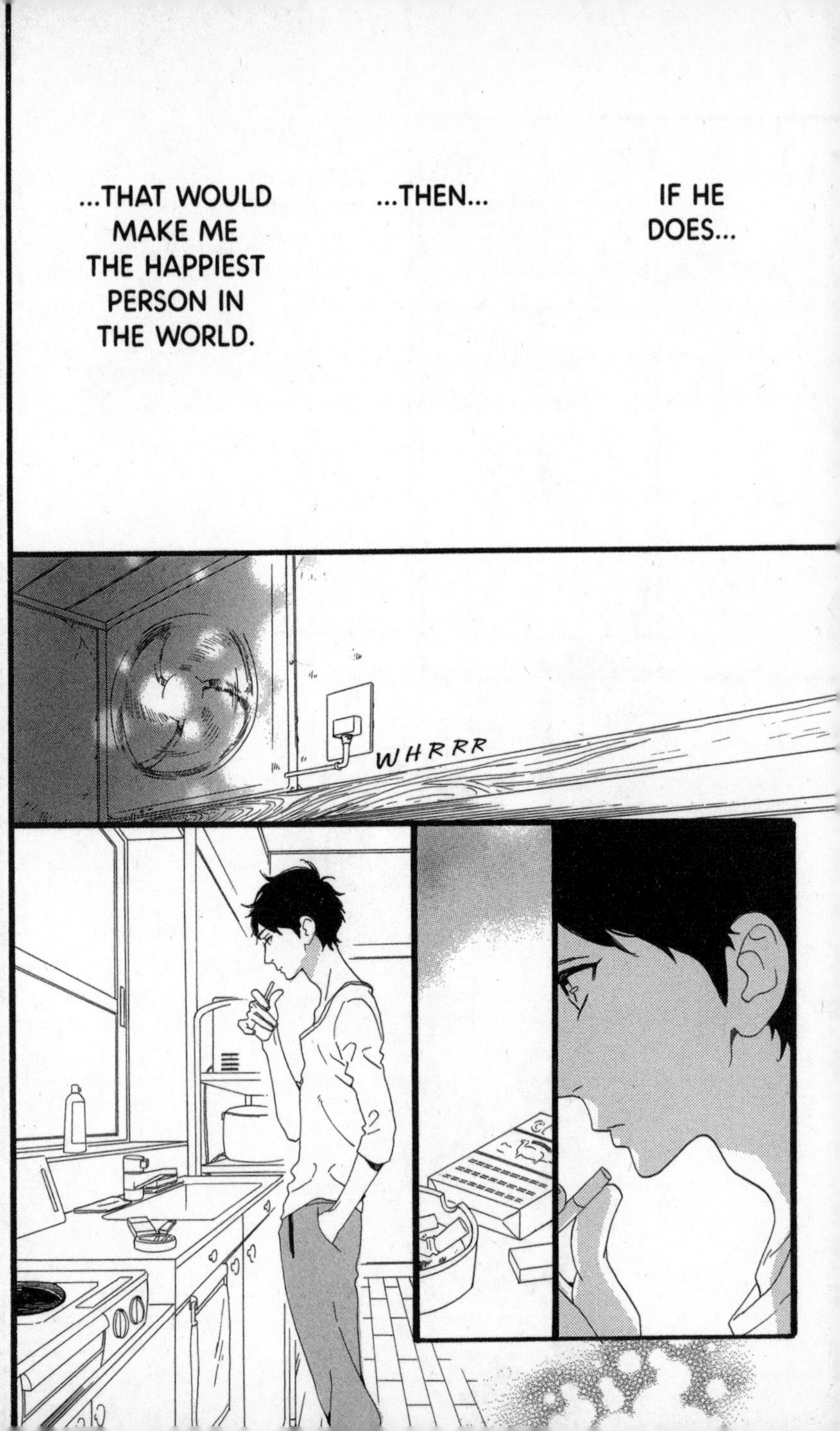
IF HE DOES...
...THEN...
...THAT WOULD MAKE ME THE HAPPIEST PERSON IN THE WORLD.
WHRRR

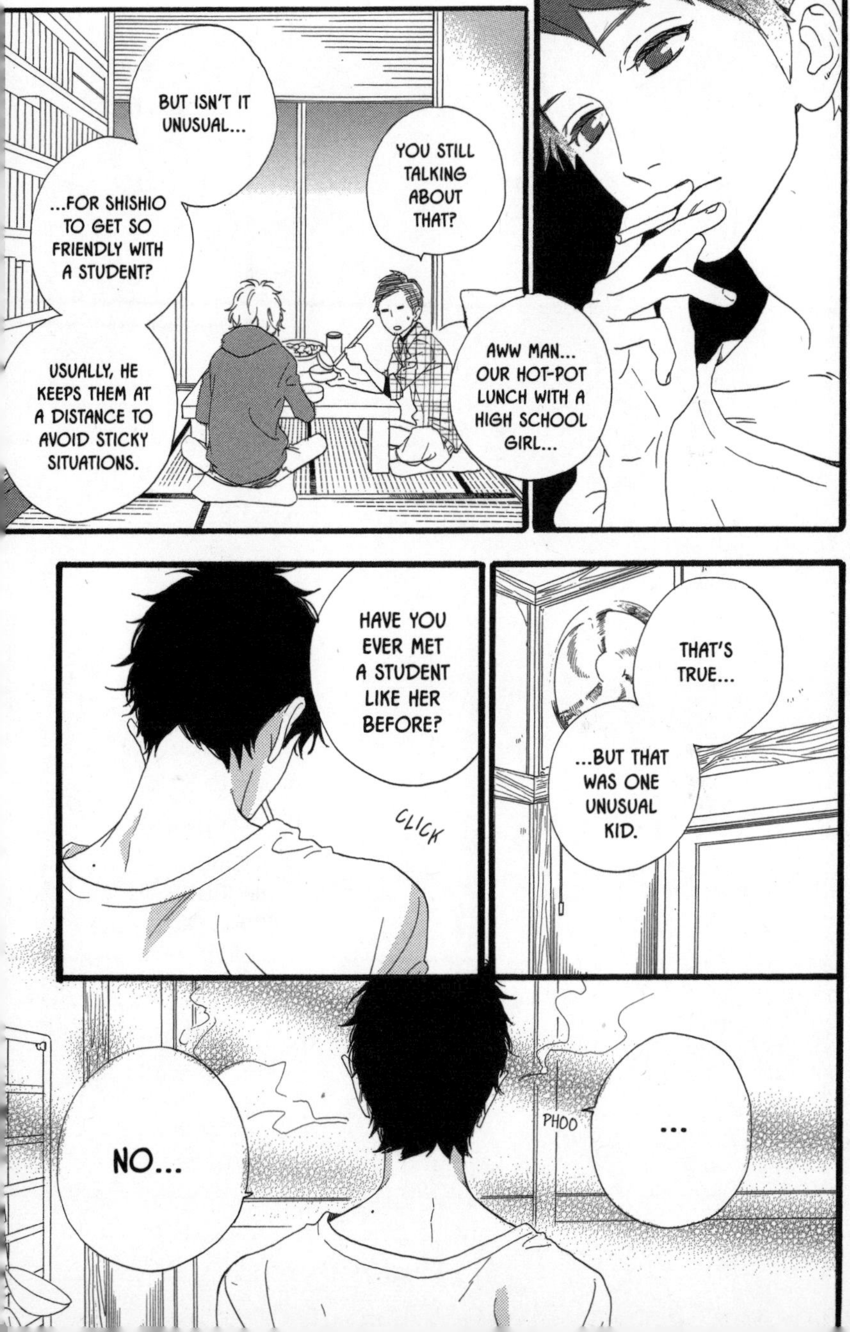
AWW MAN... OUR HOT-POT LUNCH WITH A HIGH SCHOOL GIRL...
YOU STILL TALKING ABOUT THAT?
BUT ISN'T IT UNUSUAL...
...FOR SHISHIO TO GET SO FRIENDLY WITH A STUDENT?
USUALLY, HE KEEPS THEM AT A DISTANCE TO AVOID STICKY SITUATIONS.
THAT'S TRUE...
...BUT THAT WAS ONE UNUSUAL KID.
HAVE YOU EVER MET A STUDENT LIKE HER BEFORE?
CLICK
PHOO
...
NO...

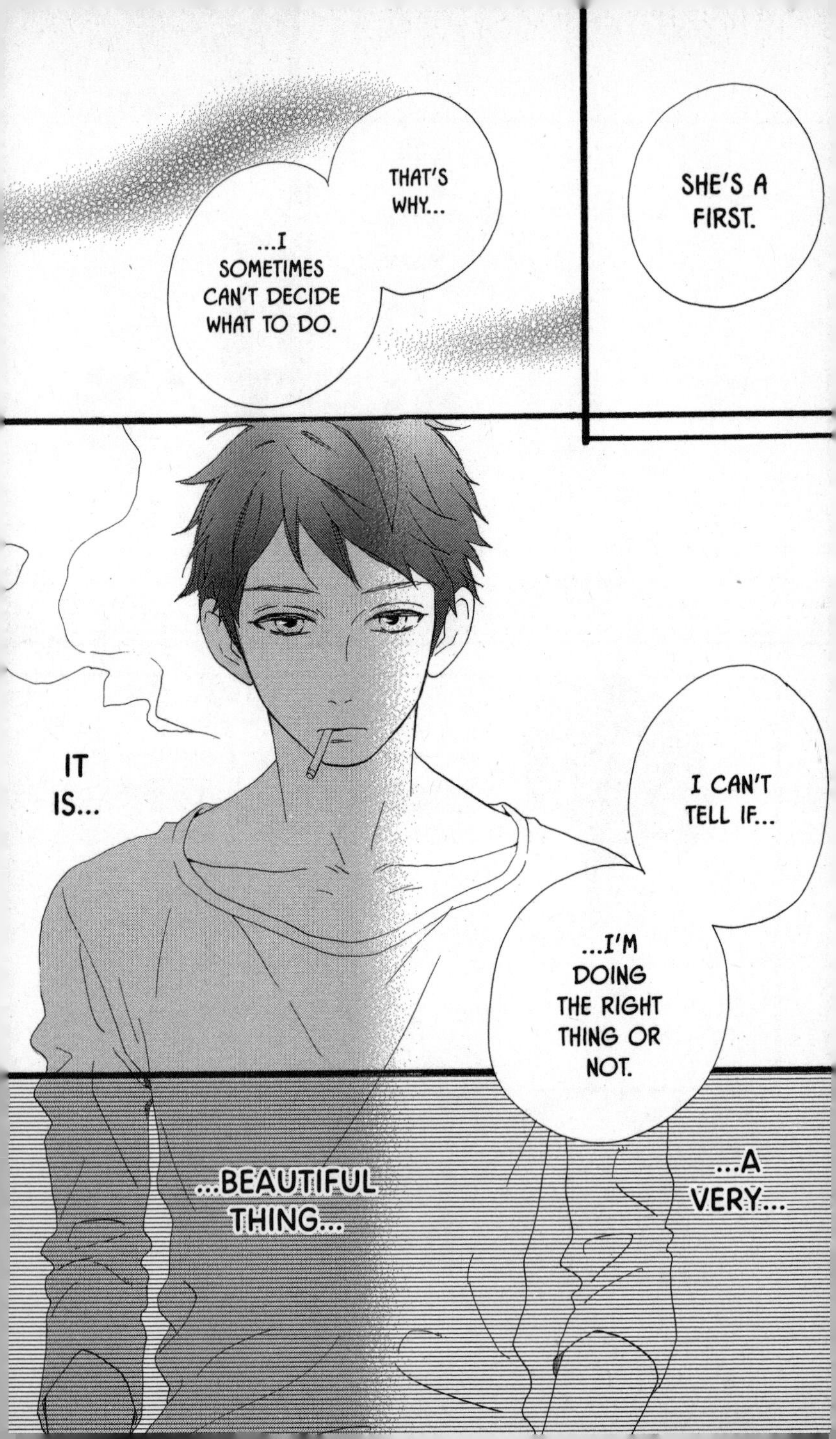
SHE'S A FIRST.
THAT'S WHY...
...I SOMETIMES CAN'T DECIDE WHAT TO DO.
I CAN'T TELL IF...
...I'M DOING THE RIGHT THING OR NOT.
IT IS...
...A VERY...
...BEAUTIFUL THING...

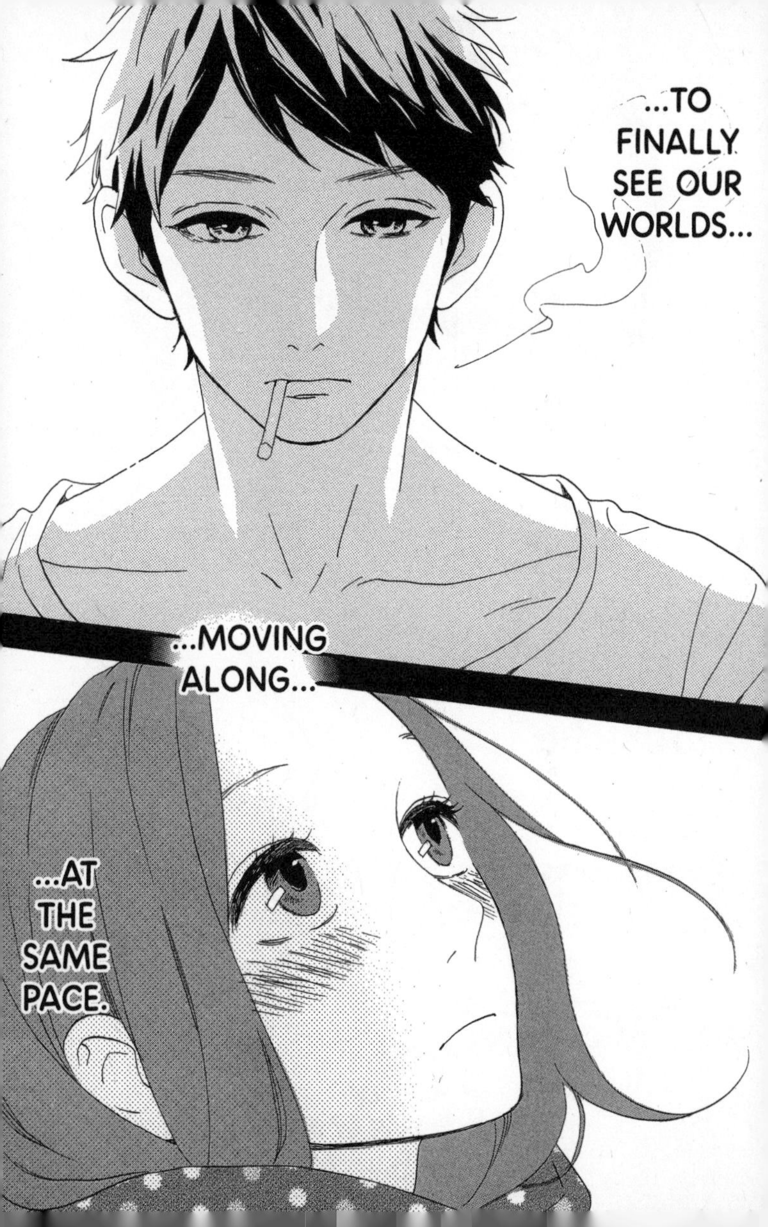
...TO FINALLY SEE OUR WORLDS...
...MOVING ALONG...
...AT THE SAME PACE.

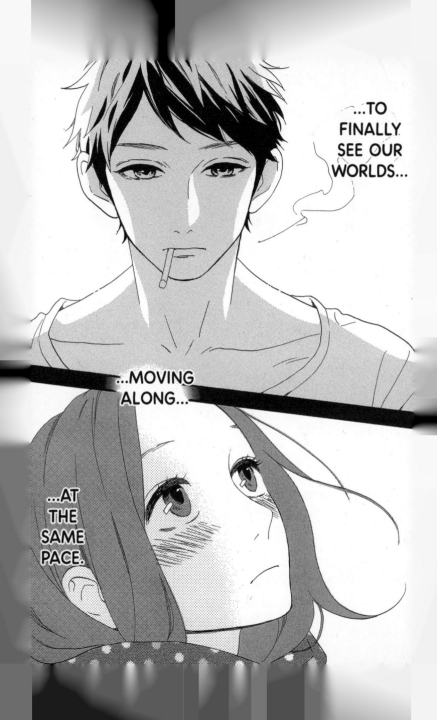

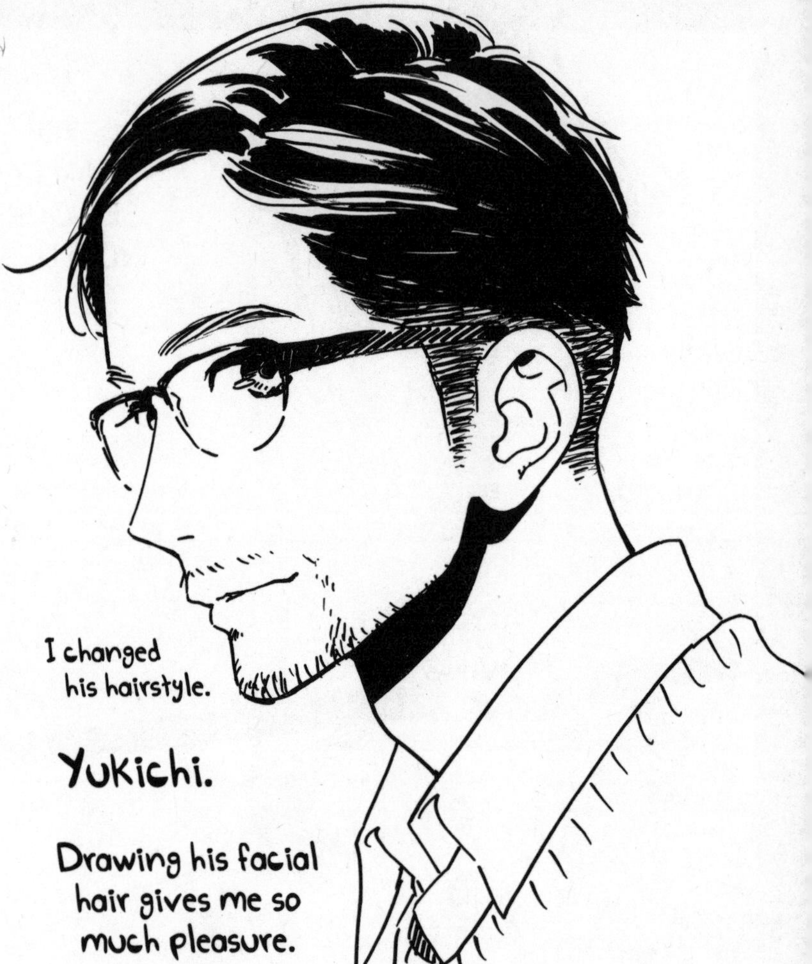

I changed his hairstyle.

Yukichi.

Drawing his facial hair gives me so much pleasure.

His glasses and beard go together like *yakiniku* and beer. Am I the only one who thinks that?

RAIN
LOOKS
GOOD
ON
HER.

TsuYuKaoru

SHAAA
GOOD MORNING, MORINO.
MORNING.
LOOK AT THIS! I'M SOAKED DOWN TO MY SWEATER.
I'VE GOT THE WORST LUCK.
THAT DOWN-POUR CAME OUT OF NOWHERE.
YEAH, BUT WHY AREN'T YOU WET?
I ALWAYS CARRY AN UMBRELLA.

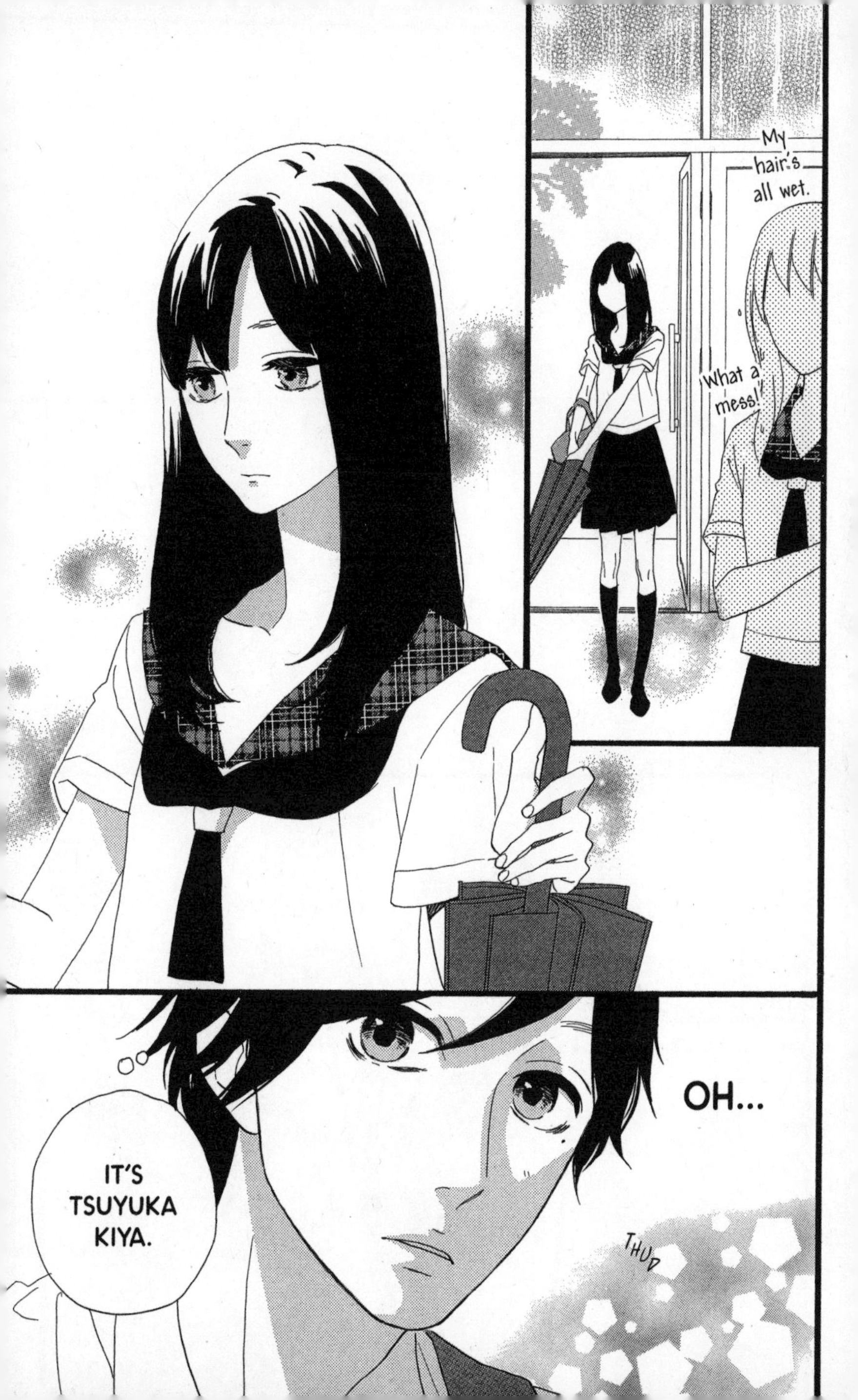
My hair's all wet.
What a mess!
OH...
IT'S TSUYUKA KIYA.
THUD

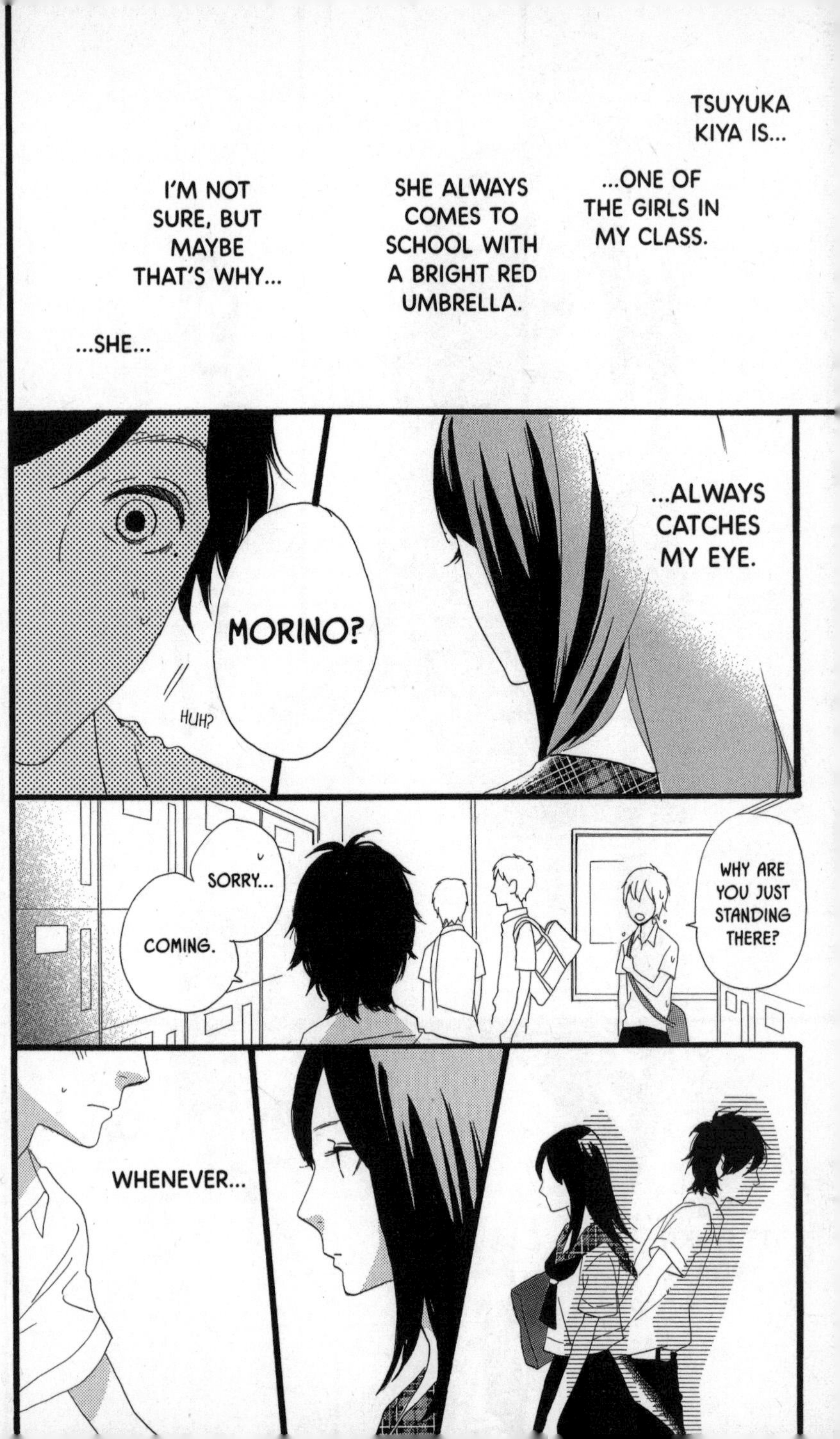
TSUYUKA KIYA IS...
...ONE OF THE GIRLS IN MY CLASS.
SHE ALWAYS COMES TO SCHOOL WITH A BRIGHT RED UMBRELLA.
I'M NOT SURE, BUT MAYBE THAT'S WHY...
...SHE...
...ALWAYS CATCHES MY EYE.
MORINO?
HUH?
WHY ARE YOU JUST STANDING THERE?
SORRY...
COMING.
WHENEVER...

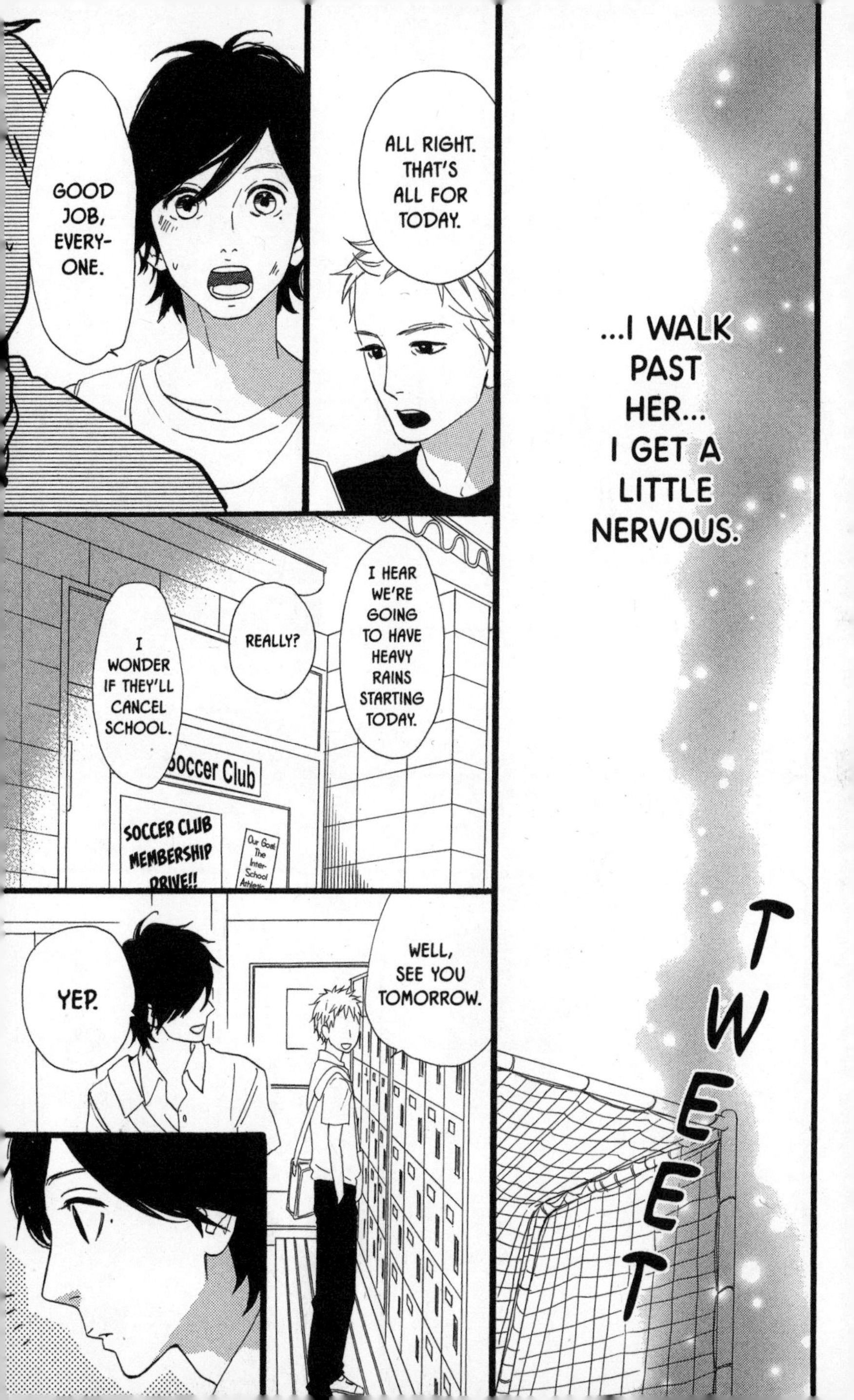
...I WALK PAST HER... I GET A LITTLE NERVOUS.
TWEET
ALL RIGHT. THAT'S ALL FOR TODAY.
GOOD JOB, EVERYONE.
I HEAR WE'RE GOING TO HAVE HEAVY RAINS STARTING TODAY.
REALLY?
I WONDER IF THEY'LL CANCEL SCHOOL.
Soccer Club
SOCCER CLUB MEMBERSHIP DRIVE!!
Our Goal: The Inter-School
WELL, SEE YOU TOMORROW.
YEP.

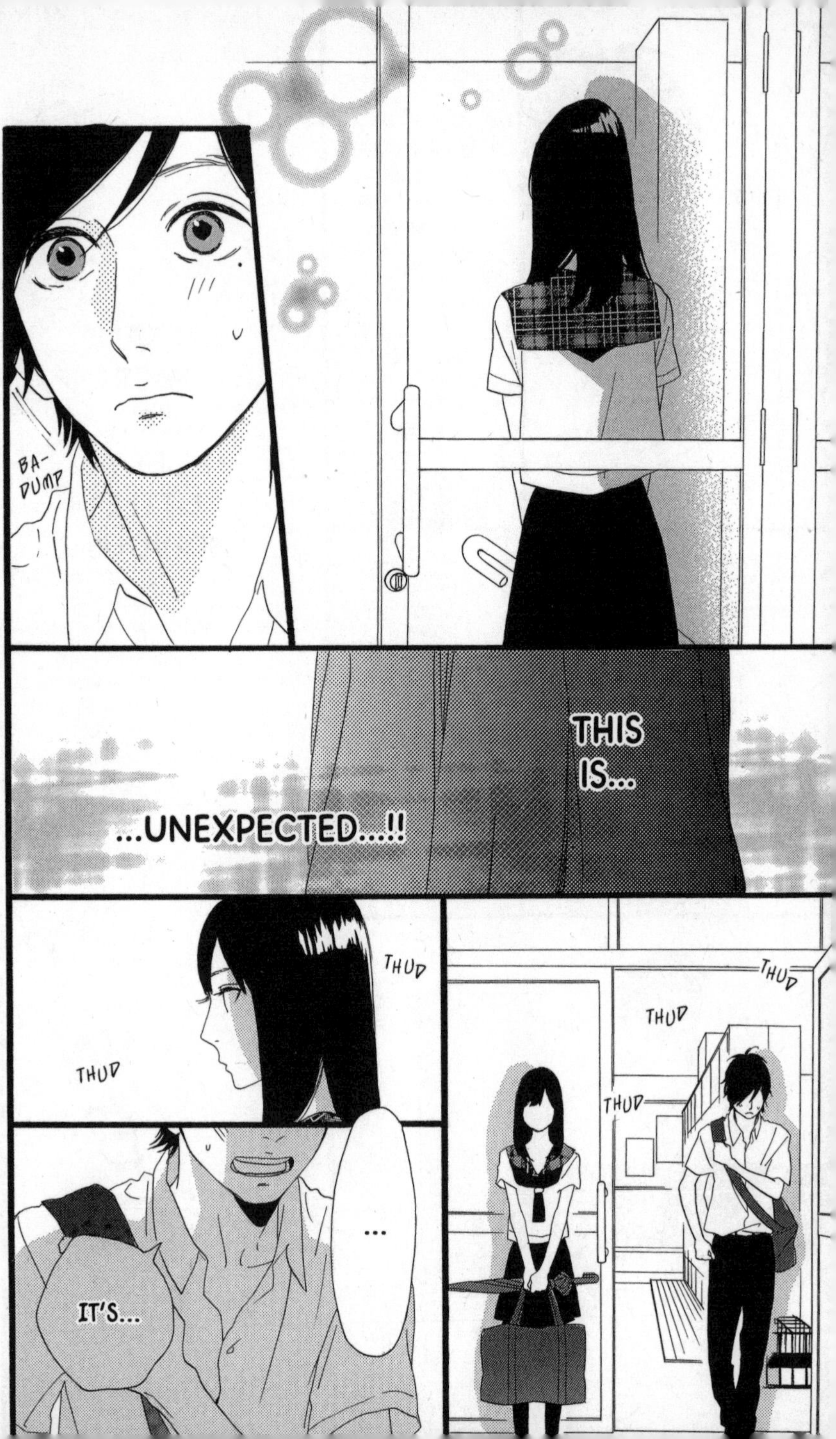
BA-DUMP
THIS IS...
...UNEXPECTED...!!
THUD
THUD
THUD
THUD
THUD
...
IT'S...

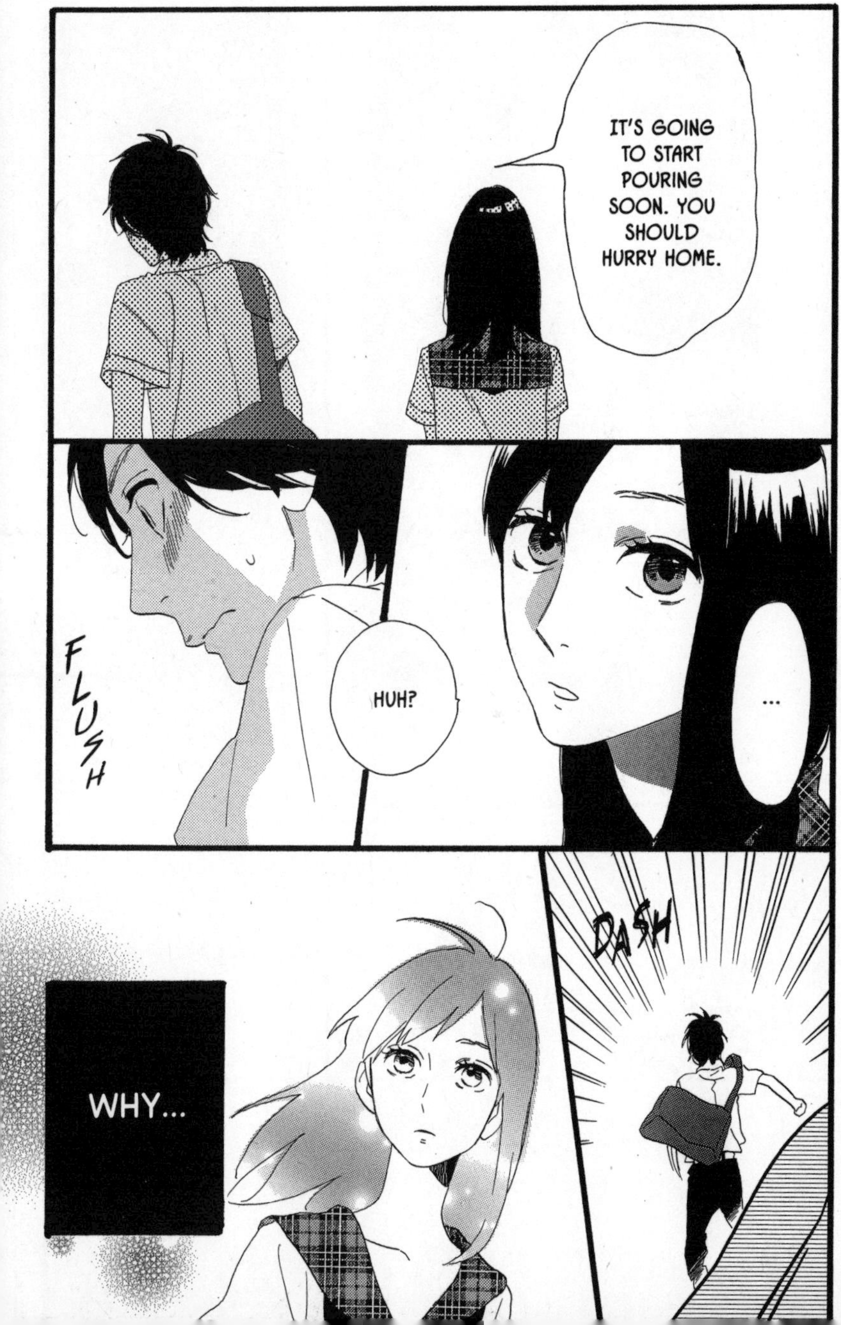
IT'S GOING TO START POURING SOON. YOU SHOULD HURRY HOME.
...
HUH?
FLUSH
DASH
WHY...

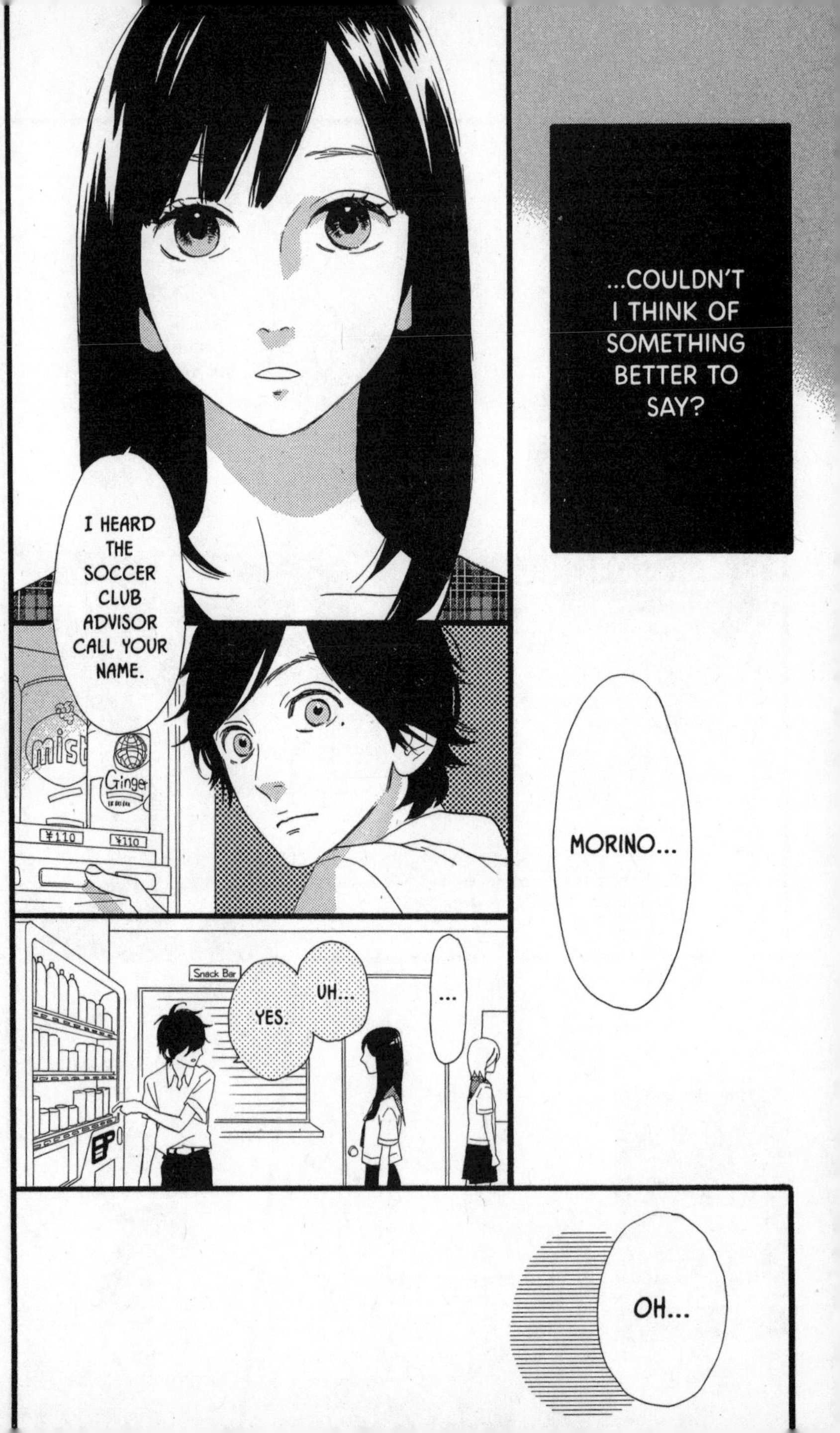
...COULDN'T I THINK OF SOMETHING BETTER TO SAY?
MORINO...
I HEARD THE SOCCER CLUB ADVISOR CALL YOUR NAME.
mist
Ginger
¥110
¥110
...
UH... YES.
Snack Bar
OH...

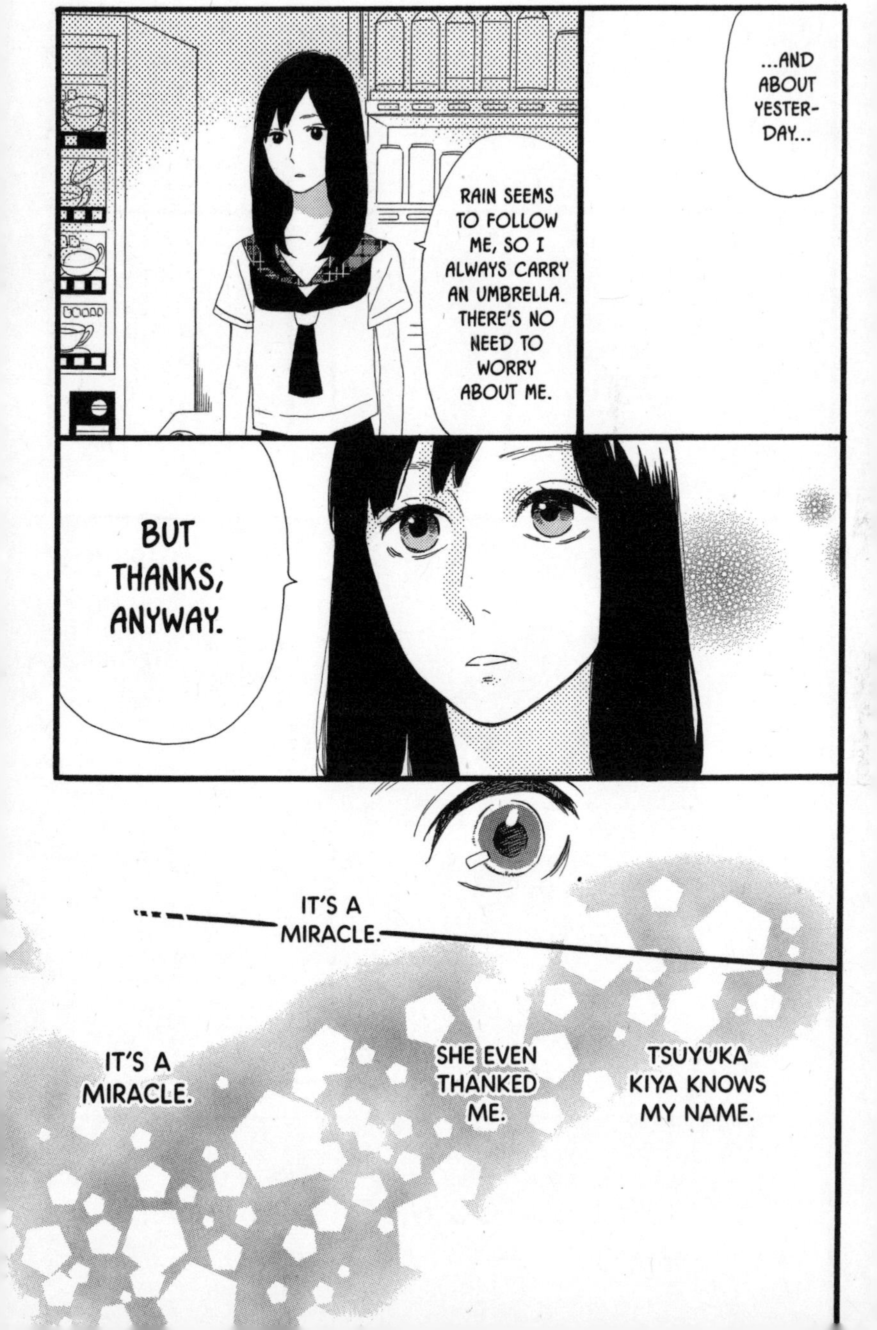

...AND ABOUT YESTER-DAY...
RAIN SEEMS TO FOLLOW ME, SO I ALWAYS CARRY AN UMBRELLA. THERE'S NO NEED TO WORRY ABOUT ME.
BUT THANKS, ANYWAY.
IT'S A MIRACLE.
TSUYUKA KIYA KNOWS MY NAME.
SHE EVEN THANKED ME.
IT'S A MIRACLE.

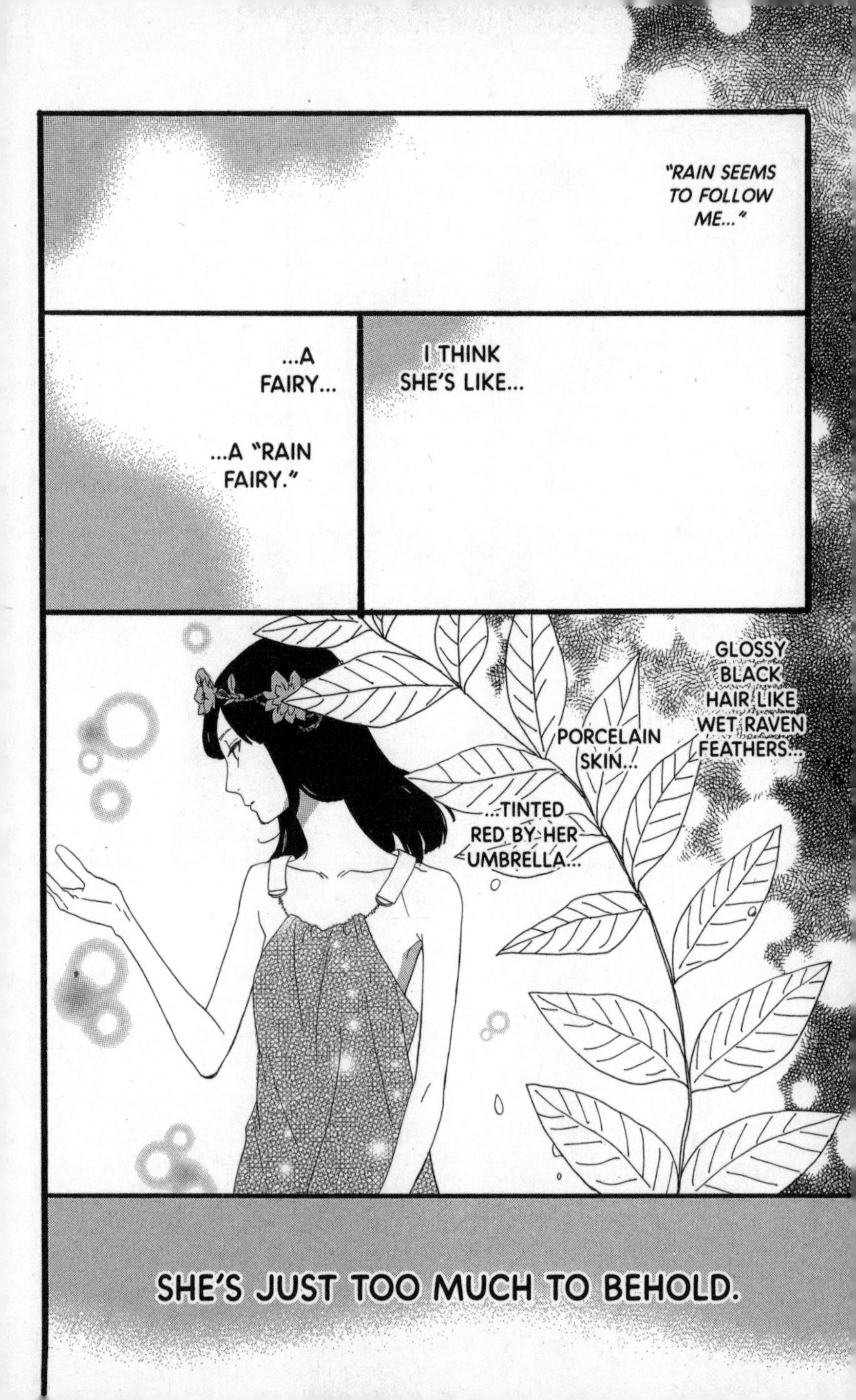
"RAIN SEEMS TO FOLLOW ME..."
I THINK SHE'S LIKE...
...A FAIRY...
...A "RAIN FAIRY."
GLOSSY BLACK HAIR LIKE WET RAVEN FEATHERS...
PORCELAIN SKIN...
...TINTED RED BY HER UMBRELLA...
SHE'S JUST TOO MUCH TO BEHOLD.

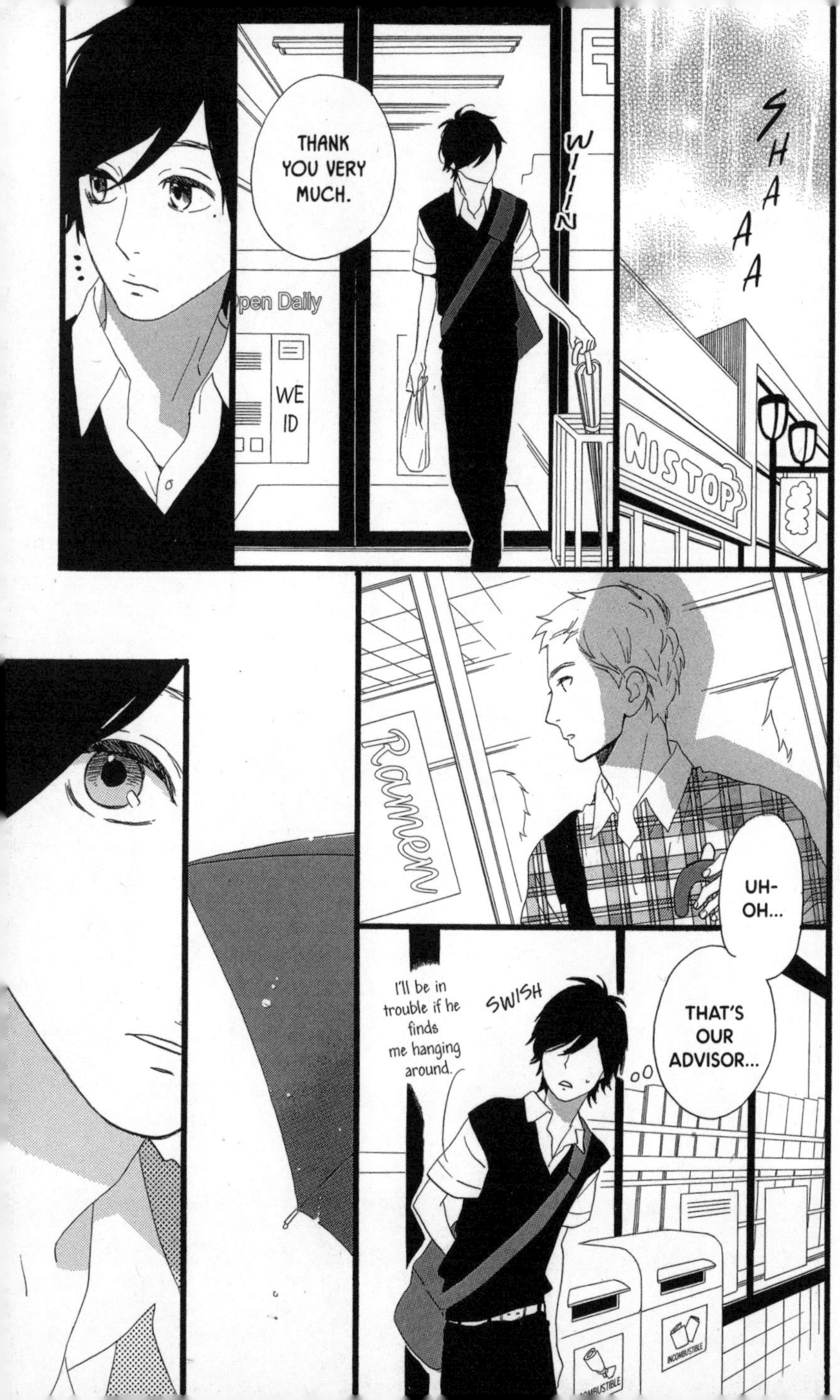
SHAAAA
NISTOP
WIIIN
THANK YOU VERY MUCH.
Open Daily
WE
ID
Ramen
UH-OH...
THAT'S OUR ADVISOR...
SWISH
I'll be in trouble if he finds me hanging around.
INCOMBUSTIBLE

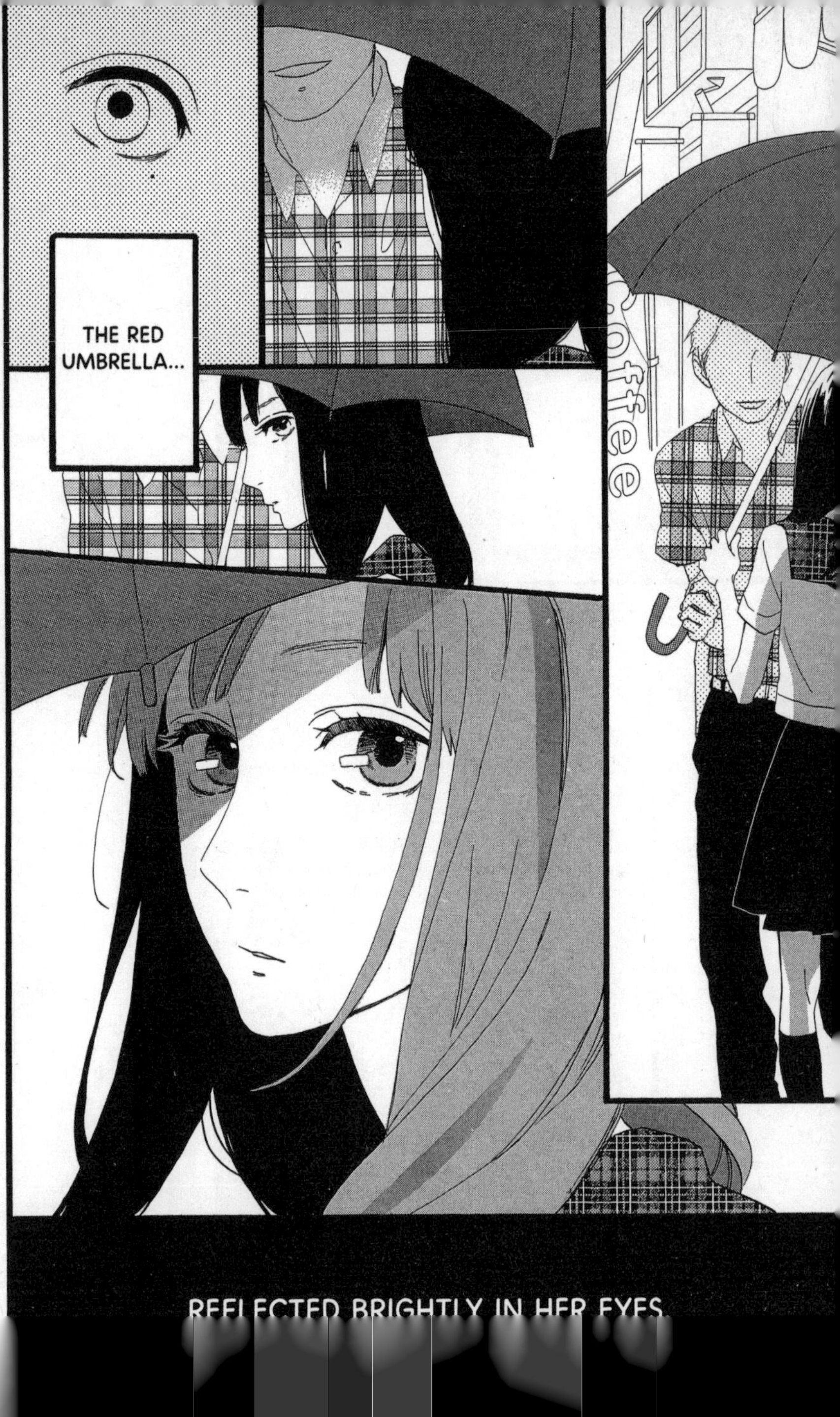
coffee
THE RED UMBRELLA...
REFLECTED BRIGHTLY IN HER EYES.

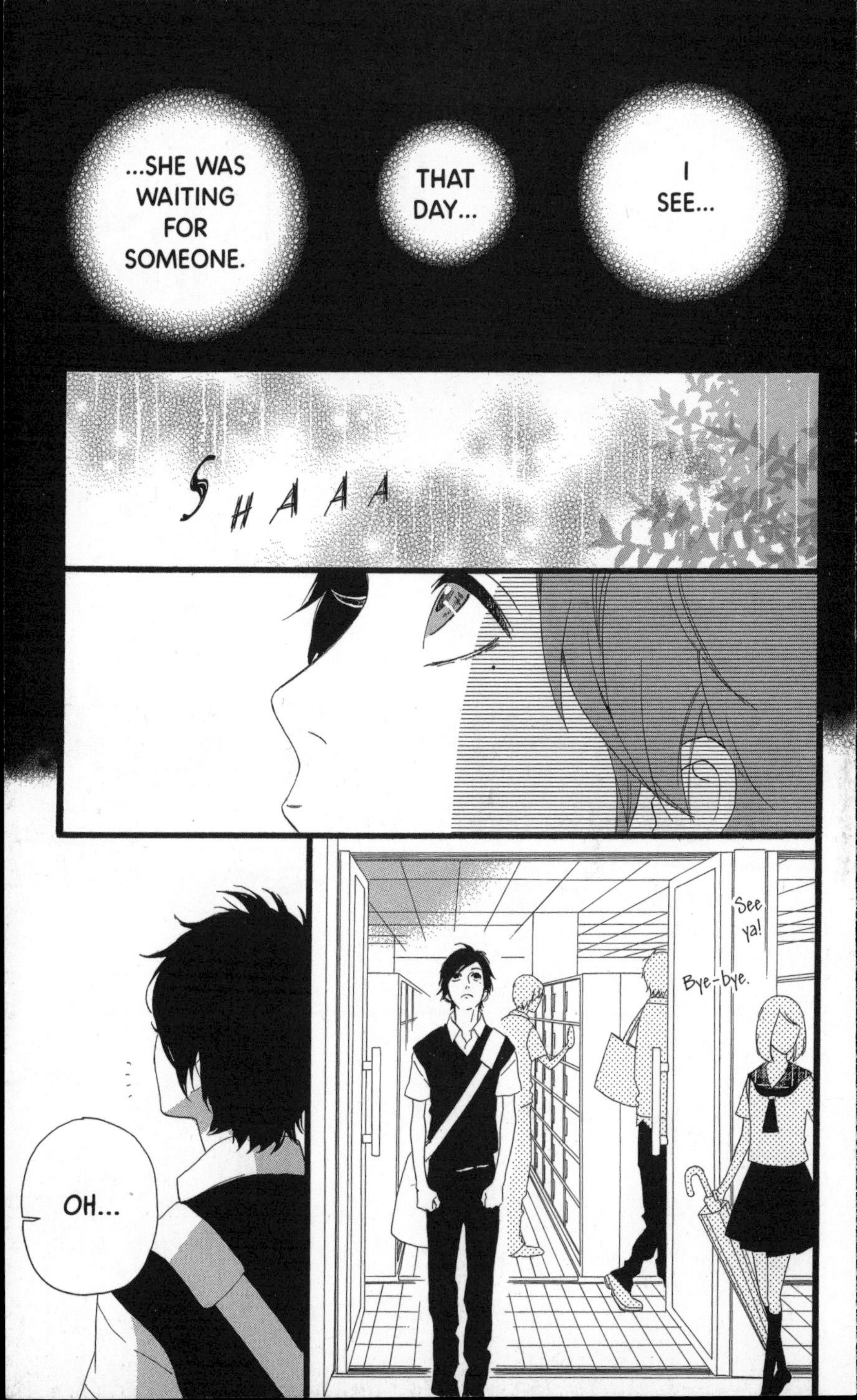
I SEE...
THAT DAY...
...SHE WAS WAITING FOR SOMEONE.
SHAAA
See ya!
Bye-bye.
OH...

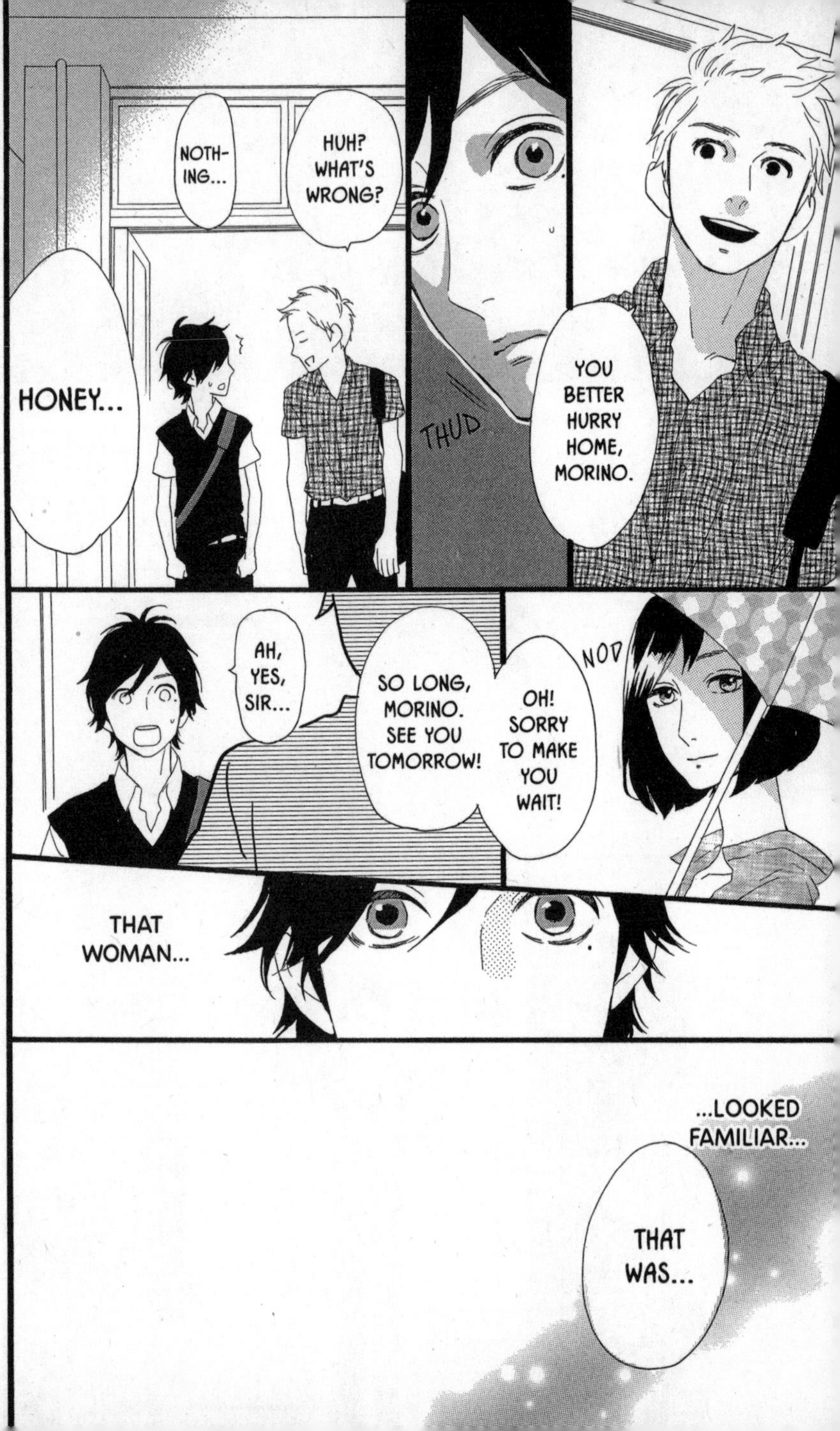
YOU BETTER HURRY HOME, MORINO.
THUD
HUH? WHAT'S WRONG?
NOTH-ING...
HONEY...
NOD
OH! SORRY TO MAKE YOU WAIT!
SO LONG, MORINO. SEE YOU TOMORROW!
AH, YES, SIR...
THAT WOMAN...
...LOOKED FAMILIAR...
THAT WAS...

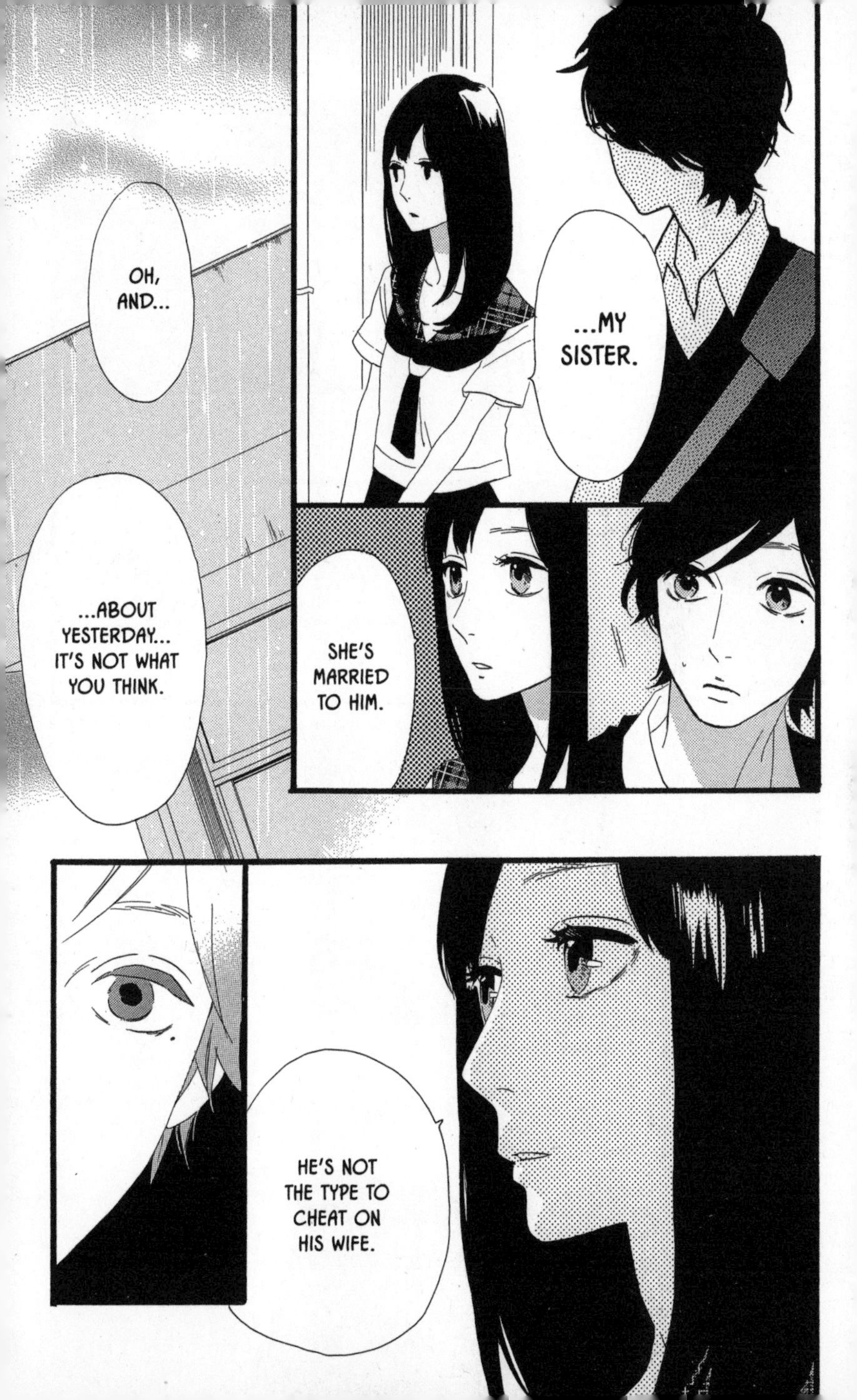
...MY SISTER.
SHE'S MARRIED TO HIM.
OH, AND...
...ABOUT YESTERDAY... IT'S NOT WHAT YOU THINK.
HE'S NOT THE TYPE TO CHEAT ON HIS WIFE.

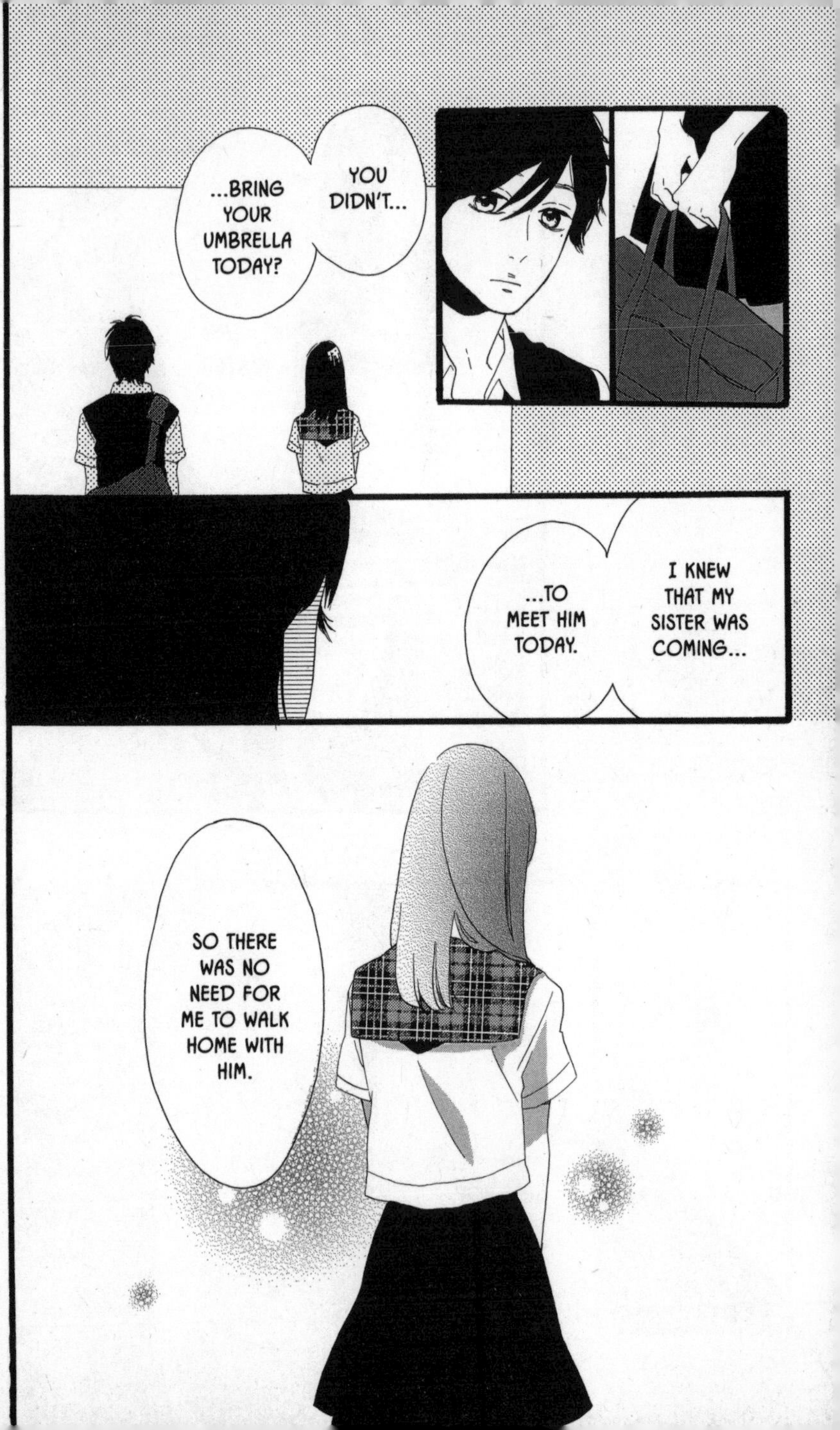
YOU DIDN'T...
...BRING YOUR UMBRELLA TODAY?
I KNEW THAT MY SISTER WAS COMING...
...TO MEET HIM TODAY.
SO THERE WAS NO NEED FOR ME TO WALK HOME WITH HIM.

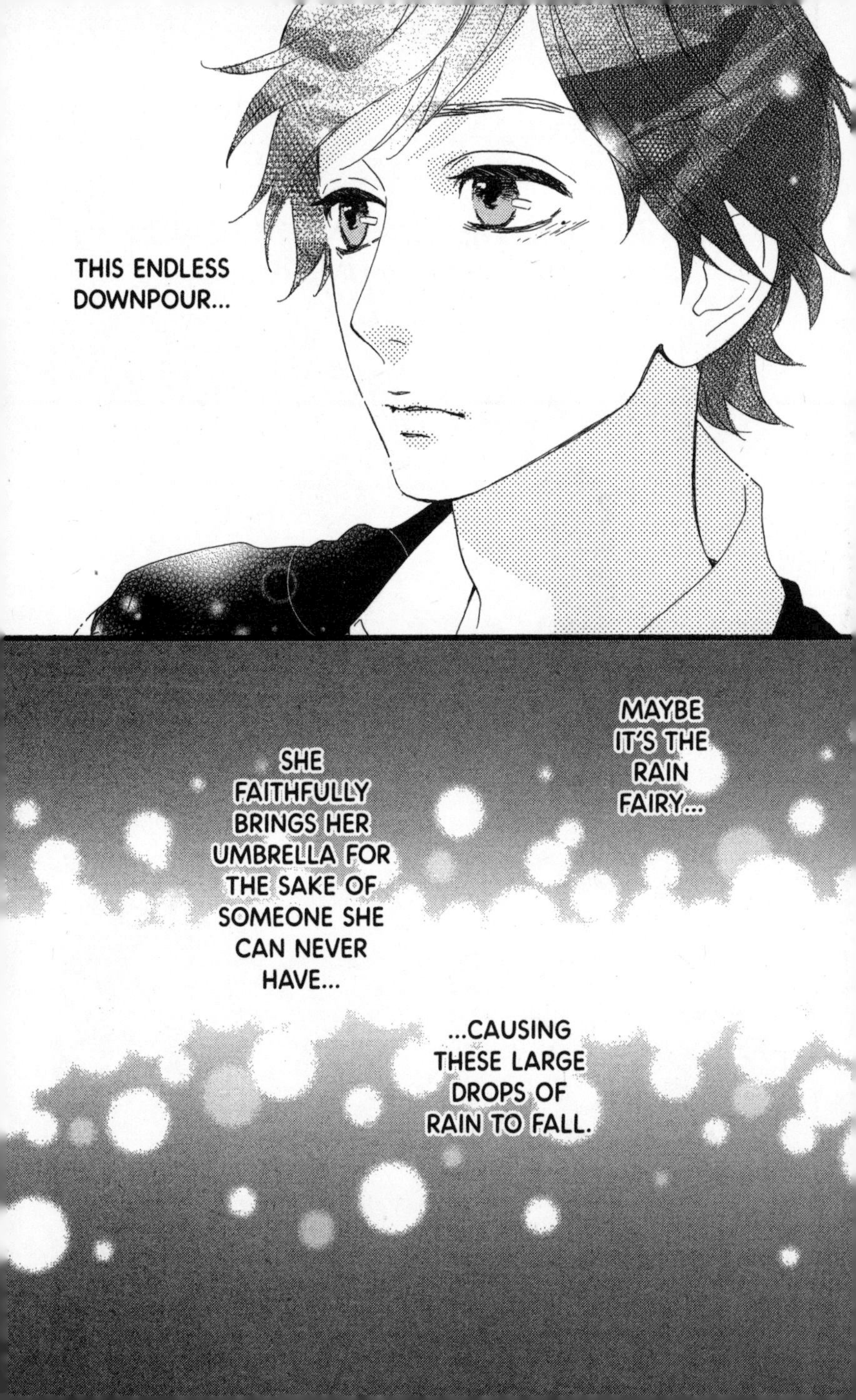
THIS ENDLESS DOWNPOUR...
MAYBE IT'S THE RAIN FAIRY...
SHE FAITHFULLY BRINGS HER UMBRELLA FOR THE SAKE OF SOMEONE SHE CAN NEVER HAVE...
...CAUSING THESE LARGE DROPS OF RAIN TO FALL.

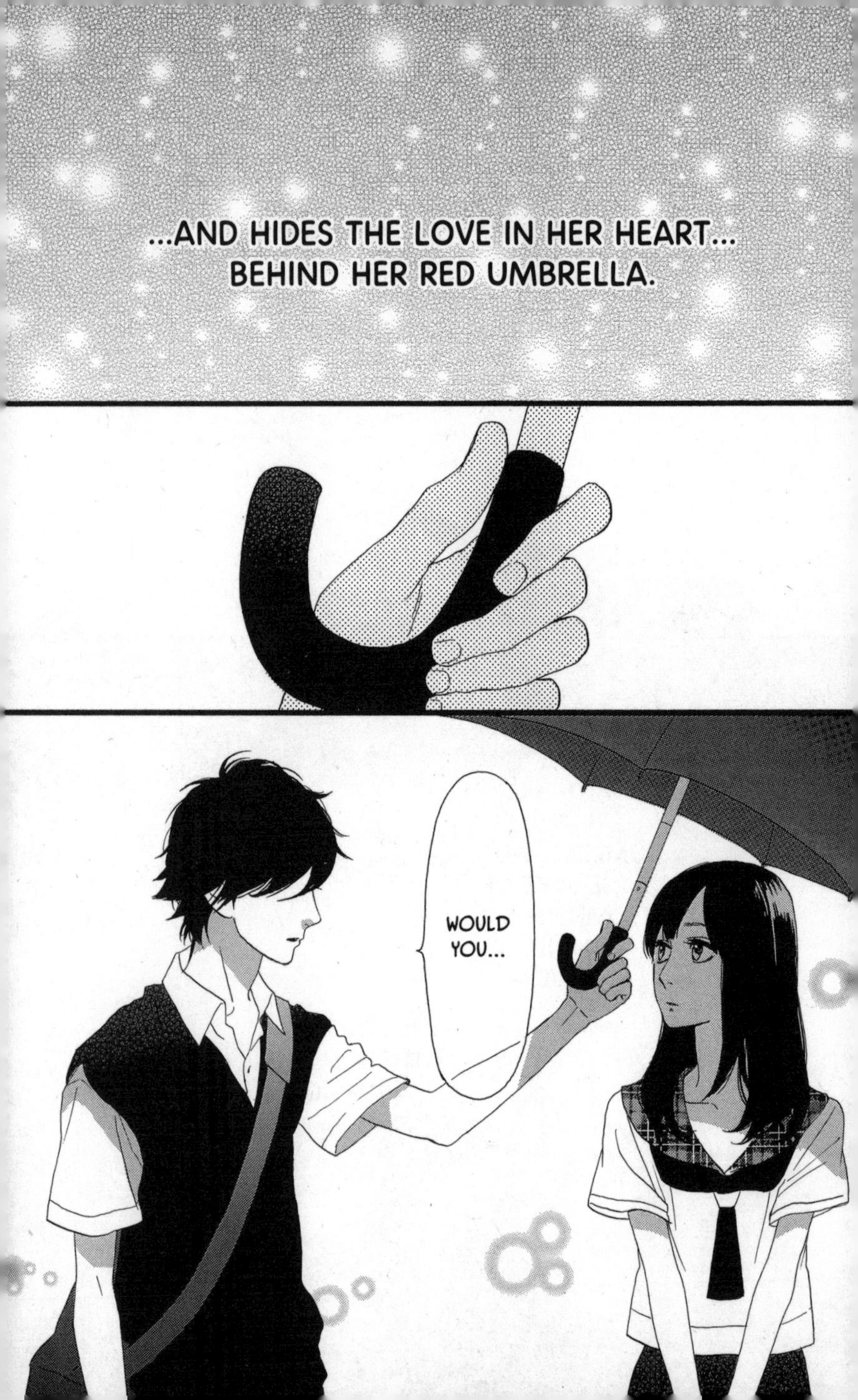
...AND HIDES THE LOVE IN HER HEART... BEHIND HER RED UMBRELLA.
WOULD YOU...

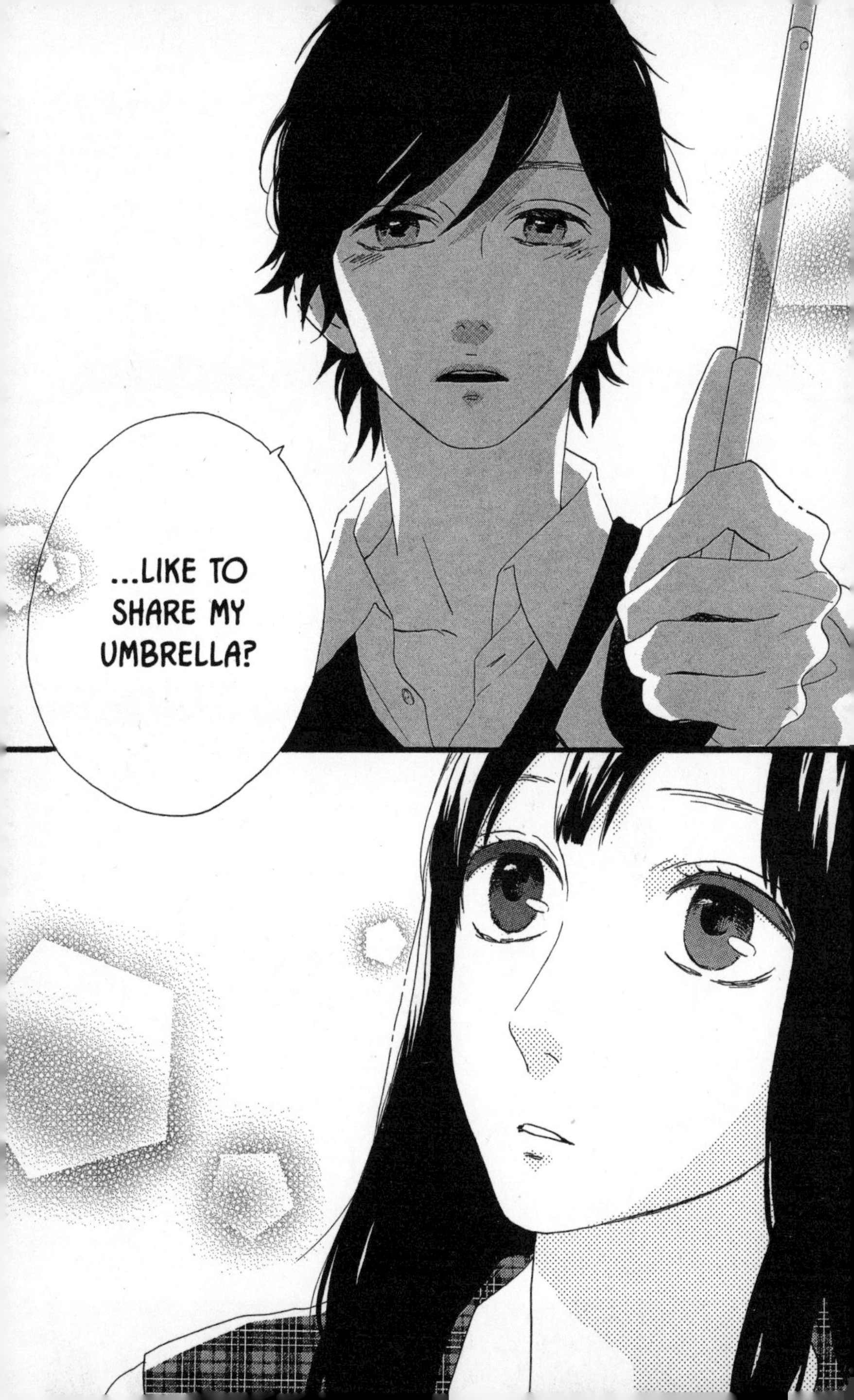
...LIKE TO SHARE MY UMBRELLA?

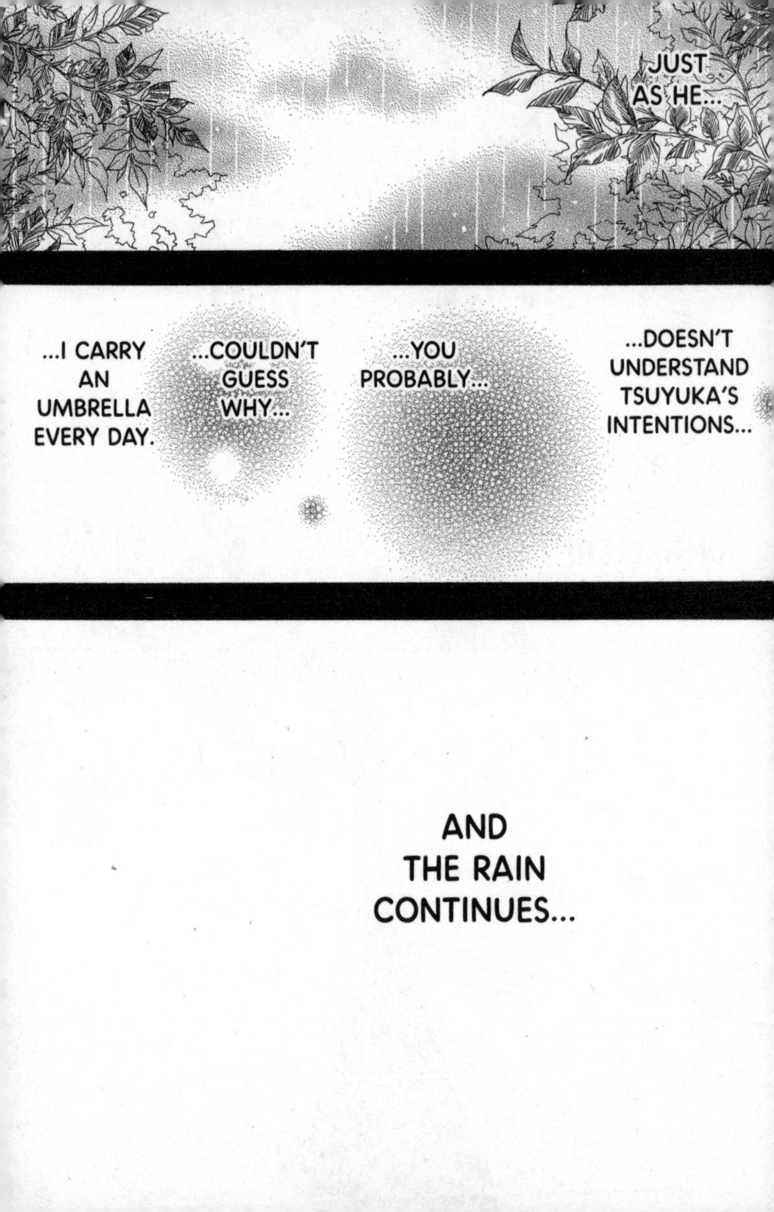
JUST AS HE...
...DOESN'T UNDERSTAND TSUYUKA'S INTENTIONS...
...YOU PROBABLY...
...COULDN'T GUESS WHY...
...I CARRY AN UMBRELLA EVERY DAY.
AND THE RAIN CONTINUES...

About
Tsuyu Kaoru.

I wrote this story to be included in this magazine's
Ateuma Extra.
Looking at my stories, including "Second Kiss"
from a previous volume, I always seem to have a
teacher character. I wonder why. Is it because I
come up with simple stories? Incidentally, I named
the main characters in this story after two of my
classmates in middle school.

And for some reason,
the girls are all
expressionless.

I guess I just like
those kinds of girls.

Tsuyuka

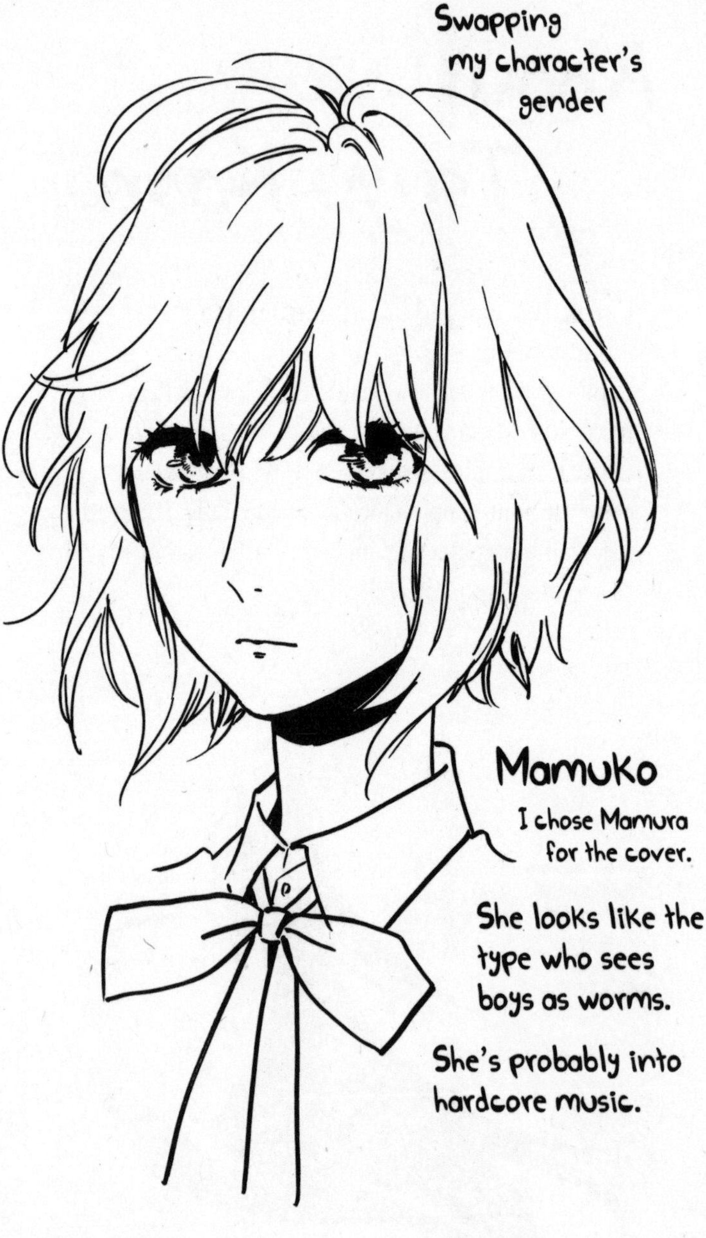
Swapping my character's gender
Mamuko
I chose Mamura for the cover.
She looks like the type who sees boys as worms.
She's probably into hardcore music.

Afterword

So, what did you think? Huh? You wanted more of Mamura? Ha ha ha. You won't have to wait much longer. I plan for you to see much more of him soon!! (Probably.)

I look forward to seeing you in volume 7.

Special ThanX ☆

Editor U,
Noborio, S, Kame,
the designers,
the editorial department,
the print staff,
my family, my friends and all of my readers.

See you Soon!

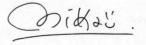

We're already at volume 6. Six was the final volume of Sugars, but it won't be for Daytime Shooting Star.

—Mika Yamamori

Mika Yamamori is from Ishikawa Prefecture in Japan. She began her professional manga career in 2006 with "Kimi no Kuchibiru kara Mahou" (The Magic from Your Lips) in *The Margaret* magazine. Her other works include *Sugars* and *Tsubaki Cho Lonely Planet*.

★DAYTIME★SHOOTING★STAR★ 6

SHOJO BEAT EDITION

Story & Art by
Mika Yamamori

Translation ★ **JN Productions**
Touch-Up Art & Lettering ★ **Inori Fukuda Trant**
Design ★ **Alice Lewis**
Editor ★ **Karla Clark**

HIRUNAKA NO RYUSEI © 2011 by Mika Yamamori
All rights reserved.
First published in Japan in 2011 by SHUEISHA Inc., Tokyo.
English translation rights arranged by SHUEISHA Inc.

The stories, characters and incidents mentioned in this
publication are entirely fictional.

Printed in the U.S.A.

Published by VIZ Media, LLC
P.O. Box 77010
San Francisco, CA 94107

10 9 8 7 6 5 4 3 2 1
First printing, May 2020

PARENTAL ADVISORY
DAYTIME SHOOTING STAR is rated T for
Teen and is recommended for ages 13 and
up. This series contains suggestive themes.

viz.com   shojobeat.com

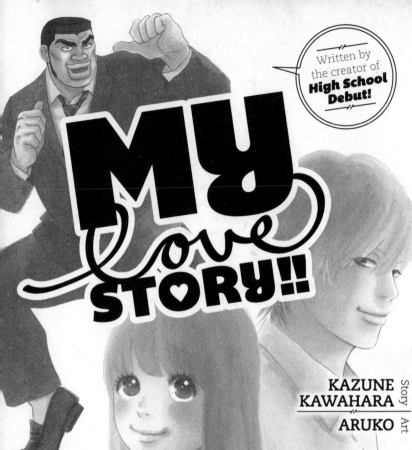

Written by the creator of **High School Debut!**

MY love STORY!!

KAZUNE KAWAHARA — Story

ARUKO — Art

Takeo Goda is a GIANT guy with a GIANT *heart.*

Too bad the girls don't want him!
(They want his good-looking best friend, Sunakawa.)

Used to being on the sidelines, Takeo simply stands tall and accepts his fate. But one day when he saves a girl named Yamato from a harasser on the train, his (love!) life suddenly takes an incredible turn!

Ao Haru Ride

STORY AND ART BY
IO SAKISAKA

Futaba Yoshioka thought all boys were loud and obnoxious until she met Kou Tanaka in junior high. But as soon as she realized she really liked him, he had already moved away because of family issues. Now, in high school, Kou has reappeared, but is he still the same boy she fell in love with?

Takane & Hana

STORY AND ART BY
Yuki Shiwasu

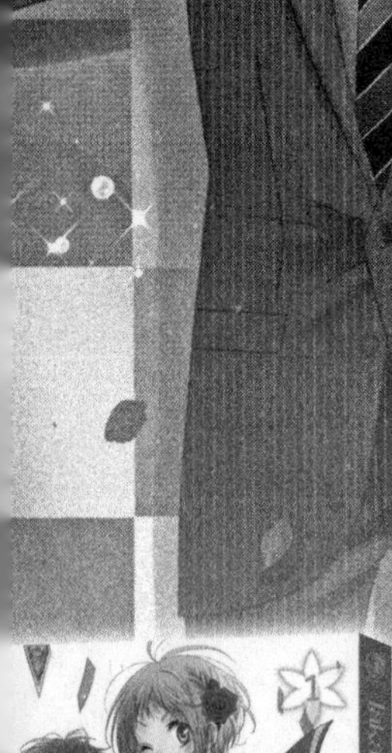

After her older sister refuses to go to an arranged marriage meeting with Takane Saibara, the heir to a vast business fortune, high schooler Hana Nonomura agrees to be her stand-in to save face for the family. But when Takane and Hana pair up, get ready for some sparks to fly between these two utter opposites!

Takane to Hana © Yuki Shiwasu 2015/HAKUSENSHA, Inc.

RATED **T** TEEN

shojobeat.com

STOP!

You may be reading the wrong way!

In keeping with the original Japanese comic format, this book reads from right to left—so action, sound effects and word balloons are completely reversed to preserve the orientation of the original artwork.

Check out the diagram shown here to get the hang of things, and then turn to the other side of the book to get started!

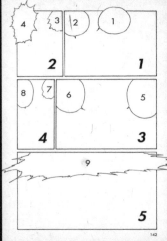

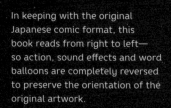